D1549763

Church of England Record Society

Volume 11

THE DIARY OF SAMUEL ROGERS
1634–1638

THE DIARY OF SAMUEL ROGERS

1634–1638

EDITED BY

Tom Webster and Kenneth Shipps

with an introduction by
Tom Webster

THE BOYDELL PRESS

CHURCH OF ENGLAND RECORD SOCIETY

First published 2004

A Church of England Record Society publication
Published by The Boydell Press
an imprint of Boydell & Brewer Ltd
PO Box 9, Woodbridge, Suffolk IP12 3DF, UK
and of Boydell & Brewer Inc.
PO Box 41026, Rochester, NY 14604–4126, USA
website: www.boydellandbrewer.com

ISBN 1 84383 043 4

ISSN 1351–3087

Series information is listed at the back of this volume

A catalogue record for this book is available
from the British Library

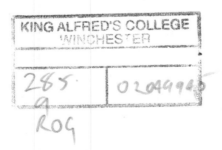
This publication is printed on acid-free paper

Printed in Great Britain by
Cromwell Press, Trowbridge, Wiltshire

Contents

Acknowledgments

The primary debt for this volume is to the Special Collections of Queens University, Belfast where the manuscript is held. The greatest thanks go to them for allowing the Society to publish this text; without such kind permission, of course, this volume would not exist. But the staff of the Special Collections have gone well beyond this, displaying an exemplary helpfulness, kindness and general amiability that made the graft of transcription a social as well as a scholarly pleasure. Ken wanted to mention W. Gordon Wheeler, then sub-librarian at the Special Collections for invaluable help in making the diary available and even offering the occasional help with transcription. I have also been welcomed at a variety of archives in the course of filling in the details, and so my thanks go to the Essex Record Office, the Hertfordshire Record Office, the Guildhall Library, the Greater London Record Office, Dr Williams's Library, the Scottish National Library and the British Library. My trips to Belfast have been funded initially by the British Academy and, more recently, by the University of Edinburgh; the work was pulled together and completed during a sabbatical granted by the latter. On a personal level my early interest was encouraged and assisted by John Morrill and, through him, by Sarah Barber, and he and Pat Collinson encouraged me to publish the text. Stephen Taylor has been a remarkably helpful, tolerant and encouraging editor-in-chief. In addition, Professors Morrill and Collinson helped to put me in touch with Ken Shipps who proved indispensable. In the instances where Rogers uses Greek, I am deeply indebted to Natasha Constantinidou who checked some of the translations, corrected others and, particularly in the last case, chased all the possibilities and very kindly refrained from laughing at my amateurish attempts. I am also indebted to Andrew Brown for checking my Latin translations. Several friends have not only provided intellectual and social support but also tolerated my endless capacity to twist conversations round to the diary. In particular, my gratitude goes to Claire Higgins, Roisín Higgins and Mike O'Brien. Ann Milović and John Morrill provided support and guidance in the trickiest of times. Above all, Ann has accepted Samuel Rogers as an uninvited addition to our household without, to my recollection, a single complaint. More than this, without her practical, intellectual and social support, this task would not have been completed.

This publication owes a great deal to one scholar above and beyond any other. Ken Shipps was the first historian to explore the journal and to realise its importance. The diary was drawn to his attention in 1969 by his then fellow postgraduate and friend J. Sears McGee as an item in a catalogue for a forthcoming sale at Sotheby's, and we all owe thanks to his sharp eyes for spotting it. My first real encounter with the text was in his article on Rogers' consideration of emigration to New England. The initial plan for publication was for the two of us to co-edit the journal and, judging by the contacts that time allowed, it would have developed into a friendship as well as an intellectual co-operative enterprise. This opportunity was a minor loss consequent upon his tragic early death in September 1996. His widow, Charlotte Kroeker, aware of Ken's long-established desire to see the diary in print, worked hard to help me make this happen. She provided Ken's transcript and notes and it was very helpful to compare the transcripts, almost to have Ken looking over my shoulder, as it were. She also provided me with a better sense of Ken as an individual, supplying me with sermons, addresses and a tribute from three colleagues and friends. Any scholar with an interest in the godly of East Anglia will be familiar with the treasure trove of his Ph.D. awarded by Yale University in 1971. Most of us will be less aware of his life combining Christianity and education, of his many publications on the place of Christianity in the colleges and universities of our time and the marvellous work he did as a tutor and then as an administrator at Trinity College, Deerfield, Illinois, Princeton, Brown University, Barrington College, Phillips University and especially at Whitworth College in Spokane, Washington. This work is dedicated to the memory of Ken Shipps and it has been an honour to bring this project, begun by Ken, to its fruition. It seems appropriate to close with a phrase from an address entitled 'Beginnings and Books' which he gave to new students at Whitworth: 'Let us never forget, however, as we enjoy our learning that the Word of God is behind and before all "beginnings and books".'

Glossary

appayed	impaired, deteriorated
awcke	confused, depressed
cleave	to adhere to, to cling to
clogge	anything that hinders action or progress; it could be a general hindrance, impediment or encumbrance or it could be a piece of wood attached to the leg or neck, usually of an animal, to impede motion or escape
currish	quarrelsome, grumpy, resembling a cur
deboising	corrupting morally, deprave by sensuality (related to debauchery)
dedolant	feeling no compunction, insensible, callous
earn	to desire strongly, to long for (similar to 'yearn')
graule	to dig a trench in, to fortify oneself in
jakes	toilet, lavatory
luskish	slothful, lazy, sluggish
maugre	in spite of, notwithstanding
misprisions	scornful actions or speeches
naughty	having nothing, empty
pullbacke	hindrance, something pulling one back
quame	pleasures, over-indulgence
slubber	obscuring, darkening
slud	mud
snibs	rebuke, snub
soder	solder, to join, to unite
squibbing	being smart or sarcastic
upreare	rebuild
wanzing	withering, fading, wasting away, becoming emaciated
warping	perverting, distorting, turning from a straight path
wowling	howling

Abbreviations

BL   British Library

DNB   *Dictionary of National Biography*, ed. Sir L. Stephen and Sir S. Lee (London, 1908–9)

ep. ded. Epistle Dedicatory

ERO   Essex Record Office

GL   Guildhall Library, London

GLRO   Greater London Record Office

PRO SP   Public Record Office State Papers

Venn   J. A. Venn and J. Venn, *Alumni Cantabrigienses* (Cambridge, 1922–54)

Introduction

Biography

A biography of Samuel Rogers will, necessarily, be somewhat cursory and stretch the definition of the genre. This is partly because he was not a minister of any importance in the sense of making any impact on the pages of traditional history, since he was of no contemporary renown as a player in religious politics, his active preaching ministry was short and he had too little time to make a reputation as a considerable minister. The main primary source for Samuel Rogers is the text that follows, as his career and its timing left little, if anything, in parochial or ecclesiastical court sources. Regarding the genre of biography, most of what follows is a contextualization as his family and his employers are more accessible to historians, were better known to contemporaries and made a greater impact on surviving traces. The 'problem' can, however, be seen as advantageous, as his diary allows us access to other figures and, more importantly, gives us access to the experience, social, political and spiritual, of an obscure minister who was an impotent observer in 'interesting times'. While an apology might be made for a biography that resembles a wedding cake that is all icing and little fruit, as it were, the icing is of interest and the fruit still excites the palate.

Samuel Rogers was the eldest son of Daniel Rogers, the lecturer of Wethersfield, Essex, and Sarah Rogers. He was born on 30 November 1613, the second child of Rogers' second wife. He had an older half-brother, also called Daniel, the only surviving progeny of Daniel Rogers and Margaret Rogers, née Bishop, the latter expiring around 1610. Samuel's mother was the daughter of John Everard, a citizen of London. They had eight children, but only five seem to have reached adulthood. The first was Hanna, and there were two younger daughters, Mary and Margaret. There was a younger brother, Richard. For most of the period before the diary begins, Samuel lived in the substantial family home in Wethersfield, where Sarah tended the house with the help of servants and her sister, Mary Everard.[1] We will return to the members of the family in greater detail shortly. An important part of his upbringing included religious instruction from an early age. His father gave his children catechizing sessions including question-and-answer exercises. Samuel, perhaps a little harshly, condemns his childhood self for answering 'like an hypocrite, when he posed mee in religious matters', as he 'lived without any reflexe thoughts', and states that

---

[1]   Diary, pp. 1, 87; H. F. Waters, *Genealogical gleanings in England* (Boston, Mass., 1901), I, 210; *DNB* s. v. Daniel Rogers; for the will of Mary Everard: ERO 54/MW5.

'I scarse knew practicallye, the right hand in religion from the lefte' (1).[2] The nature of the household, and perhaps Samuel's perspective, is revealed in that one of only two mentions of his mother throughout the journal is that he was 'very rebellious, and feirce against my mother and the servants (who yet dealt unwiselye with my childish impetuous nature)' (1), virtually accusing them of being rather too loving.[3]

In 1626, at the age of '13. and a halfe' (1) as he puts it, he left home for the first time. His father was dissatisfied with the education Samuel was getting at Wethersfield, partly because of the rapid turnover of school-masters, and Samuel moved about seven miles to the south to Felsted, where he lodged for the first year with a Mr Fitches. Felsted was an established centre for puritans. The vicar was an appointee of the earl of Warwick and the current minister, Samuel Wharton, was successor to Ezekiel Culverwell, a renowned godly preacher, and was himself an established nonconformist. The schoolmaster was Martin Holbeach, a *protégé* of John Preston, the current master of Emmanuel College, Cambridge. It is particularly noteworthy that Holbeach supervised the education of the sons of several godly ministers in the area, such as Edward Sparrowhawke, William Leigh, Giles Allen and Giles Firmin. He attracted pupils from a wide geographical area, tutoring the sons of William Fairfax and four sons of Oliver Cromwell, including Richard and Henry. It comes as no surprise, then, to learn that Rogers 'got more good in 2. yeares. with the blessing of god, upon the diligent labours of my godly master Mr Holbeach, then I got in many twoos before' (1).[4]

Shortly before he left for Felsted Samuel had what he regarded in retrospect as his first real religious experience, which amounted to a sense of guilt at his lack of guilty feelings during a family exercise on Matthew 11:2. He felt that this had been insufficient, claiming that in his first year at Felsted he had 'passed many a day of vanitye' (1). He found a more thoroughly grounded conversion experience when he accompanied a servant, Mary, to a sermon at nearby Terling given by the vicar, Thomas Weld. Weld preached on Luke 14:7–24 and the attack on earthly pleasures cut Rogers to the quick as it was a vice to which he felt particularly prone.[5]

[2] When there are quotations from the journal the reference will be given in parentheses in the text. When the text is paraphrased, the reference will be in a note.
[3] The other appearance is when she appears as a source of disapproval with him reporting a 'boyling' against 'father, and mother for the old buisinesse': Diary, p. 14.
[4] B. Donegan, 'Clerical patronage of Robert Rich, second earl of Warwick', *Proceedings of the American Philosophical Society,* 120 (1976), p. 405; P. S. Seaver, *The Puritan Lectureships: the politics of religious dissent* (Stanford, Ca, 1970), p. 182; M. Craze, *A History of Felsted School* (Chelmsford, 1989), pp. 11–12; ERO D/Q 11/33/1; GL 9537/11 fo. 139v; PRO SP 16/175/104; F. S. Moller (ed.), *Alumni Felstedienses 1564–1691* (London, 1931); T. W. Davids, *Annals of Evangelical Nonconformity in the County of Essex* (London, 1863), p. 386.
[5] Diary, p. 2. He does not make it plain whether Mary was servant to the Fitches or to the Rogers family; she is simply 'our maide'.

We might see it as quite strange that he almost celebrated the fact that his host and hostess died shortly after. This was because it led to a change of accommodation and thereafter he boarded 'at Mr Ditchfeilds, where I had incouragement and helpe, and the worke went sweetlye on, according to the light I had, then did all my former knowledge doe mee good' (2). He lodged with them for two or three years until he went to Emmanuel College, Cambridge, being admitted as a sizar, a student who served other members of the college, on 23 May 1629.[6]

Before going on to examine the next stage of his education, it is worthwhile to give some space to his family. His broader male kin are relatively well known to students of the godly ministry on both sides of the Atlantic, for he was part of the third generation of what can, with little sense of overstatement, be called one of the dynasties of East Anglian puritanism. The founding father was Richard Rogers, the lecturer of Wethersfield, who died in 1618. He was most famous in his lifetime as a preacher and as the author of the considerable tome of practical divinity, the *Seven Treatises*; he is famous among historians for this and for his own spiritual journal.[7] Susan, his second wife, was the widow of John Ward, the preacher of Haverhill in the Stour valley on the Suffolk/Essex border.[8] This meant that among Richard Rogers' stepsons were Samuel Ward, the famous lecturer of Ipswich, and Nathaniel Ward, who became rector of Stondon Massey to the south of Wethersfield in Essex and went on to take a prominent role in the foundation of Massachusetts. One of Richard Rogers' nephews was John Rogers, the godly lecturer of Dedham in north-east Essex. Mary, Richard Rogers' first wife, bore four daughters and four sons. We are not sure about the names of three of the daughters, and only two of the sons definitely survived into adulthood. The daughter about whom we know most is Mary, and she married a godly cleric, Adam Harsnett, who served Cranham, also in Essex. Samuel's better-known uncle was Ezekiel Rogers. He acted as chaplain to Lady Joan Barrington at Hatfield Broad Oak in Essex, moving north to serve a Barrington living at Rowley, Yorkshire, before emigrating to New England, ministering to a congregation at a settlement also called Rowley.

It is worthwhile to be aware of Samuel Rogers' wider family, as his godly background was an important part of his identity, but it should be made clear that, in the period covered by the diary, their appearances, if any, were rare. His grandfather, Richard Rogers, died when Samuel was four years old. He remained as an important figure of godliness. He is noted on four occasions, once when Samuel's sister died and 'wee buryed her by my grandfather' (153) and once when the renowned godly minister John Dod offered spiritual counsel to Samuel and gave thanks for his (Samuel's)

6   Venn, s. v. 'Samuel Rogers'.
7   Marshall M. Knappen (ed.), *Two Puritan Diaries* (Chicago, 1933).
8   Waters, *Genealogical Gleanings*, I, 209.

grandfather.[9] He most touchingly appears in a vision of heaven where Samuel would 'sit downe in companye, with Abraham; Paul, my grandfather, and all other blessed saints, and angels' (44). The fourth occasion related to his uncle John Rogers. Samuel never met with John Rogers in these years but the family ties were important, for Samuel noted John's death, blaming Matthew Wren and praying that God would 'let mee live his life, and dye in the faith with him; so dying I may rejoice eternallye with him, grandfather and all other the saints of god' (78).[10] The Ward part of the family make no appearance in the diary. Although, as we will see, Nathaniel Ward was close to Daniel Rogers, he had left for New England before the period covered by the diary. The only definite mention of Ezekiel Rogers is when Samuel was saddened by news of his uncle's troubles in Yorkshire at the end of 1637.[11] There is an earlier occasion when his 'burden is taken of[f]; my soule is refreshed by the coming of my deare uncle' (69), but it is unclear whether this was Ezekiel Rogers or Adam Harsnett. Whichever it is, Samuel received considerable spiritual succour, noting that his uncle was 'of a sweet incouraging spirit' and finding 'my soule inlarged with his in secret, and with his discourse' (69).

It comes as no surprise to hear that Samuel's father, Daniel Rogers, was the most influential relative, and it is worth stepping sideways, as it were, to introduce him before looking at the relationship. Like his father, Daniel Rogers was educated at Christ's College, Cambridge, becoming a fellow and receiving his BD in 1606. Before he left Cambridge in 1608 he acquired a fair reputation for scholarship and was close friends with radicals like William Ames and Paul Baynes, himself a Wethersfield boy. There is, indeed, an account, probably apocryphal, of Rogers besting a young William Laud in debate.[12] It is not quite clear where Rogers spent the immediate years after he left Cambridge. He may well have attended what was in effect a graduate seminary with Richard Blackerby at Ashen in the Stour valley. He certainly had a peripatetic preaching record, like Blackerby making himself available for nonconformist baptisms and communions in the area, guest lecturing at Groton, John Winthrop's parish in Suffolk.[13]

The next definite appearance of Daniel Rogers is his settlement at Wethersfield. His father had been succeeded as lecturer by Stephen Marshall, later a close colleague of Daniel Rogers'. Marshall had met with some success at Wethersfield and his parishioners had purchased for him a library worth £50 in exchange for a promise that he would stay with them. However, in the early 1620s Marshall married well and felt that his

---

[9]   Diary, p. 146.
[10] For the circumstances of John Rogers' death, see below.
[11] Diary, p. 129.
[12] Giles Firmin, *Weighty Questions discussed* (1692), Sig. A4.
[13] *Winthrop Papers* (Boston, Mass., 1926–43), I, 259; ERO D/ABA 1 fo. 185. For Blackerby's seminary, see Tom Webster, *The Godly Clergy in Early Stuart England: the Caroline puritan movement, c. 1620–1643* (Cambridge, 1997), pp. 30–2.

stipend failed to meet the needs of a minister married to the niece of a baronet. Upon the death of Thomas Pickering in 1625, the patron of neighbouring Finchingfield, William Kempe, saw Marshall as an attractive candidate for the vicarage. There were two other candidates, William Leigh, the curate of Denston, Suffolk, and Daniel Rogers. In the event Marshall was offered the post and his scruples were taken to a 'little Assembly of Divines' which judged his changed economic circumstances to be sufficient to waive his earlier promise. It was further decided that his successor at Wethersfield should be Daniel Rogers.[14]

It was at Wethersfield that Rogers consolidated his reputation as a godly minister, and he held the post as lecturer until his death in 1652, including the time that he was suspended from his ministry. He became an important figure in the clerical sociability of the puritans of the county, taking up a place as one of the ministers leading worship in the network of noble professors, including the Barrington and Rich families. In particular he was influential in the monthly conference established around Thomas Hooker and his students when Hooker became lecturer at Chelmsford in 1625. The flipside of this was his reputation as a nonconformist minister, making it plain that he saw compromise over liturgy without Scriptural support as wholly illegitimate.[15]

He was relatively untroubled for his nonconformity during the time of George Mountaigne as bishop of London. This was to change when Mountaigne was succeeded in 1628 by William Laud, one of the primary promoters of the heightened value of liturgical conformity along with a more tightly imposed ecclesiastical discipline. As bishop of London, Laud turned his attention to the recalcitrant ministers of Essex in his second triennial visitation at the end of 1630. Having established an improved base of informants, he was notified of Daniel Rogers' nonconformity along with that of many of his colleagues in November 1630.[16] Rogers anticipated trouble and, ahead of the arrival of the visitation, in July 1631, he canvassed support among neighbouring moderate ministers, looking for a petition to certify his exemplary ministry and lifestyle in the hope of encouraging Laud to turn a blind eye to his nonconformity.[17] This cut no ice with Laud, and when the visitation came to Braintree on 4 September he was asked to subscribe to the three articles declaring wholesale acceptance of the

[14] Anon., *Life and Death of Stephen Marshall* (1680), pp. 3–4; Giles Firmin, *A Brief Vindication of Mr Stephen Marshall*, appended to idem, *Questions between the Conformist and the Nonconformist* (1681), n. p.
[15] For Hooker and clerical sociability, see Webster, *Godly Clergy*, pp. 15–59; for the noble professors of Essex, see William Hunt, *The Puritan Moment: the coming of Revolution in an English county* (Cambridge, Mass., 1983), pp. 219–34; for preaching against conformity, see Daniel Rogers, *Naaman the Syrian, his disease and cure* (1642), pp. 524–5, 78. The ep. ded. identifies these sermons as delivered in 1630.
[16] PRO SP 16/175/104; Webster, *Godly Clergy*, pp. 187–8.
[17] PRO SP 16/196/61.

government and liturgy of the Church of England. This was beyond his conscience; he simply refused and thus had his licence to preach suspended. As he was lecturer rather than vicar he was, in effect, excluded from the pulpit for the foreseeable future.[18]

This was not quite Rogers' last appearance at the visitation. The day before he was called before Laud, he met with a number of friends and colleagues, many of whom appear in his son's diary. He was joined by his half-brother Nathaniel Ward, by Thomas Weld of Terling, Samuel Wharton of Felsted, Stephen Marshall of Finchingfield, Edmund Brewer of Castle Hedingham and Thomas Shepard of Earls Colne. According to Shepard, they 'consulted whether it was best to let such a swine [as Laud] to root up God's plants in Essex and not give him some check. Whereupon it was agreed upon privately at Braintree that some should speak to him and give him some check'. The group accordingly attended the service at Dunmow on 5 September, probably hearing the sermon promoting Laudian-style worship, and harsh words were exchanged, particularly between Laud and Weld. Shepard attempted to intervene but was restrained and led away by Martin Holbeach, Samuel Rogers' schoolmaster, and the demonstration ended with neither side converted.[19]

After this brief fracas, Rogers returned to the more protracted business of his ministry. His immediate concern was the provision of preaching in Wethersfield. This seems to have been addressed immediately, for within weeks the churchwardens, Thomas Digby and George Strawland, were presented to the court 'for maintaining a lecture without any authority since Mr Rogers suspension'. It was alleged that 'divers have preached that have not observed the Kings instructions nor read prayers before their sermon therefore [it was ordered that] they will certify the names of such have preached there since Mr Rogers suspension'.[20] Conditions do not seem to have changed when Robert Aylett used the Commissary's Court to assess the impact of the visitation and to tie up loose ends. He was 'credibly informed that Mr Attwood, a great unconformist, is there indeed a lecturer, admitted under the colour of being curate'. The churchwardens took the position of outraged innocence, claiming that since the receipt of an order threatening close surveillance, the only minister preaching there had been Stephen Marshall and he had worn the surplice.[21]

---

[18] GL 9531/15 fo. 25r–v.
[19] Michael McGiffert (ed.), *God's Plot: the paradoxes of puritan piety being the autobiography and journal of Thomas Shepard* (Amherst, Mass., 1972), pp. 50–51; Nehemiah Rogers, *A Sermon preached at the Visitation of William, Bishop of London, 3 ix 1631* (1632); PRO SP 16/499/87.
[20] GLRO DL/C 319 fo. 77.
[21] PRO SP 16/218/43; ERO D/ABA 5 fos. 135–6, 133v (interleaved). I have been unable definitely to identify Mr Attwood. There was a William Attwood who was among the commissioners for the sequestration of scandalous ministers in Essex in February 1644.

Although Rogers remained suspended for the rest of the decade, and thus for the length of his son's journal, he maintained his ministry as far as was possible. He continued to provide for the parish in his pastoral capacity, organizing and leading fasting and prayer among the Wethersfield godly, with the assistance of the Rogers' extended clerical cousinage.[22] He seems to have been fairly successful in keeping the pulpit filled, calling on friends and family, with ministers such as John Carter and Anthony Tuckney filling in for him.[23] He also took groups gadding to sermons at neighbouring parishes. The most common destination was Finchingfield, particularly to hear Stephen Marshall but also for guest preachers such as John Borodale.[24] Further afield, they went to Castle Hedingham and Stansted to hear Edmund Brewer, to Felsted and elsewhere to hear Samuel Wharton, to Barnston to hear John Beadle, and to Colchester for John Knowles.[25] In addition, he led expeditions to join exercises in Earls Colne, Sudbury and Dunmow, occasionally contributing to private worship himself.[26] On a more individual level, he could, of course, still receive visitors such as Martin Holbeach, Anthony Tuckney and John Wilson, attend gatherings of ministers and noble professors at the Barrington seat at Hatfield Broad Oak and travel to Cambridge for what were in effect puritan summits at the Commencement.[27] At the same time, he could focus on his study, and while he was silenced in the pulpit he was not in the press. Older works on practical divinity appeared; by the end of 1634 he had completed the work which was to appear in 1642 as *Matrimoniall Honour*, and he was reportedly working on 'the Sinnes of the Times here et abroad'.[28]

From the evidence of the diary, his father was easily Samuel Rogers' most important human relation, arguably the most important person in his life. This is based on the fact that Daniel Rogers' disapproval was the most feared and his approval the most valued. Although his relationship with his father improved somewhat between 1634 and 1638, this remained a constant factor. Early on, the arrival of a bill from Samuel's tutor prompted 'feare of fathers displeasure' and this 'made mee unfit to pray' (12). Shortly after this, the whole of one day's entry consisted of the following:

> This day fell out that sad disaster, my father strangely, and furiouslye fell out with mee as though he would have with words, which so distempered

Obviously this would be a like-minded minister, but it is no more than a possibility: Harold Smith, *The Ecclesiastical History of Essex under the Long Parliament and Commonwealth* (Colchester, 1933), p. 116.

22 Diary, pp. 11, 12, 115, 109, 161.
23 GLRO DL/C 319 fo. 77; Diary, pp. 11, 24, 115, 158, 161.
24 Diary, pp. 11, 12, 15, 25, 26, 98, 104.
25 Diary, pp. 14, 26, 27, 30, 98, 120.
26 Diary, pp. 3, 11, 14, 26, 78, 87, 88, 98, 100, 104, 115, 121, 161.
27 Diary, pp. 13, 24, 27, 83, 118.
28 Daniel Rogers, A *Practicall Catechisme* (1632); *idem, A Treatise of the Two Sacraments* (1633); *idem, Naaman the Syrian, his disease and cure* (1642); *idem, Matrimoniall Honour* (1642); Sheffield University Hartlib MS 29/2/7, 51a.

mee, that I knew not what to doe, till I fell downe upon my knees, where the lord melted mee and subdued my spirit graciouslye (14).

The trauma stayed with him for the next few days and even after a trip to a good sermon there was still 'a boyling I find at home ag:[ainst] father, and mother for the old buisinesse' (14). The worst spell of the relationship was caused by the time when Samuel was considering emigrating to New England, an option which had been condemned in the pulpit and later in the press by his father.[29] When Samuel broached the subject with his father, he received short shrift, and this was the first time that he seemed to be receiving conflicting messages from his earthly and heavenly fathers. 'N[ew] E[ngland] N.[ew] E.[ngland] is in my thoughts my heart rejoices to think of it; L[or]d shew mee thy way in it; and bow the heart of my father' (97). His confusion was exacerbated when it emerged that his brother took the same position as his father, and Samuel simply adopted a position of confused passivity: 'oh I wonder at my fathers and brothers sp:[irit] note it' (99). The importance of his father's opinion comes across more clearly on a happier occasion when he won his father's blessing for the prospect of becoming chaplain to the Vere family. His account was laconic, but heartfelt: 'I come to wethersf:[ield] to shew buisinesse to my father; he approves, I rejoice' (129).

He gave especial value to his father's support, career guidance and spiritual advice. He was surprised that his father's correspondence failed to prevent spiritual backsliding when he was a student, noting that 'Sophistry, credit, jollitye maugre all fathers letters, and former experience, did coole quondam zeale, fervencye, affections' (2).[30] The spiritual exercises Daniel Rogers observed with his family usually proved helpful. Even after a poor day with lacklustre preaching, 'yet someth:[ing] done at home the last sentence of my father; conc:[erning] daily applying the heart to the promise of gods love' (13). Similarly, after a day when 'My walking hath bine drowsye', he was still 'a litle warmed by familye dutye by my father' (14). In later times, when Samuel was less able to spend time at Wethersfield, visits from his father usually brought spiritual delights. 'God lightens my heart by my fathers coming; oh joyfull to see godly freinds; heavenly oh how joyfull!' (70). The very presence of his father brought spiritual joy: 'this day the L[or]d sends my father by providence to mee; who quells my spirit; and the L[or]d now is pleased still to strengthen mee in body, and to refresh my soule dailye with his peace and lovingkindnesse' (147–8). The following day he gave thanks for 'a day of libertye; and comfort' due to the Lord and 'from the joy of my fathers

---

[29] The way in which Samuel was attracted to New England and eventually lost his enthusiasm is discussed at greater length in two differing, but complementary, studies: K. W. Shipps, 'The Puritan migration to New England: a new source on motivation', *New England Historical and Genealogical Register*, 135 (1981), pp. 83–97; Webster, *Godly Clergy*, pp. 278–85.

[30] 'Maugre' means 'despite'.

presence' (148). The entry for the third day of this visit gives a slightly longer account, combining religious exercises, spiritual advice and probably very good advice to a young chaplain of a relatively wealthy woman.

> In the morning in my bed warmed and thawed, with my fathers prayer, in private; who prayed most effectually for mee; espec:[ially] that I may not loose that after recovery which I have got in sicknesse; and for present that I should wait with patience upon g.[od] in this time, when I can doe litle; oh: * I asked what I should doe ab:[out] 45r f1sh34ns heere; he says; pray; never medle except very excessive in such th:[ing]s my father would never; content your selfe; and say nothing; and ag:[ainst] try a moderation (148).[31]

The other important male figure in Samuel's nuclear family was his older half-brother, also called Daniel. He was absent for much of the time covered by the journal, as he was established as schoolmaster in Northampton. He was very much his father's son, fitting with ease into the godly milieu of Northampton.[32] Although he was unbeneficed, he is known to have preached in the main church in Northampton,[33] and when he administered the communion, he delivered it to communicants sitting, a risky endeavour under watchful Laudian eyes. Indeed, he told Humphrey Ramsdell, a promoter of Laudianism in the town, that his (Ramsdell's) life would be easier if he left the town, evidently a common opinion among the godly, as the diarist Robert Woodford saw him as a 'superstitious fellow' and prayed for his conversion.[34] We have no details of his preaching, but Woodford reported 'a good discourse with Mr Rogers who seemes to loath vayne ceremonies'.[35] Rogers' place among the godly ministers of the area appears in his performance at the execution of John Pytchley, a puritan minister gone astray. He worked with the more famous ministers John Ball and Daniel Cawdrey to deliver a face-saving display of repentance and regret to minimize the effect of an immoral puritan minister.[36] Similarly, he was

---

[31] Occasionally Rogers encodes his diary in that he substitutes numbers for vowels, '1' for 'a', '2' for 'e', '3' for 'i'. '4' for 'o' and '5' for 'u'. At most points the decoding is obvious so I have not provided a translation.

[32] For Northampton and the diocese of Peterborough, see W. J. Sheils, 'Some problems of government in a new diocese: the bishop and the puritans in the diocese of Peterborough 1560–1630', in R. O'Day and F. Heal (eds), *Continuity and Change: personnel and administration of the Church of England, 1500–1642* (Leicester, 1976), pp. 167–87; John Fielding, 'Arminianism in the localities: Peterborough diocese 1603–1642', in Kenneth Fincham (ed.), *The Early Stuart Church, 1603–1642* (London, 1993), pp. 93–113; idem, 'Opposition to the personal rule of Charles I: the diary of Robert Woodford, 1637–1641', *Historical Journal*, 88 (1988), pp. 769–88; Webster, *Godly Clergy*, pp. 215–34.

[33] New College, Oxford MS 9502, 5 April 1639, 5 August 1640 (pp. 351, 549).

[34] PRO SP 16/472/80; New College, Oxford MS 9502, 6 September 1637 (p. 22).

[35] New College, Oxford MS 9502, 9 June 1638 (p. 104).

[36] Northamptonshire Record Office Isham (Lamport) MS 2570 *passim*. For the context and a full account, see Peter Lake, 'A "Charitable Christian Hatred": the godly and their enemies in the 1630s', in Christopher Durston and Jacqueline Eales (eds), *The Culture of Puritanism, 1560–1700* (London, 1996), pp. 145–50.

xxii INTRODUCTION

among seventy ministers who signed a petition, published in 1641, promoting a campaign to convert the native Americans, in some ways a surprising signature, given his aversion to emigration noted above.[37]

Perhaps the small *rôle* he has in Samuel Rogers' diary may be related to geographical distance, but it may also relate to distance of age and the fact that any patriarchal role was more than adequately filled by their father. The one occasion when Daniel accompanied his brother on the trip from Cambridge to Wethersfield merits little comment,[38] and a little later, 'This day am I with my brother; ut solet' (58), that is, 'as usual', and it is by no means clear whether this was a positive or a negative thing. The record is rather better when the two brothers travelled with Anthony Tuckney and 'our good discourse in the journye was that which most refreshed mee' (24). When Samuel had moved to Hackney, Daniel visited for about three days and Samuel noted that 'now my brother comes, and I am refreshed; but much adoe to keep up a flagging spirit'. After they rode to Wethersfield, they both preached, and Samuel was 'much inlarged, and wee refresh the saints there my aunt Hosther, and others are comforted' (161).[39] His younger brother, Richard, is even less visible. Similarly, there was a difference of age, and he seems to have been staying with Hanna in Sudbury where he may have been attending grammar school. Samuel simply reports one visit where he felt 'joy to see some further hopes of grace' (97).[40]

Samuel's relations with his three sisters as they are expressed in his journal stand in clear contrast to those with Daniel and Richard. Even with his eldest sister, Hanna, with whom he had the weakest links, there are evidently strong emotional ties. She was already married with two children, living in Sudbury, just over the Suffolk/Essex border. He seems to have felt at least at ease in her company, and able to adopt a confident, leading *rôle* in their spiritual conversations. After some time there and in Earls Colne where his younger sister Mary lived, he reported that 'I have found great inlargement often' (26), and slightly earlier he was delighted after a trip to Sudbury, 'to Hanna, where the lord stirred up my spirit to speake freelye upon 11. Matt: before many' (14), the latter being particularly therapeutic as this was a time of trouble with his father. After December 1635, when Hanna's husband

---

37 [William Castell], *A Petition of W. C. Exhibited to the High Court of Parliament* (1641), pp. 16–19. For his opinion on emigration, see Diary, p. 99.
38 Diary, p. 10. It may be that this passes with little comment as it is a time when he neglected his diary.
39 'Hosther' was probably the daughter of Richard Rogers named in his will as 'Hassolder': Waters, *Genealogical Gleanings*, I, 210.
40 Venn noticed that a Richard Rogers had matriculated at Trinity College, Cambridge in 1640 and he suggested that he was the son of Daniel Rogers of Wethersfield. Venn suggested that Waters was wrong to include Richard as the son of Daniel Rogers, the Master of Northampton School from 1632 to 1642. Waters (I, 210) had arranged a family tree which placed Richard as the *grandson* of Daniel Rogers of Wethersfield rather than his *son*. Later letters from Daniel Rogers of Wethersfield place him as his son: BL Egerton MSS 2648 fos. 142, 144.

died, most of her appearances were dominated by pity, concern and prayers for her well-being. He saw her loss as God's punishment for the sins of the ungodly and sympathized with her miserable state: 'now hath that pore creature her heart full of sorrow; having 2. children left behind; oh how the Lord hates sin; he will punish it in his owne; by her crosses the Lord hath done her good' (40). The next time they met she was still 'desolate' although 'she hath received good by all her baskinge'. Nonetheless, his concern was far from over, for the day's entry ends with a prayer, 'L[or]d more to her, and hers' (87). His concerns were well grounded, for when they met almost exactly a year later, she was still described as 'that desolate creature Hanna' (129).

Samuel's relations were closest with his two younger sisters, Mary and Margaret, and this may be partly due to a more clearly established patriarchal relationship. They seem to have been regular correspondents, and on some occasions his rôle was almost pastoral. One entry recorded that 'I am something comforted with some fruit, the Lord hath given mee; my letters to Mary (she saith hath done her soule much good;[)] and to Margret' (52). Both sisters seem to have had ill-defined physical difficulties and Margaret, in particular, spiritual ones as well. After seeing that 'my sister peg is sweetly broken; the Lords worke is upon her soule; his hand sadly upon her bodye', he implored that the trial should continue 'so long Lord as it may doe her good' (52). This came shortly after hearing from Mary 'ab:[out] my sister Margret; that the Lord hath done her some good, oh blessed be his holy name, that snatches one brand out of the fire after another Lord perfect thy worke begun in her for thy mercyes sake' (45–6). She was still troubled when she was last mentioned, and Samuel's concern was plain: 'my heart broken toward sister Margret, whose soule the Lord hath heavilye loded oh marvailous change; blessed, be thy name Deare god, thaw her by a litle love revealed in thy promise; open the dore of hope to her sinking spirit' (58). His concerns for Mary were predominantly physical as in the following instance. 'This day I went to Colne for my sister Marye, her eye being in danger, the lord caryed mee on[,] sweetly banishing evell[,] put in some life; he mercifully delivered my sister Mary being under the horse' (12). Spiritually, they seemed more like equals, with Samuel getting as much as he gave.

> Saboath, wherin I have injoyed a great deale of god; I stay at home and M[1]ry and I are at it, and the L[or]d affords of his presence; and thawes our hearts; oh good is the L[or]d, I have tasted how good the L[or]d is, and ther[e]fore now I come unto him; yea in his armes doe I lie downe; weake, and tyred in bodye; but with my spirit up; I will sleepe in christes armes (102–3).

This sense of equality, intimacy and love is captured most clearly when Mary died, easily the longest entry in the journal. He first refers to her as 'our beloved Jonathon' (152), comparing her to King David's close friend who represents love, faithfulness and self-sacrifice. He then goes on to record how 'very pleasant hast thou bin unto mee oh my darling thy Love to mee was wonderful passing the love of women (oh my deare) for thy love was divine, and from above' (152). He then went on to praise her piety on individual, social and ecclesiastical levels, and he closes with a very moving description. She

> was a most dutifull, and loving child, as I thinke lived upon the earth, for she loved in the L[or]d; A most tender, and loving sister to her brothers, and sisters, ever studying, and praying for there good; An intire freind to the worship of Xt [Christ]; and shee againe, was the daughter, and sister, and freind of Delights (153).

Almost to provide a contrast to these good relationships, a little space must be devoted to the matter of 'M. S.' This is because it is a recurrent anxiety for Rogers and also because his anxiety is such that he encodes some relevant sections, inks out others and adopts a style that must have been clear to him but leaves the modern reader, the intruder, none the wiser. It is worth working through the references one by one, if only to suggest that what they seem to be hiding and what Rogers was worried about was, as *we* might see it, of almost no consequence (which, in itself, makes it worthy of our attention). We will work through this matter mostly chronologically, partly so that we can trace the way Rogers' treatment of it changed.

M. S. first appears on 5 March 1635. His entry for that day is as follows:

> the lord kept my heart in awe in some measure in the midst of libertye: eating sick P[words inked out] &c; with M.S. [words inked out] but my am[inked out] heart would have flowne out at night I prayed, and the Lord kept down sin, and shewed me something; but I have need of the Aaron, and Hur of dailye prayer, and watching to uphold the Moses of my soule; least the Amalekites prevaile (13).

The closing section encourages the reader to see this as a major threat, given that Moses needed Aaron and Hur to support him while he kept the rod lifted during the battle against the Amalekites. Rogers notes that, left to himself, he would have lost control; here 'libertye' is in the sense of 'libertarian', plainly a danger in Rogers' eyes. God helped him to keep his feet during the day and, in the evening, He 'kept down sin'. At the heart of the trouble is the most opaque section. He spent time with 'M. S.' but to identify the adjective he applied to his heart is little more than guesswork as all that is clear is that it opens with 'am'. From later entries, as we will see, it could be 'amorous' but there are, of course, many English adjectives beginning with 'am', so I will take it no further at this stage.

At this point it is worthwhile to take a brief step backwards, as it were, to his introductory autobiography. He noted that at Christmas 1634 he went to Colne Priory 'where I was snared with another baite; what it was I tell not; I am ashamed; but in the midst; my fathers words in the monument house with gods spirit setting them home broke mee, and made mee vow' (3).

Resisting the temptation to speculate concerning the nature of the 'baite', for we actually *know* nothing other than that it was different to his former inconsistency of devotion, we should simply note one thing. That is the 'vow' which he mentions, for it is something we will encounter below. In this particular instance, he went on to celebrate (as it were) 'a second conversion' and wonder at God's mercy in maintaining His care. He concluded this section by delivering a warning to himself. 'Yet forget not the pit, that thou wert ever caryed into, both at Braintrye and * Sudburye, about the latter end of Septemb: and begining of October; 1634. But mourne rather breake they hearte in gods bosome licke his dust, for thy basenes' (3–4). The chronology is a little confusing but it seems that something had happened or he had done something or he had felt something that he saw as requiring a great deal of humility and shame. We will gradually be in a better position to estimate what that 'something' was.

After his first mention of M. S., there followed just over three weeks of spiritual trouble, but there is little more than a gesture towards their cause. On 20 March he may have ridden with 'M. S.' to Finchingfield but the first part of the initials is heavily inked out.[41] On 29 March he was 'scared thorough an [inked out] passion' and two days later he was loath to write because of '14v2 = matters', that is, love matters. This concern can be linked to 'M. S.' through proximity, for the whole entry for 1 April is concerned with this issue.

> Overwhelmed with [inked out] melancholye, and caryd in an hurrye to passe the bounds of an everlasting vow (though rash) which yet oh that it had bine kept; remember it, your cariage with M.S. I may justlye feare that the lord will punish mee in this kind (15).

Again there is a frustratingly obliterated adjective, but there is a new element in the 'everlasting vow'. We will return to this as we can move at least from pure guesswork to estimation later on. At this point, we have little more than the fears of punishment for his attitude. It seems fair to conclude that it was no more than that, more a matter of 'thinking' or 'feeling' than of 'doing'. In any case, the issue went off the boil for the next couple of months as Rogers spent this time in Cambridge, with a short trip to Ely, suggesting that absence makes the heart grow less troubled rather than fonder, as the aphorism would have it.

He returned to Wethersfield and its environs in the middle of July, and his troubles returned with familiar opacity. On 20 July he saw his 'old weaknes of affections', brought on 'at the presence of S' (25) and three days later was 'Snared by ill affections running out upon S5'. He blamed this upon 'ocasions, for they are the dangerous things, which annoy mee, for they overcome vowes' (25). By 'ocasions' (a recurrent complaint) he means social

---

[41] Diary, p. 14.

events which he often found were distractions from his spiritual discipline, but this was the only time he blamed them for challenging vows. Similarly, at the start of August, he complained that he was 'Much troubled and ensnared with S5[;] I am unfit for a sacrament: bec:[ause] my heart is not enough broken for my b1s2 dealings with g.[od] in nibling at old v4ws' (26).

Once he went back to Bishop's Stortford his attentions were elsewhere and 'M. S.' does not seem to have troubled him. There were two incidents that may well be linked, if not specifically to 'M. S.', at least to similar challenges. On 9 January 1636 he berated himself with a note that 'I feele l1sc3v:[ious] thoughts' (40) and six days after these lascivious thoughts he looked for help, asking for 'thy filial fear [to] drop into my soule for my heart is ready to run lavish into inordinate lusts, and vanityes' (41). Other than these two concerns, hypothetically connected to 'M. S.', he was not worried about this issue until he returned to Wethersfield in April 1636. He was a little vulnerable as he had no private place in which to pray, but he also blamed 'divers companyes, and ocasions of sin'. At this point he became specific, noting 'S A' (the initials being inked out but still legible) 'after whom my [inked out] goe; and I have so snared my selfe; that I am ashamed to looke up to god'. This was followed by one of the longest lamentations in the diary, asking to be delivered from 'all my backslidings, feeblenes, and weaknesse upon all ocasions'. He did not know 'how to rise up after my fallings' because 'I dare not say I'le returne no more', concluding with a reminder to himself to depend upon God 'and the way he chaukes [chalks] out doe thou tread in; and no other' (51–2). The question of 'returne' is ambiguous: it is not clear whether he would not or could not guarantee that he would not sin in similar ways again or simply that he would not return to Wethersfield, the location of these temptations.

There are no further encounters with 'M. S.' On 1 June, by which time he was back in Bishop's Stortford, he wrote that 'I am something unsetled, wandring in my thoughts, ab:[out] commenc:[ement] and S5 which divert the streame of my thoughts, so that they cannot be for god as they should be' (57). A week later he returned to Wethersfield and on 12 June he complained that his heart was brought very low, blaming it on the fact that he was 'anoyed with other matters, troubled with h2r; a great deale of rust gets upon my soule' (59). As far as clues to the nature of the temptation goes, the only addition is that this is the first time it is plain that the temptation is a 'her', indeed it is the first time that it is definitively involves a person.

Once he had returned to Stortford and, apart from a trip to Cambridge, stayed there, he only mentioned 'the old burden' on two occasions (63, 64) until 15 September when there was a new development. He recorded that 'I am this day, perplexed with various thoughts, by reason of some hearesey of M. S. affect:[ions] towards mee; yet I have got my heart to stoop to the Lord, and his will; and have prayed heartily for h2r; that g:[od] would take of[f] all love, if it stand not for his glorye' (71). Two days later, in an almost self-congratulatory prayer of thanksgiving, he gave thanks in particular that 'in some measure he hath quieted my amorous afections; this Lord hath bine my sin, ever my ingratitude' (72). It is almost as if the suggestion made to him by some unnamed individual that 'M. S.' had affections for him had made the problem easier, in that it had externalized it, that he was now praying for someone else rather than trying to govern, or asking for help to govern, his own emotions. It came at a time when he was becoming more patient with the Holy Spirit and more adept at coping with divine absence or silence. In October he observed that 'Doubtfull things much trouble mee, and disquiett mee; as what to do in S5. buisinesse'. His response is a positively passive spirituality: 'I have engaged my selfe and it lyes glowing at my heart Lord safely deliver mee out of these snares . . . . I will yet lord looke up to thee for wisdom, and; direction, oh and thy smiles with a cleare coast between mee, and thee'. Hand in hand with this was a practical approach: 'I hope I shall be carefull to avoide' the 'snares' (75). Five days later was the last appearance of the temptation and it reads as completely under control. 'I have got my heart to stoop in S5: bus:[iness] it troubles mee not to sighing; I desire to stoop to the Lord; I cannot see him in it, therfore content' (76).

What does this scattering of concerns and incidents tell us about the nature of the problem? It seems most likely that there was a woman among the godly in his father's parish who was proving to be attractive to Rogers and that this was, perhaps, the worst possible context for such feelings to be aroused, in that he was thinking 'lascivious thoughts' at exactly the times when his mind should have been engaged in religious duties, that is to say, times when he would be most prone to feelings of guilt. In terms of actual sin, as it were, what he *actually did* with 'M. S.', the most that can be said is that it was a matter of demeanour. He regretted his 'cariage' with her (15), which is probably as much as to say that he was very nice to her. At least from some hearsay that was passed on to him, she was, we might say, charmed by him.

This leads us to the matter of some vows he had taken. It may be that it was no more than a vow to maintain chastity, in the sense that such thoughts were illegitimate outside of wedlock and that his interest broached such a vow. At its most extreme, it might be noted that some of his causes for regret were for thoughts and maybe actions outside of her company. Would it be likely that the actions were masturbation? I am inclined to conclude that they were not; this might be seen as a modern eye looking for something almost *worth* feeling guilty about, imposing our value system on Rogers when he was working within a system that considered lascivious thoughts worth putting into code. Two famous examples, in different ways, seem to back this up. Oliver Cromwell was prepared to describe himself as 'the chief of sinners' on what, to us, seems very little basis, and any familiarity with John Bunyan's *Grace Abounding to the Chief of Sinners* will guarantee an appreciation of one of the consequences of a rigorous spiritual discipline. The godly system could produce intense fear and guilt over the slightest slip even in perceptions. 'Active' sinning, in our understanding, was far from necessary. A more profitable conclusion is a greater awareness of the sense of control required for a godly life. When the slightest lapse in attention was seen as deserving the judgment of a just, albeit loving, God, the attraction of humility and passivity and, in Rogers' case, dreams of the arrival of life after death, become much more comprehensible.

To return to more solid ground, given this nuclear family, upbringing and early education of godly examples and support networks, it must have been a substantial challenge to adjust to the very different world of higher education when he left home for university. With the loss of familial support mechanisms, Rogers was exposed to the temptation of what was, at least compared to Wethersfield and Felsted, an ungodly town. In his retrospective introductory autobiography, he portrayed himself as rather naive, an over-confident spiritual stripling. 'I had thought I had bine sure (as many young converts are too apt to thinke) and by wofull examples; which were the snares of hell, woven by the wit of the devell himselfe, did catch mee' (2). While Emmanuel College, his home, was known as a godly seminary, it was by no means hermetically sealed and, under the mastership of John Preston, had been comparatively secularized in its student body.[42] From Rogers' perspective, Cambridge was virtually over-run with the ungodly.

> I have run thorough divers ocasions this day, and companyes, where I am almost drowned and lost; snared; I have recovered my selfe a litle by prayer; oh strength Lord in a sinfull university; ignorant of the power of walking with thee; few lives by faith, they live by there wits, or by there hopes; but teach mee oh father to hold close to thee and keep mee at home in consc:[ience] and trust there beyond w[ha]t I see in others (17).

A recurring problem was that he was prone to be too friendly and Cambridge offered too much social distraction. 'I have bene in a mixt company, and doubtfully jolly' (16). At one point he was convinced that there was 'Litle life yet, [and that]... I must leave this Camb:[ridge] for quickning' (21). In itself, this proved inadequate. 'This day I went upon pleasure downe to Ely; I find my hearte willing, and ready to fly out too far in pleasures; and diversitye of companyes, and objects distract mee' (23). The weakness was his own for, while Ely is a beautiful cathedral town, its most passionate defenders would not portray it as a metropolis of temptation!

The initial consequences of the changed environment were poor academic performance and devotional 'backsliding' (3). Despite being blessed with the tutelage of Thomas Hill and Thomas Goodwin, both fellows of godly fame, 'did I live most unfruitfullye' (2). Spiritually, he suffered a period which he

[42] Patrick Collinson, 'Emmanuel and Cambridge: the early seventeenth-century heyday', and 'Puritan Emmanuel', both in Sarah Bendall, Christopher Brooke and Collinson, *A History of Emmanuel College* (Woodbridge, 1999), pp. 56–90, 177–226, esp. 214–26.

regarded retrospectively as retrograde. In his autobiography he recalled that 'once above all the rest [the devil] brought mee to such a pitch as I was in my study, upon the chair musing; as that I had almost said; I will renounce all former wayes of god, I see no profit in them' (3). Fortunately, 'the Lord restrained my toung' and 'my toung therefore shall praise the Lord, as long as I live' (3). Cambridge, of course, made available public worship which could prove to be an aid, but quantity did not necessarily equal quality. While once he could report that 'I have hearde Mr Goade and Dr Sibs' and that the godly preaching of Thomas Goad and Richard Sibbes meant that 'I see a little more of the heavenlye Canaan then I did' (8), this was not always the case. A little later he diligently listened to two preachers at Great St Marys, the church at the centre of the town, but reported that he was, 'As you might suppose after 2. mary sermons, Mr meads, and Mr Howlets; Dry like the sermons in the matter of any spirituall life; and so the unfitter for to morrow saboath' (18), Joseph Mead and Richard Howlet proving to be unsuited to a puritan palate.

What came to be the antidote at university, and, it will emerge, in his later career, was supportive company and the related aid to pietistic discipline. His tutor at the time of his journal was a Mr Frost, who has proven difficult to identify with any certainty. The most likely candidate, or at least the least unlikely candidate, is Walter Frost, the Manciple of Emmanuel College. His title meant that he was the steward who bought provisions for the college, but Frost was much more than this intellectually, being a renowned mathematician.[43] A tutor in seventeenth-century Cambridge had a much closer relationship with his pupils than in current academia, acting as what we would understand as a tutor but also as a mentor and father-figure.[44] Naturally, given the nature of the source, it is the spiritual side that we have most access to, and this is true of Mr Frost's first appearance in the diary. 'The lord gave mee inlargement in prayer at Mr Frosts, the Lord heare our groanes, and unite our hearts in love; who, a companye of us have joined together to meet often to pray together, and discourse' (7). This company provided pastoral comfort and spiritual exercises, with Rogers making no distinction between what we would see as piety and training for his ministerial skills. 'The Lord hath bine pleased to warme my pore hearte in my company; ... it was my turne to pray; and the lord was pleased a litle to looke upon mee and put in some few desires to the saboath approching' (8). This even gave him confidence to accept times when God was characterized by absence rather than presence. 'This day wee fasted, and prayed, and the lord denyed audience but I will trust in the lord my strong encouragement' (10).

---

43 Collinson, 'Emmanuel and Cambridge', p. 77n.; Sarah Bendall, 'Estate management and finances 1584–1719', in *eadem*, et al., *Emmanuel College*, p. 129.
44 Collinson, 'Emmanuel and Cambridge', pp. 60–2.

In addition to Mr Frost and Rogers himself, the participants in the company, as far as they can be identified, have a fairly strong record among the godly. John Arthur became rector of Clapham, Surrey, from 1642 until his ejection in 1662. Simeon Ashe was chaplain to Robert Greville, Lord Brooke, and went on to be a major figure in the pieties and ecclesiological disputes of the 1640s. Peter Sterry went on to be one of the Cambridge Platonists, a very important figure in the later development of puritan piety and scholarship.[45] The bonds made in these exercises were substantial, as is shown by Rogers' note upon returning for Commencement in April 1636. 'I have had much good company today we joined (our old companye) in prayer together; at Mr Frosts at supper' and the following day, 'my heart yet rejoices in the choice of Sr. Sterry' as a fellow at Emmanuel (50).

In the autumn of 1635 Samuel received the news of his first post. He was to be appointed as household chaplain to Lady Margaret Denny, the elderly dowager of Bishop's Stortford, Hertfordshire. The first note is that on 28 August he was somewhat distracted due to a 'multiplicitye of ocas:[ions] and thoughts of going to my Lady Denys' (27). Three days later he took up the position. There is no positive indication within the diary of how he came by the offer, but there are two possibilities and it may have been a combination of the two. Emmanuel College had an established reputation as a breeding ground for godly ministers and had come to operate as a 'job centre' for young graduates. It was often part of a tutor's role to ease a student's transition from undergraduate to trainee minister.[46] This often involved a well-oiled gossip network, particularly present in East Anglia and its environs, and Daniel Rogers was well established as part of this community. This may well have played a part in the post being offered to Samuel Rogers as his father was a minister settled close to Earls Colne, indeed a fairly frequent visitor there.[47] This meant that he was familiar with the Harlakenden family, of whom more below. For the current purposes what is important is that Richard Harlakenden was Lady Denny's son-in-law, likely to know that she was looking for a chaplain, to have the opportunity to ask Daniel Rogers and of a mindset to value his recommendations. Thus it may be that Samuel received references, as it were, from his tutor and from his father.

In some ways, Samuel was an ideal candidate. He was from good stock, part of a family which had produced several of the major preachers in the area, and so was a good catch. At the same time, he was young and inexperienced and therefore relatively cheap, which would have been important as the Denny family were of high status but of declining wealth.

[45] The individuals discussed here are identified in Diary, pp. 8, 10. Starting points for their later careers can be found in Venn and *DNB*. There are other individuals less clearly identifiable and the possibilities are discussed in the relevant footnotes.
[46] Webster, *Godly Clergy*, pp. 36–42.
[47] For instance, see Diary, pp. 3, 98, 161.

Lady Margaret Denny was of gentle Cornish extraction, and she had been a Maid of Honour to Elizabeth I in the late 1570s and early 1580s. Around the end of 1583 she had married the courtier Sir Edward Denny and they had set up home in Tralee Castle, Munster, in the late 1580s. It was a particularly inopportune time to be part of the English ruling *élite* in the south-west of Ireland, for their worldly goods suffered severely at the hands of the earl of Tyrone and his forces in 1598 during the Nine Years War. They returned to England and, after Sir Edward died in 1599, Lady Denny settled in Bishop's Stortford, living primarily on established social credit. This must have been fairly demanding, as nine of her children survived to adulthood and seven were still financially dependent on her.[48]

While it might have been a good match in social terms, bringing cheap renown to Lady Denny and a post of some status to Samuel Rogers, it was far from perfect spiritually. A chaplaincy was more than a social flag to a gentry family, but it was also that. As Samuel noted when he went with Lady Denny to visit her brother-in-law, the earl of Norwich, Lady Denny 'makes much of mee' (77). His interests and hers were far from a good match. In fact his first account of his time at Stortford was reserved. On the first day he was 'something estranged before lying downe[;] new ocasions and companye, though lawfull, divert my heart much' and the following day he complained that he was 'somew[ha]t = streightned bec:[ause] of pl1c3' (28). As he became more and more disenchanted with his employer, in the privacy of his diary he made very unflattering allusions. On two occasions, he was convinced that 'I dwell in Meshech' (54),[49] which was as much as to say that he dwelt among warlike, barbarous people. This was almost mild compared to the scriptural model he looked to for guidance during one particularly bad spell. He was 'much disquieted with the uneven spirit of this w4m1n' and asked the Lord, 'what should Joseph doe in Potiphers house?' (71) Within two weeks he was asking for patience and wisdom 'to walke as Joseph in Potipher's company of Egyptians' (73). This was to compare Lady Denny to the wife of Potiphar who had tried to seduce Joseph and, upon being rejected, had then made false charges against him which had culminated in Joseph's imprisonment.[50]

Elsewhere Rogers compared Lady Denny to the authoritarian and quarrelsome Laban of Genesis 31: 7–55,[51] and the task of bringing spirituality to this household as being asked 'to wash Ætheopians' (78), that is, to do the impossible. At other points a scriptural education was unnecessary to decode his abuse. He employed snide sarcasm, referring to Lady Denny as 'her highnes' (71), a remark which merited a marginal note

---

48 The main source for the biographical details is H. L. L. Denny, 'Biography of Sir Edward Denny', *Trans. East Herts. Arch. Soc.*, II (1902–4), 252–9.
49 The other reference is Diary, p. 95.
50 Genesis 37:36, 39:1–20.
51 Diary, p. 102.

from Thomas Percy, later owner of the diary. Perhaps the nastiest description was when he complained that he had 'come home to my sc1b: flocke, to oynt them' (80). As far as can be certain, this was to describe the family as 'scabby' or 'scabious', as having symptoms of scabies. Thus all he could do was cope with the surface manifestations of their illness as the root cause was beyond his powers: 'though it bee but to drawe it in; that is all I can doe, and scarse that some times it breakes out; heere a push at drunkenness there a scab, of profaning gods name' (80–1).

One might be tempted to assume from the scale of this condemnation that Lady Denny was a resolute hedonist, but the condemnation reveals more about Rogers' sensitivities than Denny's sins. I am not suggesting that she was, in fact, a saint, merely that they had differing priorities. Early on in his time at Stortford he was hurt to note that 'I have bine stirred by my L.[ady] and M. E. w4rd of long prayers, &c.' (35), that is, that Lady Denny and her eldest daughter, Madam Elizabeth Earle, had had a word with him, cautioning him not to make the daily exercises too long. Evidently his appetite for prayer exceeded theirs. This was plain some time later when he noted that Lady Denny rose, presumably to leave, 'in the midst of exercise', and that the Lord 'carys mee on to gall her in duty; shee netled' (100). It may be that she had interrupted his private devotions when he complained that she had entered his chamber uninvited with the consequence that he 'could not be sweet natur[e]d all day after' (43). Her most active 'crime' was verbal, when he noted that she 'will swear by g.[od's] truth; faith; which sads my heart most heavily' (93). This helps to make the lack of common ground more comprehensible as on one particular day when he reported that 'I have had some bickering with my L1d:[y] for backing her tipling servants' (71). He reproved her lack of reproval and as a result 'All the house' were 'ag:[ainst] mee as too strict' (71).

Part of the difficulty was that Rogers had little experience of a domestic environment that was not driven by godly discipline. Even when he was an undergraduate, good preaching and godly conference had been fairly readily available. The social context of the gentry household was a different kettle of fish. Lady Denny's children failed to fit Rogers' behavioural models. He complained of 'Mr Ch:[arles'] cariage and the rest of them' (35), but it is not quite clear exactly what Charles Denny, a senior fellow of King's College, Cambridge, was guilty of. The diary is more specific with Lady Denny's eldest son, Francis. One night, 'the sad wretch Mr Francis shewed himselfe in his colours; swearing, cursing, and storming like a Bedlam' (45), which is as much as to say he behaved like a madman. His offence must have been serious, for three days later Rogers celebrated the fact that 'my lady tooke in hand Mr Francis for his swearing, spake most fully to him; oh why shouldest thou tare the name of g.[od] in peices, did he wrong thee' (46).

The social world of the gentry involved a much less avoidable ungodliness. When Lady Denny held the manorial court, by its nature it brought unattractive company: 'many ill words slip out from them; Lord thou knowest, they vexe my soule, I communicate not with them; I abhorr all ways displeasing to thee' (52). Similarly, the social *élite* of the locale did not pass muster with Rogers. The household of Lady Elizabeth Morley, an important figure in Stortford, made a particularly bad impression. They were, according to Rogers, ' a swearing, popish, profane family; my heart cold among them oh what a lamentable thing is it to be in hell, if only it were to be among swearers' (48). When he accompanied Lady Denny on a visit to the Morley household, he found himself 'entangled with a companye of forlorne fellowes' and reflected that having poor provisions among the godly was better than to be among the 'pertakers of the great abundance of the ungodly' (54–5). This could cut to the quick. In this environment, his vocation required him to participate in social gatherings where he had disdain for the company but could not admonish them. This spoiled the whole affair. When 'Stevens the caviler' was present, the gathering was ruined: 'such an one in a company is like a dead flye in a box of ointment, makes the companye unsavory' (78).

One of the most unavoidable inhabitants of Stortford, and also one who grated with Rogers the most, was the vicar, Richard Butler. He was also a clear instance of the frustration generated by involuntary tongue-biting. This was true to a certain extent at their first meeting. After a day of episcopal visitation, 'at dinner B5tler playes his p[oin]ts, ag[ainst] N.[ew] E.[ngland] the lord stird mee up ag:[ainst] him though I was faint to pinch by reason of B.[ishop']s office[r]s' (29). The pains of involuntary silence must have been exacerbated by being an involuntary recipient of Butler's preaching. Two sermons in particular tested Rogers. One exegesis of Romans 13:1, presumably upping the ante on clerical conformity, was hard to sit through. 'Saboath, this profane wretch Butler plays the wofull wretch (let every soule be subject) my heart sadded' (95–6). A performance that must have been even harder to endure in silence was one devoted specifically to the refutation of nonconformist arguments. It can only have been made worse by the fact that he seems to have set up an imaginary dispute between himself and a nonconformist. 'Butler playes his parts, shewes hims:[elf] in his colours ag:[ainst] Zelotes; brings his 25. obj:[ections] ag:[ainst] common prayer, answers them, and railes'. Rogers simply noted, 'oh what a deale of hurt does saplesse preaching' (48). It can only have confirmed his suspicions when Lady Denny joined with Butler and another guest in some unspecified wickedness. 'L1:[d y] playes the wretch still at table at noone, I silent, I have anger then shew, at my lying downe; L[or]d grant it to her also; Dr Good comes and Butler and her play the wretches, to thyne counsells; &c.' Rogers, it will have been noted, had to suffer in silence and described himself the following day as 'tamquam piscis in arido' (110–11), effectively as a fish out of water.

Rogers made many remarks about what it was like to 'live with a tumultuous companye, of vaine loose, lascivious wretches' (68), 'a most barren rotten company' (52) and in particular how he was 'full of disorder, bec:[ause] of unsetlednes in calling' (77) caused by 'many distracting thoughts, that hinder mee in my place' (63). Eventually he found order in the disorder, identifying God's purpose in placing him in this, 'my wildernes' (95). It was a purpose that was far from flattering to the Denny household:

> the Lord hath taken this course with mee to pitch mee among bryars, and thornes, that they might teare of[f] a deale of scurfe, and basenes of[f] from my spirit; I blesse thy name oh L[or]d for thy great love this weeke past (96).

Readers should not take the impression that Rogers was wholly isolated in Stortford. One major source of comfort was Richard Harlakenden, who had married Marie, Lady Denny's youngest surviving daughter, in 1634, and had possibly been a factor in getting Rogers the post.[52] Indeed, Harlakenden came to Rogers' defence when Lady Denny turned on him. 'L1d:[yship's] b3tt2r t4ng; ag:[ainst] long pr11ng[;] Mr Harlak:[enden] m4d2r1tes' (109), that is, Lady Denny turned her bitter tongue against lengthy prayers again, and Harlakenden moderated. He made a favorable impression on Rogers from their first recorded encounter shortly before his arrival at Stortford. 'I went to Mr Harlakendens, where I thought the very ayre breathed life into mee' (27–8). Virtually without exception, each encounter was a source of refreshment for Rogers. 'Oh w[ha]t an happinesse it is to dwell under the same roofe with a thorough Xian, I am much refreshed, quickned, heartned, incouraged by the company of this good man' (33). This was a constant element, albeit one reliant on his visits, with thanks being given for the fact that 'the Lord supports mee by a mighty power; and now cheeres mee by the coming of Mr Harlak:[enden] and wife; oh how deare is the company of the saints' (108). (This last was the only occasion he voiced any appreciation of Marie Harlakenden!) Richard Harlakenden certainly helped facilitate the comfort Rogers received from a Mr Archer, whom they visited together,[53] and a Mr Wilson. The latter was probably John Wilson, the nonconformist curate at nearby Elsenham.[54] Rogers' initial review was positively enthusiastic: 'oh how beautiful are the feet of such a mortified soule; I am much in love with him; and glad I have such an one that I an unworthy wretch may be acquainted withall' (29).[55]

Closer to home, he was quite successful in becoming involved in a group of like-minded parishioners in Stortford. As will be shown in greater detail in the section on spirituality below, four households hosted fasts that

[52] Denny, p. 258; genealogical details of the Harlakenden family are given in Alan Macfarlane (ed.), *The Diary Of Ralph Josselin 1616–1683* (Oxford, 1976), App. I. The family played a major role in Josselin's time at Earls Colne; cf. *idem, The Family Life of Ralph Josselin* (Cambridge, 1970), *passim*.
[53] Diary, p. 35; cf. pp. 30, 40, 67, 107.
[54] Venn; GL MSS 9537/15; GLRO DL/C 319 fo. 80.
[55] Cf. Diary, pp. 29, 31, 37, 38, 39, 63, 69, 75, 89, 92, 93, 119.

provided a fairly regular 'fix'.[56] They were referred to once as 'our weeklye meeting' (81), once as 'fasting, and prayer (secretly generale every 3. weekes)' (106). Similarly, it seems that the household staff at the Denny residence were not all beyond hope. He found particular comfort in exercises with Mary Mountfort, a rather troubled servant who gave as well as received support: 'wee pray together, the L[or]d softens us, thawes us, and gives us some heate, and warmth, L[or]d more, and more dailye ever till wee shall come to injoy it perfectlye' (100).

The greatest source of spiritual comfort, however, was a little further abroad. In his time at Stortford he established a regular and fruitful relationship with William Sedgwick, the rector at Farnham, just over the border with Essex. There is no explicit evidence of how this relationship was established. There are no signs of family connexions, and educational ties are unlikely, given that Sedgwick studied at Pembroke College, Oxford. It is most likely that he was introduced by the John Wilson encountered above, as Sedgwick accompanied Rogers on a visit to Wilson, and Wilson preached at least once at Farnham.[57] Sedgwick had arrived in Farnham early in 1634 after leaving university, and quite swiftly established himself as a rising godly preacher. In the early 1640s he was received with popular acclaim (and controversy) as lecturer in Ely and was of sufficient stature to be called to preach at a public fast before the House of Commons in 1642.[58] His later career seems to have been exemplary of the chaotic divisions among the puritans of the 1640s and 1650s, with a series of ecclesiological shifts and a fervent millenarianism which earned him the sobriquet of 'Doomsday Sedgwick'. The allegations of madness may tell us more about the hostility of critics than about any actual disorder.[59] In the period in which he was an important influence on Samuel Rogers, it seems he was a mainstream puritan critic of the status quo and a rising star of puritan preaching and politics.

William Sedgwick and his former tutor, George Hughes, with whom he was still close, filled three substantial gaps in Rogers' life at Stortford, providing three services which stopped him from feeling quite as isolated as he might have been. These were godly public worship, the therapeutic society of the saints and access to a similar perspective on ecclesiastical politics to his own. These will be treated in turn, and their importance to Rogers will become clear. The unsatisfactory provision of divine service at Stortford, at least according to Rogers' appraisal, has been touched on earlier. That this need was met by Sedgwick is plain from the entries when Sedgwick had preached. 'A litle melted by mr sedgewickes sermon; Lord still

56 Diary, pp. 32, 38, 39, 44, 53, 60, 62, 76, 79, 94, 106, 119.
57 Diary, pp. 93, 119.
58 T. W. Davids, *Annals of Evangelical Nonconformity in the County of Essex* (London, 1863), pp. 566–7; William Sedgwick, *Zions Deliverance* (1642).
59 Davids, pp. 566–7.

goe on, quicken and refresh dailye, I have continuall want of supplye' (48). This helped both his private piety and the exercises he provided for the Denny family: 'I heard Mr Sedgwicke, of holines, the Lord inlarged my heart in familye, and in secret, he drew neere to my soule' (66–7). The preaching would provide a public counter-balance to the positions promoted by Richard Butler. 'Saboath made a delight by the efect:[ual] preaching of Mr Sedgew:[ick] (son of man manifest to destroy workes of Satan) herein, my soule rejoices that all adversarys are, and shall be destroyed' (91). It should come as no surprise to find that George Hughes received equally good reviews. 'In these decaying times, the Lord hath stirred up our faithfull minister to declare the will of g.[od] closely this day; mr Hues; 4. Galati:[ans] 23. child:[ren] of promise; the L[or]d hath thawed my heart by it' (82). It should be noted that Rogers' public needs went beyond the sermon to include the sacrament. This will be developed below but here we will merely note that Sedgwick was more than satisfactory here, too. 'Saboth, and sacrament, at Farnham, much revived in spirit, and going away from gods table, as filling with marrow, and refined wines' (106).

He usually found spiritual revival from the company he met with at Farnham. 'Saboth, sadded at first; raised by the word, at Farnham; quickned by talking with some saints; much rejoycing in g.[od] in all these' (92). Such meetings helped him to see himself as on 'the right side' in society. At the time mentioned earlier when the company of Mr Good at Stortford was frustrating him, he fled, describing himself as 'at mr Sedgwicks' and quite specifically 'to avoid Good' (110). In a more positive way, when he went with Sedgwick to visit John Wilson, he reported that 'wee rejoice in each other, and animate one another to suffering; oh let my lot be with the righteous in all conditions' (93). William Sedgwick was also present at several of the days devoted to fasting and prayer in this period.[60] One day in particular can be seen to have provided spiritual solace on an individual level and to have set him among people clearly identifying themselves against the religious status quo.

> Now we fast at Farnham, the Lord inlarges mr sedgewick mightilye his sp:[irit] plainelye; the Lord thawes my heart sweetlye; and I can lye downe in some sweet assurance of acceptance through Xt; oh Lord let none of our pore suites be lost: oh dear god, be not angry ag:[ainst] the prayers of thy dear ones, who in the strength of thy command have gone out to thee; oh downe, downe with the enimyes of thy truth, and lord lift up, the heades of thy people (81).

Sedgwick and, to a lesser extent, George Hughes seem to have been central to the first possibility of a move for Rogers from the Denny household. The opportunity appears unannounced in the diary and with Rogers' gesture towards code. 'I goe with Mr. Sedgew:[ick] to Sir S. L5k: enterteined

---

60 Diary, pp. 82, 88, 94.

sweetly; discourse ab:[out] change of place' (115). We saw earlier his discontent with the Denny household, and he had complained of an inability to 'be fruitfull in both callings' (111). It was not until the day before the trip on 1 September 1637 that there is any clear indication of the possibility of new employment. On 31 August he was 'full of distracted thoughts ab:[out] change', about Mary Mountfort but also 'and my selfe' (114). It may be of significance that he ended this day's entry lying down to Simeon's song, perhaps casting Sedgwick as the righteous and devout senior man who saw the future of the infant Jesus. Whether or not this was the case, it seems that Sedgwick was the means of introducing Rogers to Sir Samuel Luke, the godly gentleman of Cople, in Bedfordshire. The diary is not wholly clear about the post for which Rogers was candidate, but we can trace the fortunes of this plan and make some educated guesses.

He must have made a good impression in the opening meeting, for nearly three weeks later he set aside a day for fasting and prayer, which shows that the plan was moving forward. The second reason he set out for the fast was 'ab:[out] the change of place, and calling; for I am to preach on Saboth' (116). Accordingly, on the following Sabbath, 24 September, he went to Farnham and heard George Hughes preach, before going on to one of three parishes called Pelham, in Hertfordshire, where he preached 'with comfortable assistance, and approbation, of Sir Sam:[uel] Luke; and Ladye, an humble gentlewoman; the L[or]d shields mee of[f] in the buisinesse' (117). Four days later the water gets a little clearer in some places, a little muddier in others. The journal notes that 'now I post to Tay: ab:[out] Capell bus:[iness] there furthered; the L[or]d upholds my sp:[irit] from sinking' (117). It seems that he visited either Great Tey, Marks Tey or Little Tey, all in Essex, perhaps about a post at 'Capell'. There are two parishes just over the border with Suffolk, Capell St Andrew or Capell St Mary which are possibilities. The best candidate is Pontisbright Chapel, which is a short distance to the north of Great Tey.[61] From the entries at the very end of the month and the start of October, it emerges that the post was parochial. On 30 September, 'I goe to Capell, on tryall, there I find loving, enterteinment; and hopes' (117). There follow two days of success and failure.

> Octob: 1. Saboath, I preach at capell twice, the L[or]d is gracious towards
> mee in assistance, and all very forward to have mee;
> 2. now Sir Sam:[uel] Luke and I goe to Bedford, for License, crost, I ready
> to be disquieted, but yet beare up my selfe by faith (117–8).

What seems to have happened was that he preached at his potential parish, possibly Pontisbright Chapel, and won the acclaim of the congregation. Then he went to Bedford with Samuel Luke in order to get a preaching licence from John Williams, the bishop of Lincoln. Williams was an

---

61   The likelihood of the post being related to Pontisbright Chapel is given weight by the fact that the vicarage belonged to Great Tey: Smith, p. 310.

attractive source as he was reliably sympathetic to puritans and was unlikely to be too testing on conformity. However, Rogers was 'crost', that is, 'crossed' in that he was refused a licence. This may have been due to the fact that he was actually eight weeks too young to be ordained and to hold a benefice. He had no clear idea for the following two weeks of what was to happen next, and felt 'Disturbed ab:[out] the place, in uncerteintyes troubles' (118). Resolution came on 16 October: 'now I am sent for to Pelham, on the sudden; and am crost in the change of my place to Sir Sam:[uel] Luke; I am troubled, yet I gather up my selfe in my god, who hath bine my comfort, and will be' (119).

This particular post had proven to be unavailable, but Rogers' appetite had been whetted and the possibility of change remained in his thoughts. 'Troubled, yet uphold my selfe by faith in Jehovah my right:[eousness] I have thoughts of removall; L[or]d guid[e] mee and find out some way of ease' (119). His trust was well placed, for the next chance appeared towards the end of November. As with the earlier negotiation, the second opportunity appears unannounced in the diary. This time the contact seems to have been made through Richard Harlakenden, although it is not made explicit.

> today greatly I delight in the humble company of Master Harlakenden; an example surely of pious humility; the honourable matron, Lady Vere (with the spiritually fair woman Mrs Watson) pleasant to be sure, in a bountiful fashion; she it is who addresses me inside the inn at Stortford; approving me as a chaplain; &c. meanwhile I await what the Lord dictates (123).[62]

A couple of weeks later he reported that Priscilla Watson, Lady Vere's secretary and close companion, 'already sends letters of hospitality to me; my God, direct my steps into your path', ending with a sense of anticipation in that 'I have beheld you thus far and I await you' (127–8).[63] His preparation for the final trial was similar too. On 9 December, two days before he was to go to meet Lady Vere again, he spent the day in private fasting and prayer. The prayer was devoted entirely to his opportunity: 'the reason is; a change of place; I surrender to the decision of Jehovah, my way, He will bring about that which bears the greatest glory to Himself, and that which is of the greatest benefit to me' (128).[64] Two days later it came to a climax and it is reported in a very concise fashion: 'I goe to my Lady Veres; the L[or]d helpes mee in the ordinance and wee strike up the match' (128).

---

[62] [This section of the diary is in Latin. Where this is the case I will give my translation in the main text and the original in a footnote.] lætor hodie quam maximè in humili societate M[agist]^{ri} Harlak; Exemplar certe piæ humilitatis; venerabilis matrona, Domina Veere (cum candidâ sp: mulier M^{ra} Watson) suavis generoso quidem modo: h: e: me: alloqoquitur; intra tabernum Storfordiensam; acceptura mea capellanum Si; &c ego interim expectam qd loquetum Dominus

[63] M^{ra} Watson literas ad me ian mittit invitatorias; Deus mi dirige gressus meas in viam tuam; Ego adhere aspexi te, atg expectabo

[64] causa est; mutatio loci; Devolvo supra Jehovam viam meam illu efficiet qd sibi maximam asferat gloriam, et qd mihi optimam est

He returned to Stortford via Earls Colne, Sudbury and Wethersfield. The purpose of the circuitous route home was to break the news first to Richard Harlakenden, then to his sister Hanna and to his father. The last was probably the most worrying as it was the most important to him and, despite the compressed entry, probably due to him being on the move, the anxiety and the relief are plain. 'I come to wethersf:[ield] to shew buisinesse to my father; he approves, I rejoice' (129). After this, breaking the news to Lady Denny seems relatively easy; perhaps now the power relations had changed and Rogers felt a little empowered. On the first day he simply writes 'I come home reveale to my Lady shee begins to stir, but I quiet her' (129). On the following day, Lady Denny seems to have accepted the inevitable with a sense of grace. 'I attend upon god, and the L[or]d gives mee favour in my Lady Dennys eyes, that I goe away suddenly shee pardons' (129).

The move from being chaplain to Lady Denny to being chaplain to Lady Mary Vere was a substantial step up the ladder of godly prestige for Rogers. As we will see, the geographical move from Bishop's Stortford to Hackney, more or less a suburb of London, exposed him to a broader selection of ministers and lay people, particularly radicals but also conservatives, but of greater importance was the family who took him on. Lady Vere's social status and marital connexions, both her own and those of her children, placed her in the influential network of puritan gentry. She was born in 1581, the youngest daughter of Sir John Tracy of Toddington, Gloucestershire. Her first husband was William Hoby of Hale, Gloucestershire and after his death she married Sir Horace Vere, later created Baron Vere of Tilbury, one of the senior commanders of the English forces in the Netherlands. He died in 1635. Her brother-in-law was Sir Edward Conway, secretary of state in the 1620s, who we will meet again. Her daughters mostly married well, both socially and in terms of godliness. Elizabeth, their eldest daughter, married John Holles, second earl of Clare, in 1626 when he was 'merely' Lord Haughton. Her second daughter, Mary, married Sir Roger Townshend, baronet of Rainham, Norfolk, the following year, and when she was widowed he was succeeded by Mildmay Fane, earl of Westmorland, in 1638. This match was a matter of concern for Rogers as he worried that Fane was spiritually inadequate, praying that 'the L[or]d pitty her, that shee may never loose any motions; but stir them up' (152). Catherine, the third daughter, married Oliver St John, son of Sir John St John of Lydiard Tregoz, Cornwall, in 1634. Similarly, when Oliver died in November 1637, Rogers was concerned about his replacement, noting that 'this is the Resolution of great ones, that Religion must complye with there state and some of there bredths yet I say not all of them bredths are sinfull' (164). She married John, Lord Paulet.[65]

---

[65] Fairly reliable biographical details can be found in *DNB* and in C. R. Markham, *The Fighting Veres* (Boston, Mass., 1888), but the introduction and notes to I. M. Calder (ed.), *The Letters of John Davenport Puritan Divine* (New Haven, Conn., 1937), are also useful.

However, the impression should not be given that these connexions were what constituted Lady Vere's importance and reputation. More significant were her piety and labour as an individual. She was one of the godly gentry who earned a substantial encomium from Samuel Clarke. He praised her 'Zeal to the worship of God' in terms of her patronage and the way she used her position to protect and advance godly ministers.[66] This can be seen in her intervention in the disputed succession to the vicarage of St Stephen's, Coleman Street, the London parochial church she most frequently attended. Upon the death of the vicar in 1624, John Davenport was chosen as successor. However, questions were asked about his conformity, partly due to his popularity. Along with Sir Edward Conway and his son-in-law, Sir Robert Harley, she was instrumental in persuading George Montaigne, the bishop of London, and George Abbot, the archbishop of Canterbury, that Davenport was a suitable candidate. Indeed, when Davenport fled to New England in 1637, Lady Vere's household looked after his infant son until the younger John Davenport joined his parents in New Haven in 1639.[67] She was held in high esteem by many of the most prestigious godly ministers. In one letter from Davenport, Richard Sibbes asked to be remembered to her and in fact Sibbes dedicated one of his most famous works of practical divinity, *The Bruised Reed,* to the Veres, describing them as 'exemplary in all religious causes'.[68]

For our purposes, the more significant part of Clarke's praise was for '*her Private Worship of God*'. According to him, 'she brought her Religion and Devotion home with her, and did not leave them in her Pue behind her ... as too many do'. There were devotional exercises twice daily, with each day ending with the reading of a psalm. Sermons were repeated to the family and servants every Sabbath and she examined the staff to ensure that they took on the preacher's message.[69] Naturally, Clarke's account is somewhat idealized and should be read against the practicalities detailed in Rogers' account. The initial impression is that there are relatively few references to the spiritual exercises and piety of Lady Vere and her family. Partly this is true: Samuel was plagued with toothache and a thoroughly unpleasant 'Ague' (143) from January 1638 through to May.[70] In addition, his sister died on 17 June[71] and this loss was to have a considerable place in his journal. In fact, the relative absence may be a good sign, given that the most

[66] Samuel Clarke, *The Lives of Sundry Eminent Persons in this Later Age* (1683), 2nd pag., p. 145.
[67] Calder (ed.), *Letters of John Davenport*, p. 2; Francis Bremer, *Congregational Communion: clerical friendship in the Anglo-American puritan community, 1610–1692* (Boston, Mass., 1994), pp. 89–91.
[68] Calder (ed.), *Letters of John Davenport*, p. 31; Richard Sibbes, *Works*, ed. A. B. Grosart (Edinburgh, 1862), I, 37.
[69] Clarke, *Lives*, p. 146.
[70] Diary, pp. 137–148.
[71] Diary, p. 152.

frequent references to family exercises in Stortford were, as we have seen, complaints. When the reader provides a closer reading, a fair assessment of Vere piety can be drawn out.

A great deal of such an assessment is quite positive. On one occasion, *rôles* were reversed when Samuel was particularly low. 'I labour under my hardness; the guilt of my levity possesses me, and I am oppressed with sadness; I go to London with Lady Vere, who strengthens and consoles me' (142).[72] Lady Vere showed an ability to embrace spiritual humility, a central part of godly piety. 'I rejoice greatly in the humble society of Lady Vere; whose soft heart displayed itself this night, through streams of tears, in contemplation of herself' (136–7).[73] This came shortly after a similar review of her eldest daughter, Elizabeth. 'I can [do] all things through the powers of Christ who gives liberty in the presence of the Countess of Clare; man is nothing, if God be present' (134).[74] A comparable assessment was earned by Catherine after the death of Oliver St John. 'Saboath; wherin the Lord is graciously with mee in a private exercise with the desolate widow Mrs St. John' (166). Indeed, shortly after his arrival at Hackney, Samuel made a rather pointed comparison. 'Saboath, the first at Hackney, the L[or]d draws neere to mee, is all sufficient, he gives mee great comfort in my Lady oh most difference between L. M.[argaret Denny] and her; oh my happy change' (130). Communal piety could also produce such enthusiasm. 'Today, we, fasting, pour forth prayers which are not scanty, in our house; the Lord melts our hearts in his breast' (170).[75] Perhaps the highlight was when he led an exercise on one of his favourite sources of piety, the Song of Songs. 'I have discussed this night, of the blessed union with Christ; and my heart rejoices in Christ, my head, vine, spouse, foundation, teacher, my King' (173).[76]

It would, however, be inaccurate to say that the relationship was wholly positive. Memories of Lady Denny must have been revived by a complaint delivered by Catherine. 'L1d:[y] tells mee I was t4 l4ng at pr1y[er] and my heart boiles ag:[ainst] her; most bitterly; A s1d w4m1n, that will have her w3l, and will not give in an 4nch; the Lord give mee a meeke, and a wise sp:[irit] to doe service in my place' (160). He was castigated for being too long at prayer and must have objected, for it is plain that Catherine would have her will and would not give an inch. Shortly after, he received an

---

[72] Laboro sub duritie mea; possidet me reatus levitatis meæ, atque premor tristatiâ; Eo Londinum cum Dominâ veere, quæ me corroborat atque consolatur

[73] Lætor multum in humili societate Dominæ veere; cuius molle cor ostendit se hac nocte per lachrymarum rivulos, in consideratione suiipsius

[74] Possum omnia per Christi vires qui libertatem dat coram Comitissâ Clarensi; nihil est homo, si deus præsens sit

[75] Hodie Ieiunantes nos, preue effendimus non ieiunas; in domu nostrâ; liqua facit dominus corda nostra in pectore suo

[76] Disservi hac nocte de beatâ unione cum christo; et exultat cor meum in Christo, capite, meo, vite, coniuge, fundamento, magistro, Rege meo

anticipatory warning that cut to the quick. After hearing Peter Sainthill preach, 'P. W1ts4n, comes to mee before repetition and tells mee; L. M1r5: would not have mee 1d: any th:[ing] to s2rm:[on] and I was much v2x2' (163). Priscilla Watson made it plain that when he led the repetition of the sermon in the afternoon he was not to add anything to it; this vexed him. Perhaps his most bitter complaint was addressed against Lady Vere and Lady Anne Wake, the stepdaughter of her brother-in-law, Sir Edward Conway. 'I mourne, yet looke toward sion, for my help comes from on high; I am greived much at the sad l2tt2r and these 2. husw3f2s W1k:[e] and V2r:[e]' (164). Unfortunately, it is not clear what the 'sad letter' was about and so we have no idea of the offence, but for Rogers, usually a stickler for social propriety, to refer to them as 'huswifes' was a serious insult, with the only precedent being his harshest condemnation of Lady Denny described above. It should, however, also be noted that these were rare difficulties, and some time before this last incident Anne Wake had been a source of delight. 'I am comforted with a letter from M W1k2r: wherin is signified that I have bin as one of 1000. to her' (157).

The new environment of London, and particularly the social network of Lady Vere, was mentioned above, and this new experience had a substantial impact on Samuel Rogers. As will be seen, the new contacts, clerical and lay, received a mixed appraisal, with some highs and some lows. Probably the biggest 'star' in the godly firmament was the elderly preacher, John Dod, who visited the household and met Samuel when the latter was ill. Dod was famed as a preacher and disputant. After he had been deprived in 1607 he found a refuge at Fawsley in Northamptonshire and worked as the leading figure in a ministerial seminary in the Midlands. He was probably best known for his numerous works of practical divinity and devotion and as a spiritual and, on occasion, political counsellor to both clerical and lay puritans. He had been a convenor of and prime contributor to conferences for puritan strategy and tactics since 1606 and was an important figure to be consulted on issues of ecclesiology in the early Stuart period. His publications were so clear on matters of practice in divine worship that Nicholas Tyacke refers to him as a representative of 'hardline nonconformity'.[77] During his visit to the Vere household he helped Samuel to decipher his illness by working through the varieties of chastisement that God sent and coming to the conclusion that it was a testing of faith which amounted to a backhanded compliment. Rogers saw Dod as an admirable veteran, noting his approaching eighty-fifth birthday and introducing him in the journal by giving thanks that 'god sent an Angel Mr Dod to comfort mee' (146). Perhaps the most moving part was the reference Dod made to Richard Rogers, the grandfather who died when Samuel was four years old

---

[77] Samuel Clarke, *A Generall Martyrologie* (1677), pp. 168–78; Webster, *Godly Clergy*, pp. 11, 25, 58, 27–8, 157–8, 301–5; Nicholas Tyacke, *Aspects of English Protestantism, c. 1530–1700* (Manchester, 2001), pp. 20, 123, 125, 66, 67 (quote).

but whose memory must have stood as a spiritual patriarch in the Rogers family. As Samuel put it, 'and so blessed mee for my grandf:[ather] and father each; and the L[or]d much refreshed mee by him' (146).

A minister who made a much poorer impression but was seen much more frequently was Calibute Downing, who became vicar at St John's, Hackney, from 1637. He inhabited the quickly disappearing middle ground of the Church of England, having godly credibility with an eye on a bishopric. In the Jacobean context, he would have been a slightly lesser version of John Williams or Joseph Hall, but the model was less workable in the late 1630s, with a constant danger of falling between two stools. By 1640 he had seen the difficulty of being a mugwump, and tested the waters of the city by preaching to the Artillery Company, declaring that it was lawful to take arms against the king to defend religion. He went on to be a chaplain to the parliamentary forces and preach to the Long Parliament.[78] At the time of Rogers' diary he was still of suspect credibility among the godly. This must be a substantial part of the reason why Rogers never had a good word for him in any of their encounters. After their first meeting, the record was relatively mild. 'God indeed denies the external, vivid word; we have Downing, a doubtful man generally self-important' (133).[79] Later on, Rogers complained that he was 'very much downe, and straite' and blamed his condition on the fact that he was 'mourning under a sad ministrye; of pore D4wn:[ing] the Civilian' (164), which was to say that Downing was not a true soldier for God's Word, that he was good as a citizen but not as a saint. One Sabbath was so bad that he judged it worthy of an asterisk so that it would not be forgotten. 'The Lord's Day * dead; on which I groan under the burden of the saddest ministry, Calibute [Downing;] have mercy on me Lord, the heart has been hard today, it is softer as I lie down' (171–2).[80] Perhaps the harshest review of his character was when he treated Downing as a symptom of the general paucity of good preaching in the 1630s: 'Saboth, sad without, and much deaded by reason of, our sad pastor; a right Ἀμφίβιον; an ambidexter' (167). This was to portray him as underhand, deceitful and as a trimmer, a chameleon capable of changing his cloth according to the company, in short, a treacherous hypocrite.

Rogers found Obediah Sedgwick a rather more rewarding preacher and companion which is just as well, as he was closer to the family, having been chaplain to Horace Vere in the Netherlands in the late 1620s.[81] By the time Samuel arrived in Hackney, Sedgwick had become established as curate and lecturer of St Mildred's, Bread Street, in London, just around the corner

---

[78] *DNB*, s. v. Calibute Downing.
[79] negat equidem deus verbum externum, vividum; habemus Downing, hominem dubium generalum sui sapidum
[80] D. Dominicus * moralis; in quo ingemisco sub onere ministerij tristissimi, Calebut: miserere mei Domine, cor durum fuit hodie, mollius est mihi recubanti
[81] Calder (ed.), *Letters of John Davenport*, p. 29n.

from George Hughes, the mentor of William Sedgwick. He was another visitor who offered help during Rogers' sickness, although the record is not quite as enthusiastic as that given to John Dod. 'Another moderate fit; comfort sent bef:[ore] by Mr Sedgewicks coming and by the gracious presence of god; who constantly reveales his lovingk:[indness] to mee' (147). He assisted Rogers in a pastoral visit to a parishioner of Hackney, a Mrs Keeling, who had particularly bad spiritual troubles although the older minister does not seem to have offered any clear assistance.[82] As a preacher, Sedgwick was damned with faint praise. After one service, Rogers described himself as 'refreshed by publique meanes, mr sedgewicke; and my soule longs for a sacrament' (151). This was a good performance compared to the first time Rogers was in his congregation. For the earlier time, Samuel simply wrote, 'I hear today Master Sedgewick preaching, pious, to be sure, as I hope, but not filled with God; he excessively savours himself; nor does he touch the very marrow of the conscience' (133).[83] Socially, he made a very poor performance. 'Mr Sedgwick is with us, frivolous in some manner, seeking applause; indeed he wastes some time with me; honourable, to be sure, and a good companion' (141).[84] Towards the end of the diary he appears as a minister who is to be tolerated with low expectations and few anticipated rewards. 'Mr Sedge:[wick] Bredstreet preaches, strangely ut solet [as usual] But I trust in God' (161).

Rogers does not seem to have had many social opportunities with John Stoughton, the permanent curate and lecturer at St Mary's, Aldermanbury in London.[85] Like St Stephen's, Coleman Street which will be discussed below, the vestry at Aldermanbury possessed the advowson of the parish and established a tradition of godly preachers, with Stoughton succeeding Thomas Taylor in 1632.[86] He was a pivotal figure in the godly network. He was consulted for advice concerning prospective ministers for vacant posts and for cases of conscience. His reputation was such that the lawyer Robert Woodford travelled down from Northampton solely to consult him.[87] He was recruited as part of a steering committee for John Dury's ecumenical project, taking part in the construction of a 'Body of Divinity' as part of this enterprise. When Rogers heard him on an 'Irenicum: for Lutherans' (000) it was probably part of this undertaking.[88] The breadth of his contacts caused concern among ther godly in 1635 when he was arrested and taken into the

---

[82] Diary, pp. 157–8, 159–60.
[83] Audio hodiè magistrum Sedgewick prædicantum, pium quidem ut spero sed non plenum dei; nimium se sapit; nec ipsam conscientiæ medullam attingit
[84] Adest nobis Mʳ Sedgewicke, aliquo modo levis, plausum querens; perdit quidem mecum aliquid; ingenuus quidem atque bonus socius
[85] A helpful, albeit brief, biography can be found in J. C. Whitebrook, 'Dr John Stoughton the elder', Trans. of the Congregational Historical Society, 6 (1913–15), pp. 178–84.
[86] Seaver, Puritan Lectureships, p. 138.
[87] J. Eales, Puritans and Roundheads: the Harleys of Brampton Bryan and the outbreak of the English Civil War (Cambridge, 1990), p. 55; Webster, Godly Clergy, p. 52.
[88] Webster, Godly Clergy, p. 257; for the enterprise as a whole, see ibid., pp. 255–67.

Court of High Commission with John White of Dorchester, and their studies were searched for subversive material. His correspondence not only covered England but reached west to New England and east to the Netherlands. He was released without being found guilty of any charges, but it was a close call, with helpful interventions and visits from Sir Robert Harley and Henry Rich, the earl of Holland.[89]

As a preacher, Stoughton was not too highly thought of by Daniel Rogers, and this appears in one review from Samuel. 'I heare Dr Staughton; of whom I thinke as my father said, there is yet aliquid amplius [something more] to be desired, but learned, witty, and godly' (159). However, on the whole, he was the minister who most consistently received positive assessments in the journal. The first full account is wholly positive. 'The Word (given today by the faithful minister Dr Stoughton) vivifies me in a heavenly manner; I am in the heavens for I am in God' (132).[90] Similarly, the next time Rogers noted that the Lord 'has given peace, consoled my soul through the evangelising of Dr Stoughton' (138).[91] Such results occur throughout his visits to Aldermanbury down to his last visit in December 1638.

> Lord's day, which the Word makes sweet, reasonably preached by Dr Stoughton; the name of the Lord to me is a tower of strength; I indeed rejoice greatly today, in this tower, my heart becomes softened and glad in Jehovah, my God (169–70)[92]

Indeed, the only time Stoughton failed, there is a note of surprise, maybe disappointment, in the entry, showing the height of Rogers' expectations. 'I have bine much kept downe in spirit this day, *even* in hearing Dr Stoughton' (162, emphasis added).

The last minister to be introduced will benefit from a little more detailed background. More accurately, what is needed is an introduction to the minister and the parish, for Rogers grew familiar with both and each needs to be known if we are to understand the other. The minister is John Goodwin and the parish is that of St Stephen's, Coleman Street. The parish was discussed above in relation to Lady Vere's part in establishing John Davenport as its preacher in 1624. Even after his departure it remained a favourite, possibly *the* favourite, parish in London she attended in the late 1630s. The parish had a tradition of radical associations and this potential was virtually institutionalized when the

---

[89] Nicholas Tyacke, *Aspects*, pp. 124–5; Webster, *Godly Clergy*, pp. 266–7; Bremer, *Congregational Communion*, p. 58; Eales, *Puritans and Roundheads*, pp. 63–4.
[90] verbum (hodie datum per fidelum dispensatorum D^{rm} Staughton) vivificat me modo cælesti; In cælis sum nam sum in deo
[91] pacem dedesti, consolatus es animum meum per evangelizationem Drs Staughton
[92] D. D. quem dulcem fecit verbum sane prædicatum D.^{ro} Stauton; nomen domini mihi est turris roboris; ego sane hodie lætor multum, in hac turre; cor meum molle fit lætumque in Iehovah Deo meo [The 'tower of strength' is a reference to Psalm 61:3.]

parish purchased the advowson in 1590. This meant that the vicar was
appointed by the vestry and they could, if they so desired, augment his
fairly paltry stipend. These circumstances gave the parish relative
independence from the ecclesiastical authorities and quite considerable
control over their vicar.[93] It did not *necessarily* follow that this would be a
particularly puritan parish, merely that it would be a fruitful environment
for godly government to take root and also for it to survive the hostile
ecclesiastical policies of the 1630s.

This potential was to be realized. Before and during the pastorate of
Davenport, most of the smaller vestry, the predominant organ of
governance, were to a greater or lesser extent men of godly sympathies.[94]
When Davenport fled to the Netherlands in late 1632, his replacement suited
this environment. Lady Vere may have been instrumental in the appointment of John Goodwin; his messy relationship with the authorities in the
diocese of Norwich, where he made his reputation, was enacted in several
towns but was mainly financed by being the rector of East Raynham, the
most valuable living in the gift of Sir Roger Townshend, her son-in-law.[95] As
will be seen, she seems to have been familiar with some of the crucial figures
at Coleman Street.

Goodwin was in some ways an archetypal godly minister and in some
ways an anomaly. He was a nonconformist and a passionate preacher. In
the 1640s he was to emerge as an important proponent of Congregationalism and an avid supporter of religious toleration. However, this was not
on the back of the familiar experiential Calvinism that was the dominant
discourse among the godly. He started off within the covenantal theology of
ministers like Richard Sibbes whose works he helped to edit. His version of
the covenant became more inclusive than was usual and his estimation of
human agency exceeded that of most colleagues and, after a long
engagement with the works of Jacobus Acontius and Sebastian Castellio,
he finally 'outed' himself as an Arminian after 1648.[96] His drift from
orthodoxy was lengthy and gradual but by the late 1630s he was regarded as
not entirely trustworthy, accounting for Rogers' reservations about his
preaching.

These reservations are revealed in the record of Rogers' first encounter
with Goodwin. It appears that he had gone with a mind to keep a close eye
(or ear) on Goodwin's doctrine in order to assess just how unorthodox he
was. 'Mr Goodwin, obscure, voluminous, preaches; about faith; I hear only
two errors; nor even after such prayers, might I have heard such confused

93 David A. Kirby, 'The radicals of St. Stephen's, Coleman Street, London, 1624–1642', *Guildhall Miscellany*, 3 (1970), pp. 99–100.
94 Ibid., *passim*.
95 Ibid., p. 108.
96 Ellen More, 'John Goodwin and the origins of the new Arminianism', *Journal of British Studies*, 22 (1982).

chaos' (136).[97] The only other time he mentions Goodwin's preaching was ten months later, when he has a less suspicious tone. Having said that, he is still far from enthusiasm and Rogers was having a generally good day, starting with a productive devotional exercise on Hosea 14:5.

> Saboth, ravished with exceeding joy in meditation in the morning; upon that promise; I will be a dew, and he shall grow as the lillye; Lord thou hast bin a dew upon my fleece this day, when others hath bin dry; Ravished by Mr Goodwins prayer (but odde preacher[)] and at sacrament (162).

His enthusiasm about divine service at Coleman Street was concentrated on the Eucharist. To a certain extent this was just part of a general appetite for the communion, a regular fix, as it were.

> Saboath, and sacrament at Coleman: and the L[or]d is most sweet ever in the ordinance; and as my sister Mary said to my father, that shee seldome received, but shee found much in that Ordinance; so I blesse God, I have received very often, and the L[or]d hath bin abundantly gracious to mee (165).

Part of this worked on an individual level, as a renewal of the covenant of grace: 'Saboath; sacrament, at Coleman refreshed, and quickened and joyed Oh that it might hold, and that I might walk worthy accord:[ing] to my covenant sealed' (159). The pleasures of the sense of proximity to the Father and to Christ are expressed in the way Rogers recorded them. 'I approach now to the table of the Lord in the congregation of Coleman oh how my mind dances in the smile of Christ; God approaches me familiarly, and my soul rejoices; your presence, Lord, is my life' (140).[98]

The greatest pleasure and spiritual gain came with a sense of *koinōnia*, the communion of saints, which he felt when the day of the Eucharist was combined with profitable conference with the saints of the parish. 'Sab:[bath] this day sacrament, at Coleman, and Spurstow afternoone; I am refreshed with the fat things of the house of my God, this day; Blesse the lord oh my soule, and all that is within mee pay tribute to him; * this is a day of gladnes and joy' (157). On this occasion the host was William Spurstow, one of the key figures in the parish, who was to go on to be an important figure in the Long Parliament.[99] The richest language was reserved for the best combination of social and spiritual communion:

> Saboth; and sacrament at Coleman: broken to peices with joy; drunk with comfort; this is a day of rejoicing, and strength; for the joy of the L[or]d,

[97] prædicat obscurus, voluminous M^r: Goodwin; de fide; duos tantum errores exaudio; nec unquam post preces tales, exaudiverim confusum chaos
[98] accedo iam ad mensam domini in congregatione Colmaneas oh quam tripudiat mens mea in risu Christi; accedit ad me familiariter deus, atque exultat anima mea; præsentia tua domina vita mea est
[99] Kirby, 'Radicals of St. Stephen's', p. 119.

hath bin my strength; A sweet communion of Saints, at mr Roules his
house at dinner; a sweet refreshing at mr Simonds; one of a most sweet,
godly spirit; and now I lye downe with praises (154–55).

After the service, he accompanied Lady Vere to dinner at the home of Owen
Rowe, a parishioner who was prominent in the government of London. He
was part of the wider godly network through being related to Susanna
Rowe, the second wife of the earl of Warwick. He was later to achieve
lasting fame by signing the death warrant of Charles I in 1649. At Rowe's
home they were joined by Joseph Simonds, the rector of St Martin's,
Ironmonger Lane, a minister who was shortly to flee to the Netherlands.[100]

With the start of 1639 Samuel Rogers almost disappears from the
historical record. According to the Candler genealogy, he was lecturer at St
Katherine Cree, London, in the 1650s.[101] Although there is no mention of
him in such a post in the parish records, a 'Samuel Rogers' does appear
among the signatories to the Protestation taken in the summer of 1641. The
likelihood of this being the lecturer is backed by the name being second in
the substantial list, immediately after the rector, George Rush, and it was
common practice for ministers to take such a place.[102] That it was 'our'
Samuel Rogers receives backing from the similarity of the signature to that
at the beginning of the diary. It is probable that he had left the employ of
Lady Vere, as she seems to have had another chaplain by 1642. The
qualification of 'probable' is due to the vagueness of his successor, John
Wallis, later the famous professor of geometry at Oxford and an early
member of the Royal Society. According to his autobiography, he was
ordained in 1640 and then 'lived as a chaplain for about a year in the house
of Sir Richard Darley at Buttercramb in Yorkshire; and then, for two years
more with the Lady Vere'.[103]

The account of the last section of his life is built upon absences. He is
absent from the fruits of the assiduous genealogical labours of H. F. Waters,
and unfortunately no will survives for Daniel Rogers, who died in 1652.
Samuel makes no more appearances in the records of St Katherine Cree. A
more positive absence, as it were, is the will of Mary Everard of 1643.[104] She
was his maternal aunt and lived in the Rogers household at Wethersfield.
Her will mentioned his brothers and sisters but *not* him. There is, of course,
the possibility of some estrangement but the least unlikely conclusion is that
between the spring of 1642, the deadline for the Protestation, and the will of
1643 Samuel Rogers had died.

[100] Ibid., pp. 104, 110, 112–13; Valerie Pearl, *London and the Outbreak of the Puritan Revolution* (Oxford, 1961), p. 324; Seaver, *Puritan Lectureships*, pp. 195, 259–60.
[101] BL Harl. MS 6071 fo. 482.
[102] GL MS 1196/1 fo. 19.
[103] C. J. Scriba, 'The autobiography of John Wallis', *Notes and Records of the Royal Society*, 25 (1970), p. 31.
[104] ERO 54/MW5.

Spirituality

As historians we tend to read texts to our own purposes and, providing that we recognize it, that is all well and good. Part of the recognition is dialectic in that it involves an appreciation of the purposes of the text in its compositional context. This is vital in this case. Reading the diary as a complete representation of Samuel Rogers gives the impression of a rather selfish individual. For instance, when he writes of the troubles of others, their difficulties, even their deaths, are often turned to their impact on him, to the lessons they offer to Samuel Rogers. To condemn this as self-centred is to misunderstand the text, in that the nature of this journal is self-centred in the full sense of it being a tool for the construction of a self, indeed to 'centre', to ground a self. This is not to say that in fact he was wholly altruistic outside of the text (we don't know), merely that it is to confuse the characteristics of the text with the characteristics of Rogers. Thus our first task is to consider some of the characteristics of the journal, the functioning of the text.

The diary can be described as having three purposes, each one contained in the one that follows, like a set of Russian dolls. The first is a source for memory and construction. Rogers recorded a selection of his experiences and dispositions and in itself this gives to the impressionistic nature of feelings a concrete, and external, veracity. At the same time these constructions become memoranda, locations of a past self to measure oneself against or to offer comfort to a present self. This is surely why Rogers marked his best, or most important, days with a marginal asterisk, in order to make them come to hand with the greatest of ease when he needed them. This purpose is linked to the second purpose, which is to provide a site for conversations. The diary is a forum for conversation between past, present and, occasionally, future. Conversations can be conducted with God (and, less often, with Christ) whether they consist, on Rogers' part, of questions, pleas, thanksgivings, complaints or apologies. There are also Rogers' conversations with himself, understandings earned by making impressions explicit, or resolutions given grounding and authority by being recorded. This section is a critical part of the third, largest, and thereby fuzziest, purpose, which is his spirituality. Some individuals who have Bunyan's *Grace Abounding* forced upon them are prone to complain that he lived in 'interesting times' but failed to make 'a decent story' in his work. Plainly this is to operate under a different set of priorities to Bunyan, for what could be of higher priority than one's developing relationship with God, the movement of one's soul towards union with its creator? This is, of course, the primary purpose of this text and it is necessary to explore the ways in which it functions as a spiritual tool, as a pietistic appliance, if this diary is to be understood.

The examination of the spirituality of Samuel Rogers will be drawn out on two levels. The first, and most lengthy, will be concerned with its linguistic operation, with language being understood as constituent rather than merely reflective. The language available to him, the parameters of expression, operated as the conduit for his piety, as the duct for his success or failure. The second level will employ the diary as a source for examining his means of spiritual succour. Among these means will, of course, be the journal.

Questions of the self seem a good place to start, given the preceding remarks, but also because it is a perpetual issue for Rogers, sometimes in a positive, more often in a negative, sense. What is particularly valuable is to maintain an effort to identify, to locate, the self, as he makes shifts within the same word. At some points, usually the worst, Rogers *is* his self.

> who am I, that I should be so beloved of gods saints, as I am generally, having such a proud heart, dead barren, awcke to good; oh Lord make mee the more to loath my selfe; for they suppose, and thinke something lovelye in mee; but I am sure I am a jakes, a cage of uncleanenesse; and I wonder that the Lord, or his servants, should looke upon mee, as comelye (58).[105]

At other times he is semi-detached, as it were, making an effort to mark distance from this self or giving thanks to God for helping him to do so. 'I will yet looke up to thee; (oh my deare father) who hast comforted mee by renouncing selfe, selfe sin, selfe dutyes, and by working thyne owne worke of faith' (4). This self, sometimes 'I', is the site of earthly pleasures and their associated flawed priorities. 'When I have a minimum of the creature, I enjoy Christ in the greatest degree' (136);[106] 'I am ready to imbrace the creature; unlesse thou dailye assist by thy grace' (50). Part of the desire to achieve separation from this self is to establish a location from which to pour scorn upon it. 'A litle sunk now, but not beate of[f] from my confidence; I will abhorre my selfe, and my flaggings, giddines, unconstancy' (29). The reverse side of this is that this self interferes, intervenes, or obstructs his vision of the Lord. 'I have had many conflicts with selfe, and sin; and can not behold the lord in the beauty of holinesse, as I would' (33).

The sense of self-abhorrence takes us into his fairly frequent perceptions of 'nothingness' which can be sources of misery and can also be turned to his spiritual advantage. He complains at several points about his 'naughty heart', that is, a heart with naught to offer.[107] At its worst, it is a perception of utter worthlessness: 'nothing, nothing, nothing; No hearte, No prayer, Noe life, No grace, No fruitfulnesse one way as other, can be discerned' (6). One Sabbath his entry is just 'pore, pore, pore, and wretched, heartlesse dead, nothing, nothing' and following day simply has 'I[bi]d' (13). However, this impotence can become a tool against pride as when he writes, 'yea Lord

---

[105] 'Awck', a favourite word of Rogers, means confused or depressed; 'jakes' is a toilet, a lavatory.
[106] Cum minimum habeam creaturæ, fruor Christo maximè
[107] See, for instance, pp. 15, 28, 33, 46, 49.

I will abhorre my selfe that am not able to stand one minute without thy helpe' (4). This can form an appreciation of God's active help: 'I have bine nothing; but the lord hath caryed mee thorough the dutyes he hath called mee to; myne eyes shall be towards him he is enough' (35). In turn this emptiness becomes empowering, provided that the external source is appreciated: 'nothing, weakenesse without thee; but when thou conveyest strength, I can doe all things' (71). Finally, this nothingness is desirable in that it can make him a vessel for the spirit as when he pleads for God to 'emptye mee, I am really nothing; and thou art all in all' (16). One day which was so good that it was marked with an asterisk had Rogers noting

> how hath the Lord wound up my heart to heaven, pitcht mee upon X [Christ]; and sent mee downe strength thorough him; and gave mee footing for faith in his promise; and great raptures of joy, and peace from thence; ... more humblenes Lord, more stillnes of emptiness and nothingnesse, and more fulnes in thy selfe (94).

At this point of success, his self has been, as far as is possible, completely abnegated.

The desire for diminution of self fits in with a common expression of spiritual delight, along with its negative counterpart, the positive side being 'melting', the negative element of stasis being 'icy'. At its least lyrical it might simply be taking a part for the whole. For instance, he described his first conversion experience by praising the performance of Thomas Weld, noting that 'his mournefull prayer melted mee in teares' (2). It appears more frequently as a metaphor chosen for the impact of divine presence: 'the Lord graciously smiles afar of[f], to the thawing of my heart' (113). It also appeared in pleas delivered in times that proved unproductive, as when he wrote that 'I cannot yet recover my selfe; Lord in mercye break this same ice, that is over my soule; thaw it by thy love, and beames of grace' (51). On this occasion the ice was just 'over' his soul; at worse times the cold went deeper, as when he complained that 'my sp:[irit] is bound, and streight, Lord in mercye, behold mee from heaven, thaw thou my frozen sp:[irit]' (55). As with the wretched self, this failure could almost be his primary characteristic, as on a particularly bad day when he castigated himself, with the judgment that 'I am icye; oh thou sun shine upon mee' (21). It reflected the demand for constant maintenance made by the godly discipline. One day he failed to start his day with private prayer and he paid for it. At the end of the day he concluded that 'I have gone drooping pitifully in the day time; and mee things [sic] the ice is growne thicke because it was not broken' (68). The warming effects of the gift of grace from God meant that Rogers employed Malachi 4:2 as the source of relief.[108] When the social distractions of the university hindered his piety, for instance, he mourned

---

[108] 'But unto you that fear my name shall the Sun of righteousness arise with healing in his wings; and ye shall go forth, and grow up as calves of the stall.'

that 'an ice got over my heart at Cambridge, and scarse is it broken yet, oh thou Sun of right:[eousness] shine upon my soule, and thaw it' (51), or, more succinctly, 'Icye, I, the sun of right:[eousness] can thaw mee' (20).[109]

The motif of nothing, with its concomitant theme of light, took Rogers to Revelation, possibly the most frequently cited New Testament book in the journal. 'Darke I; the morning star can give mee light; ... oh shine thou sun, arise thou morning star' (20).[110] Sometimes the light/dark dichotomy was stated in a plain, matter of fact way, as in 'I am in darknesse, and can see litle light' (33). On other occasions, it was a more moving mourning in the face of divine absence. 'I am pressed, sorely in my spirit; and brought low, the L[or]d seemes to be gone, and leave mee in darknesse' (74) or at an even harder time he pleaded 'oh lord let thy bowells earne[111] once more toward mee; for so long I know I shall be inlarged; but if thou leavest mee; I am a dungeon of darknesse and uncleanenesse' (8). At better times, light could capture a sense of assured comfort or even the pleasure of life after death. The first is there in a confident reassurance after a poor day, closing one day's entry with 'now I shall look into the clear sky and I shall see the light of the divine countenance; up to the point of satiety' (141);[112] the latter is in the plea ending a more frustrating time two days later when he wrote, 'I pant greatly, oh when shall I have seen you in eternal light' (142).[113]

A rather more proactive aspect to this thread of spirituality lay in variations on the theme of vision. A great deal of this comes with Rogers working with I Chronicles 4:10, one of the most popular scriptural references in the journal.[114] He is often asking for the coast to be clear or celebrating days when the coast was clear, giving him confidence either in his sight of God or in the knowledge that God was watching over him. In the former adaptation, he felt weakened, as in 'the coast is not cleare, I cannot behold the Lord so sweetlye; I will yet waite; and my old strength shall be renewed' (39). As in the preceding instance, he often ends with a patient stance of being available for visions of God should they be granted to him, a patience that is eventually rewarded. 'I have bin straitned in the day time much, but my heart lookes towards heaven, and this evening, whilest I have bine doing the Lord hath drawne neere to mee' (68). There are many days when he feels the lack of vision to be among his just deserts: 'I still looke toward heaven, the Lord smiles not sweetly; I have deserved his rod to be smarting upon mee; mine eyes oh Lord, are yet towards thee' (54).

[109] Cf. pp. 45, 70, 76, 101, 132, 137, 175.
[110] Rev. 22:16; 2:28.
[111] 'Earne' is a term that Rogers uses on several occasions, meaning 'to desire strongly, to long for', very similar to 'yearn'.
[112] atque iam cælo sereno inspiciam atque videbo lucem vultus divini; usque ad satietatem
[113] anhelo multum, oh quando viderim te in æterna luve
[114] 'And Jabez called on the God of Israel, saying, Oh that thou wouldest bless me indeed, and enlarge my coast, and that thine hand might be with me, and that thou wouldest keep me from evil, that it might not grieve me! And God granted him that which he requested.'

Sometimes the sense of punishment is made explicit, perhaps as an attack on pride, as when he feared that 'the Lord it may be drawes a curtaine before his face, because my heart is ready to be puft up' (94). At one point it seems that his sin has given God no choice: 'oh wretch, that should sin against so good a god, and *force* thee to vaile thy countenance' (65, my emphasis). He may simply plead for forgiveness ('oh Lord I have deserved thy indignation, I will beare it, and looke up' [63]) or virtually ask for parole on the grounds of promised reform ('oh that he should give a litle peeking hole into heaven againe; it is infinite mercye; for this will I praise him, and seeke him further' [22]). He may have almost a note of impatience as when he asked 'oh when shall I see him, when shall I lye in the embraces of Jesus Xt' (98) but he was more likely to stress his unworthiness. The most intense version of this is in the following entry. 'Let mee rather peep into hell, to see what sin meanes, rather then that I should be insensible, which is the heaviest burden, that a pore soule can grone under' (55). The most active plea is for a way out of a sense of indirection when he asked, 'Lord chauke [chalk] out some way to mee, wherein I may see thee clearlye and may live with peace within' (77).

This last example introduces the possibility of movement and in a variety of forms this is the most common topos in the diary. As we will see, it can involve Rogers having, or wanting, direction in his life; it can be hoping for, celebrating or mourning the lack of his movement towards God or it can be hoping for or celebrating the proximity to or intimacy with God. The most common form is probably a desire to be able to move, and especially to walk. One poor day found Rogers expressing gratitude because 'I was not laid flat upon my backe; for the Lord strengthned the legs of my soule; by beleiving' (37). Usually it was a matter of being able to 'walk' in truth: 'oh that I could walke tenderly, and closelye, Lord a dead heart remove, and cause mee to walke so before thee, that I may rejoice' (45) or, in a slightly longer perspective, he asked, 'Lord teach mee so to walke before thee heere a few dayes of my sojourning that I may at last lye downe in peace, and my end may be as the just, and upright' (61). On occasion he got more ambitious, as when the company of his uncle and his lessons of the sweetness of Christ 'hath incouraged mee to run to heaven to find more of it' (69) or when he pleaded with God for a way out of langour: 'doe thou search, and pinch mee, draw mee, and I shall run after thee' (43). As in the last example, Rogers could require active divine assistance when his movement became more ambitious. Similarly, he noted the impact of trouble at college, 'which the devell used to disturbe my mind, and beate mee backe from climbing up upon the mountaines of heaven', asking God to 'so guide mee that all petty, triviall ocasions may make mee sit loose from earth, and willing to mount to heaven' (6).

The question of agency, to which we will return, is particularly pertinent in what appear to be adaptations of Isaiah 40:31 and/or Exodus 19:4. In Exodus the power is very much the gift of God to the Israelites, less so in

Isaiah. Sometimes it is plain that Rogers is purely the recipient of the means of movement, as when he pleads as follows, 'give to me earthbound Lord the wings of an eagle, heavenly wings so that I might ascend after my spouse with soul and eyes' (122-23),[115] or when he resignedly noted that 'my strength is still in god, in whome I live, and on whom I depend, I mourne yet under my clog, and backbyas,[116] that does hinder mee from mounting with Eagles wings' (112). At other times, the source of potential success is ambiguous while the source of failure is clear: 'the lord hath also comforted mee with many secret ejaculations, and kept up my wofull flagging heart, which to my sorrow pulls mee backe, when by the wings of faith and love, I would fly to my god of holines' (4). It can be even more ambiguous where the desire is plain, when he records that despite his 'affections [being] downe; I would faine by the wings of faith, and love fly to heaven' (84), or when the entry records that 'I find flesh heavy, weighing mee downe to the creature, yet wil I raise my selfe by the weake wings of faith, and love towards heaven' (60). At his most positive he seems confident of ultimate success and seems to take credit for getting to the entrance God has made available for him. 'Downe, yet up; flying to heaven but ready to sinke downe by this clog at the heele; but I will yet fight it out, because god will have mee' (91).

Throughout the discussion of movement readers will have noted different phrases that describe the nature of failure. They fall into three categories. The first is causes of failure that imply that he was going in the right direction but not getting to his destination, being held back by impediments, as in 'Oh when shall I be rid of my clogge of hell, and hellish unthankfulnesse' (33), 'I have desired to looke toward heaven, oh the barkebyas that is as bad as a log to mee in my flying up to the Lord' (42) or 'I will recover my selfe upon the lord; who hath recovered mee from all my backslidings' (19). Perhaps the most moving instance of this failure is part of the autobiographical introduction when he felt that he was adjusting poorly to life at college, being too attached to 'carnall ease':

> yea (shall I speake it) with horror I doe; I was loath to come in to repent for my backsliding (which I knew I must doe) because I thought it would hinder the growth of my bodye; ... that he should be willing to stand at the dore, and knocke so long for mee till he bedewed his locks (3).[117]

God was available but Rogers was inadequate and couldn't come to the door. The second phrase for failure is a lack of constancy, when Rogers

---

[115] Da terrestri mihi Domine alas Aquilæ, cælestes alas, ut ascendam post virum meum animâ oculisq

[116] 'Clog' is a term for anything that hinders action or progress, usually referring to something tied to an animal; 'backbyas', as far as can be ascertained, seems to something that leads one astray, or holds one back.

[117] The image is drawn from Song of Songs 5:2 – 'I sleep, but my heart waketh: it is the voice of my beloved that knocketh, saying, Open to me, my sister, my love, my dove, my undefiled: for my head is filled with dew, and my locks with the drops of the night.'

looked to God to keep him on the right path. He asked for the Lord to 'stay my heart from swerving from thee' (45). He might note with pleasure that 'the lord hath kept mee from out strayings' (16), but it was more common to compare God's constancy with his own failure, as when

> he leaves mee not, as I have bine willing to grow loose and leave him; oh infinite mercye that when I have done many things by my swerving from him, wherby I have done as much as in mee lyes to cut my selfe of[f] from god; yet he is willing to receive mee, and lets in some beame of himselfe (52).

Perhaps the worst category is the third, where he found it difficult to be sure of his purpose. 'Still I bend toward my center, and fly to my [inked out], I am weary with flut[te]ring over the waters; oh when shall I rest in thee and never fly out more' (150). Similarly, there was a frustrated hope in the following: 'I finally do not always have freedom with Christ; now I am above the stars, now beneath the fields, even in the deepest waters; but I thus far raise the head, and I shall raise it towards heaven, and I shall look upon my hope' (175).[118]

Related to this last category of frustration, on a more terrestrial level, was the language Rogers used when he felt torn in terms of his calling. These times read as a particular frustration in that he is willing to go wherever he is called but cannot show his commitment to such a calling until he has been shown what that right calling is. Such unprofitable oscillation comes through in this example: 'my greife is that I cannot settle to any calling, I halt between two opinions; oh that I could tell, which were gods way, and I would submit to it; it disturbs my peace' (85). Such uncertainty left him unsettled and impotent, particularly in the period when he was considering emigrating to New England, as is shown in the following two instances. 'I can doe nothing, bec:[ause] I cannot pitch what to doe[;] Lord chauke out some way to mee, wherein I may see thee clearlye and may live with peace within' (76–7); 'I have no joy in England, no joy in this sad wretched familye, Lord some way, some way charte out to mee, wherin thou wouldest have mee to walke' (74). As is clear from the last quote, part of this lack of direction, or downright incomprehension, came from his low assessment of the Denny family. The same appraisal is present in the following entry in the reference to Matthew 10:16, but it it also noteworthy that he identifies two options for God, explanation or support. '[O]h what shall my troubled soule in anguish doe; I lye downe at thy feet, who either wilt find out some way for mee; or else give mee patience, innocencye, and wisdome to walke among wolves' (69). The final example is, in a sense, the happiest, in that the frustration was transformed into humility: 'faine would I goe in gods way;

---

[118] non habeo tandem semper libertatem cum Christo; iam sum super astra, iam subter agros, etiam in aquis imis; at ego adhuc caput extollo, et extollam cælum versus, et inspiciam spem meum

and as yet it is not cleared to mee, I will waite to see what the Lord will reveale to mee' (77).

It is striking that the discussion of movement should end with passivity and, as it were, positive frustration. These matters must be addressed, the former in particular as the state of passivity seems to clash with the desire for movement. To a degree this is so but only for one sort of passivity. He can be seen to be grateful for the failure of passivity in the sense that it could be worse – at least he is not going backwards. 'I am in darknesse, and can see litle light, I will not yet be beate of[f] from my confidence by the power and assistance, which my god affords mee; for indeed he beates mee downe with one hand, and yet upholds mee from sinking, with the other' (33). The dolour is emphasized in the longer version of a bad day mentioned above.

> I know to mee belongs shame for myne owne sin; the burden whereof hath so hindred mee, that I could this day scarse stirre a foote in my course, the develle by sin, snares mee, and then directes and streightnes mee; oh lord let thy bowells earne once more toward mee; for so long I know I shall be inlarged; but if thou leavest mee; I am a dungeon of darknesse and uncleanenesse (7–8).

However, it would be inaccurate to see passivity in wholly negative terms. If one has undertaken a journey with a definite destination, then the ultimate goal of arrival can involve an actual aspiration to passivity. We can distinguish between a negative passivity of incapability and a dream of positive passivity. The latter is *ultimate* in its etymological sense, *ultimāre*, to come to an end, *ultimus*, last, and *ulter*, distant. He could move from one to the others in a single day: 'oh the sad body of death that hangs upon mee; it tyes my hands, that I cannot be free, as fain I would be; oh once there will be a time, when sin will be no more for which I[' l]e waite and attend the lord in a sp:[iritual] warfare' (22–3). The obliteration of the sinful self seems to be implicit in the following vision of heaven: 'Once freed from sin I['l]le praise with heavens quire the Lord, and live in loves seraphicke fire' (28). The sense of eventual completion and distance is held in the two examples which follow. The first has the complete union of the saints, joining with models of sanctity from Scripture and family, and the completion of his perpetual quest for the sight of God in light appears in both. 'I have bine a litle in heaven now toward my lying downe; oh I can joy in meditation, that ever such a slight, giddy, proud, jolly, wretch as I am, shall be rid of all of my slud;[119] and sit downe in companye, with Abraham; Paul, my grandfather, and all other blessed saints, and angels; and be filled with eternitye, in the presence, and full sight of god' (44); 'I am much sunke, and the L[or]d seemes to frowne; yet my heart hath said and so will; that though he kill mee, yet by his grace will I trust in him; Faith shall leake a peeking hole into heaven' (89–90). The vision of an eventual escape from the vagaries of life

---

[119] Slud – wallowing in mud.

on earth, the oscillation between failure and celebration, usually informs his visions of heaven: 'I am much sunke, and pressed in spirit, and mourne under a dead, unbeleiving, disturbed heart, oh Lord, heale mee; oh when shall I come unto thee to be perfectly cured, and dwell with thee in Light' (163).[120] Sometimes the positive passivity verges on a desire for death expressed in terms of complete trust: 'woe is mee, sin is present when I would doe good; oh the day; when I shall sin no more, but dwell purely, in the glorious presence of my pure god even to eternitye' (66). This is present to an even greater extent in the following entry: 'though I cannot see so clearlye; yet the L[or]d hathe made mee to lye at his feet; and there will I perish if I dye' (38). In one short passage, he moves from desired activity through the gift of God, to greater passivity, culminating in the greatest passivity available to the saints on earth, becoming an infantile recipient: 'cause that I draw near to you; draw near to me, Lord, that from the Sacrament and the Word, just as from a breast, I may suck the milk of consolation and of nourishment' (168).[121]

An issue that has been implicit in much of this analysis, occasionally emerging, particularly in the sections regarding movement and passivity, has been agency. The forms of agency fit into three stances. There is human agency, necessarily inadequate albeit well-intended; there is divine agency, welcomed but never earned; and there is secondary human agency, entirely empowered, virtually *permitted* by divine agency. Rogers is in complete recognition of God's help when he gives thanks that he has 'lived a most joyfull life; in the morning caryd above dung, and drosse, and my thoughts, and heart where my treasure was; and supported thoroughout the day' (103). As I have argued elsewhere, Rogers embraced 'feminine' attributes almost as a get-out clause from responsibility.[122] He usually employed the Song of Songs but this instance adapted Matthew 25:10. 'A litle recovered[;] the bridegrome hath taken mee into his chanber [sic], and comforted mee with his loves, and some calmnes, and serenitye hath come into my troubled spirit' (105). It would be misleading to suggest, however, that he had a perpetual appetite for the avoidance of responsibility. The following passage is untypical only in that it makes explicit a tension that is usually implicit: 'sometimes up, and sometimes downe, ebbing, and flowing; the L[or]d shewes mee, that all is to be had in him above; and that I must live upon him in a *momentarye* dependence' (114, my emphasis), the point being that the Lord will, hopefully, be there at Rogers' weakest times but that the deal is that Rogers has to make the most of his inadequate frame.

---

[120] This vision informs most of the entries for this week.
[121] fac ut appropinquam tibi; appropinqua mihi, domini ut ex sacramento atque verbo, tanquam ex ubere lac consolationis atque nutritionis, exugam [The last image is taken from Isaiah 60:16.]
[122] Tom Webster, 'Kiss me with the kisses of his mouth: gender inversion and Canticles in godly spirituality', in Tom Betteridge (ed.), *Sodomy in Early Modern Europe* (Manchester, 2002), pp. 148–63.

This required effort fits in with the shape of the ways in which Rogers works *with* destitution and makes the best of a bad lot, as it were. Rather than solely whingeing about his failures and the distance of God (although he does do that at times) he looks for the lessons of these conditions. In a similar passage to the last one cited in the previous section, he notes, 'my heart, downe, and the L[or]d seems to leave mee'; rather than leaving it at that, he concludes, 'but it is to shew mee my nothingnesse, and that I must live by a moment[ar]ly dependence upon him' (157). There are a series of similar days when he turns similar deprivations or failures to a variety of ends. He may note that the established structure of his piety takes him to the best source for comfort: 'I have not that sweet communion with god, which I was want to have; but my heart is bent, and th[o]roughly resolved to wait ever with patience, and humble submission' (116). On another day he may find comfort in the Covenant (to which we will return) and it becomes clear to him that Samuel Rogers per se is not the focus but that his failures highlight the wonders of free grace and divine mercy: 'my heart at a low ebbe, but in the lowest, I can a litle raise my selfe, upon the promise; that god can, yea will love such a giddy, untoward, vaine wretch as I am, not for my sake, but for his free grace and mercy sake' (59). Similar circumstances could produce an appreciation of his own inadequacies, as in the following. 'I am much straitned in service, the Lord shewes w[ha]t I am, if he forsake but a day; oh Lord I have deserved thy indignation, I wil beare it, and looke up' (63). This is taken to its logical conclusion when he records that 'if the L[or]d departs, I am nothing', concluding that 'I will ther[e]fore rejoice in my infirmityes, that the power of X [Christ] may be magnified in mee' (106).

Rogers found lessons in specific troubles; with the right eyes a just order might be revealed in unpleasant situations as well as in the routine of 'regular' spiritual practice. This can be seen to develop in his treatment of grievances relating to the Denny family. The first sign was simply an expression of faith. He noted that 'Sullennesse, and melancholy discontent, takes hold on mee[;] I cannot be free in this place I am in; it is hard to conflict with great, imperious, captious, spirits; but the Lord hath set mee heere, and I believe it shall turne to my good' (54). A little later the purpose started to become clear. 'A proud heart is fearfully up, the Lord in mercye pull it downe; I see the Lords dealing towards mee in setting mee in th3s pl1ce [this place] where I am not loved; it is to pull downe this same base sp:[irit] of mine that is ready to insult upon account, and respect' (81). His final conclusion brought with it a greater appreciation of God's love: 'the Lord hath taken this course with mee to pitch mee among bryars, and thornes, that they might teare of[f] a deale of scurfe, and basenes of[f] from my spirit: I blesse thy name oh L[or]d for thy great love this weeke past' (96).

A similar exercise could be performed for the period when Rogers was ill early on in his time with the Vere family. Here I will just draw attention to two entries. The first states his condition, explains it and draws the lesson in a very succinct manner. 'I still am in dependence upon G.[od] I have no whether else to goe; in affliction wee dare not looke away from him, who beates us' (145). The second is a little longer but shows quite nicely the mixture of diagnosis, prognosis, plea and the resulting positive passivity.

> The L[or]d exercises mee with a 2d; fit; somewhat sharp; but I find more of his grace, and presense; he hath granted in my intermission some affliction grace which now I will try; oh lord give now, before new trialls; strengthen thou the hands that hang downe; my greatest burden is; that I can doe no good in my place; but it is thy will; makes mee lay my hand upon my mouth; I with Aaron will hold my peace (145).

Paying attention to Rogers' efforts to find value in difficulties takes us into the means of his spirituality as, of course, he had a minimal control over his environment, albeit more than most, and was constructing his piety in a far from perfect world. Thus part of this analysis will touch upon his difficulties, as the things that he identified as impediments can reveal his desires. It should be noted at the outset that he had, contrary to older stereotypes of 'the puritan', a general antipathy to secular or, in his terms, earthly, matters. Any day which offered non-spiritual temptations exposed the fragility of his piety: 'my heart is much downe the wind this day; and eloofe of; I have bine troubled with divers hurrying thoughts, and buisinesses; oh happy I, that have litle to do with the world' (74). One instance, which might elicit some empathy from anyone involved with current academia, was the concern expressed when the cost of his education was brought to his father's attention.

> Thoughts, and chewing upon a bill, that my father received from my tutor, and feare of fathers displeasure, put my heart out againe, made me unfit to pray; and then comes in Satan and opens the dore to jollitye; and the ocasions thereof; oh lord, more X [Christ], and less trouble of secular affaires (12).

He often found himself weakened 'when one is kept from his calling by hurrying thoughts, and much other necessary buisinesse' (27). One of the most frequent distractions was 'ocasions', usually social events which entailed mixed company, that is, saints and sinners. He found that this made his heart 'not so vivacious in the service of god' (17) as usual. After one such event he noted his pleasure in their infrequency but looked to God for help: 'oh happy am I, that I am litle troubled with these earthly matters; or am not tyed to the societye of vaine men; Lord gather up, and in all strag[g]ling thoughts and set my whole soule upon thee' (61).

The dangers of 'the society of vaine men' leads us to the matter of 'companyes' which, broadly defined, was an area of great help and great hindrance to Rogers. On the one hand, 'companyes', in the sense of social events, was draining for Rogers: 'many companyes, and ocasions have perverted my affections that they are not so vivacious' (17). Such circumstances required extra divine support to maintain his focus. 'Now busy; and full of companye frothye, I wander; never more need of new supply of grace' (50). At its most extreme, this sort of company brought complete alienation. On one of the worst days in the Denny household, he saw his 'bondage', as living 'with a tumultuous companye, of vaine loose, lascivious wretches' (68). As Rogers saw it, one ungodly individual was capable of spoiling an otherwise saintly society. The presence of 'Stevens the caviler' was enough: 'such an one in a company is like a dead flye in a box of ointment, makes the companye unsavory' (78). Hence his observation that he would be 'happy when I shall converse, with none but saints, and shall not heare the voice of any unsavory wretch' (75). However, his understanding of society was not quite so simply dichotomous. On occasion, his condemnation was not harsh so much as a matter of pity for people who were not of his mindset, who failed to share his pleasures to the full: 'oh how fulsome, and tedious to mee is the religion of such people; there discourse against the power of religion, alasse they know not the sweetnes of it, and so must seeke it in pleasures; great things in this world &c:' (68). He captured his perception of such a group early on in his time at Bishop's Stortford when he found himself 'something estranged before lying downe[;] [by] new ocasions and companye, though lawfull, [who] divert my heart much' (28). By 'lawfull' he seems to have meant formalist, even formulaic, making an effort to live as far as possible within the covenant of works but without the experiential, emotional feel of the covenant of grace.

The contrast with the positive side of 'companye' needs very little emphasis. When his friend James How left for New England, Rogers was quick to note 'how precious is the companye of the saints, and the Lord rends them from us, and gleanes away the cheife and choise, and full eares' (47). The comparison with heaven came naturally here: 'oh how joyfull is it to have the society of the saints upon earth; oh blessed is it to beleive, and meditate of that eternall societye with the Lord, holy angels, and saints' (64). At a slightly more complicated level Rogers could use the saints as a way of expressing his love for God, something he apparently found difficult to do in the abstract. 'I was much refreshed with there good companye; my delight is in those that excell in virtue and though I cannot love thee oh Lord, as faine I would, yet will I love thy people' (35). Finally, it should be noted that godly society was not wholly free from trouble. His self-examination was capable of setting off alarm bells even here. 'It is wonderfull to consider, how deceitfull my heart is; I have injoyed the company of a great many of gods people this night; and my heart trusts so much in them; that it is not so much pitched upon god as it should be; I thinke if I dwell among them, I should be too secure' (107). Indeed, his goal of a sole dependence upon God to the exclusion of all others at one point had him concluding that 'a solitary life proves best to mainteine the life of the soule' (17), which is a little unconvincing, given the many occasions when he yearned for a 'quickning companion' (36).

One form of devotion which had a substantial overlap with the positive side of 'company' was days of fasting and prayer. However, before we deal with the *social* exercise of fasting, we must touch upon the times when he fasted alone, times he described either as 'in private' or 'in secret'. On two occasions this was part of his preparation for the sacrament. The first one was fairly unsuccessful, with Rogers finding it difficult to 'get an hard heart to relent and mourne' (51). The second time he undertook 'fasting and prayer private for preparat:[ion] to sacram:[ent]' was much more successful. 'I find the L[or]d very gracious; he makes my heart bleed for the times and inlarged mee yet to mourne, and wrestle; and hath given some hints; and a sweet comfortable confidence in him that I am his, and shall be refreshed at his Feast' (157). Sometimes the 'Fasting, and prayer in secret' was to no identified purpose, apparently simply an upgraded version of his own pietistic concerns: 'sometimes up, sometimes down; difficult to flesh; I will yet rejoice in it according to the sp:[irit] my comfort is only in thee Lord in other matters I have litle joy' (65). At other times the issue was quite specific and very personal, as in 'this day I set apart for fasting, and prayer in private in espec:[ially] records ab:[out] N:[ew] E:[ngland] &c:' (97) when he was having doubts about whether or not to emigrate. Similarly, he fasted and prayed for guidance relating to the specifics of his career.

> The day is for fasting, and prayer, in a room privately, in which the Lord is near in some measure; the reason is; a change of place; I surrender to the decision of Jehovah, my way, He will bring about that which bears the greatest glory to Himself, and that which is the greatest benefit to me (128).[123]

What should be noted here is the level of passivity acquired through fasting, producing a willingness to place the difficult decision entirely in God's hands. This is most commonly shown in a willingness to 'wait', for instance when Rogers was feeling particularly weak, recognizing his dependency upon God and concluding that 'I resolve to fast, and pray, and walk before him waiting' (85). This was a day after a fast which had not been too successful, 'but I will wait, and hearken w[ha]t the L[or]d will say, for he will speak peace' (85). This will be encountered after several fasts and is present in the following entry where similar questions were addressed among broader goals.

> This day, I set apart for fasting, 1. in reg:[ard] of my selfe to get into the same communion with g.[od] which I was wont to have; and the L[or]d hath granted it in some comfortable measure; 2. ab:[out] the change of place, and calling; for I am to preach on Saboth L[or]d strengthen mee, fit an unworthy sinfull wretch to declare thy will; I have found faith more

---

[123] Dies est jeiunij, et precum, in cubiculo privatim, in quo dominus aliquo modo appropinquat; causa est; mutatio loci; Devolvo sup Jehovam viam meam illu efficiet qd sibi maximam asferat gloriam, et qd mihi optimam est

raised (the affections) espec:[ially] upon that promise; commit thy way to him, and he shall bring it to passe (116).[124]

Rogers evidently set high value upon the more communal fasts. When his sister Mary died and he wrote her spiritual remembrance, the first proof he chose as evidence of her being 'a substantiall grounded Christian' was that she was 'eminently gifted, as in days of humiliat:[ion] with Mrs Clench' (153). The appetite for such meetings appears throughout the diary. One of the mainstays of his spiritual state at Cambridge was such an informal gathering. 'The lord gave mee inlargement in prayer at Mr Frosts, the Lord heare our groanes, and unite our hearts in love; who, a companye of us have joined together to meet often to pray together, and discourse' (7). Less than a week later he was delighted to note that 'The Lord hath bine pleased to warme my pore hearte in my company'; in particular, 'it was my turne to pray; and the lord was pleased a litle to looke upon mee and put in some few desires to the saboath approching' (8). On two occasions it is clear that the meetings were explicitly fasts. The first brought the trust noted above, when 'the lord denyed audience but I will trust in the lord my strong encouragement' (10). The second fast brought more immediate rewards. 'A day of Fasting and prayer, wherein the lord went out with us mightilye, inlarged and brake our spirits; raised mee up marvailouslye; and added some power in the latter end; oh more, more' (12). It should be noted that the impact of a 'good' fast lasted, for the following day the entry was simply, 'After fasting my heart stands in some awe and see more cause to fly from my unrighteous failing prayers, and walkings to a righteous Saviour, who also hath healing in his wings for my unwilling failings' (12–13). His earlier prayer for God to 'unite our hearts in love' seems to have been answered, for the only positive note in his account of a later return to Cambridge was that 'I have had much good company today we joined (our old companye) in prayer together; at Mr Frosts at supper' (50).

He found, or maybe was complicit in establishing, a similar group at Bishop's Stortford. He recorded three fasts at the Dixon household,[125] three at the Emersons,[126] five at the Perry household[127] and one at the Ingrams' home.[128] It seems to have been part of a regular routine, although it is not quite clear how often they met. Once he refers to 'our weeklye meeting' (81) and another day of fasting and prayer is described as 'secretly generale every 3. weekes' (106). Indeed, his appetite for fasting was such that he was willing to travel some distance to take part in such exercises. He reported a trip to Hatfield Broad Oak to 'give the whole day to god sweetlye; in publique, and

124 The 'promise' is a paraphrase of Psalm 37:5 – 'Commit thy way unto the Lord; trust also in him; and he shall bring it to pass.'
125 Diary, pp. 39, 60, 79.
126 Diary, pp. 32, 38, 119.
127 Diary, pp. 44, 55, 62, 76, 106.
128 Diary, p. 94.

private together' (80), and another time at the home of the minister of Hatfield, for 'Fasting, and prayer, at Mr Harrisons' (83). There was an unsuccessful day devoted to 'Fasting, and praying', when he reported that 'I goe to Epping and am disappointed of mr Dike' (84). He had a much better experience at Farnham whether the fast was led by George Hughes or William Sedgewick. 'Now wee fast at Farnham, the Lord inlarges mr sedgewick mightilye his sp:[irit] plainleye; the Lord thaws my heart sweetlye; and I can lye downe in some sweet assurance of acceptance through Xt [Christ]' (81); 'Fasting and prayer at Farnham; Mr Hues; the Lord thawes my heart wrings out many teares and my soule can a litle rowle it selfe upon my G.[od] of peace, I will lye downe in faith, and peace' (82), or (slightly less successfully), 'Fasting at Farnham, a litle thawed; but ag:[ain] much deaded and sunke in my spirit' (88).

Two of the purposes of fasting seem to have been fairly omnipresent: spiritual unity and encouragement. After time with 'some wethersfeild company' he was '[a] litle refreshed', 'but alasse the former sweetnes, and communion I am a stranger to' (23). A more successful day had him writing in delight that 'wee rejoice in each other, and animate one another to suffering' (93). Sometimes the occasions were turned to more specific comforts. There seems to have been fasting both to restore the health of Charles Denny and to turn his demise to good purpose. 'This day fasting, and mourning, the Lord went out with us at G. D3x:[on's] Mr Charles Denny dyed; we have * a sorrowfull familye, the Lord sanctifye his heavy hand upon us, and draw our affections neere to thee; purge out the Achan from us' (39).[129] Similarly, he noted a day of

> Fasting and prayer at G. D.[ixon's] the Lord went out mightilye with us, and thawed our hearts; blessed be his name; oh Lord let us live as wee have prayed, and walke better then ever; wee prayed for J. Dix:[on] in point of mariage, and wee will wait what the Lord will answer us.

The same day ended with a section that seems to voice a frustration with ineffectual fasting: 'in point of convers:[ation] and mariage both: R. Emer:[son's] wife dyes while wee were praying for her; as Mr: Ch:[arles] Denny did, whilest I was putting up suites for him in this same place; the Lord comfort the mourning husb:[and] to whom the Lord hath surelye tryd' (60).

No such doubt appears, perhaps surprisingly, when there were more 'political' concerns in the fasts. Probably in the interests of security, he is rarely precise in the nature of the prayers, but it is a minor task of deduction

---

[129] The last section is a reference to Joshua 7: Achan had disobeyed Joshua by stealing some of the spoil after the battle of Jericho, thus bringing the wrath of God upon Israel. God would not support his chosen people in battle until they destroyed the evil among their ranks. It may be a plea over evils in the broader community but, as this is a time when he was unhappy in the Denny household, it may be closer to home.

to get the gist. After a fast at Goodman Perry's, he was delighted to record that 'I thinke I never was so caryed out espec:[ially] ag:[ainst] the enimyes of the ch:[urch] the Lord serve, and grant, and let not our trail be lost' (106). After a fast at Farnham, he prayed that their prayers should not be ignored: 'oh Lord let none of our pore suites be lost; oh deare god, be not angry ag:[ainst] the prayers of thy deare ones, who in the strength of thy command have gone out to thee'. The nature of the 'pore suites' is clear: 'oh downe, downe with the enimyes of thy truth, and lord lift up, the heades of thy people' (81). A related plea was for God to limit the impact of his wrath upon the sinful nation. 'Lord heare, Lord heare, downe with plauge sins, take away the stubble, that the fire of thy indignation may goe [inked out] out; and Lord thy destroying angel stop him' (80). Very near the end of the diary a fast was held in the Vere household which had a great deal to cover in terms of individual, familial, national and international affairs.

> Today, we, fasting, pour forth prayers which are not scanty, in our house; the Lord melts our hearts in his breast; he had grace abundantly enough, melting grace; shining and sanctifying; out of the abounding spirit he has poured forth his spirit upon me; surely great confidence in the name of Jehovah; he has suppressed the accustomed fast most willingly; and the consolation in matters concerning me, the family; concerning Lady Vere, of our church, and the Scottish [church] (170).[130]

It should come as no surprise to find Rogers' spirituality needing external support. We may recall that his relationship with God was far from consistent in its intimacy. There were many days when he felt that God was 'veiled', or 'frowning', or even 'absent'. In these circumstances, his theological context offered an alternative option to the patience and passivity mentioned earlier. The covenant had a permanent presence as opposed to a God who might withdraw. This was the case when 'the Lord is not neere, my soule is troubled; my whole trust, and wowling [that is, howling] is upon the Lord, and his full, and satisfying promise' (41). The covenant might lack the experiential value of the vision of God; it was nonetheless a reliable second choice: 'though I have not had such feeling of his love, as sometimes I have had; the Lord would have mee exercised in living by faith in a promise and not by sense, and feeling' (79). At times of neglect, the covenant could act as a safety net. One day, when he was 'sadded, and moping, only I know in whom I have believed; and whose spirit hath sealed mee; experience shall cause mee to roule my self wholly upon him, who is unchangeable in his promises backe with his oath, and seales'

---

[130] Hodie Ieiunantes nos, preue effendimus non ieiunas; in domu nostrâ; liqua facit dominus corda nostra in pectore suo; ille gratium habet abunde satis; liquantem gratiam; candescentem sanctificantamque; ex abundanti spiri tuc suum effedit super me; Ynvenio certe confidentiam magnam in Iehovah nomine; fastem solitum suppressit gratissime; atq[ue] consolationem in gratiosâ affectiae eius in rebus de ne, de familiâ; de Dominâ Veere, De Ecclesiâ nostra, atque scoticenâ

(109). The covenant could provide the framework, the spectacles, as it were, through which to see God: 'myne eyes are upon the covenant and upon G.[od] through it, there will I hang, and in the strength of it, as in the strength of god will I walke the pore time of my sojourning heere' (83). Faith and trust in the covenant could be a route to an empowering recognition of impotence.

> I adventure my soule upon the promise and if I perish, I[']le perish by cleaving to that and if I be saved, I[']le be saved also no other; and I[']le live, and dye in the faith, and hope of it; yet is thy covenant of mercye, yet thou wouldest have mee, to rejoice and, even then, when my soule is at the lowest in respect of feeling; in covenant and promise strength ther[e]f:[ore] I weaknes with live; And so when I am weake, then am I strong (82).

Given the centrality of covenant theology to puritan sacramental piety, it makes sense for this to be a recurring site for Rogers' pleasure in the covenant. It is also the place where Christ is mentioned far more than in any other context.

> Saboth, sacrament, the fruit wherof I a litle injoyed in the ordinance, and now after it in this maner; my soule is not raised to tast[e] that full sweetnes in Xt [Christ]; which I have done, and would have; but my soule lingers after him, and roules it selfe upon thy covenant which is nowe sealed; I will live, and dye upon thy promises and now sleep with it in myne armes (86).

A few days before this particular communion, his meditation took him through the old covenant of works to Christ and then on to the new covenant of grace.

> I looke toward thee, in the day approaching, and to that sacrament, invite mee Lord, and give mee a stomacke to thy daintyes, Let faith apply thy whole covenant (for pardon, healing, new creature; &c;) daily, that it being mine, may be sealed; for that also is the new Testament in Xs [Christ's] blood; 1. the new covenant (purchased by blood) signed, and sealed (86).

The sacrament functioned as a reassurance, a reminder and a spiritual 'fix' that was unmatched. 'Saboath, sacrament, at Coleman [Street] refreshed, and quickened and joyed Oh that it might hold and that I might walk worthy accord:[ing] to my covenant sealed' (159). It is useful that we take it as a reminder too, and turn our attention to the rather neglected part of puritan spirituality, public worship, and measure its part in Rogers' piety.

It is worth noting that Rogers rarely wrote about public worship per se so much as enthused or complained about 'ordinances'. At a low point he might mourn that 'I find not that sweetnes in ordinances nor the life in a Xian [christian] course, as I once found at startford in the midst of opposition' (162); public worship was a rare provider of succour in his time with the Denny family. More specifically, 'ordinances' could simply refer to *social* spirituality: 'something quickned by visiting freinds G. Dixon; sicke;

G. Dane; if any savor, lord adde more, and ever sweetnes from all ordinances, and helps w[ha]tever' (29). This could amount to a distinction between public and private, with the line being drawn between social and solitary rather than official and voluntary, as in this plea: 'oh the spirit life, and power of an ordinance what is become of it? Oh Lord I am even pulled backe in regard of outward helpes, oh Let my soule injoy thee in secret, Lord if thou departest from preaching and the assemblys' (63). Such 'outward helpes' might be closer to the ordinances of public services as in the note after a poor Sabbath when he felt that 'the life of a publique ordinance' provided 'none to that healing; and quickning; Lord in the want supply by drawing neere to mee in secret' (90).

The most frequent appearance of the ordinances is, particularly in his Stortford time, in their absence, which in itself reveals their value. 'I want the presence, and the sweetnes of Xt [Christ] in his ordinances, and thence doe I sit desolate' (81); 'where is the sweet rellish of christ in an ordinance; oh Lord more of that, and less in the creature' (73). At this time he was prone to plead for help, for 'a litle sweetnes in beholding thy face in the beautye of thyne ordinances' (41). This related to his feelings of unsettledness, wondering 'must I not remove, to search for the sp:[irit] of the ordinance' (45) and the reverse of this absence was part of his attraction to New England, as an element of his idealized vision of the colonies was perfect public worship. This appears when he followed a complaint about the Church of England by asking 'shall I one day see New England, and the beautye of thy countenance in thy livelye and pure ordinances?' (70).

The way in which the ordinances, in the narrow definition of public worship, operated was twofold. The lesser way was as a safety net, a set of comforts in the Lord's absence, as when he felt that 'my heart is ready to sinke downe to the creature; and were it not, that the lord upheld mee by the continuall dropping of something into mee in his ordinances; I knew not what to doe' (35). On its own, this offered merely short-term comfort; his heart might 'be wound up in an ordinance yet it flags soone' (37). The more common way was more productive; this was the way in which the ordinances could act as a means for him to approach God or for God to come close to him. After a visit to Earls Colne he was delighted that 'the L[or]d was with mee in the ordinance there and wee rejoice much in each others companyes' (161). On another occasion he felt that 'the Lord hath graciouslye looked towards mee, and hath not wholly forsaken mee in these ordinances; though I cannot find him in the perfection of sweetnes' (80). The first movement was present after he attended a service ministered by Edmund Brewer, when 'my soule is refreshed because I have found the L[or]d in his ordinance' (93). His delight was more passive during a visit from his father, when he noted that 'the Lord is with us in the ordinances; and drawes neere in some measure' (109).

On many occasions Rogers was quite particular about the failures and benefits of specific ordinances. Predominantly the focus of his criticism or praise was either the sermon or the communion. We will turn to the sacrament shortly but it is worth paying some attention to the preaching. The godly appetite for a good sermon is a given in studies of puritan spirituality but that does not mean that it should be skipped over. As will be seen in the text, and as has been seen above, he frequently gave a 'review' of the sermon and was rarely charitable. Concern about the absence, or even the feared absence, of good preaching should be understood as part of the godly worldview. He bemoaned his 'deadnes, and unbeleife' and directly connected this with 'my want of lively preaching' (70). The centrality and value placed upon the sermon comes across clearly in one entry: 'oh the god of the ordinance the sp:[irit] of preaching; the soule pricking, the thawing preaching; Lord shall I never injoy that againe, oh restore the power, and life of thyne ordinances' (72). The joy of a good sermon after a lapse in supply can be seen shortly after this entry, particularly in the reference to Proverbs 15:17: 'oh what a heaven is it, to injoy powerful, savory, preaching in a saboth; the life of the life; Lord find out some way, that I may lye under the power of the ordinance though with a dish of greene hearbes' (73).[131]

Before we move on to the sacramental part of Rogers' piety, I would like to propose a controversial thesis: it was possible for a godly minister to overdose on sermons! Rogers was in Cambridge when he came of age and gave himself a birthday treat:

> this day is the saboath; St Andrewes [Day] upon which I am 21. yeares old, wherein I have heard 4. sermons, and then 5. repeated, yet surelye multitude of thinges doe take away edge; I have found my heart more broken, and fitter to attend god after the hearing of one or 2. the lord hath given some meltings and joyes, but these come farre short of former, as Davids worthyes all came short of the 1. three (7).[132]

A more accurate assessment would be to note that for Rogers, listening to a sermon was a much more proactive experience than we might assume. He could only take so much because he wanted to engage with each sermon, to take it on board both doctrinally and experientially. The spiritual rigour which would take a good sermon from 'mere' theology to 'thawing' or 'melting' was a demanding process.

Similarly sustained spiritual discipline was a requisite for the sacrament. The process went well beyond the church service of the communion. Towards the end of his introductory autobiography, Rogers gave thanks for the comfort he had received over the last month, 'especiallye before, in, and after the sacrament' (4). Preparation for the Lord's Supper was often undertaken a week ahead of the service, and in itself the anticipation could be rewarding, as when he noted, 'Some thawings before the sacrament and

[131] Prov. 15:17 – 'Better is a dinner of herbs where love is, than a stalled ox and hatred therewith.'
[132] The last phrase is a reference to II Sam. 23:15–17, the greatest servants of David.

expectation raised for the good things of that feast, L[or]d fill mee ever full with thy daintys; faith love, hope; peace, comfort and joy unspeakable, and full of glorye' (38). Sometimes he noted a preparatory fast, either solitary or social, and the day of communion after one such occasion was marked with an asterisk, usually used to mark his best days; his preparation seems to have been rewarded. 'I am refreshed with the fat things of the house of my God, this day; Blesse the lord oh my soule, and all that is within mee pay tribute to him; * this is a day of gladnes and joy' (157). On one level, one particular solitary fast looks unproductive, but the truth is that as part of its purpose was to combat pride and increase humility, the superficial failure marked it as a success.

> This day have I kept a private fast; but oh porely and weakelye oh I cannot get an hard heart to relent and mourne; Lord what shall a pore creature doe; I am dead, and saplesse in my desires of X [Christ], faith downe the wind, whereas it should be upon the wing toward the sacrament; Lord I will not yet be beaten backe, for there are crums in thy sacrament (51).

Successful preparation yielded positive raptures in his journal, with sacramental piety producing some of the richest language in the text: 'oh how my mind dances in the smile of Christ';[133] 'your presence, Lord, is my life' (140).[134] At Farnham, he was 'much revived in spirit, and going away from gods table, as filling with marrow, and refined wines' (106). Most of his best sacraments were at Coleman Street, for instance the following: 'broken to peices with joy; drunk with comfort; this is a day of rejoicing, and strength; for the joy of the L[or]d, hath bin my strength' (154). Part of this exuberance came from a willingness to let go and, however briefly, to put himself wholly in the Lord's care, as after another Coleman Street service where 'the L[or]d refreshes mee more and stirs up faith to trust in him; and quickens my affections; and now L[or]d I am thyne for ever' (151).

The negative side of this can be seen at the times when his preparation was inadequate or he had a sense of spiritual inadequacy. On two occasions in the period when he was concerned about M. S. he was unsure whether he was fit to receive the sacrament. Once he thought 'I am unfit for a sacrament: bec:[ause] my heart is not enough broken for my bls3 [base] dealing with g.[od] in nibling at old v4ws [vows]' (26). A little earlier he had 'Many feares by reason of boyling corruption to come to the sacrament'. He overcame these fears and attended, albeit 'not so resolved, and prepared, as I should'. He gained some comfort, 'but alasse the fresh savor is ready to passe before night' (14). At such troubled times his language would put the emphasis on the charity of grace rather than on the 'daintys' or 'the fat things'. 'I am in a cloud; and cannot behold the Lord so sweet as faine I

---

[133] oh quam tripudiat mens mea in risu Christi
[134] præsentia tua domine vita mea est

would; yet I am upholden to seeke him; if the L[or]d will have me receive the sacrament in darknesse; yet will I looke up towards him and come for my dole' (39–40); 'my heart is at a low ebbe going to the sacrament, in a cloud, but I will looke up, and waite at the throne of grace in use of mercy for my dole' (65).

It would, of course, be an incomplete survey of Rogers' spiritual means without paying attention to his practice of keeping a diary. Surprisingly, this is the most difficult to assess from the text itself, as he never explicitly discussed why he started to write a journal. He simply opens with the remark that 'I have long bene thinking of a general view of my life' (1). The crucial word here is 'view'; writing down his assessment of each day, usually just before he retired, externalized his spirituality, literally giving him something to look at. This seems to have given him a material site for each day's 'self' and this appears to have provided access to his former state, as is shown in his practice of drawing attention to particularly important days by marking them with an asterisk, although he never actually mentions any re-reading. The nearest suggestion to that is the entry on one bad day: 'I come to the booke I confesse with litle hearte; my deare god shuts his eare, so that I have nothing to live upon, but my stocke of faith upon former experience, and yet that shall make mee call upon his name as long as I live' (9). Ironically, the best way to assess the way the diary worked is at the times when it failed him. He wanted to make a remembrance of his spiritual state on each day whether it was a positive or negative report. He was particularly down when he had a day with neither good nor bad state to report: 'No great matter to write of done; I cannot see the lord neer mee, I eloofe and he hides' (126). He was occasionally recalcitrant to open his diary, as when he was 'Loath to write, my hearte is bound by my unworthy walking' (12). Part of the practice evidently consisted of exposing himself completely to God, fully recognizing his failures. The difficulty he sometimes had in writing came from a desire to avoid such admission of guilt, almost as if the guilt was not there, was not accepted, until it was written down, as in an early entry when he admitted that, 'I was loath to come in to repent for my backsliding (which I knew I must doe) because I thought it would hinder the growth of my bodye' (3). As he adjusted to use the journal to better effect, he became better at properly embracing his inadequacies. In the following instance, he is almost self-congratulatory in his failings. 'Litle worth the writing, still I give myself ocasion to bewaile my unfruitfulnesse, and careless walking with god' (24).

The diary came to work as a site for grounding, for basic maintenance of his spirituality. This can be seen when circumstances made it difficult to keep up the practice. Early in 1635, he lost two weeks of the discipline, noting against 18 January that 'This day I went home with my brother where for want of time, but espec:[ially] spirit[,] I let this work passe; till the 2 Febru: after; most of the time being spent in recreations visitings of freinds at home, and abroad, alasse what cannot ocasions doe with my weake heart'

(10). This problem constituted the loss of a space in which to take or make a view of himself and to draw himself together each night. 'I goe to wethersfeild, where I continue some time; I want libertye of place, and I loose my heart quickly' (87). The diary was his ultimate site of privacy, a confessional booth but also a spiritual MOT agency where he could assess the trouble and start again. 'I went to wethersfeild; and there continued, where I lost my heart exceedinglye, having no convenient place to poure out my soule into the bosome of my god' (51). This last time, when he went for a week without such a place, showed that the loss of such a place led to the accumulation of daily difficulties which his self-examination without the diary could hardly cope with.

Religion and politics
If one should turn to Rogers' diary hoping for an account of a nascent revolutionary, an increasingly disgruntled radical slowly coming to the boil, one might be initially disappointed. As will become clear, most of his recorded responses were to prayer, sometimes bitterness, sometimes disempowerment. To a fair degree this is down to the nature of the source; the journal is a site for, among other things, a conversation with God and, on a more mundane level, for giving voice to resentments. Rogers comes across many times almost as the worst sort of anthropologist, standing on the margins both fascinated and disgusted with the ways of others and leaving with the reassurance that his place, his position, is better. However, he increasingly came to voice a siege mentality, allied to fears of God's wrath being delivered to his nation, his church. This took him to prayer and, later on, to watching a struggle in which he was not a participant but is very clear who he wants to succeed. Many of his grievances were *ad hominem*, gradually taking on the bigger picture.

The vast majority of his *ad hominem* bile was poured forth on ecclesiastical issues in his Stortford days, with the target being Richard Butler, the local incumbent. Butler actually worked very well as the epitome of the values of the Church of England that Rogers wanted to be changed. In addition to a style of worship far from his taste, there were three occasions when he touched on sensitive spots that bolstered his existing feelings, sharpening his disquiet and hardening his sense of identity. Serious tongue-biting was required when Butler dined with the Denny family: 'at dinner B5tler playes his p[oin]ts, ag[ainst] N.[ew] E.[ngland] the lord stird mee up ag:[ainst] him though I was faint to pinch by reason of B[ishop']s office[r]s, something; but not so heavenly as I would be' (29). His position was plain when Butler argued for ceremonial conformity using Romans 13:1, that is, on the grounds of secular authority. 'Saboath, this p[ro]fane wretch Butler plays the wofull wretch (let every soule be subject) my heart sadded' (95–6). In one sermon, Bulter was plainly preaching to the unconverted when Rogers reported that he 'playes his parts, shewes hims:[elf] in his colours ag:[ainst] Zelotes; brings his 25 obj:[ections]

ag:[ainst] common prayer, answers them, and railes' (48). He was almost driven on to the moral high ground, finding some spiritual comfort and ending with pity for those who failed to see the truth. He dismissed the

> cold doings, but the Lord hath a litle thawed my heart since I came home; in secret, and in family dutyes; (oh what a deale of hurt does saplesse preaching) a man hath no discourse for the sabbath; it dryes up a mans spirit; Lord give a blessing to a barren familye; dwell thou amongst us' (48).

A similar sense of 'goodies and baddies' with eventual therapeutic, albeit minimal, empowerment can be found when he was alert to the ecclesiastical politics of Cambridge. When he reported the 'impudent questions' of John Normanton he knew who was in the right, but admitted 'though I am not so cleare as I should be' (18). He was more confident the next time he mentioned him. Normanton was now 'that epitome of whorish impudence; that scorner of all good', and Rogers celebrated Normanton's punishment, giving thanks to God. 'Blessed be the L[or]d that some steppe in in the cause [a few words inked out] of his truth' (46). He was immediately sure when he condemned the only mention of altar policy, having heard a defence of liturgical devotion and what was probably a defence of Laudian eucharistic practices. Rogers looked for divine support in sticking to the true way in the face of such arguments.

> This day sylly D. Conghams act; ab:[out] his ceremonyes; where many things damped mee from Collins also, ab:[out] altars, supposed lawfull; till I am faint to pluck up my spirits and resolve to keepe my selfe pure, and close to the truth, and the god of truth all my dayes (19).

When he returned to Cambridge for Commencement he had the voice of an old veteran when he reported unpleasant changes, being particularly disheartened that even Emmanuel College had moved towards formalism. He looked to God for support, 'though I see universitye; yea our colledge much declined, and vanishing into shadows, and formalitye; many of the fellowes bowing at Jesus; Lord be mercifull to the place' (50). His primary concern at this point was with reining in his objections for the sake of gaining his degree: 'pride, and Malevolence about putting on my cap in a chappell; oh cursed formalists; these th:[ings] and others trouble, and disquiet my mind, and make mee feare my degree' (50). Three months later, he was rather more interested in finding protection for the whole institution. '[O]h the pore universitye, Lord pitye it in the general consent to superstition, and will worship; it is a sinfull decaying universitye; oh the strange change in 7. yeares' (61). He found some comfort when he returned in October 1637, noting that Richard Holdsworth 'does admirablye preach, kept the act, &c: the Arminians fret; Pullen playes the cursed Arminian'. Godly company at Emmanuel College encouraged him and gave a positive note to his prayer for the Lord to 'doe good to that pore colledge yet'.

Indeed, Rogers seems to have been at least momentarily empowered, in that he seems to have won an argument the following day and ended it in relative peace. 'I returne home, meet with an arminian, deboise him I lye downe in Xs [Christ's] armes' (118).

As with Holdsworth and with the earlier example of those who punished Normanton, Rogers took comfort from those who stood up to what he saw as corruptions. Given the Foxeian tradition (and *Acts and Monuments* is one of the two books that can be identified as his reading material),[135] it comes as no surprise to find that he had some appetite for at least vicarious martyrdom. A couple of weeks after Henry Burton was imprisoned in February 1637, the entry consisted of the following: 'I rejoice in the saints; and my soule abhors these cursed sycophants [presumably Laudian bishops] every day more, and more; I have re[-]read mr Burtons book, and my heart and portion be with those that contend for the faith, whether in life, or death' (93). At the start of July 1637, after some spiritual refreshment, he seemed to be yearning for the opportunity of martyrdom himself, albeit passively, rather than actively seeking it. 'I ride with Mr Harlak:[enden] sp:[iritual] talke; we mourne for Mr Burton &c the L[or]d drawes mee in some measure; my soule is yet fixed and I will waite for my charge, and for my crowne' (108). After a trip to London he noted that he had actually visited Alexander Leighton, the more obscure martyr, in prison.[136] His assessment is unclear but he was determined to find a good model in him. 'I visit Dr Laiton in the fleet; a scotch sp:[irit] right; but sure upright, and one that hath tasted of the sweetnes of X [Christ], even in this affliction' (155). This mindset turned the death of his uncle, John Rogers, the lecturer of Dedham, into a martyrdom, blaming Matthew Wren for the lecturer's demise. According to godly sources, Wren had not been able to hire horses when he was on visitation in the southern part of his diocese of Norwich and so he had, in a fit of pique, encouraged his colleague William Juxon to suspend Rogers. Juxon did so on the grounds that the lecture was a risk to public health when the plague was at its height. When the Dedham lecturer applied to take up his preaching again and was refused, he realized that he had been silenced. As Samuel Rogers and other godly observers saw it, this made Wren responsible for John Rogers' quick decline and death.[137]

> Now comes sad newes of my deare cosen Rogers of Dedham his death; our losse most sad; oh happy for him; respecting terminus a quo, as well as ad quem; for just now that cursed wren had procured London to put downe his lecture; and the Lord then takes him to himselfe; the Lord thus pluckes

---

[135] Diary, pp. 51, 91.
[136] On whom see Stephen Foster, *Notes from the Caroline Underground: Alexander Leighton, the puritan triumverate, and the Laudian reaction to nonconformity* (Hamden, Conn., 1978), pp. 14–39.
[137] For the details, see Webster, *Godly Clergy*, pp. 213–14. The truth of the story is, in a sense, immaterial. The important thing is that people of Rogers' ilk believed it.

out our stakes that are sound out of the hedges; and rotten ones are put in; how soone is such a hedge pushed downe to let wrath come in; oh let mee live his life, and dye in the faith with him; so dying I may rejoice eternally with him, grandfather and all other the saints of god (78).

As with Burton, Rogers' last note is an ambition to live like his uncle and to die like his uncle; given the opportunity, to embrace martyrdom.

Matthew Wren is the bishop who receives the worst reviews from Rogers, although his colleagues receive only slightly more gentle abuse. It might be noted that the abuse is solely *ad hominem*; he dislikes particular bishops but there is no point at which he dismisses the institution of episcopacy. As a large part of the time covered in the diary was spent on the outer limits of the diocese, it comes as no surprise to find that some of the harshest words were written during the various visitations. At the end of Wren's first visitation as bishop of Norwich, Rogers noted that a 'deep sadnes hath taken hold on mee' and the first reason was that 'the church of god [is] held under hatches, the walls of Jerusalem beaten downe; pore suffolke and northfolke lying desolate by that cursed wretch wren' (84). It is striking that he used the image of Jeremiah 39:8, identifying Wren as Nebuchadnezzar, the Babylonians and their allies although, as we will see, it was not the worst comparison he made. His next contact with Wren was during the metropolitical visitation which started 28 February 1637 in the diocese of London. Wren joined the vicar-general, Sir Nathaniel Brent, and other officials, in Stortford. From the brief entry it is not clear what Wren did, but Rogers' ire and his frustration is fairly clear. 'Visitation Archb: I goe to L[or]d of Norwich; he playes the wretch ag:[ainst] goodness; I sp:[it] but oh that I had done more' (95). During the diocesan visitation of the following September, the targets of his bile are the chancellor, Dr Arthur Duck and an unclearly identified sympathizer. 'Abo[ut] the cursed visitat:[ion] D. Duck plays the base wretch; and Mr Crause in his sermon; all formality, and bitter speaking ag:[ainst] sermons; Lord ease us; and uncloth these wolves of there sheepskins' (116). His worst experience, however, was almost sought for, when he visited London, spending his time there in Westminster Hall and Westminster Abbey before crossing the Thames to Lambeth Palace.

this day, I goe to westminster; to the Hall; to the minster, see the monuments; I was refused of the popish Clarke to go to the sword; &c: bec:[ause] I would not put of[f] my hat before the Altar; from here to a place called Hell, and thence to Lambeth to Caiphas Hall (out of the frying pan into the fire) where sat those 2. cursed traitors to X [Christ]; W.[illiam of] C.[anterbury] and M.[atthew] wren with there hangbyes; I looke above them, and have joy in G.[od] and I shall dye better then they (162–3).

Two elements here are particularly noteworthy. The first is the terms of abuse. By renaming Lambeth Palace 'Caiphas Hall', he is comparing Laud and his acolytes to Caiaphas, the high priest who 'gave counsel to the Jews, that it was expedient that one man should die for the people' (John 18:14), hardly a flattering reference. The second is the conclusion: almost a happy one, a man confident in the righteousness of his hatred and thus finding comfort in what, for him, was an awful sight.

It was not always necessary for Rogers to see symptoms of the changing church for such feelings to be provoked. They could be brought on by particular sermons. In the following instance Jeremiah Dyke had preached on Ezekiel 22:28–30, the same source Rogers had used in the lamentation for the loss of his uncle.

> This day to Epping, heard Mr Dike of the hedge broken, and not mended; one mightye in the scripture, a teaching prophet, whom the Lord hath sent as Jeremiah, and Ezek:[iel] to speak plainely among so many daubers with untempered mortar; Lord mainteine such stakes in the hedge if it be thy blessed will to doe us good (59).

More frequently, he found comfort in conventicles, being surrounded by like-minded people. Spending one night at William Sedgwick's house in Farnham, he declared himself to be 'much revived by there company, so much the more as I see more closenes in him, and opposition to these cursed times' (86). These occasions helped to sharpen the lines between right and wrong, and to bolster the siege mentality of the godly. After another fast at Farnham, his prayer caught this sense of confident humility under fire.

> Lord let none of our pore suites be lost; oh deare god, be not angry ag:[ainst] the prayers of thy dear ones, who in the strength of thy command have gone out to thee; oh downe, downe with the enimyes of thy truth, and lord lift up, the heades of thy people (81).

This perspective was maintained the following day and prompted one of the clearest (and harshest) divisions between right and wrong: 'oh thy church, thy church, Lord; restore the libertyes of thy faithfull ones; shut not thyne eares to the prayers of thy saints; but poure downe thy wrath upon the kingdome of antiX [Antichrist] shall his brats may come to revive' (81–2).

The dark side of this perspective was a fear of God's wrath being turned upon the nation as a whole. To Rogers, the cause of this potential wrath, which he feared more and more frequently as time passed, was plain.

> the Lord is angry with us a most sinful nation; witness also the heavy plauge in London, Newcastle port townes, followes the Court &c: deseases pox here, last year in Essex, these are forerun[n]ers of greater judgements as wee may justlye feare, sin gets an head; espec:[ially] sp:[iritual] sins; idolatrous superstitious Arminians carye the ball before them; they have prevailed lamentably within these 7. yeares; the Lord in mercy fight for his witnesses that seeme to be slaine now almost; Lord thy church, thy church, thy pore creatures, that know not how to keepe a good conscience in these sorrowfull times, help us, and deliver us for thy goodnesse sake (66).

It was not always clear which way God was going to go: 'my heart is looking, and sad by weighing the state of things in this wofull land; oh will the L[or]d be yet gracious to us; or will he destroy us yet further' (90). These fears were put across most sharply in an image taken from I Chronicles 21:11–12.[138] The first occasion was related to the plague, noted as starting in Gonville and Caius College, Cambridge and threatening to spread. 'Lord thou hast tried us with former favors, wee have forfeited them and the[re]f:[ore] art thou now incensed ag:[ainst] our citye, a plauge; and universitye in Kayes colledge begun; Lord stay, Lord quench; oh command back the sword, and the angel, that thou hast commanded to destroy' (79–80). A few days later, a good fast at Hatfield Broad Oak brought the image back to his mind, prompting the prayer, 'Lord heare, Lord heare, downe with plauge sins, take away the stubble, that the fire of thy indignation may goe [inked out] out; and Lord thy destroying angel stop him' (80).

It was not always clear exactly what Rogers was asking for in his prayers, as in this area his notes were often abrupt, even terse. 'L[or]d pity pore desolate England' (95); '[o]h thy church thy church; yet for England, sinfull England' (116). Perhaps he did not know exactly what he wanted to happen; he knew the desired result but, other than putting it in God's hands, as in the following example, he knew not the means. 'Lord consider the pore soules, that want food sp:[iritual] and send it to them; Lord turne the course of things, which are come to a lamentable story; make bare thy arm and strike thyne enimyes; and defend thy church' (72).[139] The scale of the change needed was apparent to him. '[W]hy not even now, Lord, something for our England, may there be peace, eternal and holy; Sion, once your delight; purify the church, and the state, found them upon your anointing, and your welcome blessed hand we beg' (171).[140] This is best seen in a short but shocking prayer: 'Lord stay also with us; purge our decaying estate; preserve thy C[ommon]w[eal]th which is now tottering; Lord preserve, and convert our King' (47). (Evidently Rogers thought that Charles had gone over to Roman Catholicism.) This uncertainty about means makes more comprehensible his passivity as news of the Covenanters arrived in London. 'I, safe and faithful, lie hidden in the arms of Jesus, even in the worst times' (170);[141] 'in you I rest, Lord, even in these times; I surely foresee the evil that is going

---

[138] 'So Gad came to David, and said unto him, Thus saith the Lord, Choose thee Either three years' famine; or three months to be destroyed before thy foes, while that the sword of thine enemies overtaketh thee; or else three days the sword of the Lord, even the pestilence, in the land, and the angel of the Lord destroying throughout all the coasts of Israel. Now therefore advise thyself what word I shall bring again to him that sent me.'

[139] He is pleading through Isa. 52:10.

[140] Quin adque domine aliquid pro Anglia nostrâ; sit paxa æterna, ut sancta; sion, olim delicijs tuis; purga ecclesiam, atq rempublicam; funda super unctum tuum, atq nos spiritum Lætus manum, supplicationum

[141] ego tutus fidusque in Iesu ulnis Latiao etiam in temporibus pessimis

to come, and I shall conceal myself in you, and I shall go forth safe, either in life, or through death' (173).[142]

He watched the astonishing developments in the north with pleasure tempered with uncertainty, anticipating change but far from sure exactly what that change would be. At its shortest, he simply asked, 'L[or]d bring good to thy church out of this Scotch buisinesse' (166). At slightly greater length, he made plain his loyalties but effectively put God in charge of the show.

> My soule still leanes on God, and in some weake measure I rejoice in g[od] and this day my heart hath bine inlarged to peice in with the Sc4ts [Scots] who begin their synod with F. this weeke and nexte; L[or]d hasten them, Lord some ease, and good ever so to thy church (165–6).

Drawing together Rogers' scattered expressions of hope, fear, disgust and concern about the politics of religion, we can make a few overall assessments. The first lesson is the intensity of his interest. This was a young minister whose life was never directly touched by the ecclesiastical authorities other than the difficulty with his ordination. But through his family, admired colleagues, worship and general perceptions he was sufficiently alienated to see William Laud and Matthew Wren as 'cursed traitors' to Christ (162). In itself this should further discourage us from assessing alienation through a simple 'counting of heads' of deprived ministers and punished laity. The particular criticisms he made are revealing, too. Apart from the unadulterated abuse, the predominant specific complaint is 'Arminianism'. This is certainly not to suggest that his only concern was soteriological, but it is noteworthy that he refers to one minister as 'popish', and raises questions about Charles I's religious loyalties, but is far more likely to complain about Arminianism. Alongside this there are two absences, one complete, the other virtual. He never raises questions about the viability of episcopacy; he does abuse particular bishops, but it is not *because they are bishops*. The virtual absence is complaints about altar policy. There is the occasion when he castigates Collins about his defence of altars and the accusation of popery relates to the minister who tried to make him remove his hat by the altar, but this is surprisingly little for a man with such a devotion to eucharistic piety. In terms of worship, his complaint is much broader, best summarized in his feeling that 'my heart grows cold', complaining that 'marthas ocasions, will scarse cary along with them, a maryes heart', (150) by which he means the complex rituals of Martha's hospitality came between her and true worship while Mary's minimalist devotions cut to the quick (cf. Luke 10:39–42). The final conclusion is his perception of his own powerlessness. This should not be used as a generalization for all his like-minded peers. Rogers was, after

---

[142] in te acquiesco domine, etiam in hisce temporibus; prævideo certe malum venturum, et abscondam me in te, et tutus ego evadem aut in vitâ, aut per mortem

all, young, unbeneficed, generally unsettled and far from overconfident. He was impotent, with only God to turn to. Having said this, the phrase 'only God' would not have made sense to him; we should avoid underestimating his confidence in God. If God chose to put things right no-one could stop Him. Having 'only God' on your side was infinitely preferable to all the earthly means available.

The Diary

Physical description of the diary   The outside covering of the diary has a full sprinkled calf-leather binding with dimensions of 17.2 by 12 cm. On both back and front covers, a border of three blind narrow strips intersect at the corners. Eight panels divide the flat spine by alternating groups of four and two fillets. On the spine the Rev. Thomas Percy, the antiquarian who had acquired the diary by 1760, has added manuscript lettering and decoration in white ink. Upside down in relation to the contents of the diary and in the second panel Percy inscribed the phrase 'A FANATICK JOURNAL M.S.' This reflected his place as a member of the Church of England with its choice of epithet to refer to nonconformists or dissenters. Above the inscription Percy drew a skull and crossbones, and below, crossbones followed by four further sets of skull and crossbones. Sewn green and white thread bands the head and the tail of the spine.

A slightly yellowed rag paper of 191 leaves makes up the interior of the diary. The leaves have a perceptible red staining on the edges but generally are in excellent condition. These leaves measure 16.1 by 11.3 cm. The collation requires 23 gatherings in groups of twelves. Gathering 23 wants a final leaf, but a surviving fragment indicates that it may have been used as a paste down. No endpapers exist for the diary. The pagination by Samuel Rogers begins on the recto of the second leaf and continues without interruption to the last complete folio. With a few double numbers and a slip in the numbering in the 300s, the pagination by Rogers runs as follows: 1–45, 45–282, 282–306, 306–13, 313–14, 215–62, 262–74; that is a total of 378 numbered pages. Within the transcript Rogers' numbering has been adopted, with the repeated paginations taken as 313a and so forth, and the inaccurate pagination of 215 onwards has been modified to 315, this judged to be least complicated and easiest for anyone choosing to compare this edition with the original. Three unnumbered folios which contain miscellaneous notes also appear, one in the front and two in the back (one formed a paste down). Each leaf of the text shows signs of having been folded twice vertically into quarters. Such folding probably helped to maintain regular margins and/or it marked the point reached in keeping up the diary. Gatherings 1–12 display watermarks like Headwood 4055,[143] described by Headwood as 'uncertain'. Gatherings 13–23, called 'pot' paper

---

[143] Edward Headwood, *Watermarks, mainly of the 17th and 18th centuries* (Hilversham, 1950).

(bearing the watermark of a pot), are like Headwood 3587, 3604 or 3627, but with the initials P/BR.

Palaeography Samuel Rogers wrote on every page of the diary. His medium-sized writing fully occupies every page, front and back, from the second through to the next to the last complete leaf. He uses some abbreviations, though he rarely employs prefix or suffix symbols. His hand reads fairly easily for the most part; occasionally he runs letters together and many pages become difficult at the bottom where he tried to crowd his thoughts into the remaining space. Since he wrote on both sides of the leaves with a finely mixed black ink, traces of the ink merge from one side into the characters of the other; this can present difficulties in reading, but fortunately such problems rarely occur. The clarity of the writing means that uncertain readings seldom arise, but readings that present such problems, usually only one or two letters, will be marked in this edition as questionable by the addition of square brackets enclosing a question mark or the statement 'illegible' or 'inked out', as appropriate. Occasionally in the text Thomas Percy has underlined a name in red, and on one occasion noted one passage with marginalia. The former have been ignored and the latter is noted. Otherwise, the writing and the marginal notations in the main body of the text belong exclusively to the pen of Samuel Rogers.

On the first and back leaves Rogers made miscellaneous notes. Thomas Percy added an inscription on the first, and unknown hands put notations on the blank back of the first leaf and the front and back of the last leaf. On the front of the first leaf Rogers had written the date of 'Novemb: 18–1634'; 'Samuel Rogers his booke'; a Latin phrase under the name which reads 'S. Ne temere. R Qui auget rem dolo augit dolorem', and a final note of 'Poet-1s' which probably refers to the price he paid for the blank book. Another inscription tops the page in what looks like Rogers' hand. It reads: 'and the Lord said unto me be of good comfort thy sins are forgiven the'. Another note, in a similar hand, in the top left-hand corner, reads 'Lib: 1.' Thomas Percy added his own vertical inscription along the left-hand side of the first leaf. After noting the date of 'Oct. 12, 1760', probably the date of acquisition, he described the volume in a way which was very much the Anglican attitude of his time: 'It was a common thing in the last century for the Puritans to draw up Narratives of their Experiences or as the favourite phrase was of God's dealings with them. The following fanatic Diary is a piece of that kind.'

On the verso of the first folio and immediately opposite the start of the diary itself, two unidentified hands have made entries. In a faded, formal hand, the following draft remarks appear:

Much estemed Honoured SSir
Whose fforme is ffamous and very
Much to be estemed in All holey

Writt: And in the Arts and Sciences
off Learning; boeth in Ethik
Logiq: Metaphisicke:
And becaus I know, know soe well
Therefore I desire Re [?]

A sum of money follows this drafted address, but the pounds are not clear; it is probably '375–18–9'. It may be the same sum and same hand that appears in the penultimate page of the diary. The only other entry on the earlier leaf is in a different hand. A sentence starts but does not end: 'It is as hard to . . .'.

After the text of the diary ends, there is one page with miscellaneous notations on both sides. On the leaf immediately facing the end of the text, someone has practised a formal hand expressing both lettering and inscriptions in Latin and English. These inscriptions run upside down in relation to the text of the diary. In the same disposition a separate hand has entered a number of monetary calculations in the hundreds of pounds. On the back face of the diary, Rogers wrote several lines denoting five different thoughts, the third beginning with an illegible clause in Greek. Written vertically from the bottom to the top of the leaf, the entries are: 'The violent, the violent take it by force; (upon 11 Matthew)'; 'the days of that ignorance G[od] winked at, but now &c.; *winked; 1. he punished it not so severelye; accord: to the analogye of other places, He that knows not his masters will, shall be beaten with stripes'; 'your father takes the libertye, that is not to be granted in reg: of betters; &c:'; 'G[od] move us to the bearing of the crosse, by our daily, and patient undergoing our pettye matters'; 'Also those sins complexionall, and habituall'. The other entry on the back page comes from an unidentified hand, the same hand that had accounted money on the previous side. Again, the entry has an accounting of sums of money in pounds, shillings and pence.

History of the diary   Any attempt to trace the passing of the diary from the provenance of Samuel Rogers until Thomas Percy obtained it is quite speculative, so what follows amounts to a possible route. It probably remained in the family after Samuel's death around 1642. If this was so, then it would have been among the manuscripts of his father until the latter's death in 1652. At this point it would be likely to have passed into the hands of his eldest son, also named Daniel Rogers. It could have been among the manuscripts that passed to Richard Baxter, including the diary of Samuel's grandfather, Richard Rogers. Some of Baxter's collection came to Roger Morrice, the late seventeenth-century dissenter whose manuscripts still form part of the holding at Dr Williams's Library in London. This much is a matter of probability but it is certain that upon the death of the younger Daniel Rogers his library came up for sale.[144] Then there is a substantial gap

---

[144] Daniel Rogers, *Variorum Librorum* (1683).

until 1760 when Thomas Percy, then a country clergyman at Easton Maudit, Northamptonshire, acquired the diary.

No evidence seems to exist to help determine how or why Percy came to possess the diary and, beyond the note in the diary itself, exactly when he came to do so. The extensive Percy papers offer no help, partly because his daily memoranda journals are missing between 24 April 1759 and 18 May 1761 and later entries fail to mention the diary.[145] It is possible that he acquired the diary through acquaintance with Richard Farmer, a young Cambridge don who had begun a career as an antiquary by 1760. By that date Farmer had already obtained an excellent collection of Elizabethan works.[146] Percy may have picked up the text in London where he had already entered the influential circle of Samuel Johnson, David Garrick and Oliver Goldsmith.[147] By 1760, aged 31, Percy had already begun to obtain older English literature, which eventually made him famous.[148]

Percy's career prospered and eventually he went to Ireland as Bishop of Dromore. He died in 1811, and most of his papers and books remained in Ireland following their purchase by the earl of Caledon. In June 1969 Sotheby's put the Caledon Percy books on sale. Queen's University of Belfast purchased the entire collection and the manuscript remains deposited as Percy MS 7 in the Special Collections Department of the university.

---

[145] BL Add MS 32,336.
[146] Cleanth Brooks (ed.), *The Percy Letters: the correspondence of Thomas Percy and Richard Farmer* (Baton Rouge, Louisiana, 1946), p. vi.
[147] *DNB*, 'Thomas Percy'.
[148] Alice C. C. Gaussen, *Percy: Prelate, Poet* (London, 1908).

Editorial Note

Since the diary has never appeared in print, and any alteration of an original manuscript can easily alter its meaning, generally the spelling and punctuation has remained unchanged. Where additions have been made they appear in square brackets. On occasion punctuation has been added in square brackets because there are occasions where Rogers neglects to put punctuation at the end of lines and this muddles the reading. However, I have erred on the side of caution. For some of his abbreviations, the text has been modified to make it plain, but this is always done in square brackets and is never done silently. At the points where leakage, inking out or where Rogers ran out of room but persevered with trying to pack his thoughts in at the expense of legibility, I have made the remaining doubts clear. For 'etc.' Rogers uses the seventeenth-century symbol similar to the modern ampersand, and the ampersand has been adopted. He occasionally goes into a form of 'code', substituting '1' for 'a', '2' for 'e', '3' for 'i', '4' for 'o' and '5' for 'u'. I have allowed the 'code' to stand, partly because his choice to encode certain sections is revealing and also because it is so easy to 'crack'. Where it is unclear, I have offered translations or possible translations in the footnotes. Sometimes he uses Latin phrases and, much more rarely, he uses a little Greek. Where the phrases are short, translations are in the footnotes, but in a few sections where Latin predominates translation is offered alongside the original. I have usually allowed the contractions in the Latin to stand, to allow the reader to consider possibilities other than my decision. The only letters to be changed are 'j' for 'i' and 'th' for 'y' where necessary. His marginal notes will be indicated in the footnotes. Rogers used the old style or Julian calendar and the dates are as Rogers penned them and, as he started the new year on January 1 rather than Lady Day, there has been no need to offer two dates such as 25 February 1635/6.

Queen's University, Belfast: Percy MS 7
A Fanatick Journal

Samuel Rogers his booke novemb 18 1634

1. I have long bene thinking of a general view of my life; and some hurrying thoughts, or other have caused mee to desist often: I am now this moneth. (Novemb: 30. 1634.) of the age of 21. So many yeares I have; Bine; but I have Lived but few of them; Sure then now I am of age; what if I count my yeares? Lord, teach mee to number my yeares past, that I may apply my heart to wisdome, to holines the few dayes, that are behind.

2. To begin then, and dally no longer; The first 13. yeares of my life. I lived without any reflexe thoughts; though I could stand, and answer my father,[1] like an hypocrite, when he posed mee in religious matters; yet was I very rebellious, and feirce against my mother and the servants (who yet dealt unwiselye with my childish impetuous nature) So long I scarse knew practicallye, the right hand in religion from the lefte; About that time (as I take it;) my father was exercising (ut solet)[2] in his familye upon the 11. Matt: & 2. last v[erses], Come unto mee, yee that are heavy loaden; &c: Art thou loaden? &c.[3] no, no; answered my soule; wherat I was a litle startled; but the hedge, (as my age,) was but low, and the devell trode it downe with ease. when I was about. 13. and a halfe, my father seing how litle I had profited under such a diversity of schoole masters, as we had at wethersfeild; sends mee to Felsted: where indeed, I thinke, I got more good

3. in 2. yeares. with the blessing of god, upon the diligent labours of my godly master Mr Holbeach,[4] then I got in many twoos before; the 1. yeare I borded at Mr Fitches; where I passed many a day of vanitye; amongst the rest, upon May day was 7. yeare; viz: 1627. I made account to adde one more, and being holyday; Mary Adams, our

---

[1]   Samuel's father was Daniel Rogers, the godly lecturer of Wethersfield in Essex. For the period covered by the diary he was suspended but far from inactive. For details, see above and Tom Webster, *Godly Clergy in Early Stuart England: the Caroline Puritan Movement, c.1620–1643* (Cambridge, 1997).

[2]   As usual.

[3]   Matt. 11:28–30 – 'Come unto me, all ye that labour and are heavy laden, and I will give you rest. Take my yoke upon you, and learn of me; for I am meek and lowly in heart: and ye shall find rest unto your souls. For my yoke is easy, and my burden is light.'

[4]   The schoolmaster of Felsted was Martin Holbeach, a graduate of Queen's College, Cambridge and a witness to the will of John Preston, written in 1618 when Preston was master of Queen's: PRO PROB 11/154.

maide aske mee if I would goe to heare Mr wells at Terling;[5] to which I answered yea; and so went skipping but why? the maine cause that I drew mee (as I remember) was that I might see a new towne; and hear a new man; *[6] Athenian[7] as I was I desired noveltyes; though with an unknowne god; But god had another end, though I knew nothing; well; Mr wells his mournefull prayer melted mee into teares (as I thinke) but his sermon expeciallye, which was upon the parable; I have bought a yoke of oxen;[8] &c; his D.[octrine] pleasures or earthly matters keepe many men from heaven;

4.   Heere was I touched to the quicke: for I knew, my play, and pleasure (to which I am beyond measure naturally prone to;) had kept mee from the way thither as yet; The whole sermon melted mee, and made mee come sobbing home; and I cast of[f] any pleasures, and desired in some pore measure to attend to what I was to doe; I could set in an hole, and cry an houre together; but many damps came upon my spirit in such a cold house as I dwelt in; but god tooke away Host, and Hostesse together, within. 3. weekes of one another then went I, and borded at Mr Ditchfeilds, where I had incouragement and helpe, and the worke went sweetly on, according to the light I had, then did all my former knowledge doe mee good; (so, let all young ones learne, though never so saplesse) the lord blessed me exceedinglye in learning, knowledge, and favour and incouragement from my freinds; Then at 17. and an halfe I was sentt to Cambridge, where I kept on the first few yeares studiously, and

5.   did continue in my old course, praying oft; but oh the weaknes, the frailtye of pore man, when god tryes him; alasse I had thought I had bine sure (as many young converts are too apt to thinke) and by wofull examples; which were the snares of hell, woven by the wit of the devell himselfe, did catch mee; Sophistry, credit, jollitye maugre[9] all fathers letters, and former experience, did coole quondam zeale, fervencye, affections; yea* that des[i]g[n] that the Lord put upon mee, moved mee not, though something at the bottome told me, god was in it, as in other things; thus did I live most unfruitfullye under Tutor Hill, Mr Goodwin;[10] &c: then was the breach made, the devell came into this

5   Thomas Weld, the vicar of Terling, was later to emigrate to Massachusetts, only to return in 1641. On his time at Terling; see Keith Wrightson and David Levine, *Poverty and Piety in an English Village: Terling, 1525–1700* (Oxford, 1995), pp. 137–9, 158–61, 179–80, 221–2.
6   Rogers marks his best days with an asterisk throughout, presumably to aid his re-reading in more difficult times.
7   There is a marginal note here which is crossed out and illegible. By 'Athenian', Rogers means ignorant and superstitious, referring to Acts 17: 22–3.
8   Luke 14:7–24.
9   See Glossary.
10 Thomas Hill BD of Emmanuel College 1633, was rector of Titchmarsh, Northants, from 1633 to 1648. Hill went on to be a prominent member of the Westminster Assembly, Master of Trinity College, Cambridge, 1645–53, and Vice-Chancellor of Cambridge University

same pore ruined citye of my soule, plaed reakes, there; yea, once above all the rest brought mee to such a pitch as I was in my study, upon the chair musing; as that I had almost said; I will renounce all former wayes of god, I see no profit in them;

6. But the Lord who ment mee better things, kept my toung that speake I could not for [heavy erasure] the Lord restrained my toung that the dev:[il] did kindled from hell; my toung therefore shall praise the Lord, as long as I live; After this many harpings upon good things, I had, and prayed I did, but porelye (the Lord knowes) and could not get of[f] from my carnall ease sometimes, otherwhile from my pride; yea (shall I speake it) with horror I doe; I was loath to come in to repent for my backsliding (which I knew I must doe) because I thought it would hinder the growth of my bodye; which indeed my sorrow at Felsted I think did; of the free love of god to such an Apostate; that he should be willing to stand at the dore, and knocke so long for mee till he bedewed his locks;[11] but oh the hellish heart that I caryed about with mee yet; I prayed after this but was unwilling that god should heare my prayer; I mean purge

7. my hearte; thus of[f], and on, I hung, as though I had bine tyed by rotten points a long time; sometimes broken sometimes sinning, and bafling my consience; in the 1. yeare of Batchlour; wherein I am sure there was little growth; though the Lord sent the 2. then at Christide 1634. went I to Colne Priorye[12] where I was snared with another baite; what it was I tell not; I am ashamed; but in the midst; my fathers words in the monument house with gods spirit setting them home broke mee, and made mee vow; wherein after (as it were) a second conversion, the Lord healed mee, comforted mee in his love; Oh the heighth, and depth, and breadth of the riches of his grace, and free mercye, who should thus dogge me as though he would not be happy without mee; thus the lord after many brunts hath caryed mee thorough the wildernes, and shewed mee this Canaan; even heaven; Oh why lord shouldest thou againe and againe reveale thyselfe to

8. [me] and leave many 1000. Apostates; Yet forget not the pit, that thou wert ever caryed into, both at Braintrye and *[13]Sudburye,[14] about the latter end of Septemb: and begining of October; 1634. But mourne

1645–7. Thomas Goodwin was a fellow at St Catherine's Hall, Cambridge at this point and went on to be a lecturer at Trinity Church, Cambridge (vicar from 1632) before he became a Congregationalist and fled to the Netherlands. He was most famous as one of the authors of *The Apologeticall Narration* (1644).

11 The image is drawn from Song of Songs 5:2 – 'I sleep, but my heart waketh: it is the voice of my beloved that knocketh, saying, Open to me, my sister, my love, my dove, my undefiled: for my head is filled with dew, and my locks with the drops of the night.'

12 Part of Earls Colne, Essex.

13 In the margin, there is '*B2t'.

14 Braintree is a parish close to Wethersfield in Essex; Sudbury is just over the border between Suffolk and Essex.

rather breake they hearte in gods bosome licke his dust, for thy basenes (oh my soule;[)] yea Lord I will abhorre my selfe that am not able to stand one minute without thy helpe; Since all these breaches the lord hath comforted me strangelye this October past; 1634. and especiallye before, in, and after the sacrament about mid: Octob: when our M[aste]r Dr Sandcroft[15] preached out of the 7. Ezra: 10.[16] though the Lord hath obscured, and absented himselfe since, I will beare this heavy chastisement of my god, bec:[ause] I have sined; I have deserved the full vialls of his wrath, yea hell upon earth, and hereafter, if it were possible; I will yet looke up to thee; (oh my deare father) who hast comforted mee by renouncing selfe, selfe sin, selfe dutyes,

9.   and by working thyne owne worke of faith, causing my soule to adventure upon the waters of thy justice, because thou hast given mee the bladders of thy sons righteousnesse; Lord, I desire to be carefull, to stand upon my watch: to claspe my unclasped armour; which the devell so unclaspes dailye; Lord, I have found, by wofull experience, that I am not able to stand, by my selfe; oh keepe thou mee by the power of faith to the day of my appearing before thee; By thy blessed spirit, guid mee thorough my conversation that it being ord[e]red aright; and I living in my uprightnes, and holines (in this valley of sin, and teares) a few dayes; may at last come to the haven of heaven; where sorrow, affliction, teares, bad companyes, secular lawfull affaires; (but oh happye) bitter sin that robs my god of his glorye all these shall be no more; but perfect is holines, joy, sight; He shall I enjoy with the Lord his angels and saints for ever. Amen;

10.   Novemb; 18. 1634. I have not walked with that sense of gods love (this day) as sometimes my god freely hath granted to mee; yet herein I praise the lord, that I have kept my hold, and confidence, which his sp:[irit] hath wrought; the lord hath also comforted mee with many secret ejaculations, and kept up my wofull flagging heart, which to my sorrow pulls mee backe, when by the wings of faith and love, I would fly to my god of holines, oh when shall I come once and appeare where sin shall be no more, nor sorrow no more; but I shall inbath my selfe in the torrent of my fathers love; and shall praise him perfectlye, whom I (though weakely) desire to praise heere;

19. X [Christ][17] said, my god, my god, why hast thou forsaken mee;[18] he had forsaken, yet he was his god; the lord this day hath closed his eare, unwilling to heare mee; Yet in the garden of anguish, (temptations,

15   William Sandcroft succeeded John Preston as Master of Emmanuel College in August 1628, moving from a benefice at Stanford-le-Hope, Essex: Webster, *Godly Clergy*, pp. 40–1.

16   'For Ezra had prepared his heart to seek the law of the Lord, and to do it, and to teach in Israel statutes and judgements.'

17   Throughout his diary, Rogers abbreviates 'Christ' to 'X' and the same is true of 'Christian' ('Xian'), 'Antichrist' ('AntiX') and related words.

18   Matt. 27:46; Mark 15:34.

untowardnes; unbrokennes in the considerat:[ion] of the same promises, and love, which often have melted me) yea in the whales belly of corruption[19] I will lye downe lookinge towards his temple;

11.   20. I was almost cast downe (with Heman) all this day;[20] my strength seemed to faile mee, but the lord faileth mee never; I walked in darknesse the former part of it; yet, I thanke the lord I strugled with my bodye of death, and the devell; and the lord now in prayer toward my lying downe hath comforted mee, and given mee some victorye; upon this experience, I will trust him, yea call upon him, as long as I live;

21. Turmoiling ocasions have, made mee unfit to pray; suppers libertyes, company lawfull all; yet I have bine too effuse in laughter (which my good father hath often told mee of) and lavish in words, I mourne lord;[21] say thou as once to David, thy sin is put away; Quin adhuc (Domine) sum * pars ædificij tui, tu totum struxisti ædificium; aptasti tu cor meum (oh miram) lapideum terranum, et coniunxisti did pexu, id structuræ tuæ: fac (Domine) ut exuberantæ huius lapidis excindatur penitus, ne sim dedecori ædificio tuo;[22]

12.   22. The lord hath inlarged my hearte to long for the saboath, now approching; and thou (deare god) as thou gavest a blessing last saboath, upon thy word, by which I lived the better all this weeke; (though oh wretched man &c., with many failings) so doe to this; then I know I shall walke livelye, both in it, and the weeke following; Amen

23. This day is the saboath; I was over taken with sleepe in the morning, and could not on a sudden get my heart warme; and surely the Lord lefte mee in some part of the day (for he cannot endure sloth, and slightnes in his dearest saints; the Lord yet a litle gratiouslye, and freelye, renewed my strength, which at prayer about 4. a clocke in the afternoone, I had thought had bine quite gone; Lord, bless all means used, for my walking, and closenes to thee in X; for this weeke approching; I fixe my heart upon thee, and desire to expect a blessing;

---

[19]   A reference to Jonah generally but in particular to 2:1–2 – 'Then Jonah prayed unto the Lord his God out of the fish's belly, And said, I cried by reason of mine affliction unto the Lord, and he heard me; out of the belly of hell cried I, and thou heardest my voice.'

[20]   It is difficult to be certain about Heman, not least because there are four 'Heman's to consider. This is probably the son of Zerah and grandson of Judah, also known as the Ezrahite (I Chron. 2:6) as Rogers seems to be refering to Psalm 88, a particularly mournful Psalm, making reference to 'the lowest pit, in darkness, in the deeps' (v. 6) and the singer is described as being 'Free among the dead, like the slain that lie in the grave' (v. 5).

[21]   In margin '2 Ephes: 21' – The text it refers to, which is not there, is Ephesians 2:21 – 'In whom all the building fitly framed together growth unto an holy temple in the Lord.'

[22]   Indeed (Lord) I am part of your building, you have built the whole building; you have changed my heart (oh wonderful) of earthly stone, and joined together the divisions in your construction; arrange (Lord) that the abundance of this stone be thoroughly destroyed, lest your building be disgraced;

13.   24. I am almost ashamed to set to writing concerning any thing; my
hearte is out of order; my thoughts hurryed and bodye, and mind out
of frame, to the service of my god; (oh spare a litle Deare Lord, and
give mee strength to recover my selfe warping[23] almost insensiblye;)
Litle or no profit either in generall, or particular calling: what shall I
then? spunge out, this day out of the booke of my remembrance, with a
perdidi diem; [loss of the day] that dolefull evensong? or scratch the
eyes of this day out; with Jobs Nailes of cursing;[24] or number it shall I,
amongst the dayes of (Nothing;) (which some of the Mexicans grant;
saying that there are some dayes in the yeare, that are dayes of nothing)
In bivio vel potius in trivio sum[25] I must end as Jonahs prophecy; in
silence; I cannot answer a word; if the lord sayes I will punish thee for
thy slightnes[26]
25. This day in mine innocencye, Salmon[27] complaines of mee to our
M[aste]r; and he ut solet[28] sharpely rebukes mee for not respecting
Masters of Arts in the teenys courte; he threatens punishment

14.   capitall; which the devell used to disturbe my mind, and beate mee
backe from climbing up upon the mountaines of heaven; oh lord so
guide mee that all petty, triviall ocasions may make mee sit loose from
earth, and willing to mount to heaven;
26. the same continue; and other mixt companyes put mee out of my
course, and my mind, wonderfully of[f] from good;
27. very pore, dead, so that the same promises the same companye; the
same words that have melted my heart into teares, doe now leave it
dead, and untoward, the lord breake mee, and teach me how to recover
my lost strength; a weak creature I am, unfit to suffer any checke; how
shall I then be willing to goe thorough the fierye triall; How? thou pore
creature? the lords grace is enough especiallye in thy weaknesse, trust
god then in the whales belly;
28. nothing, nothing, nothing; No hearte, No prayer, Noe life, No
grace, No fruitfulnesse one way as other, can be discerned; And if the
mettall of this dayes

15.   conversation should be tryed by the conning Alchymist, of conscience;
the spirits there of would be put fewe and weake;
29. Some litle life, and quick[e]ning, (blessed by the Lord for His free

---

23 See Glossary.
24 Job 3:1–3 – 'After this opened Job his mouth, and cursed his day. And Job spake, and said,
Let the day perish wherein I was born, and the night in which it was said, There is a man
child conceived.'
25 I am at a crossroads [literally, a crossing of three paths].
26 As far as can be ascertained, this may be a reference to Matt. 16:1–4; Rogers seems to be
saying that if God offers punishment then he can have no cause for complaint.
27 Either Henry Salmon, a fellow of Emmanuel 1629–34 and later vicar of Stanground, Hunts.
1634–54, or James Salmon, an undergraduate who received his BA in 1632 and MA in 1635
(Venn). As residency was not required for an MA the former is more likely.
28 As usual.

grace and love) The lord hath shewne mee in some measure that I can doe nothing; without him; oh my deare deare god, shine more according to thy ancient smiles, when it was well with my soule, when I durst freelye venture into thy presence wheras now I am afraid to enter into thy presence, who seemest a judge rather than a father; but yet thou art a father, and a loving one in thy frownes;

30. this day is the saboath; St Andrewes [Day] upon which I am 21. yeares old, wherein I have heard 4. sermons, and then 5. repeated, yet surelye multitude of thinges doe take away edge; I have found my heart more broken, and fitter to attend god after the hearing of one or 2. the lord hath given some meltings and joyes, but these come farre short of former, as Davids worthyes all came short of the 1. three;[29] Oh Felsted joyes at last

16. sacrament joyes, oh lord butres mee with the same once more;

1. December; 1634. this day I found the Lord blessing mee in my studye upon 1. Sam: 30.6. I had also a great conflict with G. Rix[30] litle done, onlye a litle confusion added to the former heape; wherin I could discerne but litle life, nor get none, the Lord discerne betweene good, and evell; my heart also is of[f] the hookes, and tumultuous companye hath snared mee;

2. The lord hath shewne mee that yester dayes affront of Mr Salmon and his former were for my good, for I can say no otherwise, but that my heart was out of tune, and very jollye, and high; and if by my ignominye, or disgrace (espec:[ially] undeserved) I may hate my selfe, and love my god more what shall I loose by that? The lord gave mee inlargement in prayer at Mr Frosts,[31] the Lord heare our groanes, and unite our hearts in love; who, a companye of us have joined together to meet often to pray together, and discourse;

17. 3. Litle done, heart cooled by the world; yet the lord brake a litle towards my lying downe, but time, and wearines, of bodye, and mind, forbade mee to follow it on hard;

4. Oh my god; why doe I sin against thee so; as thou[gh] I were made for nothing else; shall I blame thee? no farre be it from mee; I know to mee belongs shame for myne owne sin; the burden whereof hath so

---

29 Cf. II Sam. 23:15–17. The greatest among the three servants refered to here was Abishai, one of the sons of Zeruiah on whom, see below, p. 9.

30 Unidentified.

31 Mr Frost has proven difficult to identify. Possible but unlikely candidates are a William Frost, a graduate of Gonville and Caius College who was, by this time, rector of Middleton, Essex, a post he had held since 1624, and Walter Frost, who matriculated at Emmanuel College in 1636 and is thus a very unlikely candidate (Venn). The only member of staff of this name at Emmanuel at this time was the father of Walter Frost, also called Walter Frost. He was renowned for his mathematical studies but his main role in the college was as Manciple, a steward who bought provisions for the college: Sarah Bendall, Christopher Brooke and Patrick Collinson, *A History of Emmanuel College* (Woodbridge, 1999), pp. 77n., 129.

hindred mee, that I could this day scarse stirre a foote in my course, the develle by sin, snares mee, and then directes and streightnes mee; oh lord let thy bowells earne once more toward mee;[32] for so long I know I shall be inlarged; but if thou leavest mee; I am a dungeon of darknesse and uncleanenesse;[33]

5. It pleased the lord to smile gratiouslye upon mee this day; and after some great struglinges against my barren, and untoward hearte; toward my lying downe the lord gave mee some victorye and some longings to be dissolved, and to be with X, which is best of all; where no sin shall be any more;

18.   6. The Lord hath bine pleased to warme my pore hearte in my company; John Arthur; Newman, Mr. Ash;[34] it was my turne to pray; and the lord was pleased a litle to looke upon mee and put in some few desires to the saboath approching; the lord lye downe with mee, and raise mee up seasonablye that I may begin with him, and walk on in all the dutyes of the day faithfullye for X his sake; Amen;

7. This day is the saboath where in the Lord hath bine pleased sweetely to refresh my pore fainting, my lapsing hearte; I have hearde Mr Goade and Dr Sibs;[35] and I blesse god, he hath made mee to get upon the necke of my lusts, and one step up to mount Pisgah[36] where standing, I see a little more of the heavenlye Canaan then I did; oh lord more, mor[e], more, I intreat thee; it is sweete; oh grant that this whole weeke I may walke in the strength of the bread, and water I have received this day;

19.   8. The lord gratiouslye hath continued the life, he breathed into mee yesterday so that this day I have not walked so carelesslye, as sometimes; but a litle refreshed; and in feare of my good god who hath, and doth love mee freelye; I will therfore serve thee, oh lord as long, as I live;

---

32 See Glossary.

33 See Jer. 38:6–13.

34 John Arthur matriculated at Emmanuel College in 1629, graduating BA in 1633, MA in 1636, becoming rector of Clapham, Surrey between 1642 and 1662 when he was ejected. Samuel Newman matriculated at Emmanuel in 1633 (Venn). 'Mr. Ash' was probably Simeon Ashe, a graduate of Emmanuel College who was, at this time, chaplain to Robert Greville, Lord Brooke. It may be noteworthy that he was joined in this post in 1638 by Peter Sterry, another of this circle: Francis Bremer, *Congregational Communion: clerical friendship in the Anglo-American puritan community, 1610–1692* (Boston, Mass., 1994), p. 53.

35 'Mr Goade' is most likely to be Thomas Goad, formerly chaplain to Archbishop Abbot and one of the English representatives at the Synod of Dort in 1618, who was at this time co-dean of Bocking, Essex. Richard Sibbes was one of the most important godly preachers of the Stuart age; for a valuable reasessment of Sibbes, see M. E. Dever, 'Moderation and deprivation: a reappraisal of Richard Sibbes', *Journal of Ecclesiastical History*, 43 (1992), pp. 396–413.

36 Deut. 34:1 – 'And Moses went up from the plains at Moab unto the mountain of Nebo, to the top of Pisgah, that is over against Jericho. And the Lord showed him all the land of Gilead, unto Dan'; cf. Deut. 3:27.

9. I come to the booke I confesse with litle hearte; my deare god shuts his eare, so that I have nothing to live upon, but my stocke of faith upon former experience, and yet that shall make mee call upon his name as long as I live; crucifie oh lord my bubling pride, unbeleife, deadnes &c: and fit mee for thy service thou shalt call mee to;

10. my heart at sometime was untoward litle stirring in gods way; so that had I not knowne that fire some times is under ashes; life sometimes where breathing cannot be discerned; I had fainted; but the lord upholds mee; who always would be neere, but I like a wretch continually greive his spirit; oh deare god; yet thou hast elevated my hearte to heaven towards my lying downe, upon thyne allsufficiencye;

20. 11. what can I but admire at the infinite barrennes of my hearte; I can but looke upon it with admiration that grace should in appearance be shouldred out; I am weake this day with David for Abner is fallen, move, and heavenly affections are decayed and fallen, weepe with me therfore my freinds, these sons of Zerviah are too strong for mee;[37] but the lord is my strength, and therf:[ore] though I were at the pits brinke, yet would I trust in him;

12. wanzing,[38] and untoward, and unfit by eating meates disagreeing with my stomacke in a more then ordinary manner; at such a time when the bodye is unfit; it makes the mind indisposed to the service of god; oh how coole I have bine; oh miserable man that I am dr:[39] heaven once, yet, will pay for all troubles, with perfection of holines and joy for ever;

13. The lord hath a litle cherished mee with the hopes of a saboath; and put some life into mee, Lord fit thy servants to morrow to speake home to my necesityes;

21. 14. This is the saboath, wherein the lord hath justlye hidden his face, yea some times, as though he had forgotten to be mercifull; yet the lord hath put in such dispositions into mee, that I dare doe no otherwise, then seeke him and fear sin, and hate selfe more; oh worke these effects (deare god) more and then, though thou leadest mee thorough a valley of teares; thyne shall be the glorye, and myne at the last shall be the comfort;

15. The lord hath made willing to waite his leysure; oh my deare god; if thou wilt hide thy face, it is heavye, yet I will not murmure; but oh deare Lord, let mee not sin against thee and it shall be well; what thou pleasest lay upon thy servant; but oh let not sin, let not bitter sin

---

[37] II Samuel 3, particularly v. 39: 'And I am this day weak, though anointed king; and these men the sons of Zeruiah be too hard for me: the Lord shall reward the doer of evil according to his wickedness.' Joab and Abishai had slain Abner because they could not accept that he was a trustworthy ally, contrary to David's position.

[38] See Glossary.

[39] It is unclear what this could be an abbreviation of; perhaps 'driven from' or 'drawn from'.

overtake my soule;

16. I have walked unfruitfullye in my callinge to daye; and the Lord will not heare mee now at night; but seemes to keepe a distance; I have knockt, and he seems to answer mee, but then to forget mee againe; oh my god thou art angrye with mee and I have deserved it; once let mee recover my strength, and life, and sweet assurance;

22. 17. This day wee fasted, and prayed, and the lord denyed audience but I will trust in the lord my strong encouragement. al Tans Pursivalls; Mr Frost. well; stery; Mot;[40]

18. This day I went home with my brother where for want of time, but espec:[ially] spirit[,] I let this work passe; till the 2 Febru: after; most of the time being spent in recreations visitings of freinds at home, and abroad, alasse[41] what cannot ocasions doe with my weake heart; yet sometimes the lord smiled, though often justly frowned; my peace was disturbed by K!!:m^{r}s[42]

February. 2. Candlemasse day, I have bine at Finch[ing]feild sermon where litle life I got; thou lord quicken me

3. A few struglings with flesh; I nothing to contend, the lord all, some little light, and enlargement; but the lord comes as a stranger takes up his lodging with mee but for a night and behold hee is gone; oh I have deserved such desertions;

4. Alasse pore, my services so weake I am ashamed to write;

23. 5. A litle refreshed by visiting sp:[iritual] g. viall sicke of my granfathers disease;

6. The lord hath enabled mee to goe thorough my calling with comfort; the more peace I have at my lying downe;

7. Gone againe; and afraid to thinke of considering oh when shall I be rid of this slip[pe]ry heart;

8. Something got up; oh shew mee to understand thee further; that

---

40 There are several possibilities for 'well': it could have been Moses who matriculated at Emmanuel in 1627, graduating BA in 1632, MA 1635, or possibly Richard Weller, matriculated at Emmanuel in 1627, became rector of Bartlow, Cambs. in 1645 (Venn). Perhaps less likely candidates are Bartholomew Wall, a gentleman of Middleton, Essex, and John Wall, minister of St Michael, Cornhill, London in the 1640s: Harold Smith, *The Ecclesiastical History of Essex* (Colchester, 1933), pp. 292, 307, 323. Peter Sterry was later to be known as one of the Cambridge Platonists. 'Mot' was either Mark Mott, graduated BA from Queen's College in 1624, briefly curate of Stisted in Essex and later rector of Chelmsford, or, more likely, Thomas Mott who graduated from Emmanuel in 1634 and became vicar of Stoke-by-Nayland in the same year. The timing suggests the latter as the best candidate. However Mark Mott was 'formerly of Wethersfield' and his son went on to be elder of Wethersfield in the 1640s: T. W. Davids, *Annals of Evangelical Nonconformity in the County of Essex* (London, 1863), pp. 290–1. 'Tan Pursivalls' presents a difficulty: one possibility is John Purse or Pearce who matriculated in 1636, but this is little more than a guess (Venn).

41 '1633' is written in large numbers in the margin at this point.

42 Here is a mixture of letters and either indecipherable letters or 'squiggles'. What is in the text here is the best approximation of the original.

being more cleare in thy truths. I may walke more sweetlye; mee thinks I am awcke[43] to understand the things of god, espec:[ially] faith; and the miste[r]y of living by it;

9. At Mr Suttons[44] feast at Cosen Hubbarts,[45] where wee comfortablye and lovinglye enjoyed one another but my sp:[irit] flattish and untoward;

10. Shrove tuesday, heard Mr Carter at wethers:[field] and Mr Marshall at Finch[ing]f:[ield][46] but my heart Nabalish[47] yet within mee;

11. Wanzing still;[48] at the sight of J.A. out of tune; alasse I am least master of my affections; espec: that; Curbe them thou oh lord; that gettest thee a name by doing great matters; Lord deliver mee from snaring objects; and ocasions of sin; for I am weake in the presence; And in necessary ones which may cause sin, stand thou by mee, lest I offend thee;

24.   [49] 12. I heard Mr Sutton,[50] (ut solet)[51] and cannot lye downe with that cheere which I would doe;

13. A litle refreshed in hope of a sacrament, the lord fulfill the desires of my soule in it;

14. This is the preparat:[ion;] oh my sin; this body of death, lyes heavy, ease mee (deare god) in the sacrament; lantyeds sin, unloose me, I am pressed downe by it, lift thou up mine head, then shall I praise thee with cheere;

---

43 See Glossary.

44 James Sutton, the curate of Wethersfield, or Daniel Sutton who was to marry Rogers' first cousin, Mary Jenkin: H. F. Waters, *Genealogical Gleanings in England* (Boston, Mass., 1901), I, 210, 213.

45 'Cosen Hubbarts' has not proven to be identifiable. One of the daughters of Nathaniel Rogers, the son of John Rogers of Dedham, married William Hubbard, but that was after they were in New England and, as she was baptized in 1628, this is far too early. There were two ministers who were religiously like-minded with Samuel Rogers and possible contenders. John Hubbert was minister of Great Bentley, Essex, and then Boxted, Essex in the 1640s. The fact that he was educated at Pembroke College, Cambridge, lessens the likelihood of his being part of the family. Thomas Hubbard was Presbyterian minister at Cold Norton, Essex, and was ejected at the Restoration. However, these are only possibilities; Waters' diligent genealogical work offers no clues. For Hubbert and Hubbard, see Smith, *Ecclesiastical History*, p. 380; Davids, *Annals*, pp. 433–4, 431–2.

46 The visiting preacher at Wethersfield was John Carter, the son and namesake of a famous East Anglian preacher. John Carter, Jr. went on to become a well reputed preacher in Norwich during the years of the Civil War. The preacher at Finchingfield was Stephen Marshall, Daniel Rogers' predecessor at Wethersfield and one of the great figures of the Westminster Assembly. On this stage of his career see Tom Webster, *Stephen Marshall and Finchingfield* (Chelmsford, 1994).

47 That is, resembling Nabal, the husband of Abigail, a man 'churlish and evil in his doings' and 'such a son of Belial, that a man cannot speak to him': I Samuel 25, quoting vv. 3, 17.

48 See Glossary.

49 This, and the following three pages, are unpaginated in the original.

50 This is most likely to be James Sutton, as 'heard' usually means 'heard preach' and Daniel was not ordained although he was to become a minister and, as Rogers himself shows later on, it was not that unusual for an 'apprentice' minister to preach.

51 As usual.

15. Saboath, and sacram:[ent] a feast of fat things; I can say in some measure it hath bine to mee; oh more more (father) there is fulness in thine; let me receive of it;

16. I find some fruite by the sacrament this day; the lord hath banished evell in some measure; melted my heart, made it to stoope to him; fetched downe deadnes over which he hath given mee a victorye, He hath calmed my impetuous sp:[irit] these are fruites of a sacrament, and no wonder; that it is better with mee than before;

17. This day I went to Colne[52] for my sister Marye,[53] her eye being in danger, the lord caryed mee on[,] sweetly banishing evell[,] put in some life; he mercifully delivered my sister Mary being under the horse vid: plura alibi;[54]

25. 18. Thoughts, and chewing upon a bill, that my father received from my tutor, and feare of fathers displeasure, put my heart out againe, made mee unfit to pray; and then comes in Satan and opens the dore to jollitye; and the ocasions thereof; oh lord, more X, and lesse trouble of secular affaires;

19. Pore matter, to small purpose;

20. Loath to write, my hearte is bound by my unworthy walking;

21. Dead still, the lord quicken;

22. Saboath, but not like the former; I brought an heart fraught with unsavorynes and could find litle ease; and heart of a lyer, loth to stoope; yet after my fathers family prayer al [sic] night it began to give, I will waite to see if the lord will blow with a full gale of confid:[ence]

23. Dead, fore part of the day, at night the lord met, and melted mee in some measure;

Tuesday 24. Hearing Mr. Bourodell[55] at Finch[ing]f:[ield] concern:[ing] power of godlines; my heart was something cherished continue it Lord, and adde;

25. the lord hath banished evell, let in some glim[p]ses; added some holy dispositions;

26. 26. I have bine conflicting with selfe all day; refractorye I am; I will yet fight, and waite, the lord hath promised victorye;

27. A day of Fasting and prayer, wherein the lord went out with us mightilye, inlarged and brake our spirits; raised mee up marvailouslye; and added some power in the latter end; oh more, more; at G. wiggs;[56]

28. After fasting my heart stands in some awe and see more cause to fly from my unrighteous failing prayers, and walkings to a righteous

---

52 Earls Colne, a nearby parish in Essex.
53 Rogers' sister: Waters, *Genealogical Gleanings*, I, 213.
54 I see too many places.
55 John Borodale, vicar of Steeple Bumpstead, a close friend of Stephen Marshall, who was to assist his friend with the distribution of William Prynne's oppositional tracts: Webster, *Marshall*, pp. 13–14.
56 Goodman Wiggs is unidentified.

Saviour, who also hath healing in his wings for my unwilling failings; March 1. Saboath, and eloofe of from heaven bec:[ause] of a gen: and eloofe preaching; yet someth:[ing] done at home the last sentence of my father; conc:[erning] daily applying the heart to the promise of gods love;

2. Now comes in Mr wilson[57] browsing to see us as in a cave; unpreisted as he said, after his 2. voyage from N.[ew] Engl:[and] my heart a litle moved, expec:[ially] by his prayer in bed; for wee lay together

3. In the morning he calls upon g.[od] againe and also the lord was sweetly found of mee in the morning; and continued; (that sweet soule continuing all day) but removed

27.   by other objects; my father sending mee to Mr Adyes;[58]

4. not with that feeling and life, but it may be the lord will trye mee, I will waite;

5. the lord kept my heart in awe in some measure in the midst of libertye: eating sick P[words inked out] &c; with M.S.[words inked out] but my am[inked out] heart would have flowne out at night I prayed, and the Lord kept downe sin, and shewed mee something; but I have need of the Aaron, and Hur[59] of dailye prayer, and watching to uphold the Moses of my soule; least the Amalekites[60] prevaile;

6. neither life nor sp:[irit] to write, all upon a melancholye distemper taken in the day; which I could not conquer;

7. the same holds still, and scarse can find in my heart to pray; and unfit for saboath to morrow;

8. saboth, pore, pore, pore, and wretched, heartlesse dead, nothing, nothing;

9. I[bi]d:

10. Little raised yet, [inked out] matters disturbed first, and opened the way for emptines, sloth

28.   vanitye, the lord recover, light, favour, joy, peace; I am resolved not to turne backe from looking backe toward heaven;

11. Litle done yet confidence, not overthrowne, oh lord help my

[57] John Wilson, formerly a minister in Sudbury, Suffolk, had emigrated to New England in 1630 where he became John Cotton's assistant in Boston, Mass., and made several return trips to England. He was 'unpreisted' in the sense that he had left his clerical post after harassment by Samuel Harsnett when the latter was bishop of Norwich: R. W. Ketton-Cremer, *Norfolk in the Civil War* (Norwich, 1985), pp. 52–5.

[58] Edward Adey, the local physician, a graduate of Emmanuel College and a correspondent of John Bastwick: Venn; F. Condick, 'The Life and Works of Dr John Bastwick,' Univ. of London PhD (1983), pp. 54–5.

[59] Aaron and Hur supported the arms of Moses during the fight with the Amalekites, and they joined in the government of the Israelites when Moses was absent at Mount Sinai (Exodus 17:10–12, 24:14).

[60] The Amalekites were descendants of Esau (Genesis 36:12) who harassed the rear of the Hebrews soon after they had left Egyptian exile and entered the wilderness. Defeated by Aaron and Hur, God ordered their utter destruction because of their hostility to the Hebrews (Exodus 17:8–16; Deuteronomy 25:17–19).

warping[61] hearte, and quicken it;

12. I now groane, and am borne down by corruptions; they tye, and weaken the hand of my soule:

13. My walking hath bine drowsye, but at night a litle warmed by familye dutye by my father; shew (o my god) more fullnes, yea the brightnes of thy countenance.

14. This day fell out that sad disaster, my father strangely, and furiouslye fell out with mee as though he would have with words, which so distempered mee, that I knew not what to doe, till I fell downe upon my knees, where the lord melted mee and subdued my spirit graciouslye;

15. This day the former greife hath more troubled mee, then before; it runs thorough wh[at] ever I doe; though saboth;

16. I rid with Mary to Colne with a tumultuous hearte, and thense to
29.   Sudburye, to Hanna,[62] where the lord stirred up my spirit to speake freelye upon 11. Math: before many;

17. I returned to Heningham sermon,[63] where my heart was something stirred; oh lord more of it; it is sweet; but a boyling I find at home ag:[ainst] father, and mother for the old buisinesse;

18. I have got some victorye over them, I blesse the lord; oh keepe them downe more

19. Many conflicts with a stiffe sp:[irit]: I lye downe with a litle victorye;

20. the lord kept my heart in awe; that I dare not run lavish; when I rid with [possibly 'M' but furiously inked out] S. to Finch[ing]fe[ld]: and mee thinkes I find that now, which I have often done; I lye downe, full of love, as I can hold, could I not halfe dye for the man that loves mee; I speake of nat:[ural] and civill love;

21. Many feares by reason of boyling corruption to come to the sacrament; but it is not that (oh lord) to kill them; fulfill thyne ends and promise, and doe it;

22. Saboath againe, and sacrament, where though I came not so resolved, and prepared, as I should, yet
30.   yet [sic] the lord was pleased graciouslye to be found, and breake, and to open, and to inlarge at present, but alasse the fresh savor is ready to passe before night;

23. Harsh, and untoward, a great part, but the lord returned graciouslye at prayer at night, oh be thou still with mee to hold mee on, and shew mee more, and teach more;

---

61   See Glossary.
62   'Hanna' was Rogers' older sister. She was married to Roger Cockington and lived in Sudbury, Suffolk: Waters, *Genealogical Gleanings*, I, 210.
63   'Heningham' was Hedingham-next-to-Castle in Essex. At this parish the godly minister Edmund Brewer was curate and lecturer. Rogers came to this lecture on later occasions.

24. not overtaken with any wilfull sin, yet still cause to mourne under a body of death and also in some measure to say, I thanke god through Jesus X;

25. sweetly touched by Mr Marshalls[64] sermon but readye to drop againe, I have need of continuall underpropings to hold up my tottering soule;

26. Something clouded, and overshadowed by companys I am ready to loose my heart; though lawfull to a wise user;

27. Ready to be jolly, and loose my hearte, there is now an open way for Satan, but Lord doe thou dam up the way againe;

28. A most eloofe stout hearte all the day almost, but at night the lord put in more sweetnes, both of nature, and grace; oh keepe it lord, and adde more

31. 29. scared thorough an [inked out] passion, out of the Labyrinth of such affections, can I scarse evade, without the thred of the almightye power of god; and could not get my hearte to any closenes all day;

30. I visited Mr. Binks, Farrow, and Hitchin,[65] and the lord inlarged mee to speake plainelye to them but alasse straite at home, a naughty[66] hearte disordered by [inked out] objects the lord remove them, and keepe mee;

31. Heartlesse, and loth to write, bec:[ause] of 14v2 = matters;[67] [inked out underneath] oh Lord rid mee of them for thyne honors sake; that I may serve thee with alacritye;

April; 1. Overwhelmed with [inked out] melancholye, and caryd in an hurrye to passe the bounds of an everlasting vow (though rash) which yet oh that it had bine kept; remember it, your cariage with M.S. I may justlye feare that the lord will punish mee in this kind;

2. I came riding to Cambr[idge] with a sorrowfull hearte; where every thing upon ocasion brake my spirit for my former losenses with the lord presentlye after prayer when I was a litle stronger;

---

[64] Stephen Marshall.
[65] There are no clues to the identity of 'Hitchen', but 'Farrow' may be George Farrow who later went to New England, where in 1637 he settled in Ipswich, Mass. (see note below, p. 100; Henry Whittemore, *Genealogical Guide to the Early Settlers of America* (Baltimore, 1967), pp. 186–7). 'M. Binceks' was noted as elder for Wethersfield in the Presbyterian classis for Essex in 1645: Davids, *Annals*, p. 291.
[66] Rogers refers to his 'naughty' heart on many occasions. This should be understood in the sense of having naught, that is, nothing or nothingness, rather than the modern sense of being a little mischievous.
[67] At several points in the diary, Rogers uses a 'code' in that he changes the vowels in a word to numbers, 'a' becoming '1', 'e' becoming '2', 'i' becoming '3', 'o' becoming '4' and 'u' becoming '5'. It has been allowed to stay in the text for the sake of accuracy and because the 'code' is very easy to crack. I have provided 'translations' in the footnotes where necessary. He seems to do this for fear of someone reading his diary and the encoded sections are either in his spiritually inappropriate thoughts about 'M. S.' (discussed at length in the Introduction above) or where he is complaining about his employer, inappropriate thoughts from the point of view of his career.

3. Hurryed by buisinesses, things being something out of order at my studye; doe thou lord recover it;

32.   4. Barren for the most part, my mind being hurryed with multitude of buisinesse all the day; and I am faint to lye downe dead;

5. A saboth, wherin the lord hath a litle recovered; my spirit sometimes up, sometimes downe; conflicting, fighting; melted by Mr Goades sermon;[68]

6. I lye downe full of natur:[al] love; and also the love of god perswades mee, and hath softned mee in prayer; oh it is good being thus; oh Lord; Let this valley of teares have some of thy love drop dailye into it to sweeten my soure drops;

7. sin stirs not so stiffe, as it was wont to doe; my hearte is pretty well appayed;[69] oh lord quicken it more; to holines; that I may live a litle heaven upon earth;

8. I cannot lye down with that sweetnes, bec:[ause] I have bene in a mixt company, and doubtfully jolly; and have not libertye to open my soule in prayer before I lye downe, bec:[ause] I lye with Mr Burgoyne at Mills his house;[70] the lord in some measure inlarged mee before supper in our company; oh lord emptye mee, I am really nothing; and thou art all in all;

33.   9. The Lord hath enlivened, inlarged my hearte, and given sweetnes in calling upon his name; I will not dare therfore to offend him;

10. the lord hath kept me from out strayings, but how weake; how imperfect and at night now, mee thinkes I want matter to worke upon in prayer and mediation;

11. mixt companyes, and ocasions had almost made my heart willing to run after vanitye, but the lord shewes mee better satisfaction in himselfe; and therf:[ore] I hav[e] no quiet in them but only so much as I have in him:

12. Saboth, wherin I have found much sweetnesse, and if any deadnes came in, or pride stand in my face, my god of strength enabled mee in some measure to suppresse it; oh let mee enjoy thee still with this alacritye, yea with more (pardon a constant begger) and lesse sin;

13. A litle obscured, by multitudes of companyes, and words; oh but deare god depart not from thy pore weake servant; but strengthen mee

---

68 Thomas Goad, see above p. 8n.
69 See Glossary.
70 There is a good chance that the Mr Burgoyne was Roger Burgoyne, who entered Emmanuel College as a fellow-commoner on 22 Oct. 1634. He was the son and heir of John Burgoyne, Esq. (baronet, 1641; MP Warwickshire, 1645), by his wife, Jane, the daughter and heiress of William Kempe of Spain's Hall in Finchingfield, Essex. Roger was elected to the Long Parliament in December or January 1640–1 upon the Earl of Strafford's vacating a seat for Bedfordshire. He was of Sutton, Bedfordshire and Wroxhall, Warwickshire (M.F. Keeler, *The Long Parliament, 1640–1641* (Philadelphia: American Philosophical Society, 1954), pp. 122–3). As for 'Mills', this could be Thomas Mills, a curate of Kersey, Suffolk (Venn), but it could also simply be a reference to the place where the house of Burgoyne was located.

yet with thy presence, that seing thee present, I may with boldnes encounter with all mine enimyes;

34.   14. I have run thorough divers ocasions this day, and companyes, where I am almost drowned and lost; snared; I have recovered my selfe a litle by prayer; oh strength Lord in a sinfull university; ignorant of the power of walking with thee; few lives by faith, they live by there wits, or by there hopes; but teach mee oh father to hold close to thee and keepe mee at home in consc:[ience] and trust there beyond w[ha]t I see in others;

15. I am I know scarse how, at my lying downe, in a hurry of thoughts, and there arises, a kind of discontent in reg:[ard] of the estate I am in; I would faine be some body in the world; wheras in coole blood, I can say, it is best to be as I am; yet I desire to resist w[ha]tever is dissonant to the monitor within; and will goe to bed strugling;

16. unfit in body, and mind by reason I have not bine so diligent in calling this day I should have bin; and also have bine not so wise as I should have bine in mixt companye;

17. not vigorous, yet not altogether fainting, but looking still for daily peace, and grace from the founteine of grace;

35.   18. not that life which I have found, nor that desire so eager toward a saboth;

19. The lord hath kept my heart in awe, desiring to attend to his will, but oh a warping[71] hearte, that opposes, and would faine have done;

20. many companyes, and ocasions have perverted my affections that they are not so vivacious; yet my hearte is still toward heaven; I will remember the dayes of old, wherin the lord hath shewne hims:[elf] gracious in his son; and this confidence stayes my hearte, and shall make mee call upon him as long as I live;

21. some breathings after heaven; but litle life, in regard what I found, oh lord, keep mee from failing in zeale, and affection, rather increase, and quicken it;

22. Tumultuous, hurrying ocassions seeme best for body, and flesh; but a solitary life proves best to mainteine the life of the soule;

23. I have had my hearte in some awe, and filiall feare that I dare not accept many offered vanityes, and ocasions;

24. I find after jollitye, in a greate companye at Sr Arthurs chamber;[72] my heart is flagging and not so vivacious in the service of god, as I am in other matteres;

---

[71] See Glossary.
[72] Sir Arthur is probably Sir Arthur Barnardiston, one of the younger sons of Nathaniel Barnardiston, the leading gentleman of Suffolk.

36.   25. As you may suppose after 2. mary sermons, Mr meads, and Mr
Howlets;[73] Dry like the sermons in the matter of any spirituall life; and
so the unfitter for to morrow saboath

26. I could not find the sp:[iritual] breath a great part of the day; yet I
kept on my course resolving to be casting my hearte ag:[ainst] a
naughty[74] earthy disposit:[ion] and the lord bowed towards mee, in the
latter part;

27. Weake walking brings weake comforte; unsetledness, and life-
lessenesse are ofspring of a looosish conversat:[ion] yet in all, I can see
an awefulnesse[75] in my soule, that suffers mee not to run riot, and
checke me in againe;

28. Ah, pore, and feeble, because I am ready to faile in my zeale for my
god;

29. Oh deare lord, how I am ready to loose all by my undeserving
walking; I cannot hold so close, that upon all ocasions, I may come
with boldnes to the holyest; yet for this I praise the lord; that I dare goe
no whether else, but unto him for my refuge; in that awe I am
holden:

30. This day that sad wretch; Norminghton[76] of Kayes propounded his
impudent questions; one conclus:[ion] apprently was that concupis-
centia [desire] was not peccatum [a sin] his question was; that prima
praevavicatio Ada est originale pecactum; [the first transgression of
Adam is original sin]

37.   some lookes I see, and mournings toward heaven; though I am not so
cleare as I should be;

May. 1. Pitifullye on it, after 2. mary sermons by Rhodes Syd:[ham][77]

---

[73] This probably refers to sermons at Great St Mary's, the large church in the centre of
Cambridge used for many university functions, by Joseph Mead and Richard Howlet. Mead
was a don at Christ's College Cambridge and a famous author, albeit a little dry. Howlet
was the rector of Latchingdon, Essex (Venn).

[74] See Glossary.

[75] That is, a sense of awe.

[76] John Normanton, a fellow of Caius College, who, on 24 March 1633 had propounded some
unauthorized statements in a sermon at Great St Mary's on the subject of the irresistibility
of God's grace. He therefore violated the 1626 prohibition against preaching on
controversial matters. He was subsequently questioned and admonished but he persisted.
He was recognized as an Arminian and greatly disturbed puritans. Finally, sometime after
the notice of him here, he was deprived of his fellowship and dismissed from the university.
Later he went abroad and converted to Roman Catholicism: J. B. Mullinger, *The University
of Cambridge, III, From the Election of Buckingham to the Chancellorship in 1626 to the
Decline of the Platonist Movement* (Cambridge. 1911), p. 113; Venn; C. H. Cooper, *Annals of
Cambridge* (Cambridge, 1845), III, 257–8; J. Twigg, *The University of Cambridge and the
English Revolution, 1625–1688* (Cambridge, 1990). pp. 32–3; Bendall et al., *Emmanuel
College*, pp. 205–6; Anthony Milton, *Catholic and Reformed: the Roman and Protestant
Churches in English Protestant thought 1600–1640* (Cambridge, 1995) pp. 75–7, 311. Rogers
clears up some of the confusions in the evidence noted by Twigg, p. 32n. See also Margo
Todd, ' "All one with Tom Thumb": Arminianism, Popery and the story of the
Reformation in early Stuart Cambridge', *Church History*, 64 (1995), pp. 563–79.

[77] Possibly Humphrey Sydenham, a respected court preacher and future Royalist: *DNB*.

and another; fit to follow the footsteps of yesterdays companion;

2. Companye took mee up; John Kent; and Hawkins[78] &c: so that I could scarse have libertye to walke freelye; but something refreshed, and awed by Mr Wall;[79] and Mr Frosts discourse;

3. Saboath wherin I have looked toward heaven but, the lord hath denyed the former clearenes; oh shew mee thy smiles, deare father, least my heart sinkes;

4. I am faint to goe out of my study, faint and weake in regard of sp:[iritual] comforte; Oh lord doe thou raise up my sinking affections I beseech thee, and shew mee thy selfe againe; after thee doe I thirst, as he after the waters of bethlem;[80]

5. My heart is much warped;[81] and that mee thinkes insensiblye; I cannot see the loathsomnesse of sin, so much as I should, or have done; oh lord shew mee it by thy love, and make mee not to see it bitter by thy bitter hand upon mee;

38. 6. my heartlesse companye, deads mee, yet in all obscuritye, I will recover my selfe upon the lord; who hath recovered mee from all my backslidings;

7. Pore and feeble; oh publique meanes, and helpes, I much need;

8. Something refreshed by G. Motte;[82] but ready to loose all by eloofe, and carelesse companye;

9. Oh the saboath is coming; the lord hath in some measure softened mee and given mee an heart to desire it; Lord, fruite, the fruite of it;

10. Saboath, wherin the lord hath added some resolution against our cursed times by Mr Goades sermon; of; profession of our hope; 10. Heb: 23 Lord establish mee more in it against sadder times:[83]

11. This day sylly D. Conghams act; ab:[out] his ceremonyes; where many things damped mee from Collins also, ab:[out] altars, supposed lawfull;[84] till I am faint to pluck up my spirits and resolve to keep my selfe pure, and close to the truth, and the god of truth all my dayes;

12. Marvailous wea[inked out]elye, and porelye libertyes have taken

---

[78] There is no John Kent in the matriculations for this period. There is a William Hawkins, a graduate and at this point curate of Fen Drayton, Cambridgeshire. He was Master of Hadleigh School, Suffolk in 1626 and a colleague of Thomas Goad: *DNB* on Hawkins.
[79] See above, p. 10n. for candidates.
[80] This is an allegory based upon David's plea for 'water of the well of Bethlehem', II Sam. 23:15, a need answered by his three worthies, noted above. Cf. I Chron. 11:17.
[81] See Glossary.
[82] Unidentified, but see above, p. 10.
[83] For Goad, see above, p. 8n. The sermon was on Heb. 10:23 – 'Let us hold fast the profession of our faith without wavering; (for he is faithful that promised).'
[84] Probably Ambrose Congham DD, rector of Blofield, Norfolk: Venn; 'Collins' is probably Samuel Collins DD. In 1615 he was elected Provost of King's College, Cambridge and became Regius Professor of Divinity in 1617. He read his lectures twice a week for forty years, though there were accusations of negligence made against him in 1628. Later he became a Royalist: *DNB*.

away any libertye and companyes the company and sweet fellowship of the spirit;

39. Normingtons impudent position; with other ocasions, and companyes, have hurryd my minde, that I can scarse recall my selfe; oh once a time shall be, when no secular affaires shall perturbe mee in worshipping the lord;

14. weakned by great companyes, at Drapers chamb:[er][85] where the lord yet banished away much euell, which uses to offer it selfe at such times;

16. some life by hope of a sacrament to morrow; oh lord be neere be found stand not eloofe of[f] from mee:

17. Saboath, wherin I have found an heart something refreshed by the sacram:[ent] but how soone downe ag:[ain] lord, the end, the end, ever that I may walke bettere before thee all my dayes;

18. How I am willing to forget the sacrament; mee thinkes I cannot see that apparent good by it, which I would faine; oh Lord unmaske thy face, and shewe it to mee that I may serve thee sweetylye; for if thou withdrawest thy hand, I am nothing;

19. Not so heartye, as I should be, litle life stirring in the universitye oh uphold my decaying spirit from utter sinking;

40. 20. Litle, dry, pore, and dull;

21. mee thinkes I cannot tell how I am, I goe thorough many ocasions, many companyes; and am readye to loose my selfe; mee thinkes, my heart is kept in some awe; but oh the lord seemes not to be neere to mee; returne againe oh lord, and let mee see thy countenance;

22. scarse heart enough to write, I am ready to loose my selfe; oh lord recover former joyes, peace, and comfort:

23. some raisings halfe way to heaven but soone beate back againe; the lord seemes not to be neere to mee when, shall I oh lord stand in thy presence with comfort, and boldnes;

24. Icye, I, the sun of right:[eousness] can thaw mee;[86] Darke I; the morning star can give mee light; I most weake the lion of the tribe of Judah,[87] can strengthen mee; oh shine thou sun, arise thou morning star; strengthen mee oh thou lyon;

25. Pulvinariam tollo multo cum dolore, meipsum extolleir non

---

[85] Joshua Draper admitted pens. at Emmanuel on 12 August 1631 (Venn).

[86] A favourite term of Rogers, this is taken from Malachi 4:2 – 'But unto you that fear my name shall the Sun of righteousness arise with healing in his wings; and ye shall go forth, and grow up as calves of the stall.'

[87] Rev. 5:5 – 'And one of the elders saith unto me, Weep not: behold, the Lion of the tribe of Juda, the Root of David, hath prevailed to open the book, and to loose the seven seals thereof.' The symbol of the lion occurs at several times in Scripture as a synonym of strength and power.

possum, domine[88] qd pandu illud vetus, reteins hominis deprimit animam meum in te erectaou;[89]

41. 26. Hurryed along in many lawfull buisinesses of the world; where my heart is lodged; unlodge mee deare father, and quicken mee up to serve thee with alacritye;

27. Porely going on; oh lord lift up the light of thy countenance, and shew thy selfe powerfull at my low ebbe;

28. I have cause to cry out; where is my ancient life, and acquaintance with god; I am icye; oh thou sun shine upon mee;

29. I am in a whales belly; and can see no light; in a land, where darkeness dwells; oh lord I sin ag:[ainst] thee; and loose my sweetnes by my undeserving walking; I wonder that thou shouldest not lay thy hand heavye upon mee;

30. the lord justly; holds mee of[f]; but I will attend him; I know it is good praying thus;

31. Saboth, wherin I have a litle recovered my selfe, though justly; the lord holds of[f] his sweetest smiles; because I might seeke the more ferventlye to him;

42. June. 1. Disturbed with novels divinitye,[90] and other publique ocasions; as well as with a stupid kind of melancholye; oh how can I recover my selfe[;] thou canst quicken mee oh lord put forth thy hand, accord:[ing] to thy promise, upon which I dare not but yet hang;

2. Litle life yet, I thinke I must leave this Camb:[ridge] for quickning;

3. Disturbed still with abroad buisinesses, and at home; I cannot lye downe with peace, and joye; oh shewe mee thy selfe yet oh lord for thy mercyes sake;

4. weakelye, and porely the lord help mee, and revive mee;

5. my hearte is light enough all the day, and jolly in jolly companye, but oh lord, where is the true joy peace, and sweet quiet repose of my soule in thy smiles; when thou openest a crevis of light into heaven;

43. 6. Dead, and heartlesse, oh w[ha]t shall I doe for the saboath to morrow, Lord be thou in thy word, and then I know it shall be of power, to raise up my soule from this spirituall Lethargye;

7. Saboath, where yet I have cause to mourne for an unprofitable hearte, this unfruitfull tree, the lord might justly stubbe up; but Lord

---

88 'domine' is inserted between the lines.
89 I raise the anchorage with much paine, I am not able to lift myself up, Lord, because that ancient weight, of the old man, presses down my soul which is raised in you. [The 'ancient weight of the old man' refers to Colossians 3:9–10 – 'Lie not one to another, seeing that ye have put off the old man with his deeds; And have put on the new man, which is renewed in knowledge after the image of him that created him.']
90 'Novels divitye' refers to a Mr Nevel (possibly a Charles, Clement or John) who was a candidate for BD. Nevel asserted justification of sinners before God by their works and expiation of sin by outward baptism. Both were 'novel' theological positions to defend publicly and, of course, went against the older Calvinist tradition. Samuel Ward, who moderated at his presentation, openly rebuked him: Cooper, *Annals*, III, 263–4.

only prune these twigs of sin; and remove the worme that is at the roote;[91] that hinders mee from growth, which makes mee rather wanze;[92]

8. I cannot yet goe on without an heavy clogge[93] that bears mee downe from flying up to heaven; oh lord, help thy pore servant;

9. I cannot recover my selfe; oh it is my unthankfull, walking, continual that makes the lord continue his frownings upon my pore streight soule;

10. This day I came up in the schooles; tumultuous ocasions, and thoughts have taken up my mind, that I have had scarse time to collect my selfe; and now at lying downe, I am most unfit to pray, or believe, my heart, and body both are out of frame; Lord help mee;

44.   11. Something in matter of studdy, but oh the savor of a X; and the sweetnes of grace, and closenes of the lord I have scarse bine acquainted with all; and cannot ly downe with that joy, that I should doe;

12. I have cause still to mourne for, my drawing on, so heavilye; expection of buisinesse, publique; and much companye, hathe possessed my thoughts;

13. this day I declaimed in publique schooles, and in colledge also; the lord hath marvailouslye suppressed base proud thoughts, that I have her[e]tofore bubled; oh lord keepe downe everthing else, which is offensive to thee, and recover thou unto mee, the ancient bowells; tendernesse, lively and heavenly affections;

14. I find not the ancient spirit going along with the word; I have lost my hearte; and cannot recover it this saboath;

15. something in studdyes, but I want a softe hearte, filially fearing the lord, and standing in awe of him, I will yet waite upon thee, oh lord, for a better heart to serve thee better;

45.   * 16. Oh the Lord hath caused mee to melt in his bosome; and he hath refreshed my soule againe, after a sad long intermission; I wonder mee thinkes, that the lord should not rather send speedy judgements upon mee, who am so unsavory a wretch, and so unthankfull a walker as I am; oh that he should give a litle peeking hole into heaven againe; it is infinite mercye; for this will I praise him, and seeke him further;

17. this day, I have gone on pretty well in calling, and so can have the more comfort; but oh the sad body of death that hangs upon mee; it tyes my hands, that I cannot be free, as faine I would be; oh once there

---

[91] This is probably a reference to Deut. 29:18 – 'Lest there should be among you man, or woman, or family, or tribe, whose heart turneth away this day from the Lord our God, to go and serve the gods of these nations; lest there should be among you a root that beareth gall and wormwood.'
[92] See Glossary.
[93] See Glossary.

will be a time, when sin will be no more for which I[']le waite and attend the lord in a sp:[iritual] warfare;

18. something in calling; something in peace, some thoughts in discourse for heaven, some comfort; some barrenes, oh a great deale; a great deale of heart smart;

19. This day I went upon pleasure downe to Ely;[94] I find my hearte willing, and ready to fly out too far in pleasures; and diversitye of companyes, and objects distract mee;

20. Now I returne, in the morning the lord inlarged my hearte in prayer, before wee came away, in some awe I have stood, yet flesh strong, and would faine get some norishment from these ocasions; I am unfit for a saboath;

21. Saboath, wherin I have bine miserably out, I cannot rejoice, for I see not the lord cleave[95] towards mee oh returne, returne, and let mee yet taste, and see how good the lord is;

22. weakely; I have no strength; whether shall I goe? to heaven? I cannot; I am tyed, Lord loose the bands;

46.   23. A litle refreshed with some wethersfeild company, but alasse the former sweetnes, and communion I am a stranger to;

24. swerving, I cannot live an heaven on earth, because I am deprived of my joy and sweetnes in the countenance of the lord.

25. To consider how heavenly I draw on in the yoke that the lord hath put upon my necke, makes mee ashamed; I goe litle forward, and therfore I am afraid; I goe backeward;

26. my conversation is unsavory, I want quickning companye; therefore my heaven by spirits doe as it were faile; good Lord doe thou provide best for mee;

27. I am ashamed to consider this weeke past, I am wholly undeserving, dead, dull, unsavory; I have yet prayed, and will waite to see whether the lord will be gracious in the saboath to mee, Lord stir up thyne angels to stir the waters, that I may dip and be healed, and quickned to a better serving of thee;

28. Saboath; wherein I have conflicted with an unsavory hard hearte; the lord hath graunted something; but he will have mee tugge hard to enjoy my ancient clearenes of his countenance;

47.   29. Maryes[96] sermons move mee not I thinke; they may stand there all the yeare long, and there auditors goe away as wise they came, in the things of god; my hearte is stiffe, and out of kilter, Lord reduce it to thy

---

94 The small cathedral town in the Fens, close to Cambridge.
95 Rogers uses 'cleave' on many occasions in what, to us, is the unfamiliar sense of to adhere to or to cling to. This is how it is used in many places in Scripture. One that Rogers echoes most often is Deut. 10:20 – 'Thou shalt fear the Lord thy God; him shalt thou serve, and to him shalt thou cleave, and swear by his name.'
96 Great St Mary's, Cambridge.

method, and frame;

30. I am faint, to goe out of my study anxious, alasse how fruitlesse am I; I am ashamed Lord pardon, pardon, if thou regardest the sins of one daye I am undone;

July 1. Litle worth the writing, still I give myself ocasion to bewaile my unfruitfulnesse, and careless walking with god.

2. Commencem:[ent] thoughts trouble mee;[97] I still finde my hearte afraide to fly from god, and so to stand in awe, that I dare not sin wilfully; oh but this is my heavy burden; ever the burden of the song, that I cannot attend the lord all the day, and at night my heart is so out of frame that I cannot pray cordially, very generally slight, and superficiall Lord helpe mee.

48.   3. Still weake and cannot live in such obedience, as I should doe;

4. Many companyes, few holy mediatations [sic] oh how hard in ocasions to keepe close to god.

5. Commencement sermons; and the ocasions, that necessarily hang upon a man at such times; the lord kindly brake my heart by commun:[ion] with Mr Newton;[98] and melted mee sweetly, oh that it might continue and increase;

6. I loose com:[mencement] monday; many companyes still the Lord in all puts an awe upon my spirit.

7. Com[m]encem:[ent] still, alasse the heart is soone lost in a crowd;

8. I came downe with my brother to wethersfeild; Mr Tuckny with us;[99] our good discourse in the journye was that which most refreshed mee;

9. Lecture at wethersf:[ield] where, and so the day, I could not keepe a sweete hearte, and in awe;

10. Lightnes overtakes bec:[ause] neither study nor place to pray in, oh how does the heart vanish, not being imployed;

49.   11. A lazy hearte, having nothing to doe, cannot rejoice in g.[od] as I should;

12. Saboath; I am ashamed to consid:[er] litle time the lord hath of his owne day; but a most streight, untoward hearte all the day long, which I cannot ring up to praise god;

13. To Camb:[ridge] I goe with my brother In bed some sweet elevations and tendernes, oh that I could mainteine it;

14. I returne to Wethersf:[ield] having run thorough many ocasions wherin I am ready to loose my hearte;

---

[97] This was a time of both formal and informal meetings, and was often used by the godly as a time of conference.

[98] Among the many Newtons, the best candidate is John Newton, at St John's College from 1631, another product of Felsted school.

[99] Anthony Tuckney, a former fellow of Emmanuel and John Cotton's successor as vicar of Boston, Lincs. He was to go on to be very visible in the Westminster Assembly and Master of Emmanuel: *DNB*.

15. I have visited Boales, and Walfords daughter;[100] my heart is ready to be lifted up in discourse which something followes my hande

16. Drowsy, after a preaching litle searching; effectual;

17. A day of fasting, and prayer; to which I was litle prepared; many ebbs; and flowes in it; A litle refreshed, and humbled, then streight againe; I

50. have got something ag:[ainst] my lusts; I[']le waite for more; and attend the lord in his way; he hath promised to help those that trust in him and seeke him constantlye in the use of meanes;

18. Alasse porely rubbe on; dutyes are so heartlesse: and I draw on in gods yoke very heavily; oh when shall I be lightned, and eased of my wofull burden.

19. Saboath, the word so generally, and ungroundedly taught, that I cannot sucke it in as sincere milke for nourishmente; when I lye downe I can not see wherein to rejoice;

20. I have observed this day my old weaknes of affections, I cannot restraine them; at the presence of S[101] I could not hold, and I was much disturbed;

21. Through the day, though course but weake, yet the lord graciously was present at my lying downe, and renewed some of the ancient refreshings; oh continue Lord, and add more;

22. I cannot now say the same which I did yesternight; for my heart is eloofe; and heart is daily defiled with sin, which weakens my confidence:

51. 23. Snared by ill affections running out upon S5[102] and so troubled, that I cannot tell how to pray; oh Lord deliver mee from ocasions, for they are the dangerous things, which annoy mee, for they overcome vowes, and the strongest resolutions, unlesse the Lord be marvailously gracious; well I see my heart ther[e]f:[ore] to be weakenes and no strength save in heaven.

24. I have had a sad day on it, by reas:[on] of the former snaring; and forfeiting my vowes; but at last the lord hath bine pleased to gather up some strength for mee, and a litle to bow and breake and quiet my heart by breaking of[f]

25. something mollified by Mr Marshalls[103] sermon; made willing to for goe all for gods sake; Lord remove all roots of bitternes that thou that art sweetnes it selfe maist be so to mee;

---

[100] Unidentified.

[101] Rogers evidently has considerable difficulty in the presence of someone (or something) whose name has the letter 'S'. There is a first initial which might well be 'A', although it is unclear. See Introduction.

[102] As above, there is a first initial which is erased.

[103] Stephen Marshall.

26. Saboath, wherin I have not bine so livelye, as I should have bine, by reason of my unfruitfulnesse

52.   under a dead kinde of preaching; sad sutton;[104]

27. I can make a shift to hurry thorough though not with that savor I should doe;

28. Heningham[105] sermon drye discourse late with M.S. the lord awed my hearte in some measure then; oh doe it more Lord, that I may not sin against thy majesty;

29. porely out I cannot maintaine sp[iritual] life;

30. I have heard Mr Marshall of the p. gl[106] union of the soule to X; sweetly he; but my heart is sowre, I cannot find the sweetnes in such points, which heretofore I have done;

31. Drowsy, and untoward unfit for duty, and afraid to come into the presence of g.[od] bec:[ause] I cannot with that boldnes, and libertye which once I might have done;

August. 1. No great matter to write of done; I can not see the lord neer mee, I eloofe and he hides; I looke for bitternes in the end;

2. A litle refreshed by Mr Marshall; up, and downe againe; oh continue, Lord and, adde;

53.   3, 4, 5. Much troubled and ensnared with

6, 7, 8. S5[;] I am unfit for a sacrament: bec:[ause] my heart is not enough broken for my b1s3 dealing with g.[od] in nibling at old v4ws;[107]

9. Saboath and sacram:[ent] to which I d1r[e] n4[t] g41[108] bec:[ause] of the sam[e;] Lord am not I thyne; kindly looke upon mee, pardon, and restore thyne ancient affection towards mee;

10. streightened in dutyes publique; and dampish and untoward; bec:[ause] I cannot see the lord going forth with mee in anything; oh Lord I have deserved this, and greater;

11. Litle amended yet; in the secret of my soule, I cannot behold the lord cleare unto mee;

12. 13. 14. I have bine going to Sudbury

15. 16. 17. and Colne these dayes; I have found great inlargemente often; but the lord grants not the old hints of answer unto my suites; I will yet resolve to seeke, and abhor my selfe more;

54.   18. what a sad, and mournful burden doe I groane under; I cannot find the savor of prayer; nor relish X as sweet; the promise is dead to my dead heart; oh Lord if ever then now behold dead bones; and breathe:

[104] James Sutton.
[105] Castle Hedingham, Essex.
[106] This is unclear, particularly the last part. It may be 'prodigal', but also 'powerful' or 'profitable'.
[107] 'The first encoded word is most likely to be 'base', the second is clearly 'vows'. This trouble appears to be related to 'Su'.
[108] He 'dare not go' to the sacrament.

19. Pore and disconsolate; the heavens weep and the rocks give water oft, but my heart drops not;

20. Bocking[109] wedding Sr Arthurs sister; something moved by Mr Whartons[110] sermon; confuted Fenton[111] that spake baselye in an open companye;

21. 22. spent there also in recreations, and companyes;

23. Saboath, when we happilye enjoyed Mr Holbeach[112] to our refreshing; it was great mercye the lord continue the life, and adde;

24. I have found my heart very stiffe and untoward by reason: of my f1the [father] ['S' inked out] ut solet[113] to mee; harsh; and provoking as I thinke;

25. I cannot yet find the lord neere to mee; I have deserved shame, and the lord honours though I should be censured;

55. 26; I still rubbe on, with some kind of awe; I dare not let my heart run riot in sin; but in matter of sp:[iritual] evells I have cause to complaine; I find a dead unbelieving heart in all; oh mercy, mercy Lord for my unthankfulnesse, giddines thoroughout the day;

27. somew[ha]t saddened in sp:[irit] and cannot goe thorough stitch with cheerfulnesse;

28. Dry thorough multiplicitye of ocas:[ions] and thoughts of going to my Lady Denys:[114]

29. Oh hard is it to keepe from vanishing, when one is kept from his calling by hurrying thoughts, and much other necessary buisinesse;

30. Saboath troubled as before; litle heat added though grounded preaching by Cozen Hubbard[115]

31. I went to Mr. Harlakendens,[116] where I thought the very ayre

---

[109] Bocking, a parish in Essex.

[110] Samuel Wharton, godly minister of Felsted.

[111] This may be a reference to the controversial works of Roger Fenton, DD (see *DNB*) or to a catechism for admittance to Communion by Edward Fenton. It was first published in 1621 but a new edition had appeared in 1634. The third possibility is that he was delivering an admonition to a parishioner seen to have committed some social offence.

[112] Martin Holbeach, the schoolmaster of Felsted.

[113] As usual.

[114] Plainly, Rogers has agreed by this point to become the chaplain to Lady Margaret Denny. Lady Denny had married Sir Edward Denny, Gentleman of the Privy Council to Elizabeth I, who died in 1599. She survived him by forty-eight years, dying at the age of 88 on 24 April 1648. She was a Maid of Honour to Elizabeth. After spending several years in Ireland where Sir Edward was Governor of Kerry and Desmond, Lady Denny and her husband returned to their estates at Bishop's Stortford, Herts. She gave birth to seven sons and three daughters, several of whom appear below. Probably the most important for our purposes was Marie who in 1634 married Richard Harlakenden, esq. of Earls Colne, Essex: H. L. L. Denny, 'Biography of Sir Edward Denny', *Trans. East Herts Arch. Soc.*, 2 (1903–5), pp. 247–60. See Introduction.

[115] See p. 11n. above.

[116] Richard Harlakenden was the eldest son of Richard and Margaret Harlakenden and was an important layman from Earls Colne, Essex. Upon Richard's death in 1631, with his mother considered to be insane, young Richard, then 21, became the heir. He then married Alice,

breathed life into mee, inlarged I was in dutyes, and something remaining;

56. Septemb: 1. This day I came to my Lady Denys; some thoughts to heaven in the day time; but something estranged before lying downe[;] new ocasions and companye, though lawfull, divert my heart much;

2. The Lord hath put in some feare, and some life into my hearte, but I can not see that fruite and sweetnes in family dutyes; I am somew[ha]t = streightned bec:[ause] of pl1c3;

3. I can find some awe of sin in my course and company; but not that life, and freedome in publique dutyes; nor the lord neere giving some hint of answer;

4. The Lord hath directed mee in an especial maner this evening in my cariage, and espec:[ially] in prayer, went before mee, as it were to make it doctrinall to the familye, the Lord prosper it all and meanes to them, and mee;

5. The Lord hath enlarged mee in family dutyes much this day; but mee thinkes I cannot walke, or pray with that spirituall savor, and presence of the lord, which my soule desires Lord root out, whatever makes thee, and thy truth unsavory; that I spiritually rellish nothing else but thee and thy matters, others th:[ings] in subordi:[nation];

57. 6. Saboath, wherin something better then before; but the lord will not draw so neere, as he wont, but it is best, and I will beare, and beg, I have deserved eternall wrath;

7. Enlargement publique, but streightned in myne owne bowels; I cannot feele the sweet savor of the love of god towards mee, and therfore what is all to mee;

8. I can stay still, the same; oh deare god, give mee thy selfe, w[ha]tever else thou denyest; in these sad dayes, w[ha]t have I but thy love, that I can, rejoice in; oh hide not that for thy mercyes sake;

* 9. I have found some changes this day, I was at low ebbe, but I gained a prayer of my naughty[117] hearte, and some releife I have found, the lord a litle neerer, especially now I am readye to lye downe; the lord puts in the sweetest dispositions into my soul that I have found a long time, and now my eyes wett with my teares of joy; with these teares which come from the sweet meditation of the love that the lord seemes to beare mee in his, and my Christ; therefore; Once freed from sin I[']le praise with heavens quire the Lord, and live in loves seraphicke fire;[118]

---

the daughter of Sir Henry Mildmay of Little Baddow, Essex. She died shortly afterwards, for in 1634 he married Marie, the youngest daughter of Margaret Denny: Philip Morant, *The History and Antiquities of Essex* (Colchester, 1768), II, 211–12.

[117] See Glossary.

[118] Seraphic fire denotes an image of the fiery six-winged angels who guard God's throne.

58. 10. sweetly refreshed by the company of humble and gentle Mr wilson;[119] oh how beautiful are the feet of such a mortified soule; I am much in love with him; and glad I have such an one that I an unworthy wretch may be acquainted withall;

11. A litle sunk now, but not beate of[f] from my confidence; I will abhorre my selfe, and my flaggings, giddines, unconstancy;

12. Affections not much raised; but my heart is still towards god; the bent of it is not any other way save unto the Lord;

13. Saboath; something dry, and untoward, Lord quicken; else shall I be unfit to walke before thee the weeke approaching;

14. This day the court; at dinner B5tler[120] playes his p[oin]ts, ag[ainst] N.[ew] E.[ngland] the lord stird mee up ag:[ainst] him though I was faint to pinch by reason of B.[ishop']s office[r]s, something; but not so heavenly as I would be;

15. I find my heart ready to grow loose; but in that g.[od] keepes mee occupied in dutyes, he also keepes mee in awe;

59. 16. I have gone on pretty smoothly this day; yet once My toung was ready to run lavish in squ3bb3ng[121] att a pore man at the dore a gl1ss seller; Lord teach mee to rule my toung least it dishonour thee;

17. something quickned by visiting freinds G. Dixon; sicke; G. Dane;[122] if any savor, lord adde more, and ever sweetnes from all ordinances, and helps w[ha]tever;

18. I cannot see the lord cleere, I have tyed his hands by my sin, and ther[e]f:[ore] no wonder he stretches them not out to my help;

19. Inlarged in publique dutyes, and some comfort at home; but I have such a giddy, leaking heart that I can not hold anything long, the lord grant mee some consistency of sp.[irit]

---

[119] This could be the John Wilson of New England, but that is not likely since Wilson had probably boarded a ship which set sail for New England by the start of September. It is more likely to be John Wilson, a recent graduate of St Catherine's College, Cambridge, the son of George Wilson, the vicar of Elsenham, Essex, just a few miles south-east of Bishop's Stortford. John Wilson became curate at Elsenham in 1636 and was troubled for his failure to wear the surplice: Venn, GL MSS 9537/15; GLRO DL/C 319 fo. 80. There is another possibility: there was a local resident by the same name: *The Records of St Michael's Parish Church, Bishop's Stortford*, ed. J. L. Glasscock (London, 1882), p. 151.

[120] Richard Butler, the vicar of Bishop's Stortford: W. Urwick, *Nonconformity in Herts.* (London, 1884), p. 696.

[121] By 'squibbing' the glass seller, Rogers was being smart or sarcastic (*OED*).

[122] 'G' probably stands for 'Goodman'. Dane and Dixon are local residents, although Dane may be a resident of Hatfield. Some branches of the Dane family were well established, a Margaret Dane having endowed the local grammar school and both families appearing among the churchwardens: Urwick, *Nonconformity in Herts.*, p. 696; Glasscock, *St Michael's, Bishop's Stortford*, p. 114. Dane may be related to servants of Lady Denny, as John Dane, an emigrant to New England in 1635/6, mentioned that his mother was such. Lady Denny suggested a medicine for treating John, who lived in Hatfield Broad Oak, Essex. This John, and James Howe (his brother-in-law) (mentioned below pp. 36, 37, 67), emigrated to New England. See also Roger Thompson, *Mobility and Migration: East Anglian Founders of New England, 1629–1640* (Amherst, Mass., 1994), pp. 83–4, 95–6.

20. though conflicted with a deale of basenes, yet something hath bine done; so that I can lye downe with some sweetnes, and peace;

21. I am very untoward at my lying downe, dumpish, sad, irksome no heart to, nor life in prayer I will yet be in the feild where thy treasure is; continue seeking;

60. 22. I can see some awe (mee thinkes) and some generall assistance in all dutyes; but the neerenes of gods sp:[irit] in all dutyes, and in life I cannot see; I am full of wandrings, and doubts from hence; well once shall I triumph over all;

23. I have some quietnes, and peace; oh Lord set it upon firme ground[;] Be thou neere and let mee come neere to thee in purenes and holines; that I may attend thee with the more alacritye of spirit in my race;

24. The ancient assaults of strong lusts, and the untoward and awcke[123] disguisements and stiffenes leave mee; I find that I being in ore, in publique it keepes mee from rust,[124] sluggishnes and slightnes;

25. In company with Mr Archer;[125] my heart is ready to fly out in overmuch jollity and no good done by it;

26. Some breathings after heaven, and some sweet solace in the lord espec:[ially] by reading my fathers booke which the lord hath exceedingly blessed to mee this long time, I could misse any booke lesse, except bible;[126]

61. 27. I have heard Mr Bruer[127] this saboath at stansted; of the p.[ower] of love to X; many, heavenly sweet things stirring; though my heart is not so melted as it should be; Lord breake mee; and raise up this affection and make it livelye;

---

[123] See Glossary.

[124] Rogers frequently chastizes himself for having acquired 'rust' on his heart. It may simply be an adaptation of a vernacularism but it is possible that it is an adaptation of Matt. 6:19–20 – 'Lay not up for yourselves treasures upon earth, where moth and rust doth corrupt, and where thieves break through and steal: But lay up for yourselves treasures in heaven, where neither moth nor rust doth corrupt, and where thieves do not break through nor steal.'

[125] Mr Archer may have been a resident of Bishop's Stortford, or a Giles Archer, a graduate of Emmanuel College. There is an additional connexion with this Archer that may or may not be significant, in that he succeeded Richard Sedgwick as minister at Farnham in the 1640s: Davids, *Annals*, p. 285. He may also have been John Archer, the lecturer at All Saints, Hertford, a gift in the hands of the Feoffees for Impropriations. He remained there until 1638 when he became pastor to the English Congregation in Arnhem in the Netherlands. He seems to have had relatives in Bishop's Stortford (see below, p. 40) but none are mentioned in his will of 1639: PRO PCC Fairfax, 17 April 1639. The reference to an Archer family who are 'among us' (below p. 40) encourages the conclusion that this Mr Archer is a member of the Stortford community.

[126] Identifying which of his father's books was the subject of Rogers' enthusiasm is necessarily speculative. It is least likely to be *Davids Cost* (1619), a 640-page tract of practical divinity on 2. Sam. 24:24. It is more likely to be *A Practicall Catechism* (1632), a sizeable devotional guide. It is perhaps most likely to be *A Treatise on the Two Sacraments* (1633), given Rogers' delight in the Lord's Supper.

[127] Edmund Brewer, the godly minister of Standstead Mountfitchet, Essex, repeatedly in trouble with the authorities through the 1630s.

28. some litle faith in dutyes, and something the better for yesterdays sermon I have litle cause to bragge; for there is a wofull deale of slud[;][128] Oh wretched man &c:

29. I have found great ticklings of pride within mee, and cannot get a low hearte to graule[129] in the duste of god;

30. Much inlarged in publique dutyes, but not so sweet at home in myne owne heart; am dead and drowsye and litle heart to come out of it;

October. 1. I feele litle, cold prayers, cold walking a dead heart; Lord adde the life of grace; quicken mee up to a lively faith;

2. Oh that my husband would kisse mee, with the kisses of his mouth[130] and refresh my pore decayed soule and raise it up somewhat;

3. I cannot see that mortifica:[tion] within me, which I, pant after; that utter abhorring of ugly sin;

62. 4. This is the saboath, 2. Orthodoxe good sermons; but not that quickning which I would faine see; good Lord be neare, stir up in mee a zeale for thee; and a heart close in these decaying sorrowfull times;

5. I cannot, alasse I cannot find the lord so neere to me as faine I would; I have deserved hell, much more obscuritye;

6. * I have had most sweet discourse, and comfort by mr wilsons[131] company; my delight truly is in such as delight and excell in vertue; and this evening I have had a most sweet soliloquy with the lord in meditation, great joy in heaven; oh what will it be then, when this hellish clogge[132] is of[f]; then = then = oh I cannot expresse it;

7. much inlarged in family dutys, oh that the lord would more suppresse this proud heart for mee;

8. something obscured; am I not too jolly Lord wisdome in that point least I offend, and weaken that which I doe in familye by a light carriage;

63. 9. Publique dutyes keepe my heart in ore; my heart is soone downe though a litle raised; oh my pore ebbs, and flowes I[']l yet looke up to heaven;

---

[128] See Glossary.

[129] See Glossary.

[130] Song of Songs 1:2 – 'Let him kiss me with the kisses of his mouth: for thy love is better than wine.' Rogers' frequent use of Song of Songs and its place in his spirituality is discussed in Tom Webster, 'Kiss me with the kisses of his mouth: gender inversion and Canticles in godly spirituality', in Tom Betteridge (ed.), *Sodomy in Early Modern Europe* (Manchester, 2002), pp. 148–63.

[131] John Wilson appears to have become a curate for a brief time at Moreton, a Rich benefice in 1637 (see also Rockford where he served as a curate as well, unless there was another John Wilson in Essex at this time). The John Wilson who befriended Rogers was to become the vicar of Elsenham, Essex in 1638, succeeding his father: GL MS 9539A/1 fo. 66; A. G. Matthews, *Calamy Revised* (London, 1959), p. 536. A John Wilson was admitted to preach at High Ongar, Essex where he subscribed on 5 December 1638: GL MS 9539A/1 fo. 105v.

[132] See Glossary.

10. Not as I would have it; my heart not so quicke and livelye as it should be;

11. Saboath, wherin the lord was with mee in private dutyes, being debarred by raine from church, faith a litle up, though affection often downe, though I ring it up to the highest note yet that falls quickly;

12. Pretty cleere from any mainteined sin; yet I cannot see the lord so neere to my soule as faine I would; espec:[ially] now at my lying downe I find an eloofe heart.

13. I was very merry this day, yet at night, I cannot make melody in my heart to the lord; but downe, and dumpish, and hard, and alasse if I should looke to my workes, I should vaile my face least the lord of pure eyes should behold mee;

14. not that sap, nor feeling, nor sweet motions, which should be; oh stir Lord, and breath, else how can dry, dead bones praise thee;

64.   15. Some sweet breathings, by meditation before prayer, and in the duty it selfe in publique; I find the lord sweetly blessing meditation; oh that I could bend my mind towards it, more;

16. Some streightnes in my heart; though my heart be wrung up to the highest note, yet it falls downe of its owne accord to the Base, of earth, and vanitye;

17. Hardly can I wind up a downe heart, if it sinkes, there it will lye, unlesse the lord yet breath into dead bones;

18. Saboath, where I can lye downe with some peace; I have strove to hedge away evell communicat:[ion] and to season the familye with good; and this gives some comfort; though I have a dead heart, and fainted, to conflict withall;

19. some stiffenes, and untowardnes, and weaknes to god, I am towards a solemne day to morrow; and I find a very untoward heart the lord in mercye fit mee for it;

20. this day wee fasted, and prayed at Em:[133] wherin the lord went out mightilye with mee in the dutye; and a litle faith was stirring, though not that fervency of affection, which should have bine; Love a litle increased, oh Lord doe thou grant, that wee may all be the better for it, all our dayes;

65.   21. Not very well in body something aguish after the quame[134] yesternight; and so something unfit for calling, and also ready to sinke in heart, yet towards night a litle better;

22. This night M.D.[135] was 1ngry with mee [between lines] – Sc4n: in

---

133 'Em:' may refer to Emmanuel College but it is more likely that it is a contraction of 'Emerson's'. The Emerson family lived on South Street (Glasscock, *St Michael's, Bishop's Stortford*, p. 148) as did others who fasted with Rogers. Thomas Emerson was one of the collectors for the poor in 1636: ibid., p. 168.

134 See Glossary.

135 Madam Denny.

23tch ab[out] B5rly[136] – and it fr2tted in mee; oh how naught[y][137] a heart have I; I went also to R. Emers:[on's] wedding at night and kept out some sin; but cannot behold the lord with cleerenes;

23. A little sinking, oh bottome mee Lord upon thy promise; which is better then my struglings;

24. Something tough, but something inlarged by the coming of Mr Harlakenden, Lord, quicken more and more;

25. Saboath, I have had many conflicts with selfe, and sin; and can not behold the lord in the beauty of holinesse, as I would; but my heart hath bine most sweetly refreshed by the compa[n]y of that godly soule Mr Harlakenden; by naming, and feeding upon some promises;

66.   26. Oh w[ha]t an happinesse it is to dwell under the same roofe with a thorough Xian,[138] I am much refreshed, quickned, heartned, incouraged by the company of this good man;

27. The lord seemes to be far from my feeling, but neere to my pore weake faith, and that shall be enough; if the lord will frowne I have deserved it; yet it shall be for the best, bec:[ause] my god hath said it; thy promise is my strength, and shall be;

28. A litle faith stirring; though clouded with unbeleife, and a clogge[139] of corruption and untowardnesse;

29. Oh when shall I be rid of my clogge[140] of hell, and hellish unthankfulnesse; awcknes[141] to good, want of love to the lord Jesus christ; oh cover these Lord, with all my other loathsome plague sores; and spread thy skirt over mee;[142] else how shall I appeare before thy dreadfull presence;

30. I am in darknesse, and can see litle light, I will not yet be beate of[f] from my confidence by the power and assistance, which my god affords mee; for indeed, he beates mee downe with one hand, and yet upholds mee from sinking, with the other;

67.   31. I have found stirrings to heaven, some life, a litle of the breath of gods spirit; but yet a clogge[143] of unbeleife, and deadnes, and untowardnes, Lord, shake it of[f] for thy goodnes sake;

---

[136] This may be referring to 'an eitch', possibly an 'itch', to leave that a Mrs Burly has; she departs from them on November 1635 (p. 35). This, of course, leaves 'Scon:' unidentified.

[137] See Glossary.

[138] As Rogers uses 'X' for 'Christ', so 'Xian' simply means 'Christian'.

[139] See Glossary.

[140] See Glossary.

[141] See Glossary.

[142] Ezekiel 16:8 – 'Now when I passed by thee, and looked upon thee, behold, thy time was the time of love; and I spread my skirt over thee, and covered thy nakedness: yea, I sware unto thee, and entered into a covenant with thee, saith the Lord God, and thou becamest mine.' Thus Rogers is pleading to be accepted into the Covenant of Grace.

[143] See Glossary.

Novemb. 1. I have in some measure striven to waite upon the lord, and to walke with him thoroughout this day, but I find the sp.[irit] of prayer something straitned; Lord poure it out upon thy servant, for parts cannot doe it, though th[e]y can doe much;

2. something refreshed, and inlarged, oh what good waiting upon the lord, it is, for they are sure to renew there strength

3. I blesse the lord, he keepes mee from evell, and sin wasting the conscience and the soules peace; I find the lord with mee dailye according to his word, why should my distrustfull heart, be in feare; I will steppe and get the start of my unbeleife and live upon the lord his bare word;

4. Some comfort in the lord; I will yet attend him; it is good to waite upon the lord, for he will be mercifull, and shew favor to them that love him;

68.   5. This Day I have found great, inlargement for thankfulnes for the powder treason; for which never can wee enough praise the lord;

6. The Lord hath strengthned mee a litle by beleiving, and my heart hath bine lifted up to some confidence in my god in whom I have found enough; more then in creature;[144] visited, and prayed with pore sicke wench Nel.[145]

7. This, day the pore wretch dyed; I brake there garland, they vexed;[146] L1:[dy] 2x1m:[147] I have comfort in it; I want some lively help in the familye to quicken mee up; I am readye to sinke; oh Lord do thou: upholde mee; and fit mee for thy saboth; speake and to us all;

8. Saboth, I have had great struglings with a base hearte; and the devell the 2. old enimyes of gods day, thy banne all the weeke long; but shoote all there envenomed arrowes ag:[ainst] mee upon this day; the lord hath defended mee, how shall I praise him enough;

9. I cannot keepe up an heart thoroughout the day, so livelye, and heavenlye as faine I would; the lord hath this evening gone out with mee though I was at a low ebbe, I will waite upon the lord still, from whence my help comes;

---

[144] Rogers refers to himself as a 'creature' or accuses himself of accepting 'the creature' on many occasions. By this he means that he is too focused on merely earthly matters rather than heavenly questions.

[145] Nell was a maid in Lady Denny's household. She was buried on 7 November 1635: HRO D/ P 21–29/41.

[146] It has not been possible to work out exactly what Rogers means by this phrase. If it is taken literally it would be surprising to find flowers, as in a wreath, as part of early modern mourning; material expressions were mainly focused on clothes and gifts, particularly memorial rings: see Ralph Houlbrooke, *Death, Religion, and the Family in England, 1480–1750* (Oxford, 1998), pp. 220–54, 264–94.

[147] 'La: Exam:' may refer to Lady Denny's example on this day of mourning.

69.   10. I have bine stirred by my L.[ady] and M.E. w4rd[148] of long prayers,
&c. and Mr Ch:[arles] cariage and the rest of them;[149] I must looke for
some snibs[150] for X; I will yet rejoice in X; though all the transitory
world forsake mee, yet the lord is enough; I will walke before him with
a pure consc:[ience] and trust him for the love of others, or the world;
11. Oh a promise is worth the cleaving unto; my god is worthy trusting,
I have groaned under an heavy dead heart, but the lord hath in some
measure come, and poured downe some of himselfe, and his grace into
mee I am worthy of nothing, the lord of all;
12. A little downe the wind, but still heavenwards; and a promise is my
stay; and repast and shall be ever in my streights;
13. my heart is ready to lodge in the creature, I have need that the lord
rap my fingers of[f] from it, every daye; thou art sweetest oh Lord, thee
will I trust;

70.   14. Something untoward in body, thence mind a litle downe, yet I
praise the lord, I hold my confidence; oh Lord once shall I be past all
ebbings, and flowings; and have a perfect flow for ever;
15. Saboath, wherin I have bine something under hatches; but not quite
beate of[f], my hope is still fixed upon the Lord, who hath banished
much evell from us this day;
16. I have bine nothing; but the lord hath caryed mee thorough the dutyes
he hath called mee to; myne eyes shall be towards him he is enough;
17. my heart is ready to sinke downe to the creature; and were it not, that
the lord upheld mee by the continuall dropping of something into mee in
his ordinances; I knew not what to doe;
18. This day Mr. Harlak:[enden] and I visited Mr Archer,[151] where I
was much refreshed with there good companye; my delight is in those
that excell in virtue and though I cannot love thee oh Lord, as faine I
would, yet will I love thy people;

71.   19. the lord hath a little thawed my heart by mr Harlak.[enden's]
prayers in the familye; I am an unworthy wretch to injoy such helps
that the lord provides for mee; Mrs Burlye departed from us; &c.
20. I have found the lord doing my soule good, by the company of his
servants, oh how amiable is it for brothers to cherish up one another
spirit;

---

[148] Word.
[149] 'L' and 'M.E.' probably refer to Lady Denny and Elizabeth Earle (the M standing for
Madam or Mrs), her eldest daughter, who married Christopher Earle of Topsfield, Essex.
'Mr. Ch:' is Charles Denny, for twelve years a senior fellow at King's College, Cambridge
until his death on 29 December 1635. He was the youngest son of Lady Denny: Denny,
'Biography of Sir Edward Denny', p. 258.
[150] All the references to 'snibs' in Eric Partridge, *The Penguin Dictionary of Historical Slang*
(Harmondsworth, 1972), are derisory, matters of discipline. *OED* suggests that 'snibs' is 'a
rebuke', or a 'snub'. This would suggest that Rogers is either looking to find correction for
himself in the complaint or sources of correction to give to the household on Christ's behalf.
[151] For Mr Archer, see above, p. 11.

21. my heart hath bine sad and downe the wind, partly by losse of good companye; going away this day pa[r]tly body untoward, melancholy, streightned in familye dutyes; a little melted at lying downe;

22. Saboath, heartlesse preaching, litle life in it; oh a convincing minister is worth a world; Lord help in private; for my heart is ready to decay; thou canst help meanes; oh some milke to nourish my pore soule;

23. this day I have visited friends; my words, thawed a pore soule; G. H4w;[152] oh let all doe mee good; oh Lord; my heart a litle downe; but still myne eyes are towards the Lord and shall be;

72.   24. The lord upholds mee still, by the Aaron, and Hur,[153] of faith, and love, being exercised in prayer meditat:[ion] &c.; but the beauty of his countenance is not so cleare, but I will waite upon thee, that I may have all renewed;

25. I see my heart wants a quickning companion, my heart being wrung up will fall againe; Lord draw it to thy selfe, neerer I humbly pray thee I have no friend to rejoice in lest in thyselfe;

26. Doe I not a litle wanze;[154] doe I not desire to live upon meate received and not hunger after more; mr worlidge his buisinesse;[155]

27. I am nothing; slippinge, and unconstant, my confidence shall not yet be removed, for the lord will love such a naughty[156] wretch as I am; he knowes my mould, that I am but sin;

28. scarse warm, I will yet hold my confidence; the lord is my strength, though I be in darknesse, and can see scarce any light;

29. Saboath, the lord hath taught mee to walke so warilye; that much evell hath bine banished from the familye; and in it I have peace; shew mee more of thy selfe, some liftings thou hast granted; blessed; &c;

73.   24. [sic] This day the 3. wretches; abused themselves in drinking; the L.[ord] stirred up my heart against them in anger, wherin I have comfort; R. Emers:[on] and mikil manning[157] were with mee; 2. hungry soules catching at a word, the lord taught mee how to speake to them; Lord a litle of thy selfe let mee have, and thy free love, which shall be better to mee, then the world;

Decemb. 1. This day Mr Wolrich came to us, my L.[ady] tickled him;

---

152 Goodman How is likely to be James How who is mentioned again on 13 December and whose departure for New England is noted on p. 67 below.
153 See p. 13n. above.
154 See Glossary.
155 Mr Worlich seems to be a friend of Lady Denny who visits again on 1 December. There is no indication made of what 'his businesse' is.
156 See Glossary.
157 Michael Manning, like Emerson, lived on South Street in Bishop's Stortford. A relative of his may have served as the minister at Stortford in the late 1640s: Urwick, *Nonconformity in Herts.*, pp. 698–9.

my heart is ready to fly out too farre ag:[ainst] an enimy of my fathers; to scoffe at him; it is good to lay our hand upon our mouth in cases of our owne, or else to speake wiselye; the Lord hath caryed mee thorough, with enlargement; some more of thy melting having gone (Lord) doe thou drop into mee;

2. I cannot be so savorye thoroughout the day, as I should be; though the heart be wound up in an ordinance yet it flags soone;

3. A saplesse wretch preaches, my heart not stirred; the lord hath a litle raised, but I am ready to sinke; but by grace I stand;

74.   4. The Lord caryes mee thorough still, by grace I am upheld; many pull backs; the lord is strong, upon whom I depend;

5. The Lord hath graciously garded mee from evell; but oh that there were such an heart, as to love him, cleave[158] close to him, delight in him throughout the day;

6. Saboth, pore supply abroad, the Lord towards lying makes some sweet supplye; I have bine in a sweet heavenly meditation, wherin I have had more sweet joy, and comfort, then in the whole day, wherin I found great conflicts with sin, and devell, deboising[159] mee in my prayer, and yet I was not laid flat upon my backe; for the Lord strengthned the legs of my soule; by beleiving; and now I lye downe refreshed;

7. I see my selfe an unprofitable wretch in all things; oh Lord doe thou graciouslye behold in the Lord X; smile be not farre from mee, heare me love such a wretch as I am ever freely;

75.   8. I have had some pressings downe in the day, melancholy pangs, but now the Lord hath raised mee, and encouraged mee in him against all occurences whatever;

9. this day we have bine exercised with feare of Mr Charles[160] his death, but much quickned, and refreshed by the companye and sweete exhortations of Mr wilson;

10. The Lord hath given Mr Charles great ease, and raised him from death; wee have praised the Lord for him; Lord pardon my sin; I am ready to sinke now the former saint is gone;

11. my heart not so raised, as it should be; Lord quicken, and put life into these dry bones, that they may stand up, and live;

12. something downe the wind; and my heart is not raised to the pitch, to which it should be; I am awcke[161] and untoward to a saboath, oh be thou present Lord, else know I not what to doe;

76.   13. Saboath, wherin the L[or]d hath upheld mee; I have bine raised by the companye of James How; oh how beautifull are the feete of the

---

[158] See Glossary.
[159] See Glossary.
[160] Charles Denny.
[161] See Glossary.

porest, that can speake a word in season: L[or]d subdue a proud heart
cause it to stoope, and then speake peace unto mee;

14. The L[or]d hath bine a litle neere mee; I cannot walke with that
savor thoroughout the day, as faine I would, the L[or]d banishes away
much evell in the day in this place, where he hath set mee; I praise him;

15. The L[or]d hath gone out with mee this evening; in gifts; I find him
neerest, when I am in the company of his saints (mr Harlakenden) Mrs
Butler dyed this day;

16. I still looke towards the L[or]d in whom is all my strength; I am
nothing, I will yet attend upon my god, who in X can love such an
unbeleiving, hard, giddy, com[m]on wretch, as I am; oh thou
considerest my mould, and my fashion L[or]d what is a man, that
thou, shouldest looke after him;

77. 17. something sadded a long time, a great conflict with satan and sin;
but I prayed, and the L[or]d was besought in it;

18. This day we fasted[162] at E:[merson's] &c. the L[or]d went out
mightily in inlarging my heart; and though I cannot see so clearlye; yet
the L[or]d hathe made mee to lye at his feet; and there will I perish if I
dye; L[or]d answer our pore suites for our land, and selves;

19. I find some strength of sin, and the old house would faine renew its
strength, but I have fought ag:[ainst] it, and the L[or]d hath overcome
it in some measure for mee;

20. Saboath, wherin I have much comfort, that I have endeavored to
keepe my heart, and toung close; the Lord hath inlarged mee to lye at
his feet begging; I heard El: Roberts;[163] speaking well; and that she
had much profited under mee; the Lord turne her soule wholly to
him;

78. 21. Awcke,[164] and sinking; oh how hard, and how heavenly a thing it is
to walke tenderlye before thy L[or]d all the day;

22. A comfort to enjoy the companye, and prayers of the saints (m[r]
wilson) my delight is, and shall be in them, and more real joy I have in
the companye of an honest soule, then abounding with the delicacyes
of art or invention with the wicked;

23. The L[or]d still upholds mee, though I am ready to sinke; the devell
is strong, corruption too hard for mee; but thou failest mee never; Lord
pittye a pore soule, that it faile not before thy face;

24. Some thawings before the sacrament and expectation raised for
the good things of that feast, L[or]d fill mee ever full with thy daintys;
faith love, hope; peace, comfort, and joy unspeakable, and full of
glorye

---

[162] Fasted.
[163] Ea: Roberts is unidentified. That she says how she had profited from being 'under mee'
suggests that she was associated with the Denny household, possibly as a servant.
[164] See Glossary.

25. This day the sacrament; I have found my heart; something raised to believing; L[or]d thy fruite more, and more I will wait upon thee for it;

79. 26. In some darknes, but the Lord upholds my heart by looking through a cloud; to thee oh Lord will I resolve to cleave;[165] I have no whether else to flye; comforted by g. clarke;[166] I tooke the cards away;

27. Saboth, wherin my heart hath bine bent towards god, and his glorye; though I have not had such feeling of his love, as sometimes I have had; the Lord would have mee exercised in living by faith in a promise and not by sense, and feeling;

28. Mr Denny drooping; our hearts sad, myne eyes are toward heaven;

29. This day fasting, and mourning, the Lord went out with us at G. D3x:[167] Mr Charles Denny dyed; we have a *sorrowfull familye, the Lord sanctifye his heavy hand upon us, and draw our affections neere to thee; purge out the Achan from us;[168]

30. now mr charles buryed, a mourneful house, much refreshed by good mr wilson; but the coast is not cleare,[169] I cannot behold the Lord so sweetlye; I will yet waite; and my old strength shall be renewed;

80. 31. The Lord afflicts our familye exceedingly; as soone as the former buryed; 2. maids fall sicke; and 2. before; so that now 4; together; Lord doe thou humble us; and let us read our sin in our afflictions; Lord I praise thee thou hast ended another yeare; I am unworthy of any time; Pardon Lord freelye, and smile; I am thine; Lord I roule my selfe upon thee in X;

1636

January 1. Our sicke folke recover; Mrs Earlies gift;[170] my heart growes a little jollye, and stiffe; Lord quell it and thaw it, humble it, and fit it for thy sacrament;

2. I am in a cloud; and cannot behold the Lord so sweet as faine I

---

[165] See Glossary.

[166] Thomas Clarke was one of the householders noted as contributing to the funds for communion silver and so forth in 1642, so 'g. clarke' may well be of this family: Glasscock, *St Michael's, Bishop's Stortford*, p. 151.

[167] Goodman Dixon's.

[168] Joshua 7: Achan had disobeyed Joshua by stealing some of the spoil after the battle of Jericho, thus bringing the wrath of God upon Israel. God would not support his chosen people in battle until they destroyed the evil among their ranks. It was a favourite motif among puritans: see Michael Walzer, 'Exodus 32 and the theory of Holy war', *Harvard Theological Review*, 61 (1968), pp. 1–14.

[169] This phrase, which appears, in both positive and negative forms throughout the diary, is probably an adaptation of I Chronicles 4:10. 'And Jabez called on the God of Israel, saying, Oh that thou wouldest bless me indeed, and enlarge my coast, and that thine hand might be with me, and that thou wouldest keep me from evil, that it might not grieve me! And God granted him that which he requested.' In the way Rogers uses it, it is a plea for spiritual protection and intimacy, and relates to his repeated hope for the sight of God.

[170] 'Mrs Earlies' was Elizabeth Earle, Lady Denny's eldest daughter, who resided in Toppesfield, Essex: Denny, 'Biography of Sir Edward Denny', p. 258.

would; yet I am upholden to seeke him; if the L[or]d will have mee receive the sacrament in darknesse; yet will I looke up towards him and come for my dole[171]

81. 3. Saboath; dead preaching; wherby my heart hath bine something downe the wind; Sacrament, wherin I have found some comfort; oh Lord thou wouldest have mee waite and be earnest constantlye; and thou wilt grant mee what is best for mee;

4. A litle refreshed in the morning, but the day not so vivacious as a Xian should be; oh how hard is it to keepe the heart upon the wing;

5. This day I heare the newes of the death of C: Cockerton my sisters husb:[and][172] who dyed 27. Decemb: (1635;) a sad example, the Lord cause mee to profit by it, and beware; now hath that pore creature her heart full of sorrow; having 2. children left behind; oh how the Lord hates sin; he will punish it in his owne; by her crosses the Lord hath done her good; and I pray this may also be sanctified; Mr nevell (Mr Harlakend:[en] saith) is dead; a sad example Mr R: of Mess:[ing] kild his heart as he said;[173]

82. Mr Archers familyes with others are afflicted amongst us;[174] the Lord draw my soule from the vaine, and emptye creature, and set it wholly upon him, who is lasting and endures for ever;

6. something cloudy; I have bine full of merriment; I am ready to let loose thy bands too much; is it not madnes; Lord keepe my heart, that in all companyes I may not sin against thee;

7. Many ocasions are ready to divert the heart from god; oh what need of daily help have I from heaven, Lord pour downe of it I humbly pray thee; my Ladyes buisinesse ab:[out] the stone in the church;[175]

8. The coast is not so cleere; I cannot walke with that holy reverence, and awe, that I should doe; I have deserved hell; what is under is mercye;

9. I feele 11sc3v:[ious][176] thoughts; and a proud heart bubling, Lord quell them for thy mercys sake they are too strong for mee; but thy grace, and power is stronger;

---

171 The way Rogers uses 'dole' could simply mean welfare handout or charity, but he could also be using the older sense of a synonym for 'fate'.

172 C. Cockerton or Cockington was the husband of Samuel's eldest sister, Hanna, a resident of Sudbury, Suffolk. The two children left behind were named Samuel and Roger. Hanna remarried two or three times: Waters, *Genealogical Gleanings*, I, 210.

173 Mr Nevell may have been a curate or a layman at Messing, Essex, most likely a parishioner of 'Mr R', who is Nehemiah Rogers, the vicar of Messing. He was unrelated to the diarist and was far from puritan sympathies, delivering a sermon during Bishop Laud's visitation of the London diocese in 1631, explicitly supporting human inventions in divine worship: Webster, *Godly Clergy*, p. 195. Rogers is suggesting that Nehemiah Rogers killed Nevell *spiritually*, it should be emphasized.

174 See above, p. 30n.

175 This refers to the memorial for Charles Denny, still present in the church in Stortford.

176 Lascivious.

83.　10. Saboth wherin I have bine a litle warmed; but yet ready to sinke againe; how soone downe the wind; the Lord is not neere, my soule is troubled; my whole trust, and wowling[177] is upon the Lord, and his full, and satisfying promise;

11. The coast is not so cleere, as I wish it were; but the Lord carryes mee on, and through dutyes; and by them keepes my heart in awe;

12. Lord still will I lye at thy foot; unworthy to open an eye heavenward, but thou intreatest such worthlesse creatures, as I am, and ther[e]fore kicke not a pore dogge from some crumms of love,[178] and favour;

13. very untoward in body, and so in mind; A slothful heart, this afternoone overcame mee, and the lesse peace at lying downe;

14. I want some life, espec:[ially] in dutyes; and I cannot set the Lord so before mee in them as

84.　I should doe; Lord help mee in all, that thou maist have favour; and my soule a litle sweetnes in beholding thy face in the beautye of thyne ordinances;

15. The coast not cleere; the L[or]d justly shuts himselfe; I will bow; I have deserved it; I walke not so closelye; purelye humbly as I should; nor with that feare; oh thy filial fear drop into my soule for my heart is ready to run lavish into inordinate lusts, and vanityes;

16. this day I heare of Mr Goades death an heavy blow to the universitye;[179] the righteous taken way from the evell to come; G. Bowyer buryd,[180] a neighbour helpfull in good causes; much bewailed; A sermon of Mr. Butler; naked; my heart but litle moved; yet doe I, and will I looke toward heaven and there rest; accept mee deare father though naked yet covered;

17. Saboath, oh I want a searching word the sword with 2. edges; is blunted; but that I heare X preached it is mercye, and therein will I ever rejoice;

85.　18. under temptation; and my body of sin stinking hath clove fast to mee; oh when shall I once be freed.

19. I want a good companion, unto whom I may unload my selfe I will, and doe look to heaven but am troubled; I will waite, for the L[or]d will speake peace;

20. Inlarged in dutyes, and a litle quickned, but how soone downe

---

177 See Glossary.
178 Cf. Matt. 15:27; Mark 7:28.
179 The death of Thomas Goad, DD, did not take place until 8 August 1638, so it is unclear to whom Rogers refers. Either he has misinformation on the death of Thomas Goad or the loss is a member of the Scroggs/Harlakenden family (see Waters, *Genealogical Gleanings*, II, 825), although it is difficult to see how this would be such a great blow to the university.
180 Goodman Bowyer was a member of an influential family in the area: Glasscock, *St Michael's, Bishop's Stortford*, pp. 104, 146. Robert Bowyer, a linen draper, was buried on 16 January: HRO MSS D/P 21–29/41.

againe, oh hold mee up oh Lord from sinking; cause mee to walke before thee closely and not to swerve from thee;

21. the Lord keepes downe a proud heart in some measure. the old burden is still upon mee oh a litle ease give I humbly pray thee

22. still the Lord carryes mee on, I am ready to faile, but the Lord failes mee never; he that hath done thus much thus far will not leave mee, I will throw my selfe upon him still;

86.   23. The day something dull, but sweetly refreshed in meditation this lying downe; oh what is it then to praise god without any awcknes,[181] or pullbacke of hellish corruption;[182]

24. Saboath; wherin I have desired to attend unto the L[or]d what he would speake to my soule; oh what a thing is warme preaching, I find a want of it exceedinglye; Lord quicken, a litle, let mee not walke with a dead heart this weeke at preaching;

25. Oh the sweetnes of thy loving countenance (oh L[or]d) it is better then life; it is the life of life; there is sweetnes in conversing with the saints upon earth, even to behold thear faces (as mikael Manning[183] today) how much more my glimpses of thy favour;

26. The Lord upholds mee in my innocency my heart stands in feere to sin I desire still to waite upon the Lord who shall be my strength;

87.   27. myne eyes waite upon the Lord from whence comes my salvation I am ready to sinke one day to commones, and untowardnes but that the Lord quickens mee, and spurs mee on to his service; oh leave mee not oh Lord least I fall quite;

28. A common formall heart is ready to creep upon mee in the midst of meanes; the devell is so politique and malicious to deprive mee of the sweetnes in dutyes, which is to be had in them;

29. I cannot walke with that sense of the love of god, that faine I would find throughout the day; but mine eyes are still, and shall be toward the Lord;

30. I have desired to looke toward heaven, oh the barkebyas[184] that is as bad as a log to mee in my flying up to the Lord,

31. Saboath, wherin, my heart hath stood in some awe of god; and have desired to sanctifie the saboth to his honour, many sinkings, and flaggings; Lord beare mee up;

88.   February; 1. weake, and pore, in all I can doe; nothing; were not my best actions covered, where should I appeare; oh deare god looke upon a most uncomely creature, as beloved;

---

[181] See Glossary.
[182] See Glossary.
[183] See above, p. 36n.
[184] This seems similar to 'pullback' but more in the sense of leading him astray. *OED* offers no help.

2. much inlarged, but streightned in myne owne hearte; Lord, a litle love [blot] some of thy smiles, which shall be better, then the world, better then parts, credit, hopes, or whatever;

3. My heart is a cage: of uncleanenesse and sin; oh Lord whether should I sinke, were I not upheld by strong hand; oh keepe mee that am but weakenesse;

4. This day I have had some pangs, especially upon receiving of a letter from fl1[185] ut solet;[186] my heart boiles, Lord quell all, and humble thou my soule more, and more;

89. 5. This day I went to see the prince palsgrave,[187] and there state, many things passed; no thanks to meate;[188] oh Lord pardon the crying sins of England, and yet dwell amongst us;

6. A tryall between my Lady, and her son Art:[hur]; I desire to be soder,[189] oh what are our spirits, and tounges, if set on fire; Oh Lord looke upon mee, a pore weake creature not able to doe any thing without thee;

7. Saboth, I am pore, and heartlesse, thou Lord, quicken, meanes but small and not searching, but doe thou search, and pinch mee, draw mee, and I shall run after thee, The Lord hath given mee some hope of Sam: Greene,[190] pretty kindly broken the Lord continue it for his mercye sake; oh I am unworthy, and sinfull, yet thou shalt have the honour by it; Lord, let my soule be and I will forever praise thee;

90. 8. Many tumultuous words with my L.[ady] which makes mee afraid to meddle with the world, it is mercy that I have litle to do withall;

9. I am ready to be jolly, L[or]d humble my spirit, and give mee sobrietye, and wisdome to carry my selfe so in and amongst various spirits, that thy gospell may be honoured;

10. I tooke a little fret, at my L.[ady] c4m:[ing] int: ch1mb: &c:[191] and could not be sweet natur[e]d all day after; lousing and drooping heavenward, L[or]d help mee, and raise up my dead heart;

11. I would faine walke closely with thee; my heart is awcke[192] unto it

[185] 'Fal' may well be 'father'.
[186] As usual.
[187] 'Prince Palsgrave' is the Prince of the Palatine, Charles Louis, who had come to England, landing on 21 November 1635, evidently visiting Stortford: bellringers were paid 12d 'for ringing when the Palsgrave came to Towne': Glasscock, *St Michael's, Bishop's Stortford*, p. 73; Kevin Sharpe, *The Personal Rule of Charles I* (London, 1992), pp. 516–18. This was part of a campaign on the behalf of the Elector and his wife, King Charles' sister, to raise support for the recovery of the Palatinate from the Hapsburgs.
[188] That is, no grace was said at the meal.
[189] See Glossary. It may be that he wishes to be the means of bringing them back together again.
[190] Probably a parishioner.
[191] It is not clear whether Rogers is annoyed at Lady Denny coming into his chamber without invitation, as an invasion of privacy, or whether it is what she said to him when she was there that upset him.
[192] See Glossary.

oh some sweet smile shall be better then gold; oh peeke, deare god, and let mee behold thee, oh the beautifullest; and fit mee for thy worke wee are about to f1st; to morrow; goe thou along with us, that thou maist have honor all and of us peace and a gracious answer;

91. 12. This day, wee set apart at G. P2r3: [Perry][193] the L[or]d went out, and in larged us much; oh Lord the fruite; ever to be better all my dayes, more humble, more faithfull, more tender broken afected with times and zealous for thy glorye;

13. The L[or]d exercises mee still in seeking his face, which is not the least of mercyes; oh a glimpse of favour which is better then corne, and wine; a drop of grace from heaven to coole the thirst of my soule;

14. Saboath, wherin though not searching preachinge, yet many things profitable from a gifted minister; I have deserved to approve my selfe to the L[or]d in publique, and in private; the L[or]d hath kept mee from much evell; my heart is much cast downe, that I see the streame another way thy honour not god; I desire to lay my selfe downe in thyne armes, and so to lye downe in peace;

92. 15. Alasse how pore, are my services; oh Lord humble mee for all; pardon my best actions, and accept freely in Christ, in whom only I looke up to thee;

16. I have bine a litle in heaven now toward my lying downe; oh I can joy in meditation, that ever such a slight, giddy, proud, jolly, wretch as I am, shall be rid of all my slud;[194] and sit downe in companye, with Abraham; Paul, my grandfather, and all other blessed saints, and angels; and be filled with eternitye, in the presence, and full sight of god; whose countenance to see afarre of[f], while I live heere is worth a world; Lord ravish my soule more, and more and once I shall praise thy mercye without wearines or mixture of sin;

93. 17. This day I have bine troubled with cl1m4r:[ous] t4ung[195] and much disquieted; oh how happy is peace among friends; Lord shine still, and clear up the coast that I may behold thy face comfortably;

18. I have visited honest Jinnings[196] and others; wee have bine refreshed with good savory discourse; but my heart is not so warme within; I am now untoward by reason of intemp:[erance] I have not put a knife to my throate;

19. I cannot walke so comfortably, as faine I would, I have many

---

[193] 'Perry' appears frequently among the wills for this region. It may be that he was troubled at the death of a close relative, as Sara Perry was buried by her husband, Abraham, in Stortford on 9 May 1636. There is the question of why Rogers puts his or her name in code here: there is a chance that he is concerned about the rising prosecution of people participating in conventicles and is worried that this record might be used against Perry.

[194] See Glossary.

[195] 'Clamorous tongue'.

[196] A Thomas Jennings was one of the churchwardens at Stortford in the 1630s: Glasscock, *St Michael's, Bishop's Stortford*, p. 114.

pulbacks[197] and hinderances; a lazy heart to any buisinesse, Lord make mee faithfull in the place which he hath set mee;

20. I have bine dull in the day which hath bine rainye and untoward, my heart is a litle thawed oh thou sun of righteousnesse shine upon mee,[198] and let mee see thee clearely;

94.   21. Saboath wherin I have endeavored to keep my heart in awe, and to give the Lord the whole day; and much evell hath bine banished from us, for which I praise the Lord and have cause to lye downe with greater comfort, then he that hath given libertye to himselfe; Lord I looke towards thee, refresh mee with some sweeter glim[p]se of favour from heaven;

22. This day wee heare of grace wood[199] her death; how suddenly; Lord teach mee how to number my dayes, that I may passe the time of my sojourning in feare; that whether sooner, or later; all may be best;

23. I have rubbed thorough a contentious familye, as well as I can, I am almost weary of angry, and furious spirits; Lord give mee wisdome to walke so, that I may not dishonour thee in the midst of all ocasions; I have cause to blesse the Lord that he gives mee the sobrietye, and wisdome, that I can so walke before them that there is nothing but in matter of my god;

95.   24; something downe, oh I want a good lively companion, I am ready to vanish into commonnes, and jollitye; Lord stay my heart from swerving from thee;

25. An heartlesse lecture sermon; oh the power of preaching, what is become of it; must I not remove, to search for the sp:[irit] of the ordinance; Lord what a sad thing is it to mee to walke with a dead hearte heere;

26. I cannot honour the Lord so throughout the day, as I should; oh that I could walke tenderly, and closelye, Lord a dead heart remove, and cause mee to walke so before thee, that I may rejoice; this night, the sad wretch Mr Francis[200] shewed himselfe in his colours; swearing, cursing, and storming like a Bedlam,[201] oh Lord teach mee to mourne and feare;

96.   27. this day I heere from Mary, ab:[out] my sister Margret;[202] that the Lord hath done her some good, oh blessed be his holy name, that

---

[197] See Glossary.

[198] See note above, p. 20.

[199] Unidentified.

[200] 'Francis', it becomes plain when he appears again on 29 February just below, is Francis Denny MD, third son of Sir Edward and Lady Margaret Denny: cf. Denny, 'Biography of Sir Edward Denny', p. 257.

[201] That is to say, like a madman, like a resident of the Hospital of St Mary of Bethlehem in London.

[202] Mary and Margaret (later refered to as Peg) were both sisters of Samuel. Margaret was the youngest and seems to have outlived Mary, whose death is noted later in the diary: Waters, *Genealogical Gleanings*, I, 213.

snatches one brand out of the fire after another Lord perfect thy worke begun in her for thy mercyes sake; I heare also of Mr Suttons mariage;[203] a thing something strange; For myne owne heart; Lord thou that caryest mee along throughout the place thou hast set mee; warme my heart within, with the beames of thy love;

28. Saboth, I have not found that warmth of spirit which faine I would; I am blacke I can say; but Lord may I say, that I am comelye in thyne eyes;[204] oh then it is because thou accountest, and put[e]st on the garment over mee to cover all my loathsomenesse;

29. this day I note 3. th:[ings] 1. concern:[ing] myne owne hearte; I find it willing to sinke to the creature, and commonnes more than ordinarye; Lord stirre mee up and put some life into mee; the 2. is newes that I heare

97.   from Cambridge; about normington of Kayes; that epitome of whorish impudence; that scorner of all good; who for his base doct:[rine] delivered (about faith to be a new d.[octrine] &c.) was taken by Dr Smyth vicechaun:[cellor] and degraded, and imprisoned;[205] Blessed be the L[or]d that some steppe in in the cause of [a few words inked out] his truth; Thirdly, my lady tooke in hand Mr Francis for his swearing, spake most fully to him; oh why shouldest thou tare the name of g.[od] in peices, did he wrong thee; if I have; better had it bine that thou hadst strucke mee thy mother a box on the eare; most wisely, and discreetlye this and much more;

March. 1. many tumultuous lawbuisinesses about my L.[ady's] est1t have bine canvised; my head troubled, my heart a litle sunke Lord put to thyne helping hand, and comfort mee with thy flagons of love;[206]

98.   Dry and untoward; oh an unworthy, unfruitfull, unsavory, carelesse heart, what shall I doe can the Lord find in his heart to love such a cage of uncleanenesse; oh sure he can, he will cover my blacknesse, and I shall be comlye in his eyes;

3. Inlarged, yet something streight in myne owne heart; Lord a litle revive my drooping naughty[207] heart, Lord be thou stronger, so much as my helps are weake;

4. I have many things in the place I am in to content mee; yet still is my soule unsatisfyed; because it is ready to rest upon outward contents;

---

203 Daniel Sutton married Mary Jenkin, the first cousin of Samuel Rogers, his first wife: Waters, *Genealogical Gleanings*, I, 210.
204 Song of Songs 1:5 – 'I am black, but comely, O ye daughters of Jerusalem, as the tents of Kedar, as the curtains of Solomon.' This is much as to say that Rogers sees himself as a sinner but knows that God will accept him, or at least hopes so.
205 The account of Dr Henry Smyth, Vice-Chancellor of Cambridge University, having John Normanton, the fellow of Caius, imprisoned, is an addition to other accounts. Cf. above, p. 18n.
206 This plea, which occurs throughout the diary, is based on Song of Songs 2:5 – 'Stay me with flagons, comfort me with apples: for I am sick of love'.
207 See Glossary.

and the Lord will shew mee, that reall satisfaction is not in these things, but only in his love;

5. woe is mee that I want the quickning of a lively honest soule, that is acquainted with his owne heart; Lord supply it to mee, that which thou denyest by company, draw mee close to thee, and so let mee walke through thy saboath coming;

99. 6. Saboath, the Lord hath banished away much evell; and given mee that wisdome that I have walked through companye sweetlye, much refreshed in discourse with Mrs Earle; and in private dutyes, and in familye; savory truthes have bine delivered by Mr B.[208] but oh that there were such an heart; oh deare god more of thy selfe and thy love in thy X; it is the only thing that shall revive my soule;

7. this day I part with honest G. How[209] to N.[ew] E:[ngland] oh how precious is the companye of the saints, and the Lord rends them from us, and gleanes away the cheife and choise, and full eares; oh Lord thy meaning is to defend them certeinly; thou art there god, and so hast hedged ab:[out] them, and so will doe; Lord stay also with us; purge our decaying estate; Lord preserve thy C[ommon]w[eal]th which is now tottering; Lord preserve, and convert our King;[210]

100. 8. my heart can I scarse curbe from running out lavish, in speeches, cariages; jollity, levitye, Lord draw mee to thee, and cause my soule to stand in an holy awe;

9. I cannot be so fruitfull, as I should be, Lord pardon, looke upon mee in christ; A common unbeleiving heart is on foot; Lord purge it out, I humbly pray thee;

10. my heart sweetly thawed by the Lect.[ure] sermon of Mr. Harrison;[211] oh how comfortably doe they live who live under a convincing ministry, an heaven upon earth; Lord ever more give mee this bread; find out some help to raise up my dead, and untoward heart, continually;

11. My heart in the day time is ready to be eloofe of[f]; oh Lord pull it to thee, let mee not vanish into a common dead, and untoward heart;

---

[208] This may be Richard Butler, the vicar at Stortford, but it would be surprising, given the usual reviews which Rogers gives him.

[209] Probably James How.

[210] The seriousness of this prayer should be appreciated. In asking for the King's conversion, he is saying that Charles is not a Christian which, from his perspective, means that he is concerned that Charles may be Roman Catholic.

[211] This is most likely to be James Harrison, the lecturer at Hatfield Broad Oak, as Rogers visits Hatfield on several occasions. Harrison was successor to Ezekiel Rogers, Samuel's uncle, in 1626. He did face some trouble with the ecclesiastical courts in the 1630s, but survived: Kenneth Shipps, 'Lay patronage of East Anglian clerics in pre-Revolutionary England' (PhD, Yale University, 1971), pp. 108ff. and Appendix VI. There are other candidates in John Harrison, the curate of Mashbury, Essex, and a Harrison at Sudbury, but the fact that Rogers specifically mentions a lecture encourages the conclusion that it is James Harrison.

12. I find it Lord I walke closely with the old thoughts this day; Lord a litle love, that may persuade my soule;

101. 13. Saboath, I blesse the Lord that I have desired in the feare of my soule [inked out] to honour the Lord in all services in all companyes; both to doe and receive good; oh Lord cure my imperfections, and cause my soule to live by faith, as I have heard today;

14. Mr. Harlakenden come, it is a refreshing to see the face of a saint; good newes from N.[ew] England; oh the life of grace that is stirring; oh my soule enter into the counsells of those faithfull saints of god;

15. I have been much straitned this day, body out of frame, by reason of melancholy rainy weather; and mind so also; I yet lift up my soule, now looke no way but toward heaven; oh the L[or]d will not so cleare the coast; oh my deare god, I will lye and dye at thy feet;

102. 16. Untoward, earthye, sinking, oh litle savour find I in private dutyes betweene the Lord, and my owne soule; Lord a litle life;

17. A litle melted by mr sedgewicks sermon;[212] Lord still goe on, quicken and refresh dailye, I have continuall want of supplye; oh shine accord:[ing] to thy wonted favour;

18. this day, my Lady morlyes[213] men come, and fish; a swearing, popish, profane family; my heart cold among them oh what a lamentable thing is it to be in hell, if only it were to be among swearers; oh Lord in thee will I rejoice I will feare thy name though others profane it my soule feares an oath;

19. Something untoward and oh how faine would my heart vanish into a common formall course, Lord quickn mee by thy sp:[irit] to walke before thee in sp:[irit] and power, in this frozen familye;

103. 20. Saboath; Butler playes his parts, shewes hims:[elf] in his colours ag:[ainst] Zelotes; brings his 25. obj:[ections] ag:[ainst] common prayer, answers them, and railes;[214] oh cold doings, but the Lord hath a litle thawed my heart since I came home; in secret, and in family dutyes; (oh what a deale of hurt does saplesse preaching) a man hath no discourse for the saboath; it dryes up a mans spirit; Lord give a blessing to a barren familye; dwell thou amongst us;

---

212 William Sedgwick had just been appointed to the benefice of Farnham, Essex, just to the north of Stortford. He was, as is plain from the references to him, of a similar frame of mind to Rogers and often an inspiration. He was soon to be threatened with discipline and went on to be known as 'Doomsday Sedgwick', when he became preacher at Ely Cathedral in the 1640s: GL 9537/15 fo. 41v; 9656 Box 1 File 20; ERO D/ACA 53 fo. 244v; Matthews, *Calamy Revised*, p. 432.

213 Lady Elizabeth Morley, the daughter of Thomas Tresham, was the wife of William Lord Morley, fourth Baron Monteagle and eleventh baron of Morley. She was among the chief residents of Stortford. Lord Morley, a Catholic sympathizer until 1604, had learned of the Gunpowder Plot and been crucial in exposing it. His seat was at Great Hallingbury in Essex: Glasscock, *St Michael's, Bishop's Stortford*, p. 101; *DNB*.

214 Richard Butler is preaching against nonconformity. The objections are not *his*, per se, but those which he attributes to the 'zealots', plainly Rogers' choice of title rather than Butler's.

21. Something downe; Lord raise up my sinking soule; I will lye at thy feet; Lord smile a litle and it shall be sufficient;

22. Ready to be disquieted conc:[erning] my commencement; tumultuous thoughts quickly overthrow my mind, Lord, settle my heart upon thee, and so be quiet in the use of other meanes;

104. 23. I have had a cold these few dayes past; it hath more weakned mee[;] Lord strengthen mee in sp:[irit] as my decay is in bodye, so raise up my dead heart; oh how tedious is a litle swinge to young bloods; oh make mee willing to stoop;

24. This day I met with Mr Richard wiseman;[215] I am happy to be acquainted with such an one, who loves god, and the peace of his consc:[ience] before fellowships, and earthly treasures; Lord subdue my heart also, that I may willingly submit to thee, and cast my whole care upon thee though freinds forsake; and earthly hopes, but small;

25. Drunken Hurst[216] at dinner; my heart a litle downe; Lord raise it up; and enliven it up to thy service;

26. I am still downe, oh how sweet is it to walke closelye with the Lord; how shall I deeme god, A barren, naughty[217] heart overcomes mee; unlesse thou stay mee by a new supply of grace;

105. 27. Saboath, pore matters abroad, the Lord makes it up at home in some measure; warmes my hearte; oh deare god more of thy selfe, and thy love, which shall be better than the world;

28. This day I have many tumultuous thoughts ab:[out] my journ[e]y to commencement; oh how hard is it to walke with god closely in the midst of ocasions; this night, that cursed Imp F. D2nny[218] comes home; and railes like a devell; in a drunken mad hue; Lord pardon, Lord spare, and turne the heart of such a cursed hellhound if it be thy blessed will; oh turne away wrath from a familye;

29. this day I went to camb:[ridge] to visit, the Lord gave mee a mercifull deliverance; when the horse shot over even his head in a great slough coming for Mr Greenwoods;[219] my heart is a litle thawed; Lord adde more, and provide mee, against tumultuous ocasions coming.

106. 30. Litle done, tumult:[uous] thoughts assaile mee; oh how weak, and fraile is my mind, ready to be led away with every wind; Lord stay my

---

[215] Richard Wiseman is probably the second son of Henry and Mary Wiseman of Elsenham, Essex. He matriculated at St John's College, Cambridge in 1624, graduated MA in 1631 and became a fellow. He was admitted to Gray's Inn on 3 November 1637: Venn; W. C. Metcalfe (ed.), *The Visitations of Essex* (London, 1878), I, 530. His aunt Dorothy married John Rogers, the lecturer of Dedham, after Richard Wiseman (this Richard Wiseman's uncle) died in 1617: Waters, *Genealogical Gleanings*, I, 221.

[216] Unidentified.

[217] See Glossary.

[218] Francis Denny; see above, p. 45n.

[219] Possibly Rowland Greenwood, minister and headmaster of Aldenham School, Herts., until 1635. Then he became minister of Wimbish parish in Essex: Urwick, *Nonconformity in Herts.*, p. 246; Venn.

heart, and cause mee to walke closelye with thee; though I see universitye; yea our colledge much declined, and vanishing into shadows, and formalitye; many of the fellowes bowing at Jesus; Lord be mercifull to the place;

31. the Lord keepes mee from wholly sinking but oh my heart grows cold, and marthas ocasions, will scarse cary along with them, a maryes heart;[220]

Aprill; 1. Now busy; and full of companye frothye, I wander; never more need of new supply of grace;

2. I vanish more, and more I scarse can recollect of thoughts for god, Lord raise mee, who am readye to sinke;

3. Saboath, the 1. part untoward, disordered unyieldinge in bodye, and mind; a litle refreshed by supping by Gooding 2 Fryers,[221] the Lord gave inlargement in prayer; Lord adde thy blessing unto it;

107. 4. my heart very much downe, oh that I were out of this vanishing course of visiting;

5. I have had much good company today we joined (our old companye) in prayer together; at Mr Frosts at supper; yet other commencing ocasions make all lesse profitable;

6. Lord, whether doth my heart swerve I am nothing; I am ready to imbrace the creature; unlesse thou dailye assist by thy grace; my heart yet rejoices in the choice of Sr. Sterry;[222] Lord doe yet good to Emanuel Colledge;

7. Now the buisinesse with Randall and Norrice;[223] pride, and Malevolence about putting on my cap in a chappell; oh cursed formalists; these th:[ings] and others trouble, and disquiet my mind, and make mee feare my degree; oh my heart is loath to stoop to what the Lord, shall cut out for mee;

8. my heart is still excessively dejected betweene hope, and feare of my degree; yet a litle

108. supported, by something within; resting upon that promise all shall be best, whether degree, or not; at last I obteined it; and my heart leapes for joy; Lord grant that all may be for thy glorye;

9. This day a joyfull returne homeward to Starford; after my degree; blessed be thy name oh Lord who hath preserved mee;

---

[220] This is rather unclear but may be a reference to Luke 10:39–42, understanding Martha's complaints about all the rituals of hospitality while Mary simply sat at the feet of Jesus as an allegory. Those in favour of ritualist worship, who complained about the simplicity of godly worship, were missing the point: Mary's priorities were preferable to the superficial display of Martha. Mary had the heart of the matter right while Martha let the complexities of ritual come between her and true worship.

[221] Probably a place to eat.

[222] Rogers is noting, and celebrating, the election of Peter Sterry as a fellow.

[223] It is difficult to be sure who Randall and Norrice were. There was a Henry Randall at Emmanuel, a John at Queen's and a John at Pembroke. Norrice may be James Norrice, curate of Fobbing, Essex: Venn.

10. Saboath; pore helps; thence am I dull, and lowering; Lord raise; oh that my soule were in frame to honour thee with that alacritye, and fervencye that I should;

11. I cannot yet recover my selfe; Lord in mercye break this same ice, that is over my soule; thaw it by thy love, and beames of grace;

12. Exceeding jolly in the day, and exceeding untoward toward night; sad mouldy, unfit, the Lord yet caryed mee thorough dutyes sweetlye; Lord blesse all, to a pore barren unfruitfull familye, water thou, and wee shall bring forth fruite;

109. 13. This day something untoward, awcke,[224] Lord how hard a thing is it to walke sweetlye before thee through one daye; my Lld:[yship's] old humors, and misprisionions [sic][225] and groundless jealousyes vexe mee;

14. Cloudy, the coast not cleere, Lord reveale thy selfe; an ice got over my heart at Cambridge, and scarse is it broken yet, Oh thou Sun of right:[eousness] shine upon my soule,[226] and thaw it;

15. This day have I kept a private fast; but oh porely and weakelye oh I cannot get an hard heart to relent and mourne; Lord what shall a pore creature doe; I am dead, and saplesse in my desires of X, faith downe the wind, whereas it should be upon the wing toward the sacrament; Lord I will not yet be beaten backe, for there are crums in thy sacrament;

16. Oh Lord, the coast is not cleare, but blessed be thy name who upholdest my sinking soule to seeke thy face, and to resolve to

110. lye at thy feet, and come unto thy table in a cloud; shall Glover the martyr burne in desertion,[227] and shall not I receive the sacrament in one; Lord I come unto thee; oh deare god, if it be thy will unmaske thy selfe, and shine; and whet my desires after thy table;

17. Saboath, sacrament; wherin the Lord hath bine with mee, and caryed mee thorough, yet in a cloud still, oh when shall I behold thee clearely; I will waite w[ha]t the Lord wil say, for he will speake peace to my soule;

18. 19. 20. 21. 22. 23. 24. 25. I went to wethersfeild; and there continued, where I lost my heart exceedinglye, having no convenient place to poure out my soule into the bosome of my god; and through divers companyes, and ocasions of sin; S A [initials inked out but still readable] after whom my [inked out] goe; and I have so snared my selfe; that I am ashamed to looke up to god; hence dead in hearing

[224] See Glossary.
[225] Misprisions are scornful actions or speeches. Lady Denny seems to have berated Rogers for dubious loyalties.
[226] See note above, p. 20.
[227] Rogers is referring to Robert Glover, the Marian martyr. He seems to have been reading Foxe's *Acts and Monuments* later in the diary, although he may have been mentioned in a sermon. For Glover, see R. B. Seeley and W. Burnside, *The Acts and Monuments of John Foxe* (London, 1837–41), VII, 384–400.

sermons; fathers exercises; litle goode done to that, which I might
have done, Lord pardon; for thy tender mercys sake; all my
backslidings,

111. feeblenes, and weaknesse upon all ocasions, Lord deliver mee from
them, for I am not able to hold, if they are given; And now am I in a
lamentable case; for I know not how to rise up after my fallings;
because, I dare not say I'le returne no more; oh my soule stay thy selfe;
he that beleives makes not hast; stay thy selfe upon thy god, and the
way he chaukes[228] out doe thou tread in; and no other; my sister peg[229]
is sweetly broken; the Lords worke is upon her soule; his hand sadly
upon her bodye; so long Lord as it may doe her good;

26. My mind, and body unlively, because I have given way to
extravagant vagaryes; now hath my soule time to mourne, for my
sudden loosenes; Lord spare a litle that I may have time, to
recover my selfe, before I goe out of this world, and be seene no
more;

112. 27. Oh how happy are they, who mainteine a pure conscience, a cleane
soule before the Lord, with what great libertye, and boldnes may they
approch his presence daily? rust gets upon my hearte; my soule is
defiled; and the Lord layes upon mee this day sadlye; I goe drooping I
have deserved much more; I will beare the indignation of the Lord
because I have sinned;

28. This day I have gone through divers, ocasions, and companyes; my
Ladyes court;[230] many ill words slip out from them; Lord thou
knowest, they vexe my soule, I communicate not with them; I abhorr
all ways displeasing to thee; towards lying downe, the Lord a litle melts
my soule; he leaves mee not, as I have bine willing to grow loose and
leave him; oh infinite mercye that when I have done many things by my
swerving from him, wherby I have done as much as in mee lyes to cut
my selfe of[f] from god; yet he is willing to receive mee, and lets in some
beame of himselfe;

113. 29. This day I have bine much exercised with the thoughts of this
family, wherin I am; a most barren rotten company Lord in mercye
looke upon them, and beate them out of there course; I am something
comforted with some fruit, the Lord hath given mee; my letters to
Mary (she saith have done her soule much good;[)] and to Margret;
Robert Emerson; and pore Sam:[uel] Greene; Lord beat the naile home
to the head; oh suffer him not to stagger;

30. This night comes in sad suddaine newes of the death of Sr Thomas
Leventhorp, slaine in a duell betweene him, and Sr Arthur Capel at the

---

228 Chalks.
229 His sister Margaret.
230 As owner of the manor, Lady Denny held courts where assessments were made and
judgments for misdemeanours were rendered.

bowling alley at Hadham;[231] A heavy losse to that corner, a sober, judicious gentleman; Oh Lord how shall wee feare thee in thy judgements; teach mee and us all to stand upon our watch, that though thy messenger come suddenlye; yet not unexpected; For my heart; the Lord holds mee much in awe in this familye, wherin I am; my heart is not so light, and

114. giddy, as it was lately in another place; my heart bleedes over a pore wretched familye, my soule pittyes them; I have bine carefull to doe my dutye in examining some toward the sacrament; Lord blesse all to them; And for my selfe, I desire Lord to approch thy table; dost not thou invite a pore backsliding, fallen weake creature; oh Lord I come for strength, and thy promise sealed is that I shall obteine some;

May; 1. Saboath, and sacrament, wherin the Lord hath graciously met mee and refreshed my soule; oh deare god, I wonder when I consider my revolts; base dealing with thee, greiving thy spirit that thou shouldest send a tender melting, mourning heart; I praise thee for it; and that though meanes are but pore, yet thou holdest up my heart aloft; and also hast caused mee to mourne for others, and to pitty pore wandering soules in this familye;

115. 2. this day I have bine at Sr Thom:[as] L[av]enthorp[e]s;[232] and seene a sad familye, Lord cause my soule to feare thee for thy judgements; my heart is yet ready to be jollye, and perke; Lord how shall I walke soberly, purelye, and closelye with thee;

3. I goe this day with my Lady to L.[ady] L[av]enthorp[e]s againe; a sad thing to consider; I am untoward, and unlivelye, Lord quicken mee up, and refresh mee with the life of grace;

4. My heart somewhat awcke[233] in the daytime; toward my evening exercise sweetly thawed, and refreshed oh mercye of mercyes that I should not be utterlye forsaken; I consider, and see sometimes, and now at this time; that my heart was never kept cleaner, nor have I walked more closely with god in any place, as since I have come to this

---

[231] The duel took place between Sir Thomas Laventhorpe of Sawbridgeworth, Herts. and Sir Arthur Capel, the uncle of Arthur Capel of Hadham Hall, Herts.: Robert Clutterbuck, *The History and Antiquities of the County of Hertford*, III (London, 1827), 208–9. The duel was caused by an effrontery to Lord Howard by Laventhorpe, the Lord of Dover, Arthur Capel and other country gentry. In May 1636 these gentlemen had come hawking on to the lands of Lord Howard without the lord's permission, which was to treat the lord as if he was nothing more than a minor freeholder. Sir Arthur killed Laventhorpe, one of the chief magistrates of the county: Francis J. A. Skeet, 'Arthur Lord Capell, Baron of Hadham', *Transactions of the East Herts. Arch. Soc.*, 3 (1905–7), p. 314.

[232] Lady Laventhorpe was left with young children, the oldest being John, aged 6, the youngest, Thomas, having been born the previous December: Clutterbuck, *History of Hertford*, pp. 207, 209.

[233] See Glossary.

barren familye oh, great blessing that by an αντιπερίστασις'[234] I
should get heat;

116. 5. the Lord holds my heart in his feare, and to seeke him; though many
impediments; myne eyes oh Lord are, and shall be towards thee,
behold mee in thy loving kindnesse,

6. Sullennesse, and melancholy discontent, takes hold on mee[;] I
cannot be free in this place I am in; it is hard to conflict with great,
imperious, captious, spirits; but the Lord hath set mee heere, and I
beleive it shall turne to my good;

7. The Lord is now sweetly neere to my soule, I have bine troubled
with some melancholye pangs; but I have recovered them; it is a
great mercye of the Lord towards mee, that hath given mee a
cheerefull spirit; I will now throw my selfe upon thy allsuficiencye
oh Lord; and rest in thy bosome this night expecting thy holy
saboath;

8. Saboath, I doe praise the Lord for his goodnesse towards mee
this day; that he hath inlarged mee; and caryed mee with a beat of
heart towards him; and with some life, and hearte, Lord increase,
and reveale and dispense more;

117. 9. The Lord is still with mee, my comfort and my trust; oh pardon my
many failings in the day; I praise thy name that thou keepest up my
head;

10. This day have I groned, for the place I am in; woe is mee that I
dwell in Meshech:[235] it hath lay upon mee as a heavy loade; but I raise
my selfe up upon the Lord, who hath bine sweetly with mee heere and
will still bee my god till the end; and provide a fit place, for mee, when I
am fit;

11. Something melancholy still, and mourning for the place I am in,
Lord some fruit for thy mercyes sake; For myne owne part, the Lord
inlarges my heart, and gives matter, Lord also cleare up the coast, and
refresh mee with thy flagons of love;

12. I am downe much; I still looke toward heaven, the Lord smiles not
sweetly; I have deserved his rod to be smarting upon mee; mine eyes oh
Lord, are yet towards thee; and my hope of adherence is anchord upon
thee; though not of full assurance;

118. 13. this day I rode with my Lady, to the Lady Morleys (and Mr
Anthonyes)[236] where I was entangled with a companye of forlorne

---

[234] Antiperistasis: this can be seen as a 'reciprocal replacement', an 'interchange' or a contrast
of circumstances. Rogers seems to be saying either that he gains his heat from the coldness
of his environs or from his closeness to God, the more likely understanding. Thus it is an
analogy for the credit given to the sinner by the sacrifice of Christ.

[235] Meshech refers to the warlike wilderness people mentioned in Ezekiel 32:26, 38:2, 39:1.

[236] See note above, p. 48; Mr Anthony was the eldest surviving son of Sir Edward and Lady
Denny (he was preceded by another Anthony who died in infancy): Denny, 'Biography of
Sir Edward Denny', p. 257.

THE DIARY OF SAMUEL ROGERS

fellowes; I avoided there Health, and deboised it;[237] oh better is it
to live with bread, and cheese, in the refreshing company of the
saints, then to be pertakers of the great abundance of the
ungodlye;

14. Sunke a litle, in matter of feeling; the Lord frownes; oh what
shall I doe; I will yet lye at his feet, who is my Lord and my god;
oh recover my strength, thy countenance Lord, thy love reveale in
thy son, which shall be best of all;

15. Saboath, wherin I have wanted that joy in god, which
sometimes I have found; my sp:[irit] is bound, and streight, Lord
in mercye, behold mee from heaven, thaw thou my frozen sp:[irit]
Let mee rather peep into hell, to see what sin meanes, rather then
that I should be insensible, which is the heaviest burden, that a
pore soule can grone under;

119. 16. the Lord hath enlarged my heart in dutyes before strangers,
and it is ready to bubble up with pride, Lord nip it in the bud; I
have yet found streightnes in myne owne bowells; which is
heavye, Lord rouze up a dead, unbeleiving heart, that I may be
fit to praise thee, fit to fast, and pray to morrow to grovle in thy
dust;

17. this day wee fasted at G. Perryes, the Lord gave great inlargement,
but I am bound in myne owne bowells,[238] and feele my proud heart
swell, more than ordinarye, Lord, what shall I doe, thou hast done all
hitherto, conquered a dead, proud, backsliding heart, oh drive some
strength into my soule still;

18. I am downe the wind, I know not what to doe; but to throw my
selfe upon the promise though vailed;

19. this day, newes of Mr. Pasfeild's death,[239] a sad thing; we have
cause to mourne for the death of a wretch, for under him wee had
peace there, (though under a cursed banner) oh sad dayes, and worser
coming both to this towne and to the Land, Lord in mercye step in,
and stand

120. for that pore towne, and prepare a pastor, according to thyne owne
heart; and in mercye with a desolate nation, which now thou hast
visited with pestilence in London, deseases pox in Starford &c: and
a lamentable drought these 6. or 7. weekes; For my heart; it is
much sunke, the Lord frownes, oh justlye; Lord smile and thaw

---

[237] See Glossary.
[238] A common phrase in Scripture, meaning the seat of pity or kindness, and a popular term in
godly piety.
[239] Until 1636 the rector who served Chelmsford, Essex, was William Pasfield. He had served as
vicar of Wethersfield until 1631 and then moved to Chelmsford. He evidently tolerated
puritans and did not trouble them when he acted as commissioner for the bishop. He even
signed a petition in defence of Thomas Hooker, under attack from more conformist clergy
in 1629: Webster, *Godly Clergy*, pp. 152–4, 270n; Smith, *Ecclesiastical History*, p. 36.

mee; draw mee neere to thee, and declare thy lovingkindnesse to mee;[240]

20. I cannot be so profitable in my place as I should be; my heart grones for the place I am in; I cannot be free, I am in fetters, bound up, what shall I doe; Lord ease mee in thy good time, that I may serve thee with godly cheere, and alacritye;

21. I have had most strange, and sweet meditations, and musings of sp:[iritual] matters this evening; my heart elevated, and quickned; and broken; yet ready to sinke againe; Lord daily wind up the pegge that sluggs downeward;

22. Saboath, heartlesse doings at church, and sad familye at home; oh what shall I doe; my comfort is only in the Lord in secret, on whom I waite and rejoice he is found in the private closehead;

121. 23. this day I went to my Lord of Norwich with a message from my Lady;[241] courteouslye dealt withall, by my Lord; and his house; For my heart, in the morning I awaked earlye, and had most sweet meditations, and joy from them, in the dayes journye I find it hard to meditate on any thing, but passages of the journye; Lord in thyne armes lye I downe;

24. Refreshed at Mr Archers house oh how beautifull are the feet of the saints;[242] Lord quicken up my decaying spirit; raise it with thy words, which are sp:[irit] and life;

25. I make still a shell to plod on in a pore desolate familye, barren of good; the Lord keepes my heart in awe, and I think never freer from defilednes then heere by the cold antiperistasis;[243]

26. I am hurryed with discontent, and melancholy untowardnes for my Lot is fallen into a sad place, the Lord in mercye provide for mee;

122. 27. Ready to loose time by discontenting thoughts; as litle as I have to doe in the world; yet my thoughts are hurryed upon commenc:[ement] or place where I am or one th:[ing] or another, oh how happy am I that I have not the encomb[er]ing ocasions of some; Honest Mary Graves dyes this day, a crookd godly maid, oh best for her who shall be a glorious saint, and have a perfect bodye; shee cryd out for mee to speak with mee;[244]

28. I have had a litle freedome in the familye, which something refreshes

---

[240] A term Rogers uses on many occasions, taken from Psalm. 36:7 – 'How excellent is thy lovingkindness, O God! therefore the children of men put their trust under the shadow of thy wings' or Psalm. 88:11 – 'Shall thy lovingkindness be declared in the grave? or thy faithfulness in destruction?' Cf. below, p. 147.

[241] The Earl of Norwich was Sir Edward Denny, Lord Denny of Waltham, Essex. He was the son of Henry Denny of Waltham and Honora, daughter of William Lord Grey. He died on 24 October 1637 without male issue. This meant that the headship of the Denny family then came to the grandson of Sir Edward and Lady Margaret Denny, the young Sir Edward: Denny, 'Biography of Sir Edward Denny', p. 257.

[242] For potential 'Archers', see above, p. 30n.

[243] See n. 234 above.

[244] That is to say, Mary Graves cried out for Rogers because she wanted to speak with him.

mee, oh a litle with freedome, is better than abundance with putting a foot under anothers table, Lord find out some way that I may walke with freedome and alacrity before thee;

29. Saboath; most cold doings at church, Lord help mee, my Lot is sad for that; some litle light in the Lord, I will waite for more; Lord restore mee to my former joy;

30. My heart is yet kept in awe; and in feare of the Lord through my course, but oh my failings, and imperfections, Lord help; I have visited good freinds; Robert Emerson, Lord look upon him for good;

123. 31. this day, the Lord hath granted a showre of raine, after a heavye moneths drought; blessed be his name; his hand is heavilye upon our citye yet, in plauge; upon our towne, and others in pox; I am ready to be eloofe of[f] from god in the day; Lord draw mee closer; shew mee that sweetnes in thee, which I cannot find in the creature;

June. 1. I am something unsetled, wandring in my thoughts, ab:[out] commenc:[ement] and S5[245] which divert the streame of my thoughts, so that they cannot be for god as they should be Lord let a beame of love into my heart, to make mee love thee againe;

2. A company of distracting thoughts ever overrun mee; I am very melancholy, and disconsolate walking in my solitary walke; and many causes weighty I have; I now heare the certeintye of my aunt Harsnets death,[246] a most amiable wittye, godly woman, oh how great is her gaine; how deepe our losse; a goodly branch

124. slipt of[f] from the tree of our familye, alasse we are all dropping; no comfort, but in preparing to meet in heaven where no death shall be;

3. I am pressed for the sad place I live in; I am streitned in my bowells; yet the Lord gives gifts, gives utterances; Lord blesse all to most sad unfruitfull creatures; and let not all be for to make them without excuse; I am turmoiled and exagitated about hurrying thoughts, Lord gather up my thoughts to thee;

4. I have been at Hatfeild, heard good old Mr Harrison; my heart thawed, inlarged in discourse, at Mr Baringtons;[247] how sweet is it to be one houre in the companye of such as from god; oh heaven, heaven heaven, where my good aunt Harsnet is, where wee shall never part;

---

[245] Again the mysterious 'Su'. See Introduction.

[246] Rogers' Aunt Harsnett had married Adam Harsnett, the vicar of Cranham, Essex after a first marriage to William Jenkin of Sudbury. She had given birth to seven children by her first husband and others in her second: Waters, *Genealogical Gleanings*, I, 210. On Jenkin see Davids, *Annals*, pp. 543–7.

[247] 'Mr Barington' was probably Robert Barrington of Hatfield Broad Oak, the second son of Sir Francis Barrington, the premier knight of the shire at the start of the seventeenth century. Upon Sir Francis' death in 1628 Sir Thomas Barrington headed the family at Barrington Hall. See G. Alan Lowndes, 'The history of the Barrington family', *Trans. Essex Arch. Soc.*, n.s. 2 (1894), p. 24; William Hunt, *The Puritan Moment: the coming of revolution in an English county* (Cambridge, Mass., 1983), pp. 219–34. Mr Harrison is James Harrison, the lecturer encountered earlier; see p. 47n.

Lord I despise all the treasures under the sun, they are froth worse then nothing; myne eyes are to thee to whome I draw neere at thy table tomorrow[;] I have seen my good uncle,

125. 5. Saboath, and sacrament my soule thawed, and sweetly brought to beleive; and sweet comfort, in the Lord, though but litle in means, or company;

6. This afternoone most sweet meditations, and livelye; refreshing comforts, and the heart much melted and broken; and most joyfull teares oh how shall I praise the Lord enough for those sweet hints of favour, that he bestowes upon mee;

7. now I journy toward wethersfeild by Banson; heare Mr Bedle;[248] saw my broken Cousen Finch;[249] heare Mr. Perne;[250] my heart a litle up; Lord raise it more, and declare more of thy selfe to my soule;

8. This day am I with my brother; ut solet;[251] my heart broken toward sister Margret, whose soule the Lord hath heavilye loded oh marvailous change; blessed, be thy name Deare god, thaw her by a litle love revealed in thy promise; open

126. the dore of hope to her sinking spirit;

9. I returne home with my brother to our house; my heart downe; I am not doing; and so vanish; Lord gather up my disordered thoughts;

10. At mr Parkers,[252] Christianly enterteined, who am I, that I should be so beloved of gods saints, as I am generally, having such a proud heart, dead barren, awcke[253] to good; oh Lord make mee the more to loath my selfe; for they suppose, and thinke something lovelye in mee; but I am sure I am a jakes,[254] a cage of uncleanenesse; and I wonder that the Lord, or his servants, should looke upon mee, as comelye;

11. Full of melancholy pangs, and distempers, discontents; oh Lord what shall I doe in this sad place, I have no joy; myne eyes are to thee

---

[248] At Barnston, Essex, the minister was John Beadle, an appointment of the Earl of Warwick in 1632. He was a *protégé* of Thomas Hooker and had a troubled career in the 1630s: Webster, *Godly Clergy*, pp. 32, 188, 199–200.

[249] This could be William Finch, son of William of Beds. who went to Bishop's Stortford school and studied at Christ's College, Cambridge, graduating in 1632. His family probably included Martha and Thomas Finch of Wethersfield: GL MS 10,110.

[250] There are several possibilities for 'Mr Perne'. As Rogers benefits from the sermon, perhaps the most likely minister is Andrew Perne, a former fellow of St Catherine's, Cambridge, minister of Wilby, Northamptonshire in 1627.

[251] As usual.

[252] Mr Parker may be either a gentleman resident in Stortford or Francis Parker, the minister at Hatfield Broad Oak. He had difficulties with the ecclesiastical authorities in the mid-1630s for administering communion to strangers (perhaps Rogers included) and to some who refused to kneel: Glasscock, *St Michael's, Bishop's Stortford*, p. 101; Smith, *Ecclesiastical History*, p. 54.

[253] See Glossary.

[254] See Glossary.

my god all = suficient; I will not ride upon horses; Ashur:[255] &c. I am stript of content in the creature that thou maist be all unto mee which certeinly is a name used in sending mee hither;

127. 12. saboth, cold doings at church, my heart very low brought, anoyed with other matters, troubled with h2r; a great deale of rust gets upon my soule, Lord rub it of[f], and let mee shine bright in thyne eyes;

13. much prest in my sp:[irit], and streightned for place; hurrying commenc:[ement] thoughts, discontent, distrust, Lord purge out all this drosse, and provide so for mee, that I may serve thee with cheerefulnesse;

14. Many giddy thoughts, that much hinder mee in my calling, and so in my comf:[ort] Lord gather in my stragling vaine thoughts that come to litle issue, and settle my soule upon thee;

15. This day to Epping, heard Mr Dike[256] of the hedge broken, and not mended; one mightye in the scripture, a teaching prophet, whom the Lord hath sent as Jeremiah, and Ezek:[iel] to speake plainely among so many daubers with untempered mortar;[257] Lord mainteine such stakes in the hedge if it be thy blessed will to doe us good;

128. 16. much unsetlednes, and unresolvednesse of spirit; I cannot set to worke to calling, nor anything else; my head is giddy, heart running after vanityes; the Lord in mercy gather in these old vagarying stragling thoughts;

17. my heart at a low ebbe, but in the lowest, I can a litle raise my selfe, upon the promise; that god can, yea will love such a giddy, untoward, vaine wretch as I am, not for my sake, but for his free grace and mercy sake;

18. my head is so slight, and so hurryed with vagaryng [sic] nothing thoughts, that I stand, and wonder at my selfe; I am unfit for meditation, studdy, or any serious matter a dayes, onlye a perke spirit is up; Lord downe with that, put in more staiednesse, sobrietye, wisdome which I much need;

19. Saboath, most wretchedlye at church, I grone under my burden,

[255] A reference to Hosea 14:3 – 'Asshur shall not save us; we will not ride upon horses: neither will we say any more to the work of our hands, Ye are our gods: for in thee the fatherless findeth mercy.' It is thus an expression of Rogers' dependence on God alone.

[256] Jeremiah Dyke was the minister at Epping, Essex. He was a renowned elderly lecturer who had preached to the House of Commons in 1628 and had experienced difficulties for his nonconformity: Smith, *Ecclesiastical History*, p. 70; GL 9537/13 fo. 5v; Webster, *Godly Clergy*, pp. 49, 154, 260.

[257] Dyke seems to have been preaching on Ezekiel 22:28–30, a passage which is particularly noteworthy as it is an image which Rogers uses on several occasions: 'And her prophets have daubed them with untempered mortar, seeing vanity, and divining lies unto them, saying, Thus saith the Lord God, when the Lord hath not spoken. The people of the land have used oppression, and exercised robbery, and have vexed the poor and needy: yea, they have oppressed the stranger wrongfully. And I sought for a man among them, that should make up the hedge, and stand in the gap before me for the land, that I should not destroy it: but I found none.'

Lord ease mee in thy good time, so that with libertye I may walke in thy wayes, a litle inlarged in secret, else what should I doe; Lord shew mee thy selfe clearelye, and I shall have enough cause mee to disrelish other matters;

129. 20. I have had many slippery, giddy thoughts in the day, which much hinder mee in calling, and duty, yet this evening, the Lord hath poured downe a sp:[irit] of prayer in secret for my selfe, and the church; I blesse the Lord forth, for I have had much streightnes in private a great while; Lord let my soule be thawed still, and continue so in the day approching;

21. This day Fasting, and prayer at G. D.[258] the Lord went out mightily with us, and thawed our hearts; blessed be his name; oh Lord let us live as wee have prayed, and walke better then ever; wee prayed for J. Dix:[on] in point of mariage, and wee will wait what the Lord shall answer us; in point of convers:[ation] and mariage both: R. Emer:[son] wife dyes while wee were praying for her;[259] as Mr: Ch:[arles] Denny did, whilest I was putting up suites for him in this same place; the Lord comfort the mourning husb:[and] to whom the Lord hath surelye tryd;

130. 22. Many vaine thoughts; L4:[260] &c. assaile mee; Lord strengthen mee against them, draw thou my soule and cause it to conceive enough to be in thee; that thou being mine I may live without discontent, or care;

23. pore; I find flesh heavy, weighing mee downe to the creature, yet wil I raise my selfe by the weake wings of faith, and love towards heaven;

24. I am scarse my selfe in the place I live in; yet can I run to the Lord, and make my moane to him; the more I am taken from hope, and setling in the creature, the more will I looke toward him, ever my deare god, allsuficient;

25. I have two nations within mee, fighting against each other; Amalek prevailes,[261] but that the Lord upholds my hands to seeke him; which are ready to grow feeble also; Lord confound these enimyes of thy grace, as thou hast begun to slaughter so finish;

131. 26. Sabath, I goe to Stansted to heare honest Mr Miller;[262] my heart stoopes to the power of the truth; and goes along; with it; At home I have an alarm rung in myne eares from the brawling toung of an imperious woman which much disquiets mee, and unfits mee for

258 Goodman or George Dixon.
259 Elizabeth Emerson, presumably the wife of Richard, was buried on 22 June 1636: HRO D/P 21–29/41 entry on 22 June 1636.
260 The abbreviation of the sentence as well as the word make this difficult. Given the concern about vain thoughts, there is a fairly strong possibility that 'Lo:' is short for 'Love' but it may simply be an interjection of 'Lord'.
261 Rogers' enemies are the Amalekites, foes of Israel from the time of Exodus to the time of Saul and David. See above, p. 13 and n.
262 There was no incumbent by the name of Miller at either Stansted, Herts. or Stansted Montfitchet in Essex. Thus this was probably a visiting minister so it is difficult to identify him.

service, oh Lord one day ease mee of this heavy burden; and provide so, that I may not put my foot under anothers table; but that with libertye, and sweetnes I may savour thee;

27. Hope deferd breaks the heart, makes the soule unfit for better matters; my thoughts run after commencem:[ent] and hurryes mee; Lord keepe mee in the midst of all and learne mee the skill to walke in a steddy, constant course for a giddy, slight heart much wrongs mee;

28. Sunke much in the day time, I am hurryed still with many doubtful thoughts of commencem:[ent] I am not able to sit downe quiet till it come; Lord daily gather in my strag[g]ling thoughts;

132. 29. Strangely possessed with various thoughts, which hinder mee in my calling, and so in my peace, I walke about, unsetled and unable to fall closely to studdy; Lord help mee for this giddines, and longings for hope deferred; of which my heart is exceedingly impatient;

30. Many ocasions, and companyes, Dr Goades words;[263] oh happy am I, that I am litle troubled with these earthly matters; or am not tyed to the societye of vaine men; Lord gather up, and in all strag[g]ling thoughts and set my whole soule upon thee;

July 1. Mr Tendring buryed;[264] my heart downe and dull, cannot hold close to the Lord, though that course be only sweet, and comfortable; Lord teach mee so to walke before thee heere a few dayes of my sojourning that I may at last lye downe in peace, and my end may be as the just, and upright; 37 psal:[m] 37;[265]

133. 2. Much opprest, and cast downe, many thoughts, which make mee walke about disorderlye, and untoward, and unfit mee for saboath service; oh this same hope, and expectation, delayed eates up my liver; how foolish am I?

3. Saboath, dry preaching, which makes a dry, hard heart; Lord quicken it, and find out some way, that I may walke livelyly before thee;

4. 5. 6. Commencement hurryings, and thoughts, quickly ready to slip, but that the Lord daily holds mee in to work, which indeed is best for mee; oh the pore universitye, Lord pitye it in the generall consent to superstition, and will worship; it is a sinfull decaying universitye; oh the strange change in 7. yeares;

7. Many setling thoughts; litle can be done in calling, not that life, which should be;

134. 8. Litle done in calling, still vanishing, my mind moving after other matters; Lord once setle mee, and reveale thy selfe still more clearely to

[263] Dr Thomas Goad, see note above, p. 8.
[264] A gentleman resident in Bishop's Stortford, interred on 1 July 1636: HRO D/P 21–29/41, entry on 1 July.
[265] Psalm. 37:37 – 'Mark the perfect man, and behold the upright: for the end of that man is peace.'

my soule; shew mee that sweetnes in thy selfe that may make the
creature better;

9. I am downe the wind, my heart sinkes; Lord, I have no whether else
to goe save to thee, to be quickned; incouraged, and rowzed up, to be
thawed, broken, and bound up, oh doe thou all for my pore silly soule,
and fit mee for saboth;

10. Saboth, dry at church, my Lot is fallen into a sad place; my heart
sinkes, when I have no raising preaching; Lord rowze, and quicken
mee; heere Lord is my heart, and empty lamp, oh drop thyne oyle into
it;

11. the Lord hath a litle quickned mee up in private, and raised up my
spirit, oh whether should my discontented heart run, did not the Lord
in mercy gather it up, when it is strug[g]ling; oh deare god, holde it now
neere to thy selfe, make mee to walke, closelye with thee, and without
distraction;

135. 12. this day, prayer, and fasting at G. Per:[ry] the Lord graciouslye
went out with us; oh that something might sticke; that my soule might
have an utter loathing of all base earth; and that grace might conquer
in mee victorouslye, Lord pull mee closer to thee, and let mee live; oh
for thy church, pity the desolations and ruines of it for thy goodnes
sake;

13. I cannot find the Lord sweet to mee; oh I have deserved frownes for
yesterdayes worke, oh a world of selfe, and pride, Lord I would faine
conquer all as thou hast given mee some victorye, so goe on, and also
declare thy selfe to my soule, that desires to waite upon thee;

14. this day Mr. Harlak:[enden] comes, it is a heaven upon earth to
communicate, and pray with such whose soules are inflamed with the
love of X; I am tyed up, streightned in this sad place that I live in, Lord
provide for mee that I may pray freelye, and

136. walke as with life, and savor through there companyes, that I am
conversant with;

15. I have bine refreshed in the 1. part of the day; but in a most
lamentable case afterward, overwhelmed with pensive thoughts, with
desolate thoughts of my place; and sollicitude for future accomodations; Lord to thee I flye, bec:[ause] I know not what to doe;

16. this day I unbundled my heart into the bosome of B3n3ng;[266] and
had a great deale of ease; Lord thou knowest my burden, oh that my
soule were eased; help mee at thy time to thee I flye in midst of all my
distempers;

17. Saboath dry abroad, the Lord a litle lookes towards mee latward;
but oh the want of a close lively preaching; Good Lord so provide for

---

[266] 'Bining' may be Francis Bingham or a relative of his: Bingham was noted as head of a
household contributing to funds for communion silver and so forth in 1641: Glasscock, *St
Michael's, Bishop's Stortford*, p. 150.

thy pore servant; that I may walke with life, to savour, and cheerefulnesse; the way to atteine which is to be under a convincing ministrye; Lord I lye downe in thyne armes who hast assisted mee this daye;

137. 18. the old burden beares mee downe it is as lead to mee; Good Lord, some ease grant unto mee in thy good time; I am much straitned in service, the Lord shewes mee w[ha]t I am, if he forsake but a day; oh Lord I have deserved thy indignation, I will beare it, and looke up.

19. A litle lengthned out by the company of Mr Wilson and Mr Bysh:[267] oh joyfull time, when Lambs shall never be more separated, but dwell together for ever, I blesse thy name for my warmth and heate I have got by them;

20. My heart growes downe in the day, though raised in the morning Lord doe thou still uphold mee by new strength of grace, that I may not fall from thee;

21. I sigh out one day after another and litle goe forward as I should; comfort springs from diligence, and faithfulnesse in the dutyes g.[od] sets us about; but unfruitefulnesse lyes downe with sorrow;

138. 22. I cannot yet settle in my calling; I have many distracting thoughts, that hinder mee in my place, Lord remove them; I have drawne neere to the Lord by prayer this evening, and he hath a litle cleered up the way, and opened the dore to mee; oh more of this love, ever ravish my soule with thy flagon of love;

23. Lord, thou seest how heavilye I draw on in thy yoke; thou knowest my burden; and how much anguish of heart is in mee for that thou debarrest mee of holy company, and libertye and sweetnes in communion with them; Lord consider my case, and send mee some releife;

24. Saboath, dry abroade, oh the spirit life, and power of an ordinance what is become of it? Oh Lord I am even pulled backe in regard of outward helpes, oh Let my soule injoy thee in secret, Lord if thou departest from preaching and the assemblys (which deare god doe not) yet thou leavest not thyne owne people, thou dwellest with them ever; oh, with mee;

139. 25. I was much straitned, this afternoone, and the Lord shut up his loving countenance, I looked yet, and he a litle brake the clouds in prayer in the family; gave mee words (oh mercye) and spirit; put sweetnes, and mildnes of disposition into mee; when I injoy Christ most, then am I in the most melodious tune and fittest to love folke, espec:[ially] gods saints, all day long;

26. I am againe fallen into strange melancholy phansyes, and thoughts,

---

[267] For John Wilson, see above p. 29n; 'Mr Bysh:' may be William Bishop, a minister deprived at Brent Pelham, Herts: Urwick, *Nonconformity in Herts*, pp. 761–3. This is based on no more than the visitor giving spiritual comfort to Rogers and being given the title 'Mr'.

and walke, wanze,[268] and thinke out my time; Lord settle my heart
upon thee, and there let it be fixed; and set mee about that which may
be most for thy glory;

27. much care, and many pusillanimous unbeleiving thoughts come
assaulting of mee, myne eyes are yet to heaven; I have bine straitned in
dutyes, the Lord would shew mee still what I am without grace and
contin:[ued] assistance from him;

140. 28. this daye, we heare Mr wharton, and have his company, and mr
willets,[269] oh how joyfull is it to have the society of the saints upon
earth; oh blessed is it to beleive, and meditate of that eternall societye
with the Lord, holy angels, and saints; the whilest will I warre against
my enimyes, oh one day I shall triumph; oh my deare god, I beleive it,
though weaklye, and rejoice in it; Lord regard thy church sinking, the
enimyes tread it downe; the hedge is broken, and lyes open; oh set in
stakes that may uphold it; Deare god yet dwell with sinfull, rebellious,
idolatrous, oppressing, profane England;

29. This day I have wanzed[270] away my time, and have litle comfort in
it; I cannot bend my head to a serious studdye; one thought, or
discontent or other the devel intrudes upon mee which much hinders
mee in my course Lord doe thou direct mee what to studdye, and to
doe, I am almost at my wits ends; but Lord I will looke towards thee;
now newes, that the wretch that slew Sr thom:[as] Leventhorp viz: Sir
Arth:[ur] Capel is quitted;[271] oh Lord blood lyes upon us, oh pardon lay
it upon the guilty, and not us;

141. 30. Downe the wind, my heart much straitned, I am ready to sinke
dailye; the Lord keepes up my spirit by exercise; it is a great mercye if
by all meanes I may get a litle heate; oh I cannot keepe that which I get;

31. Saboth, a litle thawed by Mr Butlers sermon; oh the ancient word,
a spirit quickning for a whole weeke; oh woe is mee, that I am debarred
of it; Lord find out some comfortable way, wherin I may serve thee
sweetlye, and cheerefully;

August. 1. I am heavily depressed in my spirit, and borne downe, as
with a weight; with the old burden, good Lord, pitty thy pore creature,
and release, and chawke out some way for mee to tread in; Lord I am
bound up in my soule and cannot serve thee cheerfully in one calling
nor other;

2. I am still so pressed, that I sigh away, and thinke away most of my

[268] See Glossary.
[269] For Samuel Wharton, see above, p. 27; 'Mr Willets' is probably one of Andrew Willet's
sons, either Andrew or James. James is most likely, as he had a record of puritan sympathies
as rector of Little Chishall, Essex: Matthews, *Calamy Revised*, p. 53.
[270] See Glossary.
[271] See above, p. 52–3 and n.

time; Lord pittye a pore creature, whose sp:[irit] is bound, and I cannot serve the[e] comfortablye;

142. 3. Now I have a litle more ease in my spirit; this evening I have found my spirit loose; it pleased the Lord to give a meeke sweet kind of thawing, and brokennes in the familye; I find it a mercye to be occupied; else my heart would grow empty, for want of rubbing;

4. this day Mr Simonds;[272] a godly prayer, and good sermon; yet my heart some what straitned, and so at home in repetition; oh Lord, I will lay my selfe low, as nothing at thy feete if thou forsake, I am sin, and weaknes, and unable to performe any service I will yet looke up to thee; if thou frowne I will beare thyne indignation, I have deserved hell; and oh since thou hast delivered mee, happy I; oh wretch, that should sin against so good a god, and force thee to vaile thy countenance, in whose favour is life, joy, sweetnes, and peace;

5. this day, Fasting, and prayer in secret, sometimes up, sometimes downe; difficult to flesh; I will yet rejoice in it according to the sp:[irit] my comfort is only in thee Lord in other matters I have litle joy;

143. 6. Now heart broken still, for this desolate place I am in; my heart is at a low ebbe going to the sacrament, in a cloud, but I will looke up, and waite at the throne of grace in use of mercy for my dole;

7. Saboth; a most sad uncomfortable day, because most wretched preaching, nothing moved, there sits a congregation halfe starved for want of bread; with dead hearts, which Lord thou knowest is a heavy burden; my heart is much sadded by seeing the straine of towne, and family carelesse for gods saboath, and honor oh that I could say, I and my house will serve the Lord[;] Lord I have bine this day at thy sacrament; I went in a cloud but thou hast graciouslye dispelled it, shined upon mee, and thawed my soule; I am a litle up, but quickly downe; I lye downe in thyne armes of love, (who hast sweetly caryed mee through dutyes in the family in repeating Mr. Marsh:[all's][273] serm:[on] with circumsp:[ection]) whom though I see not so cleerlye, yet believe thee my g.[od] reconciled; so thy promise mine and this day sealed;

144. 8. my heart is full of sorrow, the Lord frownes, and I am troubled; the church sighes, and I will sigh with her; I groan for my dailye loade oh pitty mee; thou god of compassion and find out some way for my comfortable walking before thee;

9. For this cause will I praise the Lord, who hath shed abroad his love so in my heart, that it hath caused mee to love him againe, and out of

272 This could be Edward Symmons, the moderate minister of Raine, Essex on whom see Webster, *Godly Clergy*, pp. 96, 287; idem., *Stephen Marshall*, pp. 12, 23n. It is also possible that it was Joseph Simonds, the rector of Ironmonger Lane, London. Without a named location, it is unclear.
273 Stephen Marshall of Finchingfield.

love to feare him; which feare brings the most solid peace at lying
downe; but oh I cannot walke so closelye, as I would; woe is mee, sin is
present when I would doe good; oh the day; when I shall sin no more,
but dwell purely, in the glorious presence of my pure god even to
eternitye;

10. The Lord vailes himselfe, he will not smile upon my soule, as
sometimes he hath done; I have sinned, I will beare the indignation of
the Lord for I walke not so before him, as I should, oh pardon, and
cause thy pore weake creature to love thee more, and to have thee in
myne eye;

11. Much disturbed with Redmans buisinesse gathering fruit;[274] not
libertye to my selfe my sin pardon, deare god, and accept mee in thy
son; oh cleare up the coast, earthly ocasions cloud up the waye; happy
I, that have litle to doe with them;

145. 12. I am sadded under my old loade, oh what crosse to this, to live
among bryars and thornes;[275] Deare god, deliver thy pore creature, that
lookes up to thee; oh I cannot see the face of the Lord, what shall I doe;
Lord my heart breakes, if my hope be not in thee;

13. It is a sad thing to consider the sad seasons wee have had this last
yeare, and this, a most heavy drought, the last yeare in the former part
of the summer, which burnt up the grasse, scarse raine for a q[uar]ter
together, yet then a michlemasse spring; this yeare in the former part, a
sing[e]ing, yea scorching drought, heavye, gods people mourned, and
made the heavens weep; but the Lord hath turned that raine into a
crosse justlye, for it hath bine a moist uncomfortable harvest even
Aprill weather; the Lord is angry with us a most sinful nation; witness
also the heavy plauge in London, Newcastle port townes, followes the
Court &c: deseases pox here, last year in Essex, these are forerun[n]ers
of greater judgements

146. as wee may justlye feare, sin gets an head; espec:[ially] sp:[iritual] sins;
idolatrous superstitious Arminians carye the ball before them; they
have prevailed lamentablye within these 7. years; the Lord in mercy
fight for his witnesses that seeme to be slaine now almost; Lord thy
church, thy church, thy pore creatures, that know not how to keepe a
good conscience in these sorrowfull times, help us, and deliver us for
thy goodnesse sake;

14. Saboath, something better on it, then ut solet;[276] I heard Mr

---

[274] Neither the individual nor the offence have been traceable. The phrase 'gathering fruit' may
refer to poaching in an orchard belong to the family or it may be metaphorical.

[275] A popular expression for the corrupt and corrupting nature of the world. It is a reference to
Ezek. 2:6 – 'And thou, son of man, be not afraid of them, neither be afraid of their words,
though briers and thorns be with thee, and thou dost dwell among scorpions: be not afraid
of their words, nor be dismayed at their looks, though they be a rebellious house.' Cf. Isaiah
7:23–5.

[276] As usual.

Sedgwicke,[277] of holines, the Lord inlarged my heart in familye, and in secret, he drew neere to my soule; oh more of thy selfe Lord, and thy loves, ravish mee with thy flagons;

15. I wanse away my time with discontent, and unbeleiving pensivenes, and care, is not the L[or]d my god, why oh my soule shouldest thou distrust him; canst thou trust him for X, and happines, and not for life, and maintenance, I will throw my selfe therefore upon the Lord, who does regard mee;

147. 16. my heart wanzes,[278] and lingers after freedome; I cannot bring my heart to conceive, my present condition to be the best; yet the Lord will turne all to the best I will adventur[e] my selfe upon thee, and thy full promise, wherin is my comfort, and strength;

17. The Lord keepes my soule from sinking to any kind of sin; my heart is in awe of god my loving god, and father, and my soule is vexed for the barrennes, and fulsomenes of this familye I dwell in; good Lord, some fruit some fruit, that I may say, this hath the Lord done by mee; oh my heart is for the conversion of soules; Lord prepare a way to mee, if it be thy will, that I may bring honour to thee in the ministrye;

18. This day, newes out of N.[ew] England from J. How &c: and Mr Harlak:[enden][279] things goe very well with them[;] fasting ordinances, and abundance for body; blessed be thy name who hast safelye conducted them according to our prayers; my heart rejoices in this, though I have the old heavy burden upon mee;

148. 19. still the old song, or rather the old sorrow; this place is the burden of my song; Lord what shall I doe I am with a weight of lead at my heart, good father deliver a pore creature that desires to hang upon thee; libertye, Lord, some libertye of spirit for thee;

20. I have bine pressed with melancholye in the morning; comforted with R. Emers:[on] and Mr Archer sweetlye;[280] a most sweet and cleare passage given to prayer at night; I have joy in god, and in nothing so much; I see god will have mee heere a while to batter mee of[f] from the creatures; none but Christ, none but Christ;

21. Saboath, wherin I have found the L[or]d gracious; and my soule to stand in awe of him, it is a great mercy that the Lord estranges my heart more and more from sin, and sets it daily in opposition to it; much evell hath bine kept from familye, and good discourse hath had the upper hand, which is a mercye to mee in such a sad place; Lord some fruit, some blessing upon this wretched barren familye;

---

[277] William Sedgwick.
[278] See Glossary.
[279] See above p. 29. Roger Harlakenden was the younger brother of Richard of Earls Colne, Essex.
[280] For Archer, see above, p. 30n.

149. 22. I walke not with a studious heart, my mind is much taken from my studdye here of late, one dayly distraction, or other molests mee so that I cannot have that comfort in looking backe to the worke of it; the Lord hath blessed mee in familye dutyes, and inlarged mee and softned mee; Lord some fruite upon this heartlesse company, for thy names sake;

23. my heart is out of frame, oh my comfortlesse burden; Lord ease mee, and deliver mee; I am thyne, I desire to look what way thou wilt have mee walke in; Lord some favour, some glimpse of love in the face of thy son to solace my soule which hath but litle in regard of other matters;

24. I have bine this day at Mr Scrogs his house, with Mr Brograve;[281] oh how fulsome, and tedious to mee is the religion of such people; there discourse against the power of religion, alasse they know not the sweetnes of it, and so must seeke it in pleasures; great things in this world &c: oh Lord thy love I beg, and for other things thy will be done, I desire to waite;

150. 25. I have bin straitned in the day time much, but my heart lookes towards heaven, and this evening, whilest I have bine doing the Lord hath drawne neere to mee; oh more of thy selfe, thy sweetnes, thy love, which is better then a world; oh some fruit, some fruit, from this saplesse companye;

26. my bondage yet is this, that I live with a tumultuous companye, of vaine loose, lascivious wretches, no good sinkes into them; my comfort only is in thee deare god, oh smile upon mee cleare the cost, shew mee thy selfe, which shall be best of all; and in thy good time, provide that I may live sweetlye;

27. I slipt[282] this morning without private prayer by one following occasion, or other, but I have paid for it th[o]roughlye; I have gone drooping pitifully in the day time; and mee things [sic] the ice is growne thicke because it was not broken; I beare this place upon my shoulders, as my burden, the Lord ease mee in mercye; I know not what to doe; some fruit Lord, some fruit, amongst blockes;

151. 28. Saboath, my burden is exceeding heavy, under a heartlesse, pore preaching, my heart sighes and grones, Lord pitty thy pore servant;

---

[281] Neither of these men is definitely identifiable. 'Mr Brograve' probably refers either to Edward or John Brograve. Both attended Sidney Sussex College, Cambridge. John was the heir of Simeon Brograve of Hemel, Herts., who came to Gray's Inn in 1614 and married Hanna, the daughter of Sir Thomas Barnardiston of Kedington, Suffolk: W. C. Metcalfe (ed.), *The Visitations of Hertfordshire* (London, 1886), p. 33; Venn. As for 'Scrogs', Rogers could be referring to a man by that name who was a fellow-commoner at King's College, Cambridge in 1631/2, possibly John, the son and heir of Edward Scroggs of Albury, Herts. The Scroggs had married into the Harlakenden family of Earls Colne (see the will of Anne Scroggs of Earls Colne, Waters, *Genealogical Gleanings*, II, 825).

[282] Slept.

and provide that I may serve thee sweetly, and cheerefullye though with bread and water; Lord remove this dead heart; a litle thawed in family service, and inlarged, though I went sad, and nothing;

29. this day, the loade in intollerably upon mee, I know not how possibly to undergoe it; Also the Lord is angry, and frownes upon mee, oh what shall my troubled soule in anguish doe; I lye downe at thy feet, who either wilt find out some way for mee; or else give mee patience, innocencye, and wisdome to walke among wolves;[283]

30. I wanze[284] away this day, doing nothing, but walke, and thinke, and sigh away my houres; we all groane under a yoke of slaverye, imperious doings, which flesh, and blood cannot beare; but myne is greivous, my spirit is tyed, yet the Lord loosens it in dutye, oh the fruit, Lord the fruit;

152. 31. was there ever such a sad fellow as I am, who loose my time by vaine thoughts, and imaginations; and loose my sweet peace and all; oh Lord governe my heart, my thoughts; settle mee to a staid sober, wise walking before thee, and faithful in each kind of service;

Septemb: 1. my burden is taken of[f]; my soule is refreshed by the coming of my deare uncle,[285] who is of a sweet incouraging spirit; he tells mee; this is a fine dying time in reg:[ard] of the terminus a quo, and ad quem; yet expects worse, the Lord arme us with abundance of faith in these times to live, and to dye by; Lord I am thyne, and will throw my selfe upon thee, who art enough to mee;

2. Much rejoicing still in my deare Christian friends uncle; mr wilson; and uncles man, cordiall and thorough; X sweet to him; my soule inlarged with his in secret, and with his discourse; oh Lord some way that I may glorifie thee among some that feare thy name; such as excell in vertue; oh X is very sweet this evening, and the promise; oh more Lord, more, more of thy selfe of whose love I have tasted; but oh the vaile the vaile to be removed;

153. 3. The savor of my uncle remaines in family; something; (oh that there were such an heart) and in my soule; his speaking so much of the sweetnes of christ, hath incouraged mee to run to heaven to find more of it, for I have tasted of some of it, and oh more more; it shall be my heaven upon earth; Lord away with these mists; the light of thy countenance reveale, and that fully, ravish my soule with loves; I blesse the Lord the burden lyes not so heavy upon mee ut solet;[286]

4. Saboath, oh I want bread of life what shall I starve? I want livelye

[283] A reference to Matt. 10:16 – 'Behold, I send you forth as sheep in the midst of wolves: be ye wise as serpents, and harmless as doves.'
[284] See Glossary.
[285] The uncle could be Adam Harsnett, the minister at Cranham, Essex, or Ezekiel Rogers, later to emigrate to New England.
[286] As usual.

companye to cherish up my drooping soule, what shall I doe: besides all these I have looked towards heaven, and am troubled; Lord smile thou, and that shall sweeten all other miseryes, and heavy burdens; dart in some beame of love;

5. I cannot goe on faithfully, in my particular calling, I see not god cleerely before mee in any way, Lord charte out thy way; oh that I might declare thy name in

154. in, [sic] and amongst thy congregations with libertye, and peace of conscience; oh make a way; for I have no joy (every day lesse, and lesse) in this hotch-potch;[287] shall I one day see New England, and the beautye of thy countenance in thy livelye and pure ordinances?

6. oh where are those ancient beames of divine light, darted into my soule from the sun of righteousnesse?[288] where are those ancient earnings[289] of the Lord toward mee; oh I have sinned, and deserved his indignation in a high measure; but Lord, am not I thyne; save mee; wilt thou give mee thy christ, and wilt not thou make mee tast[e] of his sweetnes, oh some of his sweetnes; and thy countenance thorough him, that may ravish my soule, as with love;

7. God lightens my heart by my fathers coming; oh joyfull to see godly freinds; heavenly oh how joyfull! &c: Lord accept pore services and person this day, into thyne armes I commit mee;

155. 8. still I enjoy the sweet societye, prayer, advice of my deare father; who encourages mee in going on in this way, and place god hath set mee in; Lord I am willing to lye at thy feet, doe with mee what thou wilt; I will waite upon thee, till thou shalt chart out a way for mee in some other course; the Lord thawes mee;

9. now an ebbe againe; the Lord seemes afar of[f], what shall my pore soule doe, who have no hope; some in the Lord; why shall I cast of[f]? no I will yet waite upon him and put my trust in his name who yet is my god, though I in darknes, and see litle light, yet will I rowle myselfe upon thee my god allsuficient, and true, and will dye in thyne armes;

10. I am troubled because of the frownes of my god; I have no comfort in other matters, and I have no comfort (in reg:[ulation] of sense) in the Lord; but I resolve to hang upon him, who is my comfort, and my god;

156. 11. Saboath, oh my deadnes, and unbeleife; oh my want of lively preaching; generalls, that vanish; the Lord frownes, and I am straitned what should a pore creature doe, I will looke up to see if by the eye of faith, I can discerne the bowells of my fathers love, under an angry

---

[287] Rogers is contrasting the heterogenous beast that is the Church of England with the purity of the church in New England.
[288] See note above, p. 20.
[289] See Glossary.

countenance; I lye downe in thyne armes, at thy poole I will lye, the 38. [sic] yeares of my pore life;

12. Now the Lord smiles a litle, and my soule is comforted, and inlarged; nothing, weakenesse without thee; but when thou conveyest strength, I can doe all things; oh more of the sweetnes of christ; oh more of thy deare, and tender love, more strength ag:[ainst] the great oppositions, which I have within, and without dailye;

13. I am in a great streight, in point of studyes; if I thinke of divinitye, I am quashed with the first thought, times grow worse every day, sorrows abound, with sin; if on physicke, no helpes, bookes, nor parts I thinke that way; if on new England; too many there; (what shall I doe?) if on familye, sad doings, comfortlesse; but god* will provide[;] I sinke in this water, but that faith treads water;

157. 14. I see a litle light, but yet but shimmering and afar of[f], oh infinite mercye, that such a wretch should not be utterly left to despaire; oh my god in thee will I rejoice, and comfort my selfe, who strengthenest mee to goe thorough what thou callest mee unto;

15. I am this day, perplexed with various thoughts, by reason of some hearesey of M. S. affect:[ions] towards mee;[290] yet I have got my heart to stoop to the Lord, and his will; and have prayed heartily for h2r; that g:[od] would take of[f] all love, if it stand not for his glorye; I have had some bickering with my L1d:[y] for backing her tipling servants;[291] I told her highnes[292] that it was fit they should rather be reproved; then backed; she a litle quailed; All the house ag:[ainst] mee as too strict; but I have comfort in it, at my lying downe;

16. I am much disquieted with the uneven spirit of this w4m1n; I cannot rejoice one whit in this sad, dead unsavory place; oh Lord what should Joseph doe in Potiphers house?[293] What should I doe livinge among briars and thornes; Lord thou hath set mee heer, shew mee the reason; and give strength, sp:[iritual] courage, zeale with

158. wisdome, til thou shalt chauke out some other way of subsisting for mee; oh that I might live to pray, and joine with those that know thee;

17. I blesse the Lord, who keepes mee in perfect health a dayes, a precious mercye; keepes infectious deseases from us, pox, plauge, raging in city, &c: all other favors that I enjoy, and that I can in some

---

[290] Again the mysterious 'M.S.'. This is the first time that there is any indication of mutual interest.

[291] Rogers has evidently castigated some of the household servants for being a little too liberal with drink. See Introduction.

[292] Marginal note in Thomas Percy's hand: 'her Highness'.

[293] This is a comparison that is far from flattering to Lady Denny. Joseph was sold to Potiphar while the Israelites were in exile in Egypt, Potiphar being a captain of the guard or an officer of Pharoah. Joseph advanced to a position of management in the court through his trustworthiness, despite the fact that he was a slave. However, Potiphar's wife tried to seduce him and, having failed, then preferred false charges against him, which Joseph denied. This led to Joseph's removal to a state prison (Genesis 37:36, 39:1–20).

measure walke in some tendernes, and thawednes of heart; even by an antiperistasis[294] of cold and for that sweetnes that I find in a X, and a promise, that the Lord upholds mee begging, gives daily supply to my weaknes; oh that my soule could but joy in my god, and were but mightily inlarged with thankfulnes to him; for all, and that in partic:[ular] in some measure he hath quieted my amorous afections; this Lord hath bine my sin, ever my ingratitude; pardon, pardon, and now accept my pore desires, who am about to lye downe in thyne armes; rejoycing in my god; Yea and in him I will rejoice;

159. 18. Saboath; unlivelye, doings, oh the god [sic] of the ordinance the sp:[irit] of preaching; the soule pricking, the thawing preaching; Lord shall I never injoy that againe, oh restore the power, and life of thyne ordinances, Lord consider the pore soules, that want food sp:[iritual] and send it to them; Lord turne the course of things, which are come to a lamentable story; make bare thy arme and strike thyne enimyes; and defend thy church;[295] the Lord hath exercised and inlarged my faith to trust beyond feeling this evening; his name * righteousnesse; and g.[od] mercifull is that which I have trusted in in my partiall desertion this evening;

19. I have walked in darknesse, and saw very litle light; I have not knowne what to doe with my dead, base, barren heart; ther[e]fore were mine eyes towards thee; a litle thawed in familye dutyes; oh more of thy selfe, Lord, and thy sweetnes satisy my soule with it, and I shall have enough, though litle of other matters;

20. my heart yet lookes toward the Lords, and is much refreshed with the company of John wright,[296] it is a joy to mee to pray, where he is, or

160. with any godly soules, any teachable, it hath bine my burden to pray, and be among pitifull, unsensible creatures; Lord yet prevaile with some of them; especially pore G. Wright oh dart something into him, that may doe his soule good;

21. my heart is really enlivened in dutyes and inlarged by the company of g. wrig:[ht] whom god hath in mercye sent hither to cherish mee, and to take of[f] the burden from mee, under which I gro[a]ned; Lord continue him heere; And to mee, Lord new grace, and supply from heaven; new love, and sweetnes in thy favour and love revealed in the face of thy son;

---

294 See p. 54, n. 234, above.
295 This may be an adaptation of Isaiah 52:10 – 'The Lord hath made bare his holy arm in the eyes of all the nations; and all the ends of the earth shall see the salvation of our God.'
296 John Wright is difficult to identify with any certainty. Internal evidence suggests that he was older than Rogers and trained for the ministry. A John Wright was admitted to preach at St Martin within Endgate in London in June 1632: GL 9538A/1 fo. 19. However, if the 'G. Wright' is the same man then he would be unlikely to be a minister if the 'G' is for Goodman, although 'G. Wright' may be kin of John Wright. There were some Wrights on the parish register at Stortford: Glasscock, St Michael's, Bishop's Stortford, p. 150.

22. I am straitned; and cannot see my deare god, yet my confidence is not wholly removed; myne eyes yet looke to heaven and the name of the Lord, my right:[eous] and g.[od] mercif:[ul] gracious &c: and allmighty and ther[e]f:[ore] I will lye downe in his armes;

23. Heaven, heaven; where no cloud shall be; but I shall see the Lord face to face; and never be removed; oh a litle the whilest to comfort mee in this valley of teares; where I have no comfort but in the Lord;

161. 24. something sicklye, and feaverish; oh the time, when sicknesse shall be no more; Lord beate of my hearte from health, jollitye, hopes, things below; whatever is too sweet to mee; oh some of thy sweetnes reveale to mee, even more of it every daye;

25. Saboath, oh what a heaven is it, to injoy powerful, savory, preaching in a saboth; the life of the life; Lord find out some way, that I may lye under the power of the ordinance though with a dish of greene hearbes[;][297] And now draw neere to mee, and shed thy love abroad in my heart, and let mee lye downe in thy embraces;

26. where is the sweet rellish of christ in an ordinance; oh Lord more of that, and lesse in the creature; pardon my weaknesse in walking before thee this day;

27. My heart is kept in an awe of god, he it is who both hath shed his love, and his feare into my heart; but oh more communion, draw neere Lord to my soule; this night I made L.[ady] D.[enny] acquainted with my intended journeye to Hatf:[ield Broad Oak] to heare mr Dike; granted ut putes[298]

162. I had borrowed S. horse before; he tells h2r; shee stops it to hinder mee, out of a peevish, penurious, and jealous conceit (oh base!) Did ever man sigh out a life amongst such uneven tempers, Nabalish dispositions, as I;[299] Lord ease, if it be thy will; I groane; else thou canst give pat:[ience] and wisdome to walke as Joseph in Potipher's company of Egyptians αμέμπτως;[300]

28. I have bine at Hatfeild sermon mr Dike[301] the L[or]d yet finds out, heere, and there a portion for mee in this barren wildernesse; my heart hath not bine so thawed at the sermon as sometimes; He hath a way of

---

[297] A common plea with Rogers, possibly a reference to Proverbs 15:17 – 'Better is a dinner of herbs where love is, than a stalled ox and hatred therewith.'

[298] This is unclear: 'pernes'; 'prones'?

[299] Nabalish, that is, churlish or miserly: I Sam. 25. As far as can be ascertained, Rogers seems to have borrowed S's horse without asking permission and, although he has borrowed the horse before, S complained and Lady Denny forbade Rogers from taking it. Rogers saw this as a spiteful action (although it might be admitted that he seems incapable of seeing any fault in himself on this!).

[300] άμέμπτως: blamelessly or righteously.

[301] Jeremiah Dyke.

his owne wittye, and stuffe, but farre short of Hooker Shephea[r]d &c:
faith a litle on foot to day, else what should I doe;[302]

29. Now discourse with mr Cooke[303] ab:[out] N:[ew] E:[ngland] my
heart closes with it more, and more the Lord hath pretty well knocked
mee of[f] from hence; if I could but perceive the Lords mind beckning
mee thither; Lord shew mee thy will every day more clearelye; heere I
lye at thy dispose; doe with mee, what thou wilt; And for the present
some beames or else sheere faith in darkenesse;

163. 30 Now in companye at mr Reades,[304] how suddainelye am I ready to
loose my heart; mee thinkes I find some strangenes to godward; oh
Lord draw neere to a pore creature, and reveale thy selfe fully;

October 1. my heart is much downe the wind this day; and eloofe of; I
have bine troubled with divers hurrying thoughts, and buisinesses; oh
happy I, that have litle to do with the world; this same mr stephens[305]
his companye is sad to mee; one not savoring goodnesse; but secretly
disapproving it, oh what a cub it is to mee; oh the company, that I live
withall, the companye which hath a transforming quality in it, unlesse
the Lord were the more mercifull to mee, else heart breakes; I have no
joy in England, no joy in this sad wretched familye, Lord some way,
some way charte out to mee, wherin thou wouldest have mee to walke;
oh discover, I am in a streight betweene twoo studyes;

164. 2. Saboath, damped by the company of this sad stevens, that hath
shewed his heart; a litle thawed by mr sedgwicke, and inlarged in
familye, wher[e] litle else but dislike and opposit:[ion] Lord strengthen
mee still, and give mee new supplye of zeale, and wisdome to oppose
and beate downe opposition;

3. I am pressed, sorely in my spirit; and brought low, the L[or]d seemes
to be gone, and leave mee in darknesse I am much damped in this
barren place, my heart naught;[306] and the Lord gone too, oh what shall

---

302 Rogers sets out his preferences in preaching style, advocating the more direct style of Thomas
Hooker and Thomas Shepard, both ministers from his father's social circle and both likely to
have been seen by Rogers in his youth. Hooker had been lecturer at Chelmsford, Essex and
Shepard at Earls Colne, Essex. Both eventually emigrated to New England, Hooker ending up
in Connecticut and Shepard in Cambridge, Massachusetts. For their time in England, their
pietistic style and their troubles with the authorities, see Webster, *Godly Clergy*.
303 The chances are that Rogers is referring to someone from the Cooke family of Earls Colne,
Essex. George and his older brother Joseph Cooke had emigrated to New England in the
summer of 1635. It is possible that one of them had returned to England, telling of their
experience and attempting to 'recruit' others, or it may just have been an account shared
from correspondence. See Thompson, *Mobility and Migration*, p. 188.
304 Possibly William Read, a churchwarden at Bishop's Stortford: Glasscock, *St Michael's,
Bishop's Stortford*, p. 114. There was also an Alexander Read who served as minister to
Fifield, Essex: Matthews, *Calamy Revised*, p. 162.
305 Thomas Stevens was recorded as the head of one of the households contributing to the
funds for communion silver and so forth in 1642; he was one of the collectors for the poor in
1636 and churchwarden from 1647 and 1648: Glasscock, *St Michael's, Bishop's Stortford*,
pp. 163, 168, 114.
306 See Glossary.

I doe; oh I know; I will beare the indignat:[ion] of the L[or]d; and yet I will not be beaten from his name; yet will I shroude myselfe in the secret of his tabernacle;

4. I have a heavy pulbacke, by my dry, dead, company that I live withall; oh the burden of a dead decaying heart; Lord in mercye raise mee for I sinke exceeding much oh leave mee not in these streights I have no help but in thyne allsuficiencye;

165. 5. much estranged, and disheartned by my sad companions; something inlarged, and refreshed by the company of mr wilson; oh happy when I shall converse, with none but saints, and shall not heare the voice of any unsavory wretch;

6. Doubtfull things much trouble mee, and disquiett mee; as what to doe in S5. buisinesse, and in cr4mw:[307] I have engaged my selfe and it lyes glowing at my heart Lord safely deliver mee out of these snares; I hope I shall be carefull to avoide them; I will yet lord looke up to thee for wisdome, and; [sic] direction, oh and thy smiles with a cleare coast between mee, and thee;

7. I am in a lamentable streight my comfort, and light gone, no comfort in place; what shall I doe, I study not I know not what to studdy nor which way to take; and the th[in]g upon 6. day hang upon mee, and I lye downe full sad;

166. 8. this day at Hatfeild; much out of frame for the former crosse doubtfull buisinesses; the Lord seemes to be gone, out of deep anger; sweet discourse with that precious woman Mrs Barington[308] but oh the streightnes of a base cursed heart, that scarse will stoop to the government of christ espec:[ially] in some odde humor; L[or]d help mee I am in a heavy streight[;] oh smile, and deliver mee for thy goodnes sake; one peeke into heaven, one crevis of light;

9. Saboath, the L[or]d hath banished away other distracting thoughts, and caused mee to rejoice in the saboath, and in the ordinances of it; I have hea[r]d at mr Bowles at Farnham,[309] someth:[ing] of that; to you that believe he is precious;[310] oh my X precious, sweet, amiable, and precious faith, that applyes him oh more precious faith L[or]d, that

---

[307] 'S5. buisinesse' is probably the amorous fears touched upon above. See Introduction. The nature of 'cr4mw' (cromw) is unknown.

[308] This Mrs Barrington is possibly Dorothy Barrington, the wife of Robert Barrington of Hatfield Broad Oak, Essex.

[309] Possibly a preacher at Farnham. There are several possibilities. Narrowing it down to the more godly ministers, given Sedgwick's position and Rogers' enthusiasm, the best candidates are Samuel Bowles, an Emmanuel graduate and fellow; Richard Bowles, born at Wethersfield and an Emmanuel MA in 1613; Edward Bowles, St Catherine's College, Cambridge MA and a prominent preacher during the 1640s: *DNB*, Venn and Matthews, *Calamy Revised*.

[310] Bowles preached on I Peter 2:7 – 'Unto you therefore which believe he is precious: but unto them which be disobedient, the stone which the builders disallowed, the same is made the head of the corner.'

may derive some more of his preciousnesse; and sweetnes into my soule
And now thou Sun of righteousnesse shine into my soule;[311] and it shall
put out my starlight; and the candle which anything of myne may light;
and the sparks which I am ready to kindle to encompasse my selfe
withall;

167. 10. now wee hurry to Colchester Hall[312] Lld: &c: where I have not
wholly lost my heart; but yet ready to sinke, having powerlesse
company, oh Lord quicken mee; and cleare the coast daily more, and
more more of thy selfe, and thy sweetnes, which is best of all;

11. I have got my heart to stoop in S5: bus:[iness] it troubles mee not to
sighing; I desire to stoop to the Lord; I cannot see him in it, therfore
content; the Lord is with mee to give some content in this place in John
wright, I account it as a precious mercye, that the Lord hath brought
him hither; and George is coming I hope; Lord pull him out, oh that
there were such a heart; Lord some fruit grant unto thy pore servant in
his endeavors; one smile now at lying downe which shall be enough to
mee;

12. I am heavily tormented with w4m[en']s tatlings, and bargaines my
eares glow with still the same song; what shall I doe for good company,
it were a heaven upon earth; L[or]d doe not thou absent thy selfe, what
shall I doe;

168. 13. I find a wofull deale of barrennes, coldnes, disorder of thoughts,
giddines, in my course which costs mee deare; the Lord smiles not, but
hides himselfe and my heart is gone toward fasting, and prayer; but
Lord prepare my soule, and bow thyne eare and meete us in the
ordinance;

14. this day wee fast, and pray at perrye['s], the Lord drew neere;
humbled our pore soules; and more will I wait for; at night I meet Mr
Harlak:[enden] oh happy day, that I may pray, and converse with such
an one; oh heaven, heaven; where I shall have none but such;

15. oh sadly; because I was hurryed to a journye, before I had a good
prayer next my heart; yet something refreshed by Mr Harlak:[enden's]
companye oh deare god, now a litle meat that the world knowes not of;
some sweet tast[e] of the sweetnes of christ; some beames of thy favor
which may make mee refreshed, and may thaw my dead heart;

169. 16. Saboath; my heart downe the wind, the Lord seems to be absent,
what shall my pore soule doe; I will yet rowle my selfe upon the Lord,
and staye my selfe upon my god; I will creep into the clifts of the rocke
of my salvation;

17. I am much troubled ab:[out] my studys, I can doe nothing,

---

311 See note above, p. 20.
312 Colchester Hall lay in the parish of Takeley, Essex, just south of Elsenham in the hundred of
Uttlesford. The estate appears to have belonged to the Wyberd family: Morant, *History and
Antiquities of Essex*, II, 572–3.

bec:[ause] I cannot pitch what to doe[;] Lord chauke[313] out some way to mee, wherein I may see thee clearelye and may live with peace within; oh rid mee of this saplesse dead place that I may serve thee freelye;

18. I groane under this heavy burden first of sin, deadnes, unbeliefe, awckn[ess][314] to good and exmide,[315] frownes from heaven; and the coast darke; And then this saplesse place, that I live in, barren of any love or power of godlinesse; oh Lord, thou knowest, I cry out for anguish of spirit; oh when shall some way be made that I may serve thee comfortably, though with bread and water;

170. 19. now I goe to the Earle of Norwich[316] his house; L1d:[y] makes much of mee; but I returne to Epping heare mr simson;[317] of D.[ear] G.[od] is faithfull; a sweet comfort for the soule to rellish in the midst of these billowes of temptat:[ion] and sorrowes abroad, and at home; the L[or]d hath inlarged my heart now to rowle my selfe upon faithfulnesse and the G.[od] of truth; I have got a litle start of unbeleife; Lord more; Let the life, that I live be by faith in the son of god;

20. A litle up, quickly downe; oh dead hearted companye, what a heavy pulback is it in my course; Lord some way, where I may honour thee, with a free conscience; without regrette, though with a dish of greene hearbes, with a threadbar[e] coate; And now a litle of thy selfe, that I may rejoice in thee, however Let thy faithfulnesse uphold mee and that to the end;

21. I live uncomfortablye by reason I am not setled for calling, I know not what to doe; faine would I goe in gods way; and as yet it is not cleared to mee, I will waite to see what the Lord will reveale to mee;

171. 22. full of disorder, bec:[ause] of unsetlednes in calling; and this sad deading company in the familye; Lord draw neere to mee, and uphold my spirit from failing, put in zeale new, and wisdome, to deale with rugged dispositions, uneven tempers that litle regard the power of religion; And now Lord, some of thy selfe that I may lye downe in thyne armes, Let mee be safe in the secret of thy tabernacle;

---

313 Chalk.
314 See Glossary.
315 The word 'exmide' does not appear as such in *OED*. The nearest possibility that has been identified is 'ex' added to 'mid' meaning 'out of in the midst of', that is, isolated, excluded. However, this can be no more than a suggestion.
316 Sir Edward Denny was the Earl of Norwich who died in 1637. He resided at Waltham, Essex: Denny, 'Biography of Sir Edward Denny', p. 257.
317 The Wednesday lecturer at Epping could have been one of several 'Simson's, for instance the chaplain of Sir Gilbert Gerrard, part of the Barrington circle. It may well have been Sidrach Simpson, a rising star who would have appealed to the congregation at Epping. He had attended Emmanuel and held a curacy at St Margaret's, Fish St, London. He had been troubled in the metropolitical visitation of 1635 and less than a year after this date he emigrated to the Netherlands, joining William Bridge and others to develop an independent congregation at Rotterdam. He was later famous as one of the 'dissenting brethren' promoting Congregationalism in the Westminster Assembly: *DNB*; Paul Seaver, *The Puritan Lectureships: the politics of religious dissent, 1560–1662* (Stanford, CA, 1970), p. 257.

23. Saboath, sadded, because of Stevens the caviler;[318] such an one in a company is like a dead flye in a box of ointment, makes the companye unsavory; oh Lord, that I might live among thy servants, though with bread, and water; oh some mercy, some waye make that I may serve thee sweetly and not allways among bryars, and thornes, and to wash Æthiopians;[319]

24. I am hurryed with endless thoughts and cannot settle to worke, and have the lesse comfort, at lying downe yet the Lord hath a litle thawed my heart this evening, in the midst of opposition, he caryes mee on, Lord I blesse thy name that leavest mee not;

172. 25. my burden is yet upon mee, and I groane under it; the L[or]d yet a litle rejoices mee in this, that he hath sent one into the familye, that is capable; J.[ohn] W.[right] with whom I may pray; and he is yet present with mee to inlarge mee in the midst of discouragements; oh Lord yet more of thy selfe; there is litle else that I can rejoice in;

26. Now comes sad newes of my deare cosen Rogers of Dedham his death; our losse most sad; oh how happy for him; respecting terminus a quo, as well as ad quem; for just now that cursed [Bishop] wren had procured London to put downe his lecture; and the Lord then takes him to himselfe;[320] the Lord thus pluckes out our stakes that are sound out of the hedges; and rotten ones are put in; how soone is such a hedge pushed downe to let wrath come in; oh let mee live his life, and dye in the faith with him; so dying I may rejoice eternallye with him, grandfather and all other the saints of god; He dyed the 19 of the monthe; buryed 21. Mr Knowles preaches;

27. who am I, pore dust, that I should live that I should have one morsell to refresh mee, one libertye to pray, oh how many of gods deare ones injoy not the tithe And yet oh base unthankfull, and discontented heart;

173. 28. Now I goe to Colne, my hearts loade is removed for a litle time, I rejoice to breath with the saints; yet the Lord sees it best for mee to live with bryars, and thornes; oh Lord, the use; the use; even to rub of[f] the rust that is behind;

29. the Lord inlarges mee in that familye; I am happy, when I can but pray among the saints; Yet my heart puffs; Lord, Lord convey some of

---

318 See above, p. 74 and n.
319 The last part is a gesture towards Jer. 13:23 – 'Can the Ethiopian change his skin, or the leopard his spots? then may ye also do good, that are accustomed to do evil.'
320 Samuel's uncle, John Rogers, the renowned lecturer of Dedham, Essex. After a long career, with occasional disciplinary troubles, Bishop Wren of Norwich in a fit of pique apparently asked Archbishop Laud to silence Rogers, when he found that no horses were available to him in Ipswich because they had been taken by people travelling to hear Rogers preach just over the county border in Dedham. The lecture was suspended on the grounds that it was likely to aid the spread of disease but, when Rogers requested to have his licence renewed, he was refused. As the godly saw it, this hastened his death. His funeral sermon was delivered by John Knowles of Colchester. See Webster, *Godly Clergy*, pp. 213–14.

thy Lord Jesus his humilitye into my breast, else this proud heart, will disquiet mee, and overthrow my sweet peace with thee; I am something sadded by reason of Wethersf:[ield] b5s3n:[ess] g3rl:^{s} are s111c34s;^{321} and I am troubled to heare it; Lord help mee from such sad pangs for thy goodnes sake;

30. Saboath; very much sadded with melancholy pangs; followed with them; I have my loade upon mee, in respect of meanes without place; and my distempers within; oh Lord give strength against them, that I may serve thee sweetly; and may find sweetnes in nothing but X;

174. 31. Downe the wind, my heart is at an ebbe; I mourne, that I cannot so walke with god in the day, that I can rejoice in him at lying downe; oh some sweetnes yet Lord for thy tender loves sake;

Novemb: 1. Something refreshed by Mr Fullers^{322} sermon mariage of Xt, and the soule;^{323} and by the communion of saints; oh more brokennes, tendernes, sweetnes in thy love, some of thy mariage love oh my husband;

2. I make a shift to rub on porelye, and disconsolatelye in this wretched place Lord help mee, I groane under this burden; shew thy selfe more clearelye, reveale thy love, to comfort my distressed sp:[irit] and shew mee some way, wherin I may walke;

3. the desire of my soule is toward the Lord, oh that my heart were so prepared, that I could walke more sweetlye, and closelye with him; oh pardon my weakenesse, and if thou Lord canst spye out any integrytye, accept mee in thy son; And yet shine more clearelye into the darke corners of my soule;

175. 4. this day I have set apart to seeke the Lord in secret; and about 5. went to Dix:[on's] for a meeting; but I cannot find the presence of Xt as faine I would; yet the Lord has raised faith a litle to take hold of his strength, and make peace; oh smile now, at lying downe, that I may rejoice in thee;

5. this day wee give thanks to the Lord for he hath caused us to triumph over our, and his adversaryes; mr Lee preaches out of 21 psal:[m] 11.^{324} they intended evell ag:[ainst] thee; they imagined a mischeivous device, but they could not prevaile; a fit text; Lord thou

---

^{321} It is not at all clear what the 'Wethersfield business' was that prompted Rogers' conclusion that 'girls are salacious'.

^{322} It is not possible to identify this Mr Fuller from among the many Fullers serving as ministers in East Anglia at this time.

^{323} Fuller is preaching on the Song of Songs. See Webster, 'Kiss me'.

^{324} Mr Lee may well be Thomas Leigh, the schoolmaster at Bishop's Stortford on whom see Venn; Urwick, *Nonconformity in Herts.*, pp. 124, 696, 699; Smith, *Ecclesiastical History*, p.56. If this was the minister, then he was preaching the day after he had buried his son: HRO D/P 21–29/41, entry for 4 January 1636/7. Another possibility is William Leigh, the minister of Groton, the home town of John Winthrop. The Scripture was Psalm 21:11 – 'For they intended evil against thee: they imagined a mischievous device, which they are not able to perform.'

hast tried us with former favors, wee have forfeited them and the[re]f:[ore] art thou now incensed ag:[ainst] our citye, a plauge; and universitye in Kayes colledge[325] begun; Lord stay, Lord quench; oh command back the sword, and the angel, that thou hast commanded to destroy;[326]

6. Saboath, and sacrament, the Lord hath graciouslye looked towards mee, and hath not wholly forsaken mee in these ordinances; though I cannot find him in the perfection of sweetnes; oh but he hath made mee to rowle my selfe upon his covenant, sealed, and willingly to

176. seale backe to him againe; oh my god, I will take hold of the strength; the strong mercyes of my god in his praise confirmed this day; and so will I make peace with him;

7. myne eyes yet wait upon the Lord, but I have cause to mourne, that by reason of unresolvednes in studyes I pitch upon nothing, but thinke and sigh away most of my time[;] oh Lord shew some way, wherein with cheerfulnesse, and setlednesse I may honor thee; oh that in the ministrye; rather had I convert one soule then cure many bodyes; thy way yet would I faine choose;

8. Now I goe to Mr Baringtons,[327] the L[or]d inlarges mee, gives mee freedome in speaking; my heart rejoices in the sweet societye of the saints; my Lady Massam makes very much of mee; Mrs Barington excells in vertue I scarse know 2. in there places alike;[328] my heart rejoices in my new acquaintance;

9. now wee fast, and pray at Hatfeild wee give the whole day to god sweetlye; in publique, and private together; the L[or]d goes out with mee Lord heare, Lord heare, downe

177. with plauge sins, take away the stubble, that the fire of thy indignation may goe [inked out] out; and Lord thy destroying angel stop him;

10. Now I come home to my sc1b:[329] flocke, to oynt them; though it bee but to drawe it in; that is all I can doe, and scarse that some times it

---

[325] Gonville and Caius College, Cambridge.

[326] The image is taken from I Chron. 21:11–12 – 'So Gad came to David, and said unto him, Thus saith the Lord, Choose thee Either three years' famine; or three months to be destroyed before thy foes, while that the sword of thine enemies overtaketh thee; or else three days the sword of the Lord, even the pestilence, in the land, and the angel of the Lord destroying throughout all the coasts of Israel. Now therefore advise thyself what word I shall bring again to him that sent me.'

[327] The home of Robert Barrington at Hatfield Broad Oak.

[328] In meeting Lady Elizabeth Masham and Dorothy Barrington, Rogers was meeting two of the leading patrons of the puritan ministry in Essex. Masham was the daughter of Sir Francis Barrington and married Sir William Masham of Otes in High Laver, Essex. One of their chaplains had been Roger Williams of Rhode Island fame. See Hunt, *The Puritan Moment,* pp. 219–34; Arthur Searle (ed.), *Barrington Family Letters 1628–1632, Camden Society,* 4th ser., 28 (1983).

[329] There are a couple of options for the meaning of 'scab'. It could be an abbreviation for 'scabrous', that is, roughened or indecent, salacious or difficult to deal with. From what follows it is more likely to simply be an abbreviation for 'scabby', that is, covered in scabs

breakes out; heere a push of drunkenness there a scab, of profaning gods name; &c A proud heart is fearfully up, the Lord in mercye pull it downe; I see the Lords dealing towards mee in setting mee in th3s pl1ce[330] where I am not loved; it is to pull downe this same base sp:[irit] of mine that is ready to insult upon account, and respect;

11. wee have had our weeklye meeting this night, the L[or]d lef[331] mee not; it is mercye he should not, considering what an intolerable proud heart I have oh some ease of it Lord; it is that thou knowest, that disquiets mee, and cuts the bond of sweet peace betweene mee, and thee; oh an humble heart, and broken for these wretched times;

178. 12. I beg, but the Lord is angry for the base pride of my heart, for my lightnes, selfe seeking; oh Lord I desire to lay them downe oh that I might be strengthened to overcome them; Lord thaw, Lord humble Lord cause my soule to beleive, and draw thee neere, and smile, and give mee satisfying peace;

13. Saboath oh I want bread ther[e]fore is my soule so leane; I want the presence, and the sweetnes of Xt in his ordinances, and thence doe I sit desolate, and like a mourning dove but yet myne eyes are towards thee I will stay my selfe upon my G.[od] and my Lord; and I shall face my beloved again after a while;

14. the Lord sweetly keepes my heart in tune to seeke him; though his backe be turned; yet certeinly it is to weep, and he will say at last, he is Joseph,[332] I will waite to heare what the Lord shall say; for he will speake, and by speaking create peace;

15. my heart is much damped, and sadded my sp:[irit] is much bound up, and straitned, oh unloose mee Lord, and put in a bleeding, broken heart; in my sorrows looke upon mee, and that shall quiet mee; I will yet looke toward thee;

179. 16. Now wee fast at Farnham, the Lord inlarges mr sedgewick mightilye his sp:[irit] plainleye; the Lord thawes my heart sweetlye; and I can lye downe in some sweet assurance of acceptance through Xt; oh Lord let none of our pore suites be lost: oh deare god, be not angry ag:[ainst] the prayers of thy dear ones, who in the strength of thy command have gone out to thee; oh downe, downe with the enimyes of thy truth, and lord lift up, the heades of thy people;

17. there is some effect yet remaining upon my heart of the fast, my soule looks yet towards the house of mourning; and I will peice in with them; myne eyes wait upon there; oh thy church, thy church, Lord;

---

or, perhaps a little more delicate, for 'scabious', that is, having symptoms of scabies. Thus his ministrations can, at best, treat the surface molestations of the disease without completely removing it.

[330] This place.
[331] 'Left'?
[332] Probably a reference to Gen. 45:1–15 when Joseph reveals himself to his family after a long separation, removing their fears and delivering promises of happier times.

restore the libertyes of thy faithfull ones, shut not thyne eares to the prayers of thy saints; but poure downe thy wrath upon the kingdome of antiX[333] shall his brats may come to revive;

18. I am under hatches now; oh what am I in all services, if the L[or]d of strength leave mee; feeble and weaknesse; oh deare god, some of thy selfe; Let that good sp:[irit] of thyne bee a * Comforter to mee; I have litle else to joy mee in the wretched place I am in;

180. 19. the lord strengthens mee to hang at the breasts of a promise and to sucke for milke; and though but litle comes, yet still I am strengthned to sucke; oh I will wait upon the Lord, it is good dying while I lye at gods feete, looking up, though troubled;

20. I adventure my soule upon the promise and if I perish, I[']le perish by cleaving to that and if I be saved, I[']le be saved also no other; and I[']le live, and dye in the faith, and hope of it; yet is thy covenant of mercye, yet thou wouldest have mee, to rejoice and, even then, when my soule is at the lowest in respect of feeling; in covenant and promise strength ther[e]f:[ore] I weakenes will live; And so when I am weake, then am I strong;

21. I am bound up, by reason, either of imperious, or false spirits; thus am I faint to groane under this burden, I know the Lord aimes at the pulling downe of my proud heart; if I were amongst some that should embrace mee, my heart would be lifted, and that much worse then * streightnes;

181. 22. In these decaying times, the Lord hath stirred up our faithfull minister to declare the will of g.[od] closely this day; mr Hues;[334] 4. Galati:[ans] 23.[335] child:[ren] of promise; the L[or]d hath thawed my heart by it;

23. Fasting and prayer at Farnham; Mr Hues; the Lord thawes my heart wrings out many teares and my soul can a litle rowle it selfe upon my G.[od] of peace, I will lye downe in faith, and peace; the Lord hath drawne neere my soule, and I will praise him; and lye downe in the armes of my first husband;[336]

---

333 Antichrist, that is, an agent of Satan sent to corrupt the church and the world.

334 This is George Hughes who was suspended by Laud from his lectureship at All Hallows, Bread Street, in London in 1635. He had earned his BD in Oxford, and while he was there he had tutored William Sedgwick, who was at Pembroke College. Hughes contemplated emigrating to New England but was dissuaded by John Dod of Fawsley, Northants. Shortly after 1635 he was chaplain to Lord Brooke at Warwick Castle. In the 1640s he became the leading Presbyterian minister in Plymouth, Devon: *DNB*; Matthews, *Calamy Revised*, pp. 281ff.

335 Galatians 4:23 – 'But he who was of the bondwoman was born after the flesh; but he of the freewoman was by promise.' Probably a sermon on the covenant between God and the Elect; Rogers frequently refers to 'the promise' and 'promises'.

336 A reference to Hosea 2:7 – 'And she shall follow after her lovers, but she shall not overtake them; and she shall seek them, but shall not find them; then shall she say, I will go and return to my first husband; for then was it better with me than now', the point being that Rogers knows that all other interests are secondary to his relationship with God.

24. my soule is yet among the mourners my thoughts are still upon zion, oh thy church, thy church in Eng:[land] Lord preserve it; turne away thyne angry countenance from the prayers of thy saints, and yet smile upon them, and make us yet the joy of the earth;

25. my hope yet is anchored upon my God and All-suficient: upon him will I wait to renew strength, oh hold mee up from sinking in this desolate place;

182. 26. Oh a straite hearte, a great while, but a litle loosened bef:[ore] I lye downe; myne eyes are upon the covenant and upon G.[od] through it, there will I hang, and in the strength of it, as in the strength of god will I walke the pore time of my sojourning heere;

27. my heart hath bine much sadded this day; the mournfull times, the wretched unspirituall ministry, that I live under the fruitlesse, saplesse familye that I sigh out, some time in; give mee my load; I can see litle of god in all of them; the Lord goes away also, but it is to shew mee my heart; he meetes mee a litle now; I will hang upon him, that weaknesse may be made strong;

28. yet looke I up to heaven, though not cleare; the L[or]d smiles not but it is to make mee more eager after him;

29. I goe to Mr Baringtons; rejoice in that good companye; my heart sweetly thawed by Mr Spurstows prayer, and exercise;[337]

183. 30. Fasting, and prayer, at Mr Harrisons my soule rejoices to be with the mourners in sion,[338] that I may peice in with them, the day is finished in private by mee upon 8. psal:[m] the Lord gave inlargement, yet a dead child I, will yet hang upon thee and wait; Lord doe but cast but for mee this hellish proud base heart,

Decemb: 1. I returne home, visiting G. Goldsmith[339] pray with her: inlarged toward her quickned at home; but yet the L[or]d is not neere with his smiles to my soule; my selfe ends, and proud heart grieve his sp:[irit] and send it sad to heaven; I will lye in the dust; Lord purge mee from all base wayes, make mee a cleane temple, and dwell with mee;

2. my god is still angry with mee, for the proud risings of my sp:[irit] for my base selfe ends in those companyes ut sup:[ra] the promise that no sin shall have dominion and the death if Xt applyed a little supples my heart and untyes it, oh more, yea establish mee by thy * free sp:[irit]

---

337 William Spurstow, an Emmanuel MA of 1630. His whereabouts are fairly vague in the 1630s; by August 1637 he had moved into the circles of John Hampden and took Hampden's home benefice of Great Hampden, Bucks. in 1638. He was later a major figure in the religious politics of the 1640s and 1650s, partly as one the Smectymnuans, the authors of the early anti-episcopacy treatises.
338 A reference to Isa. 61:3 – 'To appoint unto them that mourn in Zion, to give unto them beauty for ashes, the oil of joy for mourning, the garment of praise for the spirit of heaviness; that they might be called trees of righteousness, the planting of the Lord, that he might be glorified.'
339 Probably Agnes Goldsmith, married to Edmund, residents of Stortford: Glasscock, St Michael's, Bishop's Stortford, p. 152; HRO D/P 21–29/39, 9 March 1616.

184. 3. some smiles after conflicts, the Lord will love mee, but not my pride, not my selfe seeking; I will ther[e]fore be as I am, even nothing, and then shall I be encircled with free love; oh more, more warmth of soule by thy beames from heaven;

4. Saboath, oh I groane under an unsavory, rowling, roving fellow; oh I am starved for want of bread; Lord find mee out some redresse; oh thy gospell, with greene hearbs, and thread bare clothes;

5. A deep sadnes hath taken hold on mee many motives; 1. the church of god held under hatches, the walls of Jerusalem beaten downe;[340] pore suffolke and northfolke lying desolate by that cursed wretch wren;[341] the plauge abroad; 2. this wofull place; in whose companyes I am afraid to be for feare of some evell speech spil[l] out from an evell heat; oh my burden is intolerable; Future accomodations much perplexe mee; oh Lord, some way for preaching; oh my soule is in N;[ew] E:[ngland] 3. my g.[od] in covenant frownes.

185. 6. I arose with a dead, unbeleiving heart, the L[or]d gave mee a sweet frame of a broken sp:[irit] upon eager begging; (oh what doe I loose by drowsines) and yet are myne eyes to heaven, in a most pitifull barren familye that is enough to breake the heart did not the L[or]d uphold strangely;

7. Fasting, and praying; I goe to Epping and am disappointed of mr Dike my heart so sad and awcke,[342] that I could hardly get it up; and partly for that, a tyring journy, makes mee unfit for all things; my heart yet joines with the mourners, and myne eyes look up;

8. Some streightnes by reason of my carelessenes in preparation to dutye; affections downe; I would faine by the wings of faith, and love fly to heaven;

9. A great deale of discontent, and awcknes[343] arises; place; &c: unresolvednes for future; oh that I could get the start of all these hinderances; and could live above them by faith;

186. 10. myne eyes are yet toward heaven; oh I am pore, and weake, and sinfull every day; and it is free grace, I am not sent to hell but the compassions of the L[or]d faile not, he is mercifull every day; he knowes my mould, and fashion; he pardons; and yet is good to my soule;

11. Saboath, wee stay at home, and sweetly inlarged, and refreshed; L[or]d blesse all, to this pore dead, wretched family; and now drawe

---

[340] There are several candidates for this image, for instance Nehemiah 4:7, but the best candidate is Jer. 39:8 – 'And the Chaldeans burned the king's house, and the houses of the people, with fire, and brake down the walls of Jerusalem', which would equate Bishop Wren with Nebuchadnezzar, the Babylonians and their allies.

[341] Rogers is bemoaning the impact of the visitation of Bishop Matthew Wren, his first after his arrival in the diocese of Norwich: see Webster, *Godly Clergy*, pp. 207–14.

[342] See Glossary.

[343] See Glossary.

neere to mee in secret; oh thy love cleared and the coast so too; draw neere to mee; oh give mee thy presence and it shall suffice, in this woful world; Remember Sion; upreare[344] the broken wall;

12. I blesse the L[or]d; who upholds mee from sinking in this barren wildernesse; for new supply of sp:[irit] and gifts, inlargement this night; and that he hath cleansed mee from the filth of sin in some measure; oh a blessed thing; that my proud heart lustfull, and unbeleiving is banished; oh more strength for thy goodnesse sake;

187. 13. the L[or]d meetes mee a litle in private; but oh the fulnes of his love; yet infinite mercye that I may heare his voice though hid in the rocke, and his ha[n]d before mee and I cannot see his glorye; yet is his voice; the L[or]d gracious mercifull; &c; in the strength of this, will I goe out to fasting, and mourning the day approaching;

14. this day wee fast, and pray in private, the L[or]d caryes mee on through the day and gives mee strength he humbles my soule, and brings mee to stoop; but I cannot find the thawing, and melting, that I would; but I will wait, and hearken w[ha]t the L[or]d will say, for he will speak peace

15. I have not that sight of gods love, which faine I would, but the L[or]d upholds my heart from sinking, and causes mee to depend upon him, and I resolve to fast, and pray, and walk before him waiting;

16. my greife is that I cannot settle to any calling, I halt between two opinions; oh that I could tell, which were gods way, and I would submit to it; it disturbs my peace;

188. 17. Now have I gained some sweet thawings, and the Lord hath taught mee to lay hold upon his strength; to trust in his name whence my heart is sweetly pacified, and rejoices in the Lord; thus the L[or]d teaches us the lesson of beleiving, while wee are upon our knees; oh I will never depart from thee, but give the calves; &c:[345]

18. Saboath, not joyous, because of an heartlesse minister; Lord the meanes of grace, with bread, and greene herbes; oh some way, wher[e] I may honour thee, either in preaching, or hearing; oh bread, bread, what shall I doe without it; And now at my lying downe reveale thy selfe, that I may rejoice in thee;

19. By occasion I slipt the time of duty bef:[ore] familye exercise; and I find the want of it in much; the L[or]d hath raised my heart now to some confidence, and faith in his covenant and there I will lye; but for pardon and healing; this day note the bick:[ering]

---

[344] That is, rebuild.
[345] Possibly a reference to Hosea 14:2 – 'Take with you words, and turn to the Lord; say unto him, Take away all iniquity, and receive us graciously: so will we render the calves of our lips.'

betweene L.[ady] D1n:[ny] and E. E1rl. high sp3r[it]ˢ: though loving cannot cotton,[346] note; it:

189. 20. I have bine so dull, and untoward this afternoone, that I have bine unfit for any service to god, or in calling, unlesse my heart should be daily wrung up, I should not know w[ha]t to doe; I looke toward thee, in the day approaching, and to that sacrament, invite mee Lord, and give mee a stomacke to thy daintyes, Let faith apply thy whole covenant (for pardon, healing, new creature; &c;) daily, that it being mine, may be sealed; for that also is the new Testament in Xs blood; 1. the new covenant (purchased by blood) signed, and sealed;[347]

21. Fasting, my heart very streight, and awcke[348] to the dutye, as ever I felt it; oh pore meanes without; and discouraged within, yet mine eyes are towards thee;

22. my faith is in some measure a foot, to apply the covenant that same new testament in his blood; sealed to mee; oh thy table L[or]d, and those daintyes are in myne eyes; I will come, and take my food, bec:[ause] thou invitest mee;

190. 23. Straitned in dutyes, but the L[or]d does it, to shew mee, what is in my heart; I will abhor my selfe yet more; and though in darkness I will trust in his name; I shar[349] my Right:[eousness] and my g:[od] mercifull, gracious &c: there I will sleep, live and dye;

24. I have bine much straitned this day, and bound up: oh Lord unloose mee; that with libertye, and alacritye I may come to thy saboth, and sacrament, oh let desire, and faith be upon the wing; and let mee rejoice in that feast made unto my soule;

25. Saboth, sacrament, the fruit wherof I a litle injoyed in the ordinance, and now after it in this maner; my soule is not raised to tast[e] that full sweetnes in Xt; which I have done, and would have; but my soule lingers after him, and roules it selfe upon thy covenant which is nowe sealed; I will live, and dye upon thy promises and now sleep with it in myne armes;

191. 26. this night at mr sedgewickes, much revived by there company, so much the more as I see more closenes in him, and opposition to these cursed times; I lye downe rejoicing in god, staying my selfe upon his covenant sealed; I will love the Lord (how can I choose?) and feare him all my dayes;

27. Much refreshed, and inlarged by the company of some honest

---

346 Rogers notes that love cannot 'cotton' or succeed in resolving a dispute between Lady Denny and her daughter, Elizabeth.
347 Here Rogers is referring to the old Covenant of Works being taken over by the new Covenant of Grace in Christ's sacrifice.
348 See Glossary.
349 End of word lost at side of page.

young man, coming to prayer; Mich:[ael] Manning, &c;[350] my soule rejoices in them; though pore and weake; bec:[ause] of perfect hearts, as I hope; as our point was; Lord I give up my selfe unto thee; and lye downe in thyne armes; I am thyne save mee;

28. I went into Essex to uncle Longs: met Betty, and M. Fink:[351] I cannot use libertye, porelye, but there is some staine left behind oh I cannot be watchfull as I should bee; L[or]d take it of[f] and shew mee thy selfe againe, and let mee enjoy freedome;

192. 29. I goe to wethersfeild, where I continue some time; I want libertye of place, and I loose my heart quickly;

30. Libertyes, and companyes take of[f] my edge, and I cannot retire my selfe to gather of my lost strength;

31. Sports, shooting; &c; still eate into mee; I see it a mercye, that I am in a place, where I am restrained, if I should have full scope, it would be worse;

New yeare Jan: 1. [1637] unpreparednes to saboth makes it the more unwelcome; yet some sweetnes I find; but my eyes are caryed to vanitye and the wings singed;

2. I goe to Sudburye; delivered in journye, meet Richard,[352] joy to see some further hopes of grace; meet Hanna, desolate, yet her sp:[irit] tauzd, [sic] and she hath received good by all her baskinge; L[or]d more to her, and hers;

193. 3. I goe to Colne, the L[or]d caryes mee thorough service there, but oh a dead child within, I am not so lively, and sweet as I was wont, by reason of such a deale of defilement got upon mee;

4. I returne home, safe untoward indisposed; now I have yet some time to gather up my thoughts;

---

[350] See p. 36n. above for Michael Manning. This young man may have served as curate at Stortford in 1647. There is no record of a university education but this would be of no surprise in the conditions of the late 1640s: BL Landsdowne MSS 459 fo. 109. A Michael Manning was baptized in Stortford in 1609; if this is the same Michael, he would be four years older than Rogers: HRO D/P 21–29/39, entry for 16 July 1609.

[351] The identity of Uncle Long is unknown. It is possible for him to be a 'proper' uncle, as Daniel Rogers, Samuel's father, had three sisters about whom we know little (Waters, *Genealogical Gleanings*, I, 210), and it may be that one of them married into a family surnamed 'Long'. There is even less success with 'Betty' and 'M. Fink', in fact none at all. A later reference (below, p. 99) gives little further help, merely mentioning an Aunt Long. The close association with carrying his sister Mary may encourage an estimate that the Longs may have lived in or around Earls Colne. They may simply have been aunt and uncle as a term of affection, which would make establishing a connexion difficult.

[352] Richard may well be Richard Rogers, Samuel's younger brother. At this point it appears that Richard is living in Sudbury, perhaps with his sister Hanna. He may have been attending the grammar school there.

5. Hurryd to Downe Hall,[353] something awcke,[354] still, alasse happy they that have litle to doe in divers ocasions, and objects to snare them;
6. Not quiet in myne owne sp:[irit] bec:[ause] of the former flawes oh to keepe the consc:[ience] tender and clear (though without the sense of gods love) is a joyfull feast; L[or]d purifie it;
7. still so, scarse ready, be:[cause] of it; L[or]d teach mee how to rub of[f] this rust, and to be watchfull ag:[ainst] the time to come;

194. 8. Saboath; much deadnes, and hardnes I labour under a burden that I have laid upon my selfe; by my slightnes, impure use of libertyes want of place to gather up my selfe dailye, I am so sunke, that it must be a great power of the Lord to raise up my spirit; oh put away my transgressions, and receive mee againe into favour; shew mee, oh shew clearely the beauty of thy countenance, the sense of which I have lost;
9. Up, and downe yet much darkned and straitned, over that which was wont; L[or]d cleare up, that I may behold thee; there is nothing but bitternes in deceitfull sin there is nothing but sweetnes in X; oh my love let mee understand the sweetnes of thy mouth;
10. I meet with S. Shephead &c;[355] a great joy to see any that excell in vertue; oh that my habitation might be amongst them; now the L[or]d this evening hath drawne a litle neere to thaw my heart for my carelesse walking befor[e] him; oh L[or]d what a deale of gall

195. and anguish is there in deceitfull sin; I will therefore loath it, and make a covenant with myne eyes, and lips, that they goe not out to folly any more;[356] (Lord give grace on ocasions unavoydable) oh the sweetnes of Christ to the soule that rellishes nothing above him; oh thy selfe, Lord, thy selfe, and faith to be my evidence of things not seene;
11. Fasting at Farnham, a litle thawed; but ag:[ain] much deaded and sunke in my spirit; oh the sp:[irit] of holines being greived and sent sad to heaven by my vanitye and loosenes at wethers:[field] (where I have bine often foyled nota:) is not easily brought back from heaven; L[or]d

---

[353] There were two Downhalls in Essex. One was in the parish of Rawley in Rockford Hundred and seems to have belonged to the Clopton family early in the seventeenth century. The other manor and mansion was in the hundred of Dengie and the parish of Bradwell near the sea. It belonged either to the Mildmays or the Everards in the 1630s: Morant, *History and Antiquities of Essex*, I, 277; II, 376–7.

[354] See Glossary.

[355] This S. Shepard was probably Samuel Shepard, who emigrated to New England in 1635 with Joseph Cook and Roger Harlakenden. He was the half-brother of Thomas Shepard, the minister at Cambridge, Mass. In 1635 Samuel and the Cooks had registered as servants of Roger Harlakenden, but they soon became freemen in Massachusetts: C. E. Banks, *Planters of the Commonwealth, 1620–1640* (Baltimore, 1972), p. 168; *Winthrop Papers* (Boston, Mass., 1929–), IV, 124; Michael McGiffert (ed.), *God's Plot: the paradoxes of puritan piety being the autobiography and journal of Thomas Shepard* (Amherst, Mass., 1972), pp. 38, 64. Shepard may have returned to England with one of the Cooks to encourage others to emigrate.

[356] In margin: large '*'.

I will seeke thee; oh be fe[a]red and help mee to overcome all my corruptions in the habit of them;

12. Not that perfect peace in G.[od] which my soule would have; nor the wound of conscience so healed; but I will lye in gods way; I will beare his indignation; yea though he suffer satan to stir up guilt, and horror;

196. 13. my heart is in a great deale more quiet from the former guilt; and a litle of my faith, and peace I have recovered; Oh my soule, never returne any more to follye; what fruit? &c Look to thy lips, to thy heart, to ocasions, which have been often the candle to sing[e] thy wings;

14. now I can say most comfortablye, G.[od] is my refuge, my rocke, in him will I trust; he hath (after some conflicts this day) new opened the clefts and let mee into them, where I will sleepe safe this night;[357] Lord more faith every day, wherby I may dwell in thee; and be above the feares of the world;

15. Saboath, a litle refreshed; and setled; my thoughts are toward heaven; I want meanes food, and bread, bread of life but the L[or]d will either uphold mee with small helpes; or else provide better for mee; I will waite to see gods way, and hearken what he will speake, for he will provide, that which shall be best for mee, it is his promise sealed;

197. 16. something sadded by my blrr:[en] c4mpln:[y][358] L[or]d myne eyes are towards thee; oh support my sp:[irit] I am sunke but raise my heart to beleiving thy covenant, and living upon it;

17. my sp:[irit] falls; and the greived sp:[irit] seemes to be gone sad to hear oh I will beare; &c: but I will yet stay my selfe upon my god;

18. I am much distempered with thoughts of future accomodations oh that I knew gods way: Lord shew mee it; that I may serve thy providence in it; Lord nowe let mee lye downe in thyne embraces, even with joy and well afraiednes;

19. Some comfort in good companye mr wilson, and mr sedgewicke; and in family dutys; I find the Lord drawing neere to mee oh more of thy selfe, Lord, and remove all my sin guiltines, and let the coast be cleare;

198. 20. Good company cheares mee at G. Jinnings; Mr wils:[on] sedgewick: &c[359] oh how beautifull is the face of a godly man; Lord thou knowest my soule closes with them; And I lye downe with them in my bosome; oh let mee lye downe in thyne;

21. I am much sunke, and the L[or]d seemes to frowne; yet my heart

---

357 Song of Songs 2:14 – 'O my dove, that art in the clefts of the rock, in the secret places of the stairs, let me see thy countenance, let me hear thy voice; for sweet is thy voice, and thy countenance is comely.'
358 Barren company.
359 The name 'Jinnings' is common in Hertfordshire and in Stortford itself: Metcalfe, *Hertfordshire*, pp. 147–8; Glasscock, *St Michael's, Bishop's Stortford*, pp. 140, 166, 187, 193.

hath said and so will; that though he kill mee, yet by his grace will I trust in him; Faith shall leake a peeking hole into heaven;

22. Saboth; discomfort, and sadnes suficient without and within; but the L[or]d supports mee; so that I looke towards him; but oh the life of the publique ordinance, none to that healing; and quickning; Lord in the want supply by drawing neere to mee in secret;

23. Sadded with the unsavorines of this place; who are whole, and no need of the physician; hig[h]ly conceited, without bottoms; L[or]d; L[or]d; some good, some fruit; And now smile on mee;

199. 24. Ebbing, and flowing; in heaven in the morning; sunke ag:[ain] by night, and the L[or]d leaves mee to a streight heart, to shew mee my heart what is in it without his contin:[ued] grace; but yet my confidence is not removed; thou art my god, in thee will I trust;

25. I am much unsetled by reason of an unresolved mind; I am halting still betweene 2. opinions Oh Lord to thee I looke; I am in a great streight; In my sp:[irit] I am sometimes up; somet:[imes] downe; the Lord still shewes mee my insuficiencye; and his Allsuff:[iciency] to which I looke, and am refreshed;

26. my heart is looking, and sad by weighing the state of things in this wofull land; oh will the L[or]d be yet gracious to us; or will he destroy us yet further; I Lord will hide my selfe under thy fe[a]thers and there shall I be safe;[360] and in thyne armes will I now sleep;

200. 27. I cannot have that full, and complete peace in my god, bec:[ause] I have not setled to my study, thoughts take mee up; and I knowe not which way yet to take; L[or]d point mee out some way, and establish mee in it; And for thy favour I blesse thee; and that I yet feare thy name; and walk in some light, which is as life;

28. my heart above the creature, and sweetly rellishing the love of god in the morning; but yet sinking quicklye; yet always my heart is fixed, and so shall be; in thyne armes will I sleepe;

29. Saboth; most uncomfortable, bec:[ause] the bread which I have had, hath not bine well moulded, nor well baked; oh how does such stuffe make a saboath unwelcome, and undelightsome; Lord drawe neere to mee now; my soule is towards thee; cleare the coast, and let mee see thee;

30. sadded, by reason of unfruitfulnes in calling; and roving thoughts, that have hindered mee in studyes; L[or]d pardon and settle my mind; and shew mee thy selfe;

201. 31. I cannot walke so fruitfully as I should doe, and therf:[ore] have not that comfort; yet God hath sweetly drawne neere to mee this evening; gives inlargement and some sweet communion with himselfe; and now

---

[360] Psalm 91:4 – 'He shall cover thee with his feathers, and under his wings shalt thou trust: his truth shall be thy shield and buckler.'

I am in his armes I will dye, if he will have mee; This night as I was reading Mr Hoopers story; where he cryes out I am hell; &c.[361] I laid (m2g:) flat;[362] who is allwayes jangling very unsavorilye; the fruit of her carnall reason; Lord remove these far from them and give them to rellish sp:[iritual] truths more then ever; L[or]d grant it; L[or]d grant it; February 1. greived to consider my unfruitfuln:[ess] L[or]d pardon it to mee; and yet count mee as one of thyne beloved; I will sleepe in the armes of thy covenant;

2. Downe, yet up; flying to heaven but ready to sinke downe by this clog[363] at the heele; but I will yet fight it out, because god will have mee; I thankfully acknowledge L[or]d, thy goodnes in bowing the hearts of the 2. M:[adam] D2:[nny] and E. E.[364] in outward subjection, being commenced; How far thy comfort in J. Wright and Mary;

202. 3. mourning for warpings,[365] and not fruitfull in honoring g.[od] in my calling; yet blessing the L[or]d for the integritye, and sinceritye of my heart in the midst of failings; I am thyne, and I would walke still better;

4. melancholy pangs assaile mee, make mee unfit to praise the Lord, yet have I in some measure over come them; and see some footing in god for faith; I will yet roule my selfe upon my god, he is my help, in him will I trust living, and dying; Let thy saboth be my delight;

5. Saboath made a delight by the efect:[ual] preaching of Mr Sedgew:[ick] (son of man manifest to destroy works of Satan) herein, my soule rejoices that all adversarys are, and shall be destroyed, I will stand still, and see the salvation of the L[or]d; the L[or]d is my god, in him doe I trust in his armes I sleep, I live, I dye;

203. 6. my heart is fixed; yet in some darknes; but my whole stay is in the Lord my Allsuficiencye, for my self, and his ch:[urch]

7. the bent is yet towards heaven but many flaggings; Earthly discourse by Mr H2rl1c:[kenden] hath made heaven a litle strange; but myne eyes looke up yet, and shall doe;

8. the Lord is yet neere mee; and my god of whom may I be afraid; he is my joy, from him have I all sweetnes, and comfort; oh more of it, deare god in this valley of teares and sinfulnesse;

9. my burden is my unfruitfulnesse in calling; and this unfruitf:[ul] family; my joy is in the Lord, who leaves mee not, but supports mee daily with new strength of grace, wisdom and courage; and now Lord shew mee some good, ever lift up the light of thy counten:[ance]

---

[361] Rogers has been reading an account of the martyr John Hooper, the bishop of Gloucester and Worcester, in Foxe's *Acts and Monuments*: Seeley and Burnside, *Acts and Monuments of John Foxe*, VI, 636–58, but especially p. 657.

[362] This may be a reference to Lady Denny as 'Meg' but this is unlikely as Rogers usually uses an abbreviation of Lady Denny. It may be that 'Meg' was a servant in the household.

[363] See Glossary.

[364] Madame Denny and Elizabeth Earle, her daughter. See above, p. 35.

[365] See Glossary.

10. myne eyes are yet to heaven, and my hope is in my god Alls:[ufficiency;] I mourne that I can love him, feare and obey him no more, and bring no more honour to him: oh heaven, heaven, when I shall;

204. 11. now I visit mr wilson, quickned, and refreshed; sadded by the coming in of that wretch J. Wiseman;[366] (Remember him and by the pain) Lord thou art my hiding place, ther[e]fore am I safe;

12. Saboth, sadded at first; raised by the word, at Farnham; quickned by talking with some saints; much rejoycing in g.[od] in all these; oh who am I that I should have a naile in gods temple; and now heare of the victorye, that X hath got over all the works of Satan, and his accomplices; 92. Psal:[m] 5.6.7.[367]

13. my bent is to serve the L[or]d in my innocencye, and uprightnes; oh pardon for my weaknesse, and failings;

14. now wee hurry to ware[368] in the coach, I, the more comfort, because I am called; my heart is framed yet towards the Lord; and I find more content, and sweetnes in him, then the world can in the creature, He is my Lot, hiding place, inheritance; I will dwell in him, and cast my care on him in welldoing;

205. 15. my soule is yet inlarged to run in my race, though weakely, and slowly; oh pardon, and yet quicken mee; Let my soule prosper as my body doth; oh thy church;

16.[369] my soule this day rejoices in the saints, my portion oh L[or]d let it be with thyne in my estate soone; the L[or]d hath sweetly ravished my heart at lying downe, and made mee to weep for thankfulnesse, ever teares of joy; oh blesse[d] be thy name for my Xt given, and with him all things;

17.[370] my head is now inflamed with love to Xt; and his saints; I see the L[or]d drawing neere to mee in thankfull praising his name, for his exceeding much favours, which he hath given to mee; gifts, strength, ag:[ainst] corrupt:[ion] hell; courage in this place this night; I lye downe with abundance of peace in sp:[irit] plainely; &c. Mrs Roe buryed;[371]

18.[372] Thou hast ravished my heart with thy flagons; thou hast given mee the witness of

---

[366] John Wiseman was probably the eldest son and heir apparent to Henry Wiseman of Elsenham in Essex: Metcalfe, *Essex*, part I, p. 530. As noted above, Wilson was probably the curate of Elsenham where one branch of the Wiseman family lived.

[367] Psalm 92:5–7 – 'Oh Lord, how great are thy works! and thy thoughts are very deep. A brutish man knoweth not; neither doth a fool understand this. When the wicked spring as the grass, and when all the workers of iniquity do flourish; it is that they shall be destroyed for ever.'

[368] Presumably to Ware, Herts.

[369] In margin: '*'.

[370] In margin: '*'.

[371] A Stortford resident: HRO D/P 21–29/41.

[372] In margin: '*'.

206. Xs blood to sprinkle mee so that thou shouldest passe mee over unpunished;[373] justifye &c: of water by sanctific:[ation] and myne new sp:[irit] declaring arguments from heaven, and thy sp:[irit] sealing mee; thou hast shewed thy selfe to mee (14: Joh:[n] 21:)[374] oh let that sp:[irit] be a sp:[irit] of thankfulnesse;[375]

19. Saboath, wherin the L[or]d still caryes mee aloft by Mr Bruer at takely[376] oh my soule is refreshed because I have found the L[or]d in his ordinance; the saboth is my delight I will ever joy in god; my god; oh when shall I be with thee forever;

20. A litle downe againe; a great reason bec:[ause] I hath not my bredth in preparation to family dutye; but L[or]d thy selfe; more love more grace; my heart is fixed;

21. L[or]d my heart is yet inclined to walke before the L[or]d; inlarge mee daily, that I may run; pardon failings; pore service and accept mee; I will live, and dye in thyne armes;

207. 22. There is a vexing emptines in the creature; there is a satisfying fulnes in god, and ther[e]fore my heart is united to him, and resolved never to start from him to folly, and dry pits; I hear M. D2; will swear by g.[od's] truth; faith; which sads my heart most heavily;[377] L[or]d teach mee; &c

23. I rejoice in the saints; and my soule abhors these cursed sychophants every day more, and more; I have re[-]read mr Burtons book, and my heart and portion be with those that contend for the faith, whether in life, or death;[378]

24. this day, mr sedge:[wick] and I goe to mr wilsons; wee rejoice in each other, and animate one another to suffering; oh let my lot be with the righteous in all conditions;

25. A litle downe, but I will goe on in my uprightnes, and see for more

---

[373] Rogers moves from an image taken from the Song of Songs to a plea related to the passover when the plague sent to Egypt excepted the people of Israel: Exodus 12.

[374] John 14:21 – 'He that hath my commandments, and keepeth them, he it is that loveth me: and he that loveth me, shall be loved of my Father; and I will love him, and will manifest myself to him.'

[375] In margin: '*'.

[376] Edmund Brewer, minister of Castle Hedingham, preached at Takeley, Essex.

[377] Evidently Lady Denny made an oath 'by God's truth' which disturbed Rogers who, like many like-minded people, tried to refrain from swearing by anything in ordinary conversation.

[378] Rogers could have possessed *For God and King*, the two sermons that Henry Burton, the minister of St Matthew's, Friday Street in London, had preached against bishops, the referent, presumably, of the phrase 'cursed sychophants'. Burton had called the bishops caterpillars and 'antichristian mushrumps'. Charges of sedition came forth immediately, and when Burton did not appear, he was suspended and an order issued for him to be apprehended. On 1 February 1637 Burton had his doors forced and his study searched. He was taken to the Fleet prison, soon to be joined by William Prynne and John Bastwick. It is possible that Rogers may have read another of Burton's works upon hearing of his fate. See Stephen Foster, *Notes from the Caroline Underground: Alexander Leighton, the puritan triumvirate, and the Laudian reaction to nonconformity* (Hamden, Conn., 1978), pp. 46–56.

from him who hath forgiven much; oh the saboath and fasting, strength faileth;

208. 26. Saboath; quickned toward night, and rejoicing in god; my delight is in the Lord, his saints, and truth oh more of thy selfe Lord, for I have none in earth but thee;

27. this day this wretched t4r1n: hath vented his f5ry ag:[ainst] F. Wr3gh:[t] and M1r:[y] and ag:[ainst] religion;[379] this is your country profess:[ion] all of you so proud; oh cursed venom of a guilty consc:[ience] Lord humble the proud insolent serred heal of the one; and discover the holownes of the other, and make them thyne, that thou maiest have glory by them; I am heart sicke of them;

Lord myne eyes are towards thee for the fast, I come to thee in thy strength, this strength of thy grace and covenant; oh help us, and poure downe of the sp:[irit] of repent:[ence]

28.[380] this day wee have set ap:[ar]t for fasting and prayer, at G. Ingh:[381] the Lord mightely went out with mr sedgew:[ick] and with mee, more then ever I found I thinke; oh how hath the Lord

209. wound up my heart to heaven, pitcht mee upon X; and sent mee downe strength thorough him; and gave mee footing for faith in his promise; and great raptures of joy, and peace from thence; oh a thankfull heart for his exceeding goodnes; more humblenes Lord, more stillnes of emptiness and nothingnesse, and more fulnes in thy selfe;

March 1. A litle downe, but yet I will raise my selfe up againe by the promise[;] pressed, but not oppressed; the Lord it may be drawes a curtaine before his face, because my heart is ready to be puft up by extraordinary revelat:[ions] and gifts yesterd:[ay] but I know his grace is sufficient, and ther[e]f:[ore] I will stay my selfe upon my god;

2. Dampt, but elevated ag:[ainst] satan strives; and I fight by strength given; the Lord sometimes seemes farr; but appro[a]ches ag:[ain] oh the admirable comfort in a cleare cause; a pore heart; and the smiles of god upon it;

210. 3. Downe the winde; sinking, but catching at the twig, and there will I hold; bound up, but the L[or]d will either inlarge mee, or else his grace

---

[379] The identity of the name 'toran' does not appear to be recoverable. There is no apparent scriptural source. It may refer to Robert Tournay, the minister of Springfield, Essex, but the connexion would be undemonstrated and unlikely. Perhaps 'toran:' refers to a torrent of anger against F. Wright and Mary which came from someone in the Denny household. It may well be about two people, as in the following prayer he seems to be pleading for God to take on two individuals. It is difficult to decipher, not least because of the term 'serred'. This may be 'close-packed' and maybe in the sense of intransigent; this would fit in with a contrast between the two people involved. Even this is strained and it is best left to readers to interpret for themselves.

[380] In margin: '*'.

[381] There was an Ingram family within Stortford parish: Glasscock, *St Michael's, Bishop's Stortford*, pp. 70, 142.

is sufici:[ent] to support mee; much vexed with Mr Newcom:[en][382] for his cavilling and base discourse; &c

4. the frame of my heart is to honour god, and to serve him in purenes of conscience, and faith; my heart is sometimes lifted up to heaven; and tast[e]s some hidden Manna oh my daily portion of it, Lord, I intreat thee;

5. Saboath, the L[or]d graciously looks upon mee; and gives mee some sweetnes, hath inlarged my heart, and ther[e]fore will I run his way; oh thy church Lord, what shall pore England doe our eyes are towards thee;

6. Free within; the son, and the truth of the promise hath made mee free indeed; I will walke before the L[or]d therf:[ore] in that glorious freedome of the son of god; L[or]d pitty pore desolate England;

211. 7. Downe a litle; but my heart is yet to heaven, hearkening, oh pardon my weaknesse, and untowardness;

8. Visitation Archb:[ishop] I goe to L[or]d of Norwich; he plays the wretch ag:[ainst] goodnesse:[383] I sp:[it?] but oh that I had done more; I heare Mr Dike; goe to Lady Massams;[384] well entertained a godly Lady, and the face of the familye is good; but remember the guilty consc:[ience] of h3m: Mr Bp: dead;[385]

9. I return to Meshech;[386] yet the L[or]d is as neere mee in this my wildernes, as in other places, upon him I will yet live;

10. In this I have comfort, that my heart is fixed to choose the L[or]d to be my god upon all termes; and I desire to fear him, love him; and depend upon him, in his sure promise; oh how I shall be thankfull enough to him;

212. 11. pressed much in spirit; and being for a while in darknesse; but supported; and a litle chearing toward lying downe; L[or]d some fruit to those that have a name, with Sardis,[387] but dead I feare and oh thy ch:[urch] when L[or]d, when;

12. Saboath, this profane wretch Butler plays the wofull wretch (let

---

[382] Possibly the Thomas Newcomen who lived on High Street, Stortford: Glasscock, *St Michael's, Bishop's Stortford*, pp. 146, 175.

[383] Rogers describes the metropolitical visitation of the diocese of London which began on 28 February 1637. On 8 March, the Vicar-General, Sir Nathaniel Brent, and other officials, notably Matthew Wren as indicated by Rogers' reference to the 'Lord of Norwich', met at Stortford. The visitation was seen as a serious threat to many of Rogers' friends and colleagues. See Webster, *Godly Clergy*, pp. 235–45.

[384] Jeremiah Dyke and Lady Masham of High Laver, Essex.

[385] 'Mr Bp' may be William Bishop, the minister deprived of a benefice who was mentioned earlier; see above, p. 63.

[386] See above, p. 54n; Ezekiel 32:26, 38:2, 39:1.

[387] Revelation 3:1–6. The church in Sardis was falling away from the true way although there were a few 'which have not defiled their garments' (v. 4); this is plainly an allegory for the Church of England as Rogers saw it.

every soule be subject)[388] my heart sadded; but at Farnham Mr
simson;[389] revived, and much comforted; L[or]d let it hold, and sweeten
all my life still with thy favour;

13. Sad bec:[ause] I can be no more profitable thorough the day; L[or]d
pardon all my lustishnes; &c; I rejoice yet in the L[or]d, a great joy in
M1r:[y] Mountf:[ort] the L[or]d caryes on his worke secretly in her;
L[or]d doe more for her; I lye downe in my gods armes; mourning for
the glory of Israel which seemes to be departing; L[or]d stay, let the
Ark of thy presence continue with us;

14. I mourne, that I doe so litle good in my calling; bec:[ause] of
unsetlednes; L[or]d pardon my heart is yet comforted that the L[or]d
my glory is with mee, in whose armes I sleep;

213. 15. the L[or]d is my help at hand, he strengthens mee to speake to the
consc:[ience] of these, by his owne rule; oh that he would sp:[eak] it to
them; (but oh how I feare that speech; pray no more for this people)
the L[or]d gives mee a clod in token of my inheritance;

16. my soule rejoices in good company oh pardon all failings; and
warme mee with thy love; susteine mee from sinking in this wretched
place;

17. pressed, and loded, and streightned and clouds arise betweene
g.[od] and my soule, but the L[or]d shewing mee his frownes does it;
that I knowing his wrath might persuade, these pore blind creatures;
and the L[or]d hath more than ordinarily poured downe a sp:[irit] of
pitty and compassion to those that are without mercye; the L[or]d
drawes neere, and came soe to feare his name, and trust in it;

214. 18. the Lord hath taken this course with mee to pitch mee among
bryars, and thornes, that they might teare of[f] a deale of scurfe,[390] and
basenes of[f] from my spirit: I blesse thy name oh L[or]d for thy great
love this weeke past; oh more of thy selfe; I beg not for riches or
honour;

19. Sad by our old wretch Butler;[391] quickned by Hatf:[ield] sermon; the
Lord gives now, and then, a precious bit, to the nourishing, and
strengthning of my soule; I blesse thy name who hast made thy saboath
my delight accord:[ing] to the inward man; cary mee on oh L[or]d;

388 Butler was preaching on Rom. 13:1 – 'Let every soul be subject unto the higher powers. For
there is no power but of God: the powers that be are ordained of God.' From Butler's earlier
remarks on conformity and so forth, it seems likely that he was pressing ceremonial
conformity as a spiritual requisite.
389 This may be Sidrach Simpson, at this stage lecturer at St Margaret's, Fish Street, London.
He had been part of the Feoffees for Impropriations, an earlier scheme promoting godly
preachers. He was troubled during the metropolitical visitation and, although he submitted,
he emigrated to the Netherlands in 1638. When he returned, he became an important figure
in the 1640s, not least as one of the authors of the Apologeticall Narration (1644).
390 Rogers is refering to scurf in the sense of flaky or scaly matter adhering to or peeling off a
surface rather than dandruff.
391 Richard Butler.

20. the L[or]d is good, and gracious yet; he is my god in him will I trust; blessed be thy name for any life, sweetnes in X, porenes[392] mainteined; oh who am I a wretch that should have so much from thee;

21. I am disheartned, and melancholy for this sad familye; but my peace, and joy is from heaven, and my reward, and crowne is there, I will waite for it in well-doing;

215. 22. Downe the wind, discontent, untoward in reg:[ard] of place, accommodat[ion] future; oh how shall I know gods way that I may walke in it, that I may trust him in it;

23. my service is pore, and ragged, yet is my heart toward heaven; L[or]d pardon the once, and accept the other freely thorough Xt;

24. I goe to Hatfeild, revived, and comforted in sweet freinds, and the L[or]d drew nigh; yet there is a difference between my self abroad, and at home; that I might love home better;

25. still there, my heart rejoicing in the word, good company; and heart leaping at N:[ew] E:[ngland] whence clm[e] a freind with g44d n2w:[s][393] blessed be god who yet prospers his; oh L[or]d shew mee thy way, and I will walk in it;

26. saboth, downe, yet heart is fixed, and feares the L[or]d, and my trust is in him my rocke;

216. 27. I am in darkes, yet will I feare thee oh my god; thou art my sheild, my rocke, my god in thee will I trust;

28. myne eyes are towards thee; oh satisfye my soule with thy loving kindnesse, crowne mee with it; others say who will shew us any good, my good is thy smiles;

29. the coast is not cleare, L[or]d take away these clouds, and refresh mee with thy favour; I yet looke up; oh look thou downe; shew mee the way, wherin I shall goe;

30. my heart is marvailouslye inlarged for N:[ew] E:[ngland] in the company of Mr Simson;[394] and other such freinds; L[or]d thy way shew it to mee; and thy lovingkindnesse;

31. N[ew] E[ngland] N.[ew] E.[ngland] is in my thoughts my heart rejoices to think of it; L[or]d shew mee thy way in it; and bow the heart of my father; I am thyne I lye downe in the shadow of thee my almightye;

217. April: 1. this day I set apart for fasting, and prayer in private in espec:[ially] records ab:[out] N:[ew] E:[ngland] &c: the Lord hath sweetly drawne neere to mee and given mee an heart to blesse his name for his goodnes to mee the more of N:[ew] E:[ngland] I have, the more of god I injoy; L[or]d yet further shew mee thy selfe, thy lovingk:[ind-ness] and also the way wherin I shall walke;

---

[392] 'Poorness'.
[393] Evidently a friend came from New England with good news.
[394] Possibly Sidrach Simpson.

2. Saboath, comfort at Hatfeild; my hearte is above, rejoicing in god, and his saints; these 2. dayes have bine sweet to mee; and the more I have of god, the more I sigh after N.[ew] E.[ngland] and the more I thinke of that, I thinke I find the more of god; L[or]d find then out my way thither if it be thy will;

3. strong for N:[ew] E:[ngland] and my peace much in the love, and smiles of g.[od] upon mee; my hope is only in him; I will walke before him in a perfect way till I come to sion:

218. 4. My hope is yet in my defence and rocke, he is my god, I will not be afraid; I will resolve to love him the more, and cleave[395] still closer to him;

5. The Lord shewes mee my selfe to be nothing without his continuall assistance; he shewes mee also his favour, he gives mee sweet peace, and he will pardon and doth my weaknenesse; oh help mee to delight greatly in thy commandments;

6. my soule longes to injoy god in the puritye of his ordinances; and to walke in his way; oh when shall I see him, when shall I lye in the embraces of Jesus Xt; when will he kisse mee with the kisses of his mouth, amongst those that excell in vertue;

oh blesse the Lord, oh my soule, for that sweet communion I have with him in secret; for that horen [horn] full of hidden manna,[396] which he hath given mee this day; and a great while;

219. 7. my brother comes, my sp:[irit] sunke myne eyes are towards thee, I visit Thom:[as] Dixon; hopes;[397] L[or]d doe good to his soule; thaw his spirit; and bestow free compassions upon him; now Lord goe out with mee, and lead mee in thy way;

8. wee goe to Hatfeild, something sinking; and home rejoice in our friends; it is a mercye that wee in any peace may see one another;

9. Saboth, sweetly thawed in the morning before the sacrament, and in it, and much after it; oh let my soule savour of it all my dayes;

10. A litle drye, yet revived ag:[ain] oh how hard is it to keep life in varietye of ocasions and companyes, and out of a mans place is it not, that the L[or]d would have mee rejoice in doing my proper place;

220. 11. Heare Mr Marshall;[398] quickned goe to Colne, refreshed with the societye of the faithfull, Lord evermore of this bread;

12. wee goe to Colchester, at Mr Knowles,[399] thawed, and comforted; it is mercye that I heare now and then some word of life, and comfort;

---

[395] See Glossary.

[396] Rev. 2:17 – 'He that hath an ear, let him hear what the spirit saith unto the churches; To him that overcometh will I give to eat of the hidden manna, and will give him a white stone, and in the stone a new name written, which no man knoweth saving he that receiveth it.'

[397] Rogers receives a visit from his brother, probably Daniel who, we learn a week later, did not favour Samuel's emigration. He is later cheered by Thomas Dixon, a resident of Stortford.

[398] Stephen Marshall.

[399] John Knowles, the lecturer from Colchester.

13. Heare my brother; X redemption; varietye of companyes ready to doe mee hurt; I pray at Mr Purples with freedome, and inlargement; the companye sweetlye affected;[400] L[or]d some good to heare pore soules, and I shall have enough; oh purge out all dayes of pride

14. Now wee part I cary Marye; great worke ab:[out] N:[ew] E:[ngland] (oh I wonder at my fathers and brothers sp:[irit] note it)[401] I come to aunt Longs; lovinglye and sweetly enterteined by all; cousin Jenkens;[402] freedome there oh some fruit, and remember them;

15. I part with all, and returne to my mill oh my heart fails; but I will waite till god shew mee his way;

221. 16. Saboth, sadded at first, a litle revived at Aubury, by mr Good; and so at home, I see Thomas Dixon full of comfort (after stormes;) a dying; Blessed be thy name who hast done much in answer to prayer for him;

17. I goe to Mr Good at Aubury,[403] Drye, as a bone; my heart is sunke; I am ready to loose it abroad, and can hardly find it againe; oh L[or]d thy presence; it is life and marrow; give mee it;

18. something gained from heaven; a litle tendernes; for my pride, self ends, slacknesse, wantonnesse, that were ready to overtake mee at wethersf:[ield] L[or]d recover to mee thy smiles, and shine, and I shall have enough

19. my soule mourns after the L[or]d; oh my unsetlednes, unfruitfulnes lasines, pardon; accept mee; oh thou dost; dost thou not? now the court comes; sadding my spirit with those unsavory base spirits;

222. 20. Court companions sad mee; I can see nothing of g.[od] at table, and my soule is pained; loathes these base wayes; pore Mary Mountfort,

---

[400] Rogers appears to have heard a sermon by his half-brother Daniel, and then gone to the house of a Mr Purples. A Christopher Purpill, gent., lived at Wethersfield, where he died in 1643; this was probably father of the Christopher Purple of Essex who matriculated at Emmanuel College in 1649: Venn.

[401] Before coming to his Aunt Long's, Rogers seems to have convinced Mary, his sister, that the idea of emigration is a good one, but then notes the opposition from his brother and father (see above, p. 97).

[402] Presumably the Jenkens mentioned here was William Jenkyn (1613–85), the eldest son of William Jenkyn, the vicar at Sudbury, Suffolk until his death in 1618. The younger William's mother was a sister of Daniel Rogers, Samuel's father. Her name was Mary, and after the elder William's death, she had married Adam Harsnett of Cranham, Essex: Waters, *Genealogical Gleanings*, I, 210. Jenkyn, through the efforts of his mother, obtained an excellent education at St John's College, Cambridge and then at Emmanuel College, moving to Emmanuel with his tutor, Anthony Burgess. His whereabouts are uncertain until 1639. In 1641 he left a lectureship at St Nicholas Acons, London, for a rectory in Colchester, returning to London in 1642. He was a strong Presbyterian spokesperson, barely escaping execution in 1660 and becoming famous as a preacher against and resister of conformity: DWL 'Life' in John Quick's MSS 'Icones'; *DNB*; Matthews, *Calamy Revised.*

[403] Mr Good of Aubury was possibly either the William Good who represented Hertfordshire in the Westminster Assembly (Urwick, *Nonconformity in Herts.*, pp. 395–6) or he may be Thomas Good or Goad LL.D, Regius Professor of Law at Cambridge. He served as a civil lawyer and was a friend of Archbishop Laud: Brian P. Levack, *The Civil Lawyers in England, 1603–1641* (Oxford: Clarendon Press, 1973), p. 233.

disconsolate, in the deepes; wee pray together, the L[or]d softens us, thawes us, and gives us some heate, and warmth, L[or]d more, and more dailye ever till wee shall come to injoy it perfectlye;

21. my heart mournes, bec:[ause] god seemes to stand afar of[f]; and to draw the curtaine; oh I have done very foolishly in greiving the L[or]d; by giving way to my selfe at D5nm4[w];[404] ag:[ain] oh that I might doe so no more but that with modesty I might walke; and L[or]d heale my consc:[ience] and distempers, put away my sins, and let the coast be cleared;

22. why standest thou afar of[f], oh my deare god, why hidest thou thy selfe from mee; my heart is yet fixed, greives for my loosenes, folly; I will come unto thee, oh my first husband, oh hugge mee in, thyne armes, and I shall be safe;[405]

223. 23. Saboth; held under in regard of sight, yet my soule feares the L[or]d; and ther[e]f:[ore] trusts in his name; and there I stay; oh remove all guilt, and rust, and restore to mee as much, as ever I had, and adde more; M. M5mf:[ort] pray; with mee this night; gives thanks for that which god hath done by mee; oh unworthy wretch I; oh blessed be thy name;

24. my soule yet hangs upon the promise, fearing the L[or]d; oh but my failings and weakenesse in the day, L[or]d pardon, and cleare, and now I will lay mee downe quietly bec:[ause] thou makes mee to dwell in safety;

25. my head is running, and giddy by reason of abundance of ocasions, and companyes; oh how unfit am I to beare them L[or]d thy selfe, thy selfe, put thy gladnesse into my heart and I shall be satisfyed;

224. 26. Drooping by reason of unfruitfulnes and giddines, the L[or]d supports my spirit yet to looke to him; L1d:[y] rise up in the midst of exercise; the L[or]d carys mee on to gall her in duty; shee netled; I quickned, comfortd, having peace I rejoice; J. W.[right][406] G. Farrow, M. Mountf:[ort] and I joine while 2. a clocke, our soules caryd aloft; and now will I lye downe in gods arms thankfully,

---

404 Dunmow was a parish in Essex. It was a place where Rogers visited his cousins.

405 The 'first husband' is taken from Hosea 2:2 – 'Plead with your mother, plead: for she is not my wife, neither am I her husband: let her therefore put away her whoredoms out of her sight, and her adulteries from between her breasts'; that the plea is of an adulteress rather makes the question about God's distance rather a rhetorical question.

406 All of the people in this passage (John Wright, Mary Mountford and Farrow) prayed with Rogers on a fairly regular basis, and throughout the previous week Rogers and Mary had prayed together frequently as if something special was at hand. Farrow may have been George Farrow who went to New England in 1637 and settled at Ipswich (Whittemore, *Genealogical Guide*, pp. 186–7). Those plans for emigration could have played a part in the gathering that took place this 26 April. Certainly a group from Hatfield left for New England around 24 April, when Lady Judith Barrington recorded gifts at their 'going to New England', gifts of 5s to 'Goodman Graves daughter' and £1 to 'Goodman Howe': ERO D/DBa A2 fo. 29v.

27. sometimes downe, but raised this evening, thawed; a comfortable tranquillity in my mind; Xs peace, though tribulation; oh that my soule were filled with thankfulnesse for that which I have found; I cannot see him clearly; but yet thorough a glasse, darkelye;[407] I cannot open the casement, yet I can see him thorough the quarrells though sometimes the soile be upon them; and a dew; yet the beames of his love dissolve them; oh comfortable ways; this god I shall one day see clearlye as faith, faith to waite;

225. 28. my heart comforted by N:[ew] E:[ngland] sparke dining with us; litle drooping ag:[ain] and shut up; yet lying down a litle opened, and raised; and will cast my soule, and confidence upon my dear g.[od] for more;

29. much damped this afternoone, but the L[or]d does it to shew mee my selfe; I will then be nothing and it is free grace; and free love that shall comfort mee heere and save mee hereafter; the L[or]d hath a litle softened my sp:[irit] and inlarged me to faith, by which I will run my selfe into him my hiding place, and sleep safelye;

30. Saboath, wherin my bent is to god; and my greife is in my straitnes, and unbeliefe, and I mourne, that there are any clouds; and any dew upon the glasse thorough which I should see him, whom my soule loveth;

226. May. 1. L[or]d pardon all weaknesse, all hideboundnes, deadnes, disquiet, unbeleife, folly; and subdue all for thy servant; and draw neerer yet to my soule, that I may be safe;

2. Held under (a guilt, of my unfruitfulnes, giddinesse; old sins and most scarse rubbed of[f]) a great while; at last I have gained a prayer of my strait, dead heart; and the Lord hath graciouslye smiled upon mee; and given mee a comfortable answer; oh I will love the L[or]d forever;

3. A sweet serenitye possesses mee in the mor[n]ing; I rung up the pegs, and set all in pretty tune; but yet are ready to fall againe; I am faint to ring them up yet againe; I have smoothed the banke and it crumbles, and I must smooth yet againe;

4. my soule is fixed upon my god; I will believe in his name; he is my allsuficiencye; he is my Sun; he hath given grace (some thawings, meltings humblenes faith he pardons all) and he will give glory at last;

227. 5. the Lord hath drawne neere to mee; smiled, thawed mee, made faire weather in my soule; oh how shall I praise him; I will walke before him in a perfect way; I will beleive him;

6. my heart is resolved to depend upon the L[or]d; I mourne that I can walke no closer with him; oh help mee; and shew thy selfe unto mee;

7. Saboth, sadded with poison in stead of bread; I goe to Hatf:[ield]

---

[407] I Corinthians 13:12 – 'For now we see through a glass, darkly; but then face to face; now I know in part; but then shall I know even as also I am known.'

there a litle revived; the L[or]d drawes neere in the familye, and
supports mee gives mee inlargement in the companye of good people;
G: Dane;[408] I rejoice in the saints of god, my delight shall be in those
that excell in verture;

8. visiting G. Jinnings; oh how good is it to see his heart taken from
clods; and flying higher; and thom:[as] Dixon; L[or]d strengthen, and
answer all his scruples; G. Mountfort; L[or]d pitty her;[409] my heart is
toward thee; oh cleanse mee and love mee;

228. 9. Yet my soule is heated, and my life is sweet, because I injoy god,
who is the life of my life; I will hang upon thee; I will praise thee;
bec:[ause] of that glory, which thou hast given mee; who will also give
more;

10. Still shall my soule praise the L[or]d who gives a serenitye; and
heavenly smiles; he meetes mee in the morning; in the day, in the
company of the saints; N:[ew] Eng:[land] going away; and revives my
sp:[irit] pore M1r5:[410] tormented with this furye[;] the L[or]d *
eminently supports, and gives her a blessed use of all; oh how shall
wee be thankfull enough for all his goodnesse to us;

11. Blessed be the L[or]d, who hath crowned mee with lovingkindnesse;
who hears mee; smiles upon mee; who denys mee creatures, and gives
himselfe; he dwells with mee, by his good sp:[irit] and walks with mee; I
will be thyne; to praise thee of day and to eternitye;

229. 12. I am pressed heavily with the hellish sp:[irit] of thy cursed J2c1b:
continuall brawling espec:[ially] with M2r:[y] and J.W: my soule is
vexed with her abominable courses; L[or]d redresse, and deny not the
presence of thy sp:[irit] while I am Labans houle;[411]

13. I goe to Hatfeild, refreshed, by uncle;[412] Mrs Baring:[ton] &c: oh
how pleasant is the presence of the saints; my delight; &c: I will lye
downe in thyne armes; I will dwell safelye;

14. Saboath, wherin I have injoyed a great deale of god; I stay at home

---

408 G. Dane is among those who depart for New England on 21 May 1637 (see. p. 103 below).
He is probably related to John Dane who had emigrated earlier and later left his famous
autobiography: 'John Dane's narrative, 1682', *New England Historic and Genealogical
Register* (1854), pp. 147ff., esp. pp. 152–3. See above, p. 29.

409 Rogers prayes that God might pity 'G. Mountfort'. This was because her husband William
Mumford had died that day: HRO D/P 21–29/41, entry for 8 May 1637. Mary Mountfort
may have been a member of this grieving family, providing at least a partial explanation for
her feelings during this period.

410 Perhaps 'Maru:' is Mary, but any more than that would be a guess.

411 Jecab or Jacob, the crafty but unfortunate son of Isaac and Rebekah, continually quarrelled
with his uncle, Laban, and Laban's son. Yet though Jacob remained tied to Laban's
household, God intervened to limit the arbitrary actions of Laban and his sons: Gen. 31:7–
55. Rogers pleads for God's spirit since, as a Jacob, he feels captive to the household of
Lady Denny as his Laban.

412 Presumably, Rogers met his uncle, Ezekiel Rogers, at the Barringtons. Ezekiel had served as
chaplain to the family in the 1620s before Sir Francis presented him to a rectory at Rowley,
Yorks.: Hunt, *Puritan Moment*, pp. 221–4, 232.

and M1ry and I are at it,[413] and the L[or]d affords of his presence; and thawes our hearts; oh good is the L[or]d, I have tasted how good the L[or]d is, and ther[e]fore now I come unto him; yea in his armes doe I lye downe; weake, and tyred in bodye; but with my spirit up; I will sleep in christes armes;

230. 15. Sadded, that I cannot be so faithfull, and fruitfull in my studys, as I should bee; I mourne for it; L[or]d direct mee and shew mee thy selfe in my studyes; settle my head, to thy service in my calling; Oh thou lettest mee lye downe in thyne armes, and ther[e]fore I am happy;

16. the Lord does yet support mee in this wretched place; he is not wholly absent from mee, I desire to depend upon him, oh help mee to walke before thee in my integritye; oh my failings, oh my comings short, and drawings backe;

17. My soule rejoices in thee; creatures are vile; oh blessed be thy name who hast blessed mee with all sp:[iritual] blessings in thy Christ; and for the support and strength in this place; among tygers, and wretches, among bryers, and thornes;

231. 18. I come with praises to thee oh L[or]d, who from day to day dost carry mee on with calmnesse, and sense of thy favour; thou hast crowned mee with lovingkindnesse, which shall make mee glory in thee; G. Mountfort with mee; litle thawed, in returne to praier oh praised by thy name;

19. my sp:[irit] is a litle flagging, oh how shall I ascend, where my head is;[414] my head is yet fixed; I breake m1tch: betw:[een] J.W:[right] and G. B:[415] Lord stay ther: sp:[irits] I will yet lye downe in thyne armes;

20. my heart melts to see this family yet so unsavory, and there creaturelynes; I am unsetled; L[or]d provide some way; L[or]d let me live, under the roofe of those, that feare thee; though with greene hearbes; when L[or]d shall, this be granted; oh give mee this; w[ha]t ever thou denyest; that I may have the companye of those that fear thus; I should sinke, but that the L[or]d supports mee;

232. 21. Saboath, I have lived a most joyfull life; in the morning caryd above dung, and drosse, and my thoughts, and heart where my treasure was; and supported thoroughout the day; at night our N:[ew] E:[ngland] company; G. Dane; Blakely; Chandler; &c:[416] gave mee

---

[413] This Mary may be Samuel's closest sister rather than the Mary Mountfort at Stortford.

[414] Rogers may well be using 'head' in the sense of 'leader', that is, 'Lord'.

[415] G. B. is hard to identify with any certainty. It may be Goodman Bull, mentioned earlier, or Goodman Blakely who appears two days later.

[416] Evidently Rogers was present when a group or company of those people in his neighbourhood heading for New England met for prayer before they departed. Of those mentioned, only the identity of 'Chandler' is traceable. This is probably William Chandler who ended up in Roxbury, Mass. in 1637: Whittemore, *Genealogical Guide*, p. 82. Of G. Dane and Blakely little more can be said other than that they may be members of families who had already emigrated: ibid., p. 44. See above, p. 29.

occasion of inlargement, and the L[or]d was with us graciouslye, and draw neere, and made us happy; oh blessed be the L[or]d for his unspeakable goodnesse; I will depend upon him [for] my help, my comfort, my allsufficiencye all my dayes;

22. my heart is sadded much; (our N:E: neighbours wee take our leave of) and the untoward buisinesse of M. M45nt:[fort] falls out; her fall into a heavy agony; but the Lord answered at Embusons; where a private ch1mb:[er] was called for; never forget it; L[or]d doe more, and sanctifie it; it c1m[e] by the 1. s3te; hidden half a year, now revealed by a providence, L[or]d, L[or]d, thou god of extremityes, be at hand; help, and ease;

233. 23. I have found the L[or]d gracious to mee, revealing still his love to mee; Blessed be his name; this pore wretch M1r: M:[ountfort] is yet under an heavy burden L[or]d ease, for thy promise sake, and let s3n be for good; that well may praise thee;

24. much distracted, and pestered by these hurrying thoughts, and they come in to trouble mee in dutyes, Lord help, and command in all, that I may walke before thee in a perfect way, that thou maist come unto mee;

25. I visit thom: Dixon, raised in spirit; oh an happy returne of prayers; wee blesse thee oh L[or]d; I am pressed, and sunke, a wretch, a litle revived at night; oh more, more; I will cast my selfe upon thee;

26. Now the tearfull falling out, betweene ML1rg: and S1m:[uel][417] playes the devell ag:[ainst] M1ry M:[ountfort] J[ohn] W[right] and S1m:[uel] Lord gave

234. S1r:[ah] patience,[418] that fettered her heart; Lord free all miscariages and speak peace, yet, and then all tribulat:[ion] withal shall be nothing;

27. We goe to Topsfeild;[419] the L[or]d supports mee,

28. 29. and the Saboath, sweetnes by companye

30. 31. with us, a great deale of joy in

June 1. them, and so in hearing at Finch[ing]field;

2. and goe to wethersf:[ield] and Sudburye; and

3. returne home this 3. June; I have bine sometimes up, sometimes downe; many ocasions, (though lawfull) and vaine ty[p]e of companyes, are ready to snare mee; oh hard, very hard to keep sweet comunion, and close fellowship with god; oh L[or]d it is my desire; and mourne that I cannot serve thee better, and cleave[420] unto thee, without distraction;

---

[417] The names of 'MLarg:' and 'Samuel' remain unidentified. Samuel may refer to the J. Samuel mentioned below.

[418] For the scriptural Sarah, see Gen. 17:15–19, 21:1–3. She was the wife of Abraham, who was barren but gave birth to Isaac at the age of 90.

[419] Perhaps Rogers goes with Lady Denny to Toppesfield where her daughter, Elizabeth Earle, lived, and then he separately made the rounds of his family, all of them being in Essex, except for Richard and Hanna, just over the border in Suffolk.

[420] See Glossary.

4. Saboath, my soule is fixed; yet a litle eloofenesse of spirit I find in mee; and the L[or]d seeminge to stand afar; and the old burden of familye pressing mee; L[or]d ease, L[or]d ease; declare thy selfe and shew mee thy way;

235. 5. A litle recovered[;] the bridegrome hath taken mee into his chanber [sic],[421] and comforted mee with his loves, and some calmnes, and serenitye hath come into my troubled spirit; oh L[or]d, more of thy selfe; it is my joy, and my strength; oh provide a way for mee; L[or]d grant mee to live among thy saints;

6. the joy of my god, is my strength I have nothing, that comforts mee but only the refreshings that I have from heaven; L[or]d evermore of this food, oh suffer mee not to be distracted with creatures but pitch my soule upon thee, oh let my heart be taken up;

7. I have seene the frownes of my god, this day, I have prayed, and beheld trouble, and distemper, in his wrath, and in this wretched familye; L[or]d I have prayed, that thou wouldest looke upon mee, and provide a place; yet if thou hast no pleasure in mee, behold heere I am; and yet will lye at thy feet;

236. 8. much inlargd, by the incouragm:[ent] from G. prestlands company; and quickned by G. Brewster &:[422] oh Lord in thy saints is all my delight; oh find out some way, that I may injoy thee in them; though meanlye; L[or]d more of thy selfe; I will sleep between the breasts of my beloved;

9. I lye under hatches this day; much sadded, that I pray among stocks, and stooles, carnall, undiscerning spirits, that rellish not the things of god; Lord this * one thing, have I prayed long for, that thou wouldest shew mee a way to serve thee comfortablye; oh that I may dwell among thy saints; I have bine under thy frownes; thou leavest; and I am weake and goe without courage in this disheartning place;

10. I goe to Hatfeild; refreshed with good companye; oh that I might but injoy it; L[or]d more of thy selfe, yet will I fix my heart upon thee, oh let the coast be cleare and let faith be yet stronger to a[p]pear,

237. 11. Saboath, the L[or]d keepes mee from sinking; quickens mee in some measure, gives mee an heart desirous to walke before him in a perfect way;

12. the L[or]d is yet gracious to mee; I am ready to droop, then he raises mee; he lets mee sometimes lye in the grave, but suffers mee not to see corruption;

13. Drooping, and something straitned, if the L[or]d departs, I am

---

[421] An adaptation of Matt. 25:10 – 'And while they went to buy, the bridegroom came; and they that were ready went in with him to the marriage: and the door was shut', part of the parable of the wise virgins.

[422] The names of Prestland and Brewster do not appear among the parish records of Stortford, although they appear to be local people.

nothing, I will ther[e]fore rejoice in my infirmityes, that the power of X may be magnified in mee;

14. I cannot keepe so close, as faine I would, nor be so fruitfull; it is my burden; and greife; oh L[or]d yet my heart is towards thee, and I will wait for thee; and in this, that thou leavest mee not, but caryest mee on with daily smiles (now and then) and favour I will praise thee;

238. 15. the Lord is with mee and I will rejoice in him; he hath brought perfect peace to mee, who hath inlarged my heart to stay my selfe upon him;

16. my heart is yet above clods, and dirt, and my god is my best portion, he is enough for mee, the more I mediate of him, the more I love him; I would faine walke better before him, ever in truth and with a perfect heart, and mourne that I can cleave[423] to him no surer;

17. the coast is comfortably cleared; and I doe yet behold the brightnes of his face; oh why L[or]d shouldest thou shew thy selfe unto mee, and reveale so much to mee who have forfeited all, as much I thinke, as a pore wretch in a great way of mee; oh free mercy to heale my backslidings, and receive mee graciouslye; I rejoice to thinke of thee, and thy saboath, and the daintys prepared for mee in word, and seale

239. 18. Saboth, and sacrament, at Farnham, much revived in spirit, and going away from gods table, as filling with marrow, and refined wines; oh that my soule could but be thankful;

19. my heart is yet fixed, though I feel still the backbyas,[424] much thawed by the company of Thom:[as] Dixon;[425] who lyes most heavenly, rejoicing in god and triumphing in the expectation of his crowne;

20. the Lord is yet with mee, and myne eyes are towards him, oh that I could but see him face to face; oh the glasse is something sullyed, and I see him but darkelye;[426]

21. this day fasting, and prayer (secretly generale every 3. weekes) at G. Perryes the L[or]d went out wonderfullye with mee; I thinke I never was so caryed out espec:[ially] ag:[ainst] the enimyes of the ch:[urch] the Lord serve, and grant, and let not our trail be lost;

---

[423] See Glossary.
[424] See above, p. 42n.
[425] Rogers describes the condition of young Thomas Dixon, who had lain ill for many months and had profited from Samuel's frequent ministrations. Though Rogers does not mention it, Dixon died and was buried on 3 July 1637: HRO D/P 21–29/41.
[426] I Cor. 13:12. See above, p. 101.

240. 22. Yet my heart is upon the L[or]d, in whom I must only trust, for he hath snatched away J. Wright from mee,[427] and this unworthy family; I must stoop, since the L[or]d will have it so; but I must live above creatures; upon a naked g.[od] without a powre; and more of thy selfe, I blesse thee for that I find in thee;

23. I sinke, but the L[or]d supports mee, and gives mee yet more of himselfe, renews my strength, according to his promise sealed to mee; the joy of the L[or]d is my strength; and carys mee above currish[428] natures, to trample all under my feet;

24. the Lord indeeres my heart to himselfe, more, and more; he overcomes mee with renewed favour, and smiles; I have enough; he takes mee into the moment of transfiguration and talks with mee; and sweetly witnesses to mee, that he hath graven mee upon the palmes of his hands; (Isia: 49:16)[429] oh then he will often looke upon mee, and also I shall never be put out; oh believe, and be thankfull;

241. 25. Saboath, wherin the L[or]d is graciously present to mee, and gives mee a great deale of comfort in pore m1ry m45n[tfort] whose head is much raised with joy, and peace; and in prayer with mee, gives abund:[ance] of thanks her heart, and mine, are brim full and running over;

26. the coast is a litle mistye, and I wonder, that the Lord should doe any thing to such a vile wretch; that he should vaile himselfe to mee, and reveale so much to mee; L[or]d pardon the hypocrisye, giddines, and unbeleife of a pore wretch, oh L[or]d I am hell, and thou art heaven;

27. It is wonderfull to consider, how deceitfull my heart is; I have injoyed the company of a great many of gods people this night; and my heart trusts so much in them; that it is not so much pitched upon god as it should be; I thinke if I dwell among them, I should be too secure;

242. 28. At Mr Archers a great conflict ab:[out] s2p1r1:[tion] to litle purpose;[430] my body a litle dumpish, but my faith not wholly downe; Jesus X yesterday, and to day, and for ever the same;

29. I am nothing but the L[or]d is all unto mee; oh who am I, a lump of sin, that the L[or]d should reveale himself so much unto mee; oh I cannot run over with praises, and thankfulnes sufficientlye to so good a god;

---

[427] John Wright, who has served as Rogers' spiritual companion in the Denny household, moved to another location. As Wright reappears later on in the diary, it is unlikely that New England was his destination.

[428] See Glossary.

[429] Isaiah 49:16 – 'Behold, I have graven thee upon the palms of my hands; thy walls are continually before me.'

[430] This may be John Archer, the minister at Hertford, or a local resident named Archer. Interestingly, after this 'great conflict ab:[out] separa:[tion]', John Archer, the minister, did leave for the Netherlands, so the dispute could have been about separating from the Church of England. For broader possibilities, see above, p. 30n.

30. I goe to Mrs Baringtons,[431] the L[or]d is with mee; but yet there is something in mee, mee thinkes, that I am not at home; the L[or]d would have mee love home better; a proud heart and selfe disquiets mee;

July. 1. there still, my heart sinkes, the L[or]d crosses mee in a place; he tyes mee yet to be among bryers, and thornes; the L[or]d shew mee his way; and give mee an heart to keep it; my heart is something sunke, be yet towards that oh my deare god;

243. 2. Saboth, something in a cloud, but my heart is fixed, and stayed upon the L[or]d, and that continues mee in peace; L[or]d teach mee to live upon feelings, and sight; let mee ever both in darknesse light trust in it;

3. the L[or]d denyes, what he hath formerly afforded; he frownes and leaves in some part, that I may know what is in mee; ever weaknesse, and nothing, and in the L[or]d is my strength; oh be my god, and depart not from a departing creature; but cleare away all my drosse and dwell with mee;

4. my heart seems to be a litle aloof of; but yet standing toward the L[or]d, who is my stay, and strength; L[or]d teach me to live by faith purely, and cleave[432] unto thee for ever without distraction; I have this night prayed with Mrs Earle being sicke;[433] her sp:[irit] much stooping; her consc:[ience] awake; complaining of her selfe; I have dealt plainely with her; L[or]d sanctifie all unto her;

244. 5. the Lord supports mee by a mighty power; and now cheeres mee by the coming of Mr Harlak:[enden] and wife; oh how deare is the company of the saints;

6. I rejoice in the L[or]d, who is my strength, he is my refuge, my resting place, my help, in whose presence is a confluence of all happinesse; in his bosome doe I lye downe;

7. I meet M[rs] Br4gr15;[434] a sp:[iritual] w.[oman] I ride with Mr Harlak:[enden] sp:[iritual] talke; wee mourne for M[r] Burton[435] &c the L[or]d drawes mee in some measure; my soule is yet fixed and I will wait for my charge, and for my crowne;

8. the L[or]d is with mee, caryes mee on in my course; gives mee daily

---

431 It is not clear which of the Barringtons he visits, but it is probably Dorothy, the wife of Robert and close friend of Daniel Rogers. Samuel Rogers probably would have said 'Lady' Barrington if he was referring to Lady Judith or Lady Joan Barrington, just as he notes 'Lady' Masham.

432 See Glossary.

433 For Elizabeth Earle, Lady Denny's daughter at Toppesfield, see above p. 35n.

434 Mrs Brograu may be either Dorothy Brograve, the wife of Simeon Brograve of Hemel, Herts. or her daughter-in-law, Hanna, the daughter of Sir Thomas Barnardiston of Kedington, Suffolk: Metcalfe, Herts., p. 33; see reference above to Brograves, p. 68n.

435 Henry Burton.

more of himself; and will still be mine, therefore I['lle not feare what man can doe unto mee

245. 9. Saboath, my heart much downe in the morning, straitned, we goe to Farnham, a litle thawed; Mr Harlak:[enden] gives us some thing at night; my heart thawed, and caryed above; but a deale of hypocrisye, and boasting comes in; and the L[or]d seemes to send mee a prick in the flesh to try mee; (his frownes, and a sad dull heart) but his grace is enough for mee;

10. my heart droops; be:[cause] I am out of exercise; Mr Harl:[akenden] doing all; but the L[or]d is not wholly absent; drawes neere; and quiets my soule, he is my support and refuge; I shall be safe in him; though I passe through the shadow of death;

11. my father comes, my soule rejoices in them both delivered; and now does my soule lye downe in thy presence for therin I have had fulnes of joy by beleiving this evening; often some clouds; oh blesse the Lord;

246. 12. my father heere still the Lord is with us in the ordinances; and drawes neere in some measure, thaw the heart, and increase faith, L[or]d yet more, that I may praise thee; I will lye downe in thyne armes;

13. the Lord was wonderfully with mee this evening; L[or]d fall downe selfe; and shew thy selfe still gracious, and every moment revere love least I should be exalted, the L[or]d set mee as a pricke in the flesh, L1d:[yships] b3tt2r t4ng; ag:[ainst] long pr11ng[;] Mr Harlak:[enden] m4d2r1tes;[436] L[or]d shew mee thy way and, that shall give mee strength, when I have it no where else;

14. I feele a boiling selfeloving heart ag:[ainst] h2r: vexing, there is yet a great deale of poison in mee, to be purged out; yet in duty at night, and since my heart hath bin in a most sweet, and heavenly frame; I behold the L[or]d loving mee, and giving mee his hand and su[illegible][437] to mee; I also will be his for ever;

247. 15. yet my heart is bent for god, and I can rejoice in him; up and downe; oh who am I, a warping[438] pore creature, that the L[or]d should acquaint mee with hims:[elf] and reveale more, then to the world;

16. Saboath, pressed, but not oppressed, still there is something, that carys mee out of my self to X my right:[eousness] and g[od]. my g.[od] in him, who is yet with mee ag:[ainst] the shadow of death;

17. sadded, and moping, only I know in whom I have believed; and whose spirit hath sealed mee; experience shall cause mee to roule my selfe wholly upon him, who is unchangeable in his promises backe with his oath, and seales;

---

[436] Lady Denny repeated her complaints about the length of Rogers' prayers and Harlakenden seems to have 'moderated', that is to say, tried to reconcile the two.

[437] As far as can be ascertained from the text, this might be 'sucaring', perhaps 'suckling'. This is, it should be noted, supposition upon supposition.

[438] See Glossary.

18. Raised againe, my confidence is in god my god; and I mourne that I should play the Sadducee to erre so often, in not knowing the scripture and the power of god;[439] now the promise is sweet, and the power of g.[od] to my word is great; I believe L[or]d; oh help mee ag:[ainst] my great unbeliefe;

248. 19. the Lord denys that sense, that I might live by faith upon a naked god, and a bare promise; my heart is fixed; I am much perplexed about my condition of changing; L[or]d guide mee for the best; let mee see thee in all; that I may praise thee;

20. the L[or]d clears, the coast in some measure reveales himselfe; oh sinfull wretch I, unfruitfull, creaturelye, vaine, dead unbelieving; oh that g.[od] should count mee as precious, and honourable, and smile upon my soule, and indeare my heart unto himselfe by his chaines of love;[440] L[or]d I am thyne I am thyne; I am overcome by thy looks, thou hast ravished mee with thy looks oh L[or]d Jesus;

21. sadded much, by this r13l4ng; Sh3m23;[441] who hath plaid the devell this night with F4g: ab:[out] M. M5mf:[ort] and ab5s2d h2r most basely, and hellishly; L[or]d shew the course, thou wouldest have h3m visit and yet more purified; L[or]d the art just ag:[ainst] h2r, for thou wilt have thyne not give way to any lies L[or]d, keep h3r and pardon, and humble

249. 22. now Jesus X is come, now, faith hath overcome my doubts, and distractions without; L1:[dy] playes the wretch still at table at noone, I silent, I have anger then shew, at my lying downe; L[or]d grant it to her also; Dr Good comes and Butler and her play the wretches, to thyne counsells; &c. with this generat:[ion] Lord I am thyne, thyne, and I will not feare thou I am a worme;[442] no not in the shadow of death; bec[ause] thou art with mee;

23. Saboath, downe, at mr Sedgwicks to avoid Good;[443] I am tamquam

439 A Sadducee was a member of the Jewish priesthood. In New Testament times they clung to the letter of the Jewish law and they outraged the people with harsh codes. They lacked a certain piety found in the Pharisees, and were seen as holding on to the letter of the law but losing the spirit: Mark 12:18, Acts 23:8.

440 This may be from Song of Songs 4:9 – 'Thou hast ravished my heart, my sister, my spouse; thou hast ravished my heart with one of thine eyes, with one chain of thy neck.'

441 Shimei was David's bitter enemy; he cursed the fugitive monarch. David's triumphant return to power brought Shimei to abject penitence, and David finally pardoned him: II Samuel 16:5ff., 19:17ff. The preceding word is probably 'railing' despite the last vowel appearing to be an 'o'. The object of his complaint is, unfortunately, unclear. The person involved abused Mary Mountfort to 'Fog' which seems to be an abbreviation for someone unknown.

442 Cf. Psalm 22:6 – 'But I am a worm, and no man; a reproach of men, and despised of the people.'

443 Dr Good, who appears earlier in the diary, causes some problems in the Denny household, and so Rogers attends Farnham in order to avoid Good's service at Stortford. See above, p. 99.

piscis in arido;[444] out of imployment; though litle comfort, yet it is to be doing; I lye there, I get a litle from heaven;

24. there still, the L[or]d caryes mee thorough the dutys gratiously drawes neere to thaw; and humble; L[or]d I am thyne be with mee still, pardon all selfe ease, creaturely drowsines, unbeleife, and strength L[or]d ag:[ainst] all;

250. 25. my soule blesse thou the L[or]d who hath forgiven thy daily deadnes unbeleife, unfruitfulnes; &c: and healed the corrupt:[ion] in some measure, and crowned thee with lovingkindnesse, and tender compassions; I have seen his salvation, and ther[e]f:[ore]; L[or]d now, where thou wilt, thy will be done; yea come L[or]d Jesus, come quickly, oh times, times, L[or]d pitye,

26. my greife is, that I cannot be fruitfull in both callings; I mourne that I can live no more in heaven and above creatures; oh pardon, oh draw neere; irradiate thyne owne graces in mee; let in thy beames continuallye;

27. I have bin with Mary Milton;[445] a most sad example of a wretch; who set her selfe ag:[ainst] the power of godlinesse, and now lyes sicke like a Nabal; with her; Mr. Wharton preaches;[446] 4 d: my heart a litle downe; but myne eyes are fixed; and my heart is towards him, I know in whom I have believed, and thee I will stay; oh faith, faith, to trust not in sense, but in the name of the L[or]d Jesus, Jehovah my right:[eousness] &c

251. 28. Straitned, and drooping, and melancholy; oh I am weake L[or]d, I am pore, and nothing, and darke without thy beames; thou wouldest have mee stoop; L[or]d I lye at thy feet; and there a pore dog is content to licke up crumbs;[447] A litle fruit toward lying downe;

29. the L[or]d affords some faith, to teare downe distempers, to comfort in disquiet; the L[or]d does not so perfectly cleare the coast, yet he gives an eye to see a beame coming thorough, the cloud, and the god above the clouds does irradiate the grace he hath put in;

30. Saboath, G.[od] hath gone along with mee graciouslye; though my heart flags, and sinks; if the L[or]d remove but a minuit, I have no hope, or help; I will take hold of the name of the L[or]d Jesus for my right:[eousness] and shelter; Holinesse shall not save mee teares prayers; &c: are dung and drosse in point of X, my saviour; there is my hold, and the L[or]d will make mee as mount Sion;

---

[444] Just like a fish on dry land.
[445] Mary Milton may be a woman, 'widow Milton', mentioned in the churchwarden's book of Stortford, living at Hockerall: Glasscock, *St Michael's, Bishop's Stortford*, p. 151.
[446] Samuel Wharton, the minister of Felsted, Essex, seems to have preached at Stortford on this occasion.
[447] See p. 41n above; Matt. 15:27; Mark 7:28.

252. 31. In some darknesse, I want at last, the ancient serenitye, and calmenesse; my confidence is yet in my g.[od] my rock, and deliverer; and in this trust, will I lye downe in peace;

August: 1. I am cast downe, yet upheld from failing; my head wanders; and I am disturbed with my sad companions (Mrs hotbolt note her)[448] but the L[or]d a litle peekes out of the clouds, and smiled on mee now this evening oh I will blesse him, and lye down in his armes;

2. the L[or]d caryes mee on in this wretched familye, inlarges my heart toward them L[or]d some fruit, some fruit, thou that hast granted some, give more; thou seemest to stand behind the curtaine, but yet puttest it aside, thou art yet my God, and in thee will I trust;

3. this day Mr Symonds of Raine[449] declares himself a wretch; out of Amos: 5.13.[450] wrested to his owne destruction without mercye; Lord save mee from this forward generat:[ion] I blesse thee, who hast plucked mee from in; and into thyne counsells; now Lord will I lye downe in thy bosome;

253. 4. the L[or]d keepes mee downe in some way; in regard of that cleare sight of himselfe, yet supports my spirit to seek him, and caryes mee o[ve]r comfortably among bryars, and it shall suffice;

5. my strength is still in god, in whom I live, and on whom I depend, I mourne yet under my clog,[451] and backbyas,[452] that does hinder mee from mounting with Eagles wings;

6. Saboth; the L[or]d appeares, and makes mee lively sometimes; he withdraws yea but a litle, and I am left to deadnes; that I may know G.[od] is my life comfort; &c.

7. the L[or]d is yet my portion, and carryes mee on from day to day; why should I distrust him; I have chosen the L[or]d, and he mee; I am thyne keep mee from this current generation; thou hast so; both from hell, and men; praised, be thy name;

254. 8. still I hold upon G.[od] my rocke of ages; he gives strength from day to day; oh pardon L[or]d yet my pore service and obedience, oh wash away, my hypocrisye, selfe unbeleife, and all my drosse;

9. I visit G. Bull, miller;[453] ravished in sp:[irit] sings sweetly like a swan: without almost any doubtings; litle to resist; and so the more faith, and

---

[448] Unidentified.

[449] See above p. 65n.

[450] Amos 5:13 – 'Therefore the prudent shall keep silence in that time; for it is an evil time.'

[451] See Glossary.

[452] See above, p. 42n.

[453] Both Bull and Miller families lived in the parish of Stortford: Glasscock, *St Michael's, Bishop's Stortford, passim.* It is possible that he is mentioning Goodman Bull who was a miller. 'John Bull the elder' was churchwarden in 1631, 'John Bull' was churchwarden the following year and one of the collectors for the poor in 1642, 'Ralfe Bull' was churchwarden in 1641 and 1642 and 'Ralph Bull' was churchwarden in 1643: Glasscock, pp. 114, 168.

peace; my soule is stayed on my G.[od] allsufficient, who confirms mee
with perfect peace;

10. the Lord is my portion, in his name is my sure confidence; to him I
looke, and am againe lookt upon, he refreshes mee from above; Blesse
the L[or]d oh my soule; who hath crowned mee with his lovingkindnesse; oh my god, forgive the weakenesse; selfe, hypocrisye, deadnes,
unbelief of my soule;

11. some straitnes, yet faith in some measure up; Lord pardon my pore
service, I am thyne, maintain mee at thy cost be thou my All-sufficiencye;

255. 12. now he is come graciously, hath made the winds to cease, and
brought a calme upon my spirit; oh blesse the L[or]d, oh my soule; the
L[or]d let mee dwell in thy presence;

13. Saboath, my heart fully fixt, and bent for god, and never well, but
when thoughts and words tend that way, yet not that freindly
communion, and fellowsh:[ip] that I have injoyed; L[or]d pardon all
sins, and subdue daily;

14. the Lord graciously smiles afar of[f], to the thawing of my heart,
lifting up of my soule to heaven, he hath given some seale, and shewne
mee the glory, that I wait for, and shall have shortly;

15. somew[ha]t pincht in the day, but graciously inlarg[e]d, at lying
downe; oh he is come, he is come; oh that I might dwell in thy presence,
and never be removed from thee;

16. the L[or]d is still my portion, his presence is my joy, and
gover[n]ment; he doth shew great, and hidden things, while I am calling
on him; Jer:[emiah] 33.3[454] caryes mee through this wildernesse;

256. 17. Ebbing, the L[or]d sees it best, that I should not even be up; but he
gives mee an heart loving him, hank[e]ring after him; and mourning,
that I can honour him no more;

18. mr wall comes, refreshes mee;[455] I am thyne oh L[or]d, who art my
stay, and my comforte; I fly only to thee for new supply, thou acceptest
mee com[e]ly, pardonst mee uncomelye;

19. I have injoyed much sweetnes in god this day, but yet some rust is
ready to get upon mee, and some guilt hinders mee (that I draw on the
more heavilye); ever of my unfruitfulnesse, that I doe so litle in the day
for god, or in calling;

20. Saboath, somew[ha]t straitned, corruption n1t:[456] stirring; L[or]d
ease deliver mee out of distresse; forgive daily, and heale my deseases;

21. my heart is ready to sinke; Mr Symonds[457] comes, such common

---

[454] Jer. 33:3 – 'Call unto me, and I will answer thee, and shew thee great and mighty things,
which thou knowest not.'

[455] This may be the Mr Wall from Emmanuel College, whose identity is touched upon above, p.
10.

[456] Either 'natural' or 'national'.

[457] Unidentified.

company does litle good; where litle of god, and much of the creature; oh a mercy to mee, that I injoy god a dayes, and other folke discontenting vanitye;

257. 22. my heart is something downe, body awck,[458] companys; yet I have no other in heaven, or earth, but thee; L[or]d smile on mee, for in thee is my mercye, yea my life;

23. much pressed in spirit, I can scarse keep my selfe from rust in civill companyes; Mr Symons; &c: Lord shine thou, yea yet more clearely I have none on earth but thee;

24. yet my heart is fixed upon god my portion; and my reward; and I find nothing but sweetnes, and strength in his way; and distemper when I start out of it;

25. sometimes up, and sometimes downe, ebbing, and flowing; the L[or]d shewes mee, that all is to be had in him above; and that I must live upon him in a momentarye dependence; L[or]d pardon L[or]d heale, L[or]d draw neere, and absent not thy selfe;

258. 26. the L[or]d goes on graciouslye with mee, gives mee assistance and daily something to support mee he feeds mee as with hidden manna; L[or]d pardon my frailtyes;

27. Saboath, a litle up in the morning, ready to contract guilt, and rust which sinkes my spirit; the L[or]d is only my light, and life, if he withdraws, I am darkenes, and a breathing log;

28. A litle darke, yet faith is upon the wing; and overcomes straitnes bears downe doubts, and feares; and supports oh but thy amiable presence; Let mee dwell in it; it is sweet;

29. weak, and pore, when g.[od] absents I am nothing; I must live upon renewed mercy; L[or]d I am nothing, nothing; Thou art my god, and my all

30. Now falls out the desperate b45 ab:[out] M1r: they part; J. S1m: in a distressed condit:[ion] yet braces hims:[elf] up in set[ting upon] g.[od] and lights upon ps: 37 out of providence;[459]

259. my heart sweetly thawne, and meltd and much of god, I find; oh thou art my joy; and thy countenance hath, and shall make mee exceeding glad; sorrow without and peace within;

31. I am full of distracted thoughts ab:[out] change; ab:[out] M1r5 M:[460] and my selfe; I am my wits end but that I have a gracious, and loving father to fly to, in whose armes I am; whose name defends mee; whose countenance quiets my soule, and ther[e]f:[ore]

---

458 See Glossary.
459 This seems to be an argument relating to Mary Mountfort. J. Samuel seems to have been upset about abuse regarding some religious matter because he found solace in Psalm 37, which offers comfort and reassurance to the godly under fire.
460 Possibly Mary Mountfort.

I can lye downe with Simeons' song, L[or]d now &c: for I have seene; &c:[461]

Septemb: 1. I goe with Mr. Sedgew:[ick] to Sir S.[amuel] L5k:[e] enterteined sweetly; discourse ab:[out] change of place;[462] the L[or]d guid[e] mee in the matter, L[or]d some way, far ease, and that I may honour thee, and win soules;

2. A litle cloud, daily rust gets upon mee; much adoe I have to rub it of[f]; L[or]d clear the coast; I[']l wait upon thee in well doing;

260. 3. Saboath, sweetly refreshed and comforted in god my shephea[r]d, M1r:[y] M:[ountfort] prayes, most sweetly in S1m:[uel's] way; it joyes my heart; pore Bess: Brewster refuses my sp:[irit] this night;[463] L[or]d I thanke thee, who hast heard my prayer, and hast given in twoo pore soules; oh unworthy wretch I that ever I should be the intrument of doing any g[ood]; not unto mee: &c;

4. much vexed by this old w4m:[an] crost in Colne journey and no rule over my selfe; much troubled ab:[out] resetling; L[or]d find out some way, where I may live with some sweetnes; oh that I might preach thy gospell;

5. I goe to taine;[464] find good successe; and to Colne the L[or]d stayes my heart upon him; but yet something eloofe of, being out of action;

6. there still; inlarged much, yet some streightnes, and damp; L[or]d more of thy selfe;

7. I goe to wethersfeild; sad sutton preaches;[465] I goe to Dunmo[w], visit freinds; ready to be vaine in company of cousins L[or]d pardon;

261. 8. I returne home sad; some flaw I feele, and some damp; and I mourne under it; M. Mountf.[ort] sicke; a sicke sad yeare it hath bin the L[or]d is angry with us oh pardon, and heale;

9. Drooping, I get not up I recover not my self; I am weake in ocasions; the L[or]d mercifully takes them from mee; oh heale my peace, and be my god;

10. Saboath, wherin I mourne after god, but cannot finde that I would, but I blame my selfe; L[or]d pardon, and restore lovingkindnesse;

11. sunke, sunke; If the L[or]d be silent; I am like those that goe downe into the pit; L[or]d restore mercy to mee; and hide thy face from my sins;

---

[461] Simeon's Song refers to the righteous, devout old man, Simeon, who took the infant Jesus in his arms and blessed him when he was presented in the temple: Luke 2:29ff.

[462] William Sedgwick goes with Samuel to call on Sir Samuel Luke of Cople in Bedfordshire. Luke was the eldest son of Sir Oliver Luke of Woodend, Beds. Sedgwick's connection with Luke may have been from his days in Oxford or through George Hughes, an old friend. There was some communication that helped Rogers to make contact with people who might help him to find a more fruitful employment. See Introduction.

[463] These people, Mary Mountfort and Bess Brewster, have prayed with Rogers before. It appears that he compares Mary's style with that of the Old Testament figure, Samuel.

[464] Either Taine, Essex or Taye, a place he later visits.

[465] Daniel Sutton, the rector of Wethersfield.

262. 12. Much troubled, and cast downe, for the Lord is justly silent; I was carelese in comp:[any] 1n:[n] scr4g; and cousens at D5nm:[ow];[466] and some guilt is upon my sp[irit]; oh L[or]d rub it of[f], and wash mee as with pure water;

13. Abo[ut] the cursed visitat:[ion] D. Duck plays the base wretch; and Mr Crause in his sermon;[467] all formality, and bitter speaking ag:[ainst] sermons; Lord ease us; and uncloth these wolves of there sheepskins; the L[or]d hath bin gracious to mee removinge the guilt of my sin in some measure; myne eyes are towarde thee still;

14. A litle revived, I mourne for my unfaithfulnesse, and awcknes[468] yet god is good to mee, he is my all-sufficiencye; and my god pardoning sin;

15. pore, and weake, fruitlesse, and comfortlesse, the L[or]d seems to withdraw, and I sinke but yet my resolution is such; though I dye yet will I trust in him;

263. 16. I mourne for my wandrings, and unfruitfulnesse, deadnes, and unbeleife; L[or]d pardon; oh reveale thy selfe to mee; and shew mee thy way;

17. Saboath, my heart is somew[ha]t straitned; the Lord will shew I am nothing without him; I am weak but let mee be strong in thee;

18. I have not that sweet communion with god, which I was want to have; but my heart is bent, and th[o]roughly resolved to wait ever with patience, and humble submission; Oh thy church pitty; wee grow worse; oh amend thinges for thy goodnes sake;

19. The L[or]d is very gracious to mee, I am sinking, he upholds mee, and carys mee thorough a difficult place with some sweetnes; though sometimes in a cloud; Blesse the L[or]d oh my soule; &c: Oh thy church thy church; yet for England, sinfull England;

264. 20. This day, I set apart for fasting, 1. in reg:[ard] of my selfe to get into the same communion with g.[od] which I was wont to have; and the L[or]d hath granted it in some comfortable measure; 2. ab:[out] the change of place, and calling; for I am to preach on Saboth L[or]d strengthen mee, fit an unworthy sinfull wretch to declare thy will; I have found faith more raised (the affections) espec:[ially] upon that promise; commit thy way to him, and he shall bring it to passe;[469]

21. the L[or]d upholds mee still in some desire to walke purely before him; but in some darknes; yet my soule rejoices in Jehovah my right:[eousness] and in the feare of the L[or]d will I trust in his name;

---

[466] Anne Scrogs and cousins of Rogers lived at Dunmow.

[467] Dr Arthur Duck, a civil lawyer and the Chancellor of the diocese of London, an official of the episcopal visitation. Mr Crause may be either John or Thomas Crouch; otherwise the name does not appear among existing materials on clergy.

[468] See Glossary.

[469] The 'promise' is a paraphrase of Psalm 37:5 – 'Commit thy way unto the Lord; trust also in him; and he shall bring it to pass.'

22. now he is come, and shined into my soule, oh thou hast made a covenant of peace with mee; I will lye downe in thyne armes; L[or]d pardon my daily weaknesse and yet shew mee more glorye and I shall praise thee;

265. 23. the L[or]d is gracious to mee upholds mee, inlarges mee; oh how sweet is it to dwell in his overpowring presence; I looke up now to thee Saboth day, and preaching strength thou wilt give mee it;

24. Sab:[bath] this day I goe and hear mr Hues in Farnham;[470] thawed in something and goe to R. Pelham, preach the first, with comfortable assistance, and approbation, of Sir Sam:[uel] Luke; and Ladye, an humble gentlewoman;[471] the L[or]d shields mee of[f] in the buisinesse I must yet pray more, and depend upon him for strength to submit to w[ha]tever he shall cut out for mee;

25. I returne to Farnham, discourse with mr Hues;[472] excellent; and home; this ladye begins at her fits to yeeld; L[or]d bow her heart fullye;

26. my heart is up toward heaven, but clouds arise; oh my deare god, I want that same sweetnes in thee; oh L[or]d recover it that I may praise thee;

266. 27. something downe; I am pore; but myne eyes are yet towards thee; oh L[or]d dislodge my heart from the creature and teach mee to serve thee without distraction;

28. now I post to Tay: ab:[out] Capell bus:[iness] there furthered;[473] the L[or]d upholds my sp:[irit] from sinking;

29. now I goe to wethersf:[ield] and so to Bailye;[474] I meet with a godly woman at the Inne; I much refreshed;

30. I goe to Capell; on tryall, there I find loving, enterteinment; and hopes;

Octob: 1. Saboath, I preach at capell twice, the L[or]d is gracious towards mee in assistance, and all very forward to have mee;[475]

---

[470] George Hughes, see above p. 82n.

[471] It appears that Rogers was preaching on trial, as it were, at Pelham, in Herts. Rogers does not say which of the three possible Pelhams it was. Presumably the presence of Sir Samuel Luke, the Bedfordshire gentleman, was related to the conversation reported earlier, see p. 115.

[472] George Hughes.

[473] Rogers rides to the parish of Great Tey, Marks Tey or Little Tey, all in Essex, about the possibility of becoming minister of 'Capell'. The potential opening seems to have been at one of two Suffolk parishes, either Capell St Andrew in Willford Hundred or Capell St Mary, just across the Suffolk border in the Hundred of Samford. However, directly to the east of the parish of Earls Colne and directly to the north of Great Tey lies the parish of Pontisbright Chapel, so it may be that he was talking to parties in Tey about a place at the nearby parish. See Introduction.

[474] It is unclear whether 'Bailye' was a person or a place.

[475] Rogers went on trial possibly at Pontisbright Chapel, next to Earls Colne and Great Tey. This presents a possibly confusing situation. At this time another Samuel Rogers was the curate at Great Tey. This curate had graduated BA by 23 September 1634 when he first applied for admittance to the curacy, and had an MA by 13 June 1636 when he received a licence from the bishop to preach at Great Tey: GL 9539A/1 fo. 66v. This Samuel Rogers at

2. now Sir Sam:[uel] Luke and I goe to Bedford, for License, crost,[476] I ready to be disquieted, but yet beare up my selfe by faith;

267. 3. I goe to the commencement Dr Holsworth does admirablye preach,[477] kept the act &c: the Arminians fret; Pullen playes the cursed Arminian;[478] I meet father, brother, freinds comfortably, and many godly in the colledge incourage them, oh L[or]d doe good to that pore colledge yet;

4. I returne home, meet with an arminian, deboise[479] him I lye downe in Xs armes,

5. Disturbed ab:[out] the place, in uncerteintyes troubles, I meet Sir Sam:[uel] at Farnham, the L[or]d tryes mee; I will wait upon thee; L[or]d direct mee for the best;

6. I am full of cares, and thoughts still; oh that I had yet more faith to attend upon god in well doing, without fretting; I am thyne, oh provide for mee;

268. 7. I want faith to live by in the midst of tryalls; and thoughts; Lord I would trust in thyne all-sufficiencye; help mee;

8. Saboath, my heart is for god; I speake some truthes out of 14: Hos:[ea] 3. and th[e]y thaw, and prevailes something; Sarah Burlin affected and coyes out; not fatherlesse Lord smite upon the iron, and let it not grow cold;[480]

9. I am ready to droop, yet I depend upon god, and my heart is fixed upon him; L[or]d reveale thy selfe graciouslye unto mee; let mee have that in thee, which I cannot have in creatures;

Great Tey was probably the son of Timothy Rogers, the vicar of Great Tey and perpetual curate of Pontisbright Chapel until 1636. At this point Timothy Rogers moved to become vicar of All Saints, Sudbury, Suffolk and thus Pontisbright needed another curate. Then perhaps the diarist received a call to preach on trial. This Samuel did not obtain a licence, and instead Timothy Rogers returned to take the place at Chapel. Timothy's son, Samuel (probably unrelated) received a presentation by Nehemiah Rogers, his uncle and a Laudian (see *DNB* on Nehemiah), to the vicarage of Great Tey on 27 January 1638 (a vicarage formerly held by his father, see *DNB* on Timothy). Cf. Smith, *Ecclesiastical History*, pp. 109, 310.

[476] Rogers and Sir Samuel Luke rode to Bedford which was in the diocese of Lincoln. The bishop of Lincoln was John Williams, known to be fairly sympathetic to puritans. Though confident about obtaining a preaching licence in Bedford, Rogers writes that he was 'crost', i.e. 'crossed': he failed in his efforts. He may have been refused because of a technicality. He did not turn twenty-four until 30 November, so he was technically not old enough to be ordained and to hold a curacy.

[477] Dr Richard Holdsworth was elected to the Mastership of Emmanuel College, Cambridge on 25 April 1637, thus keeping the post in fairly reliable godly hands.

[478] The most likely candidate is Samuel Pullein DD, who became chaplain to Aubrey de Vere, Earl of Oxford, during the Civil War and later became the Archbishop of Tuam: see *DNB* on Pullein.

[479] See Glossary.

[480] Rogers preaches on Hosea 14:3 – 'Asshur shall not save us; we will not ride upon horses: neither will we say any more to the work of our hands, Ye are our gods: for in thee the fatherless findeth mercy', a text he has referred to in his personal piety earlier in the diary, see p. 59 above. He probably preached in Stortford, as the name Burling appears frequently in those parish records: Glasscock, *St Michael's, Bishop's Stortford*, pp. 145, 176, 182.

10. something downe, but my thoughts are yet upon god my rocke; in his name doe I trust, I will roule my selfe upon him in well doing;

269. 11. A little obscure, but comforted at last in my god; faith doth yet bare mee up; and my joy is in god;

12. Sometimes up, and somet:[imes] downe, the L[or]d will shew the difference of via, and patria; but the kingd:[om] is before mee; and I['] le presse hard, by thy grace; oh nowe poure out an extraordinary measure of thy sp:[irit] I am to meet thee;

13. now wee fast; and pray at Emers:[ons] the L[or]d caryes mee thorough the dutye, graciouslye; and though affect,[ions] not so up; yet faith, in some measure is upon the wing, and now I lye downe in his armes;

14. A litle cloud, yet some beames thorough it; I desire yet to depend upon him, who is my portion, and in whome alone I trust;

270. 15. Saboath A litle sadded in the day, but a litle refreshed, and comforted in god at last; the L[or]d is my comfort, and stay, in whom I may trust; now this night comes M1r5: s1r:[ah] the c44k and pore B2ss to my chamber, and bemoane there departure;[481] I hope the L[or]d hath done there soules good; oh whom am I, that the L[or]d should make mee an instrument to doe good to soules;

16. now I am sent for to Pelham, on the sudden; and am crost in the change of my place to Sir Sam:[uel] Luke;[482] I am troubled, yet I gather up my selfe in my god, who hath bine my comfort, and will be;

17. Now wee goe to Farnham, Mr Sedg:[wick's][483] child baptized; mr wilson preaches p4rl5; the L[or]d was with mee in dutys in the family and pride is ready to stand up; L[or]d help mee; and guide mee on, and doe mee good;

271. 18. At Mr Sedgewicks; with good company; a litle downe, but yet I hold my confidence, and I know in whom I have beleived, who will carry mee on to heaven; oh that I could make things present to mee;

19. Troubled, yet uphold my selfe by faith in Jehovah my right:[- eousness] I have thoughts of removall; L[or]d guid[e] mee and find out some way of ease;

20. My service is so pore, that I am ashamed of it; L[or]d pardon, and accept it freelye; I am nothing; I praise thee for that which I have tasted from thee;

21. L[or]d, I mourne, that I should honour thee no more in my life; and

---

[481] Mary Mountfort, Bess Brewster and Sarah the cook meet with Rogers. He does not specify the nature of their departure.

[482] Evidently Rogers received some sort of invitation to go to Pelham, where Sir Samuel Luke may have resided. The potential move did not happen, which was probably due to the difficulty in getting a licence. It may have been that Luke was looking for a curate as well as or instead of a chaplain.

[483] William Sedgwick.

that I want that sweet familiaritye that I was once wont to injoy with thee;

272. 22. Saboath; my heart is straitned by the absence of god; I must learn to live upon a naked god, and promise; to trust in a name when I have no token or pawne of mercye;

23. I lye downe melancholye, and sad, I have very litle comfort without; and litle within; my heart is streight, and I mourne under it;

24. I live yet in a dependence upon my god; though I injoy not that which I have done; now G. B5l: M. M. and pore B2s: pray together at midnight;[484] the L[or]d is with them wonderfullye; I am yet something bound, but my soules desires are with g.[od] and I will be content; let him doe with mee what he will;

25. some clouds, but myne eyes are towards heaven; I have none in heaven but thee; oh looke downe with favor pardon my pore obedience;

273. 26. the Lord is with mee in this familye, caryes mee on, gives mee gracious assistance, and throwes in 2. pore soules in answer to my pore labours, M1r M. and pore Bess: Brewster; oh that the L[or]d should honour such a sinfull creature as I am to doe good to soules; now John wright prayes, and parts from us; the L[or]d be with him, and us;

27. the L[or]d now shines upon mee, gives mee some sweet glimses of favour; oh L[or]d, I am thyne thyne, not myne owne; oh pitty pore England; oh shew mee, which way I shall goe, that I may honour thee;

28. Now honest Bess: Brewster goes away; the L[or]d takes away my comforts; L[or]d goe along with her and carry thyne owne workers; Oh give mee in thy selfe, that which I injoy not in the creatures;

274. 29. Sabo:[ath] I am somew[ha]t clouded, yet my heart is fixed to see when the sun will brake thorough; The L[or]d is my portion, and in his armes I lye downe;

30. my soule is fixd still upon my g.[od] all-sufficient; I have none but thee in heaven; now Mr Harlak:[enden] comes, and refreshes, oh how joyfull will heaven be, where now be such; I will waite a litle while;

31. the Lord hath manifested himselfe sweetly to mee this day; oh pore wretch that I am, that the Lord should look upon mee; be my husband; I a wife, that walke not so as I s[h]ould[;] G. Plum buryed;[485]

Novemb: 1. I goe to Felsted, and Ba[r]ns[t]on, refreshed by mr Bedle,[486] sweetlye; preachinge, and discourse; inlarged at aunt Longs; ready to goe out in myne owne strength; Lord pardon; oh I see a cause, why the Lord hath hampered mee among bryars, and thornes;

---

[484] G. Bull, Mary Mountfort and Bess Brewster pray together with Rogers.

[485] G. Plum was probably a member of the Stortford parish. An Edward Plum was collector or overseer of the poor in 1642 when he was head of a household who contributed to parish funds: Glasscock, *St Michael's, Bishop's Stortford*, pp. 151, 168.

[486] John Beadle of Barnston, Essex.

275. 2. Damped, and downe, yet my soule depends; upon my god; oh inlarge mee to walke before thee in a perfect way; and doe thou come unto mee;

3. Downe, but stil staying my heart upon god; mourning for the barrennes of my company, L[or]d ease, and provide that I may dwell among thy saints;

4. Now I goe to Priory,[487] the L[or]d is with mee, I lye downe something darkelye, but my heart is fixed, and I depend upon Xs strength for to morrow;

5. Saboath, g.[ods] treasure I preach twice at Priory (with some difficultye) the L[or]d is with mee; and strengthens mee; and some savour I see left upon them; Amuck, and cousens exces:[ses] In gods love, and respect;

276. 6. Now I returne to my dead companye; sadded; I goe to G. m45ntf:[ort][488] I find my sp:[irit] flat, and untoward other inlargement; oh L[or]d why is it, that thou seemest to be gone; and to leave mee in a cloud; oh L[or]d, put it away, and sp:[eak] least I be like those, that goe downe, into the pit; oh pardon the sins of my helplesnes;

7. I have bine much pressed this day, and straitned; but now at lying downe, the Lord drawes neere and smiles, and cheeres my sp:[irit;] softens mee, stirs mee up to faith obedientiall; oh more, more sweetnes; and make mee love thee more;

8. the Lord is yet neere mee; L[or]d let it close mee; I am nothing, sinfull, and pore in services, and dutyes in the day time; oh pardon;

277. 9. The Lord refreshes mee most sweetly, raises up my flagging spirit, and carryes mee above creatures; Blesse the L[or]d oh my soule, who hath crowned; &c; oh that I could walke worthy of thy humbling, softning, pardoning, sanctifying grace, and might not turne it into wantonesse.

10. I goe to Mr Reads;[489] shee I hope honest, and savorye; my Lady ut solet;[490] the L[or]d tempers my sp:[irit] that I debauch them with the sp:[irit] of meeknes; the L[or]d causes mee still to live upon hims:[elf] oh my pitifull flesh; L[or]d some fruit;

11. The Lord is gracious to mee, supports mee from day to day in this barren wildernesse, I know not how, but still I am caryed on, and sinke not whollye; oh blesse pore endeavors; some fruit some fruit; Thou letest mee now lye downe in peace in thyne armes;

---

[487] The Priory was part of Earls Colne, Essex, the home of Richard Harlakenden. Another possibility is the Barrington residence, the Priory House, in Hatfield Broad Oak: Arthur Searle (ed.), *Barrington Family Letters 1628–1632*, Camden Soc. 4th ser., 28 (1983), p. 4.
[488] Goodwife Mountfort.
[489] See above, p. 74n.
[490] As usual.

278. 12. Saboath, my confidence is in god, and my joy; my sorrow is that I walke not worthy of so great mercy, and love revealed, L[or]d pardon;
13. G.[od] is my hope, harbour, and strength, and ther[e]fore I cast my selfe upon him; I have litle: but g.[od] hath given mee contentednes, and hims:[elf] to make up all; and I desire to beleive in well doing for the time to come;
14. the Lord gives mee something still that keepes mee from sinking; my way, I commit to him, and my thoughts are established;
15. A litle downe, but my heart fixed; m. m45ntf:[ort] stoopes after the crosse c1r1ge on saboth; my sp:[irit] over comes; it is good to overbeare such sp[irit]s L[or]d give mee wisdome, and grace;
16. satisfied with peace and glory, oh sinfull wretch I, that the L[or]d should drawe neere to mee; oh but yet more till I come to see face to face;

279. 17. Faith yet beares up my sp:[irit] ab:[ove] creatures; by it I will run into the name of the L[or]d, my strong tower, and be safe;[491]
18. my sorrow is from my selfe that there is such a deale of corruption within mee; I sinke this day in dutyes, bec:[ause] the Lord withdrawes, but my heart still hankers after G.[od] and in him doe I trust though I dye;
19. Saboath, not so cleare, as at sometimes, but my trust is in his name, whose name is my tower;
20. Somew[ha]t flat, but my soule depends upon him, in whom I have beleived; he is my harbour, and my strength, and my contin:[ual] rejoicing; the joy of the L[or]d is my strength;
21. I rejoice in X my life; who hath dyed, that I might live; yea that he might live in mee and the life which I now live, through not always in feeling is yet by faith in the son of god;

280. 22. the Lord is still with mee, and reveales more, and more unto mee;[492] video (modo invisibili) Christum meum ascendentem ad patrem suum, et patrem meum, ad deum suum, atq ad Jehovam meum; ad gloriam suam, atque ad meum gloriam; ille fidelis mediator (et Advocatus) perficit coram deo, qd reliquum est sacerdotalis oficij; Da terrestri mihi Domine alas Aquilæ,[493] cælestes alas, ut ascendam post virum meum animâ oculisq;

[22. I see (in an invisible way) my Christ ascending to His Father and my Father, to his God and to my Jehovah; to His glory, and also to my

---

[491] Taken from Psalm 61:3 – 'For thou hast been a shelter for me, and a strong tower from the enemy.'
[492] In the margin there is a note reading 'John 20.17'. The Scripture it refers to is as follows – 'Jesus saith unto her, Touch me not; for I am not yet ascended to my father; but go to my brethren, and say unto them, I ascend unto my Father, and your Father; and to my God, and your God.'The Scripture is not in the diary, only the reference.
[493] An image of strength taken from either Exodus 19:4 or Isaiah 40:31.

glory; that faithful mediator (and Advocator) performs in the presence of God that which is remaining of priestly business; give to me earthbound Lord the wings of an eagle, heavenly wings so that I might ascend after my spouse with soul and eyes;]

23. Christus mihi vita est, ille enim pro me mervit, ille applicat per suum spiritum, vitam* iustitiæ,* sanctitatis, atg * gloriæ vitam; in Christo itag vivo ego, hinc est qd quotidie morior; iam Deus meas osculo labra mea compri mit, nide est qd iam caput tutissimo Componam sopore; lætor hodie quam maximè in humili societate M[agist]ʳⁱ Harlak; Exemplar certe piæ humilitatis; venerabilis matrona, Domina Veere (cum candidâ sp: muliere Mʳᵃ Watson)⁴⁹⁴ suavis generoso quidem modo: h: e: me⁴⁹⁵ alloqoquitur; intra tabernam Storfordiensam; acceptura mea capellanum Si; &c ego interim expectam qd loquetum Dominus;

[23. Christ is life for me, for He has earned for me, He is dedicated through His spirit, to a life of * justice, * sanctity and * a life of glory; and so in Christ I live, because I am dying every day; now my God with a kiss my lips He presses, then I now may entrust [lit. settle my head] my person to the safest repose; today greatly I delight in the humble society of Master Harlakenden; an example surely of pious humility; the honourable matron, Lady Vere (with the spiritually fair woman Mrs Watson) pleasant to be sure, in a bountiful fashion; she it is who addresses me inside the inn at Stortford; approving me as a chaplain; &c. meanwhile I await what the Lord dictates;]

281. 24. Post magnam serenitatem exortæ sunt nubes quædam tempest atesg; in quibus tamen nomen Christi deig patris mei, mihi terris secura est,⁴⁹⁶ in quâ dum latitem sine luce, sine fenestris securus dormio;

[24. After a great serenity certain clouds and storms have arisen; in which nevertheless the name of Christ, and of my Father, is a secure tower for me, in which while I lie without light and without windows, securely I sleep;]

25. Eo iam visum magis: Scrogs, de rearduâ, inter M. Hawksby, et illum, litem aliquo modo componimus; vir sane minimè ingenuus; appropinquat dominus mihi publicè oranti; in cuius brachijs tutus sum;

⁴⁹⁴ Lady Mary Vere, the daughter of Sir William Tracy of Toddington, Glos. and the widow of William Hoby, lived at Hackney in Middlesex. For further details, see Introduction, above. Mrs Watson was the life-long servant and companion of Lady Vere. One of her services was the writing of Lady Vere's letters: I. M. Calder (ed.), *Letters of John Davenport* (New Haven, Conn., 1937), pp. 77, 83.
⁴⁹⁵ The abbreviated words make this unsure.
⁴⁹⁶ Another image of strength and security taken from either Proverbs 18:10 or Psalm 61:3.

[25. I now go to see Master Scrogs, concerning this arduous business, between Master Hawksby, and that man,[497] we will settle the quarrel in some manner; a man to be sure in the least wise honourable; the Lord approaches me openly praying; in whose arms I am safe;]

26. Dies Dominicus; in quo cerno quidem sed per speculum, et per ænigma, sed cor meum fixum est et lætor maxime in Christo iustitiâ; ego equidem nihil sum;

[26. The Lord's day; in whom I see, to be sure, but through a glass, and through a riddle, but my heart is firm and I rejoice greatly in Christ's justice; I indeed am nothing;]

27. Ad hoc deus mihi omni = sufficiens est; creatura mànis certè est, atq plena molestiarum; exorandus est domine ut trahas cor meum (quam creaturale) ad te Deum, h: e: misericordiam, amorem, peccata, etiam aversiones meas corantem;

[27. For this God is all providing for me the created thing is certainly a shade, and full of annoyances; it is implored, Lord that you draw my heart (how creaturely) to you God, who is caring for my misery, love, sins, even the aversions of my heart;]

28. Lubens ego ascenderem ad Christum meum sed motum hunc multa et intus, et foras impedimenta conantur retardare; Intus reliqiæ

[28. Willingly I should ascend to my Christ but many impediments, inside and out will try to slow this movement within me, the remains]

282. veteris hominis; miser ego, quis tandem eripiet me ex catenis hisce? extra satanæ potestas, atg invidia; (at verò potentior deus est) mundi dein ocasiones variæ licitæ quidem, sed captautes animam imbellem; hodie visito M[agistri]. Sedgewicke; atg B. Breuster;[498] preces effundimus; illorum corda mollia redduntur; meum quidem superbum est, ego me quæro, et perdo consolationem; reatus sequitur; condona domine in omnebuis opere bono qd meum est, (etiam lava lachrymas) qd tuum est in Christo advocato meo aecipias velim;

---

[497] Rogers does not give enough information to clarify what 'arduous business' is at hand. Master Scrogs may be related to Anne Scrogs, who lived at Earls Colne; perhaps he was her father, Edward Scrogs of Aldbury, Herts. For more, see above, p. 68n. The Mr Hawksby may well be the elderly pastor at Earls Colne. Earlier in the year Hawksby had admitted that he 'sometimes administered the sacrament of Baptism without using the sign of the cross, and sometimes administered the Holy Eucharist to non-kneelants'. The vicar-general released him upon the vow that Hawksby would conform thereafter: Smith, *Ecclesiastical History*, p. 52. Perhaps he had run afoul of the ecclesiastical authorities again.

[498] William Sedgwick and Bess Brewster.

[of the old man; I wretch that I am who finally will rescue me from these chains? outside is Satan's power and envy (but God is truly more powerful) the various occasions of the world, then, are surely permitted, but they are alluring to the weak soul; today I visit Master Sedgwick and B. Brewster; we pour forth prayers; their hearts have been made soft; indeed mine is proud, I seek myself and I lose consolation; same follows, pardon, Lord, in every good work that which is mine, (even wipe my tears) that which is yours I wish that you should accept it, in Christ, my advocate;]

29. parem possum in vocatione, nec generali nec particulari, labitur dies, q[uo]d ego?

[29. I am able to do little in my duties, neither in general nor in particular, the day glides past, what do I do?]

282. [498a]dum creseimus, vita decrescit; attanem ego per inconsistentiam meam multas perdo horas; condona Deus mie; Ad gratia tuam, confugio, tanquam ad asylum; In tenebris sum, parum splendoris ad est; confido tamen et adhere Jehovæ nomini, atg deo meo inniter; in cuius manibus somnio securus;

[while we have grown, life diminishes; but yet I, through my inconsistency, lose many hours; forgive me, my God; to your grace I flee as if to an asylum; I am in darkness, too little splendour is here; I trust nevertheless even now in the name of Jehovah; and I lean on my God; in whose hands I sleep securely;]

30. vidi iam annos 24: natalis meus est; vixi verò circa decem;[499] hodie diversæ turbæ animum distorquent, fælix ego sum, qd prudentissimus deus servum suum a consortio mundi multum liberavit in mihi rideas Domine;

[30. I have seen 24 years already: it is my birthday; in truth I have lived about ten; today different crowds twist the soul, I am happy, because a most prudent God his servant from participation in the world has been greatly freed; may you smile on me o Lord;]

283. Decemb: 1. Doleo inconsistentiam, et cordis, et capitis; miser deploro corpus hoc mortis; cerno quidem stagnum peccati, ex quo oriumtur nubes tenebrosæ faciem domini abfuscantes; tandem aliquando, peregrinus ego patriam attingham; oh quam anhelat anima mea, et quam totus sitio, glacitoque ut in conspectu tuo appaream semper;

498a Following p. 282, also numbered 282.
499 Cf. above, p. 1.

[December 1. I grieve at inconsistency both of heart and head; mournful I lament this body of death I see indeed a swamp of sin, from which rise murky clouds hiding the countenance of God; finally, at some time, I, a pilgrim, shall reach the homeland; oh how my soul pants and how utterly I thirst and freeze, that I may appear in your sight always;]

2. per gratiam servor; gloriabar in imbecillitate meâ, ut gratia extollatur; accepti hodiè gratiam, ad humiliationem, ad remissionem, ad curationem; ut gratias quas pessim maximas Christo referam; Atq ad huc domine perge inauxilio meo; da vires mihi, etiam momentaneas, atq tuæ contendam pro te, contra hostes, inimicos tuos;

[2. through grace I am saved; I shall glory in my weakness so that grace may be extolled; today I have received grace, to the end of humbling, to remission, to healing; so that I might return to Christ the greatest thanks that I am able to return; and even so now, Lord, continue in my aid; give powers to me, even momentary, and then I shall fight for you, against your enemies and your foes;]

3. D. D. in quo facies domini non apparet admodum serena; fides ad huc per nubes volitat ad spem meam in cuius ulnis, quanquam in tenebris tutus latito;

[3. The Lord's Day, on which the face of the Lord does not appear wholly serene; faith thus far flies through the clouds toward my hope in whose arms, although I am in darkness, safe I am concealed;]

4. Quin adhuc rugas Domine liedat servo tuo in augustij suis submissè te in clamare; quid est in causâ (Deus me) si

[4. why thus far your frowns Lord? to your servant in his precarious circumstances to call out to you submissively; what may I plead (my God) on my behalf?]

284. si peccata mea, infidelites, terrietas, apostasia, inconstantia, atg corruptiones innumeræ, iustitiam tuam accendant; habes tu tecum iustum Christum meum, iustitiam meam, in cuius veste ego (nigerrimus) pulcher evado; extinguat Christus accensam iram; Si sup me integrum (quasi Hemanum)[500] incumbit ira, Da animum tranquillum, timentem tui, submissum valdè; fidem etiam ut stabilias exoro, per

---

[500] See above, p. 5n.

cuius alas in te rupem meam, in rimas promissionum tuarum confugiam, ubi securus lateam[501]

[if my sins, disloyalties, earthliness, apostacy, inconstancy, and innumerable corruptions, kindle your justice; you have with you my just Christ, my justice in whose clothing I (most black), go forth beautiful; may Christ extinguish God's inflamed anger; If, upon me, my entire being, (just like Heman) presses anger, give me a tranquil spirit fearing you, humbled greatly; I beg also that you make firm the faith by whose wings to you my rock, into the clefts of your promises I shall fly, where I shall be securely hidden]

5.[502] Iam Dom: m1rg1r2t[503] viris suum, ericat in me, in preces, grates admodum carnali spiritui, qui non sapit, quæ dei sunt; nec vidi certè feminam magis ignoranter obstinatam, atg constanter inconstantem; Cæca mater, cæcam, superbam perpuit filiam, sui similimam, Nota semper falsam istius faciem;[504] Deus mihi dedit hac nocte magnanimitaxtem spiritualem; ignorantiæ huic, superbiæ, menti verbo scrutanti adversæ liberè contradico; condona domine qd sapit carneum; atg iam in ulnis misericondiæ tuæ pastoralis acquiescam;

[5. Now Lady Margaret her poison vomits against me, against prayers, which are completely pleasing to the carnal spirit, who does not know the things of God; and I certainly have not seen a woman more ignorantly obstinate and consistently inconstant; Blind mother, has produced a blind, proud daughter, just like herself, Always note the concealed face of that one; God to me gave, on this night, spiritual maganimity; against this ignorance, this pride, this mind opposed to the scrutinising word I speak against freely; forgive O Lord that which knows the flesh and now in the arms of your pastoral mercy I shall rest;]

285. 6. Multæ me interpellant cogitationes vanæ; mens mea valdè exagitata est per sordidas, atg minime generosas mulierum mores; Ascendo tamen pennis aquilæ per gratiam, atg spiritus vires, supra omne qd pietati contradicit; Inveni orans præsentiam domini, hac nocte, multum; Bona nova animum mealsium iactah exhilarant; M[ra] Watson[505] literas ad me ian mittit invitatorias; Deus mi dirige gressus meas in viam tuam; Ego adhere aspexi te, atg expectabo;

---

[501] Song of Songs 2:14 – 'O my dove, that art in the clefts of the rock, in the secret places of the stairs, let me see thy countenance, let me hear thy voice; for sweet is thy voice, and thy countenance is comely.'

[502] In margin: '*', or, more accurately, a large 'X'.

[503] Lady Margaret Denny. This seems to be along similar lines to Lady Denny's earlier objections to the length of Rogers' prayers.

[504] In margin: large 'X'.

[505] Mrs Watson, Lady Vere's servant: see above, p. 123n.

[6. Many empty thought disturb me my mind is surely agitated through the filthy, and minimally noble customs of women; I ascend, nevertheless, by the wings of an eagle, through grace and the powers of the spirit, above all which speaks against piety; I have found, praying, the presence of God, much, this night Good new things exhilarate my mind; Mrs Watson already sends letters of hospitality to me; my God, direct my steps into your path; I have beheld you thus far and I will await you;]

7. nunc ridet Christus in me, candidè me alloquitur, hinc meæ lachrymæ consolationis lachrymæ Inflammerunt Radij huius solis animam meam amore cælesti; omnes irradiarunt spiritualis in me habitus; denig dubios nodos ques non potuit sancta ratio desecuere;

[7. Now Christ smiles upon me; clearly he addresses me, hence my tears are tears of consolation; the rays of this sun kindle my soul with heavenly love; they brighten all the spiritual disposition in me; firmly they have cut off the knots of doubt which holy knowledge was not able to;]

8. Iam angestijs sam, et liberat me dominus; In fluxus, et refluxus, mentique meæ; in tutis Christi ulnis dormio; video in me corpus mortis; oh quis liberabit me? tandem domine videam te in cælis;

[I am in narrow straits, and the Lord delivers me; in ebbing, and flowing, of my mind; in the safe arms of Christ I sleep; I see in me a body of death; oh who will free me? at length Lord I will see you in heaven;]

286. 9. Dies est ieiunij, et precum, in cubiculo privatim, in quo dominus aliquo modo appropinquat; causa est; mutatio loci; Devolvo supra Jehovam viam meam illu efficiet qd sibi maximam asferat gloriam, et qd mihi optimam est;

[9. The day is for fasting and prayer, in a room privately, in which the Lord is near in some measure; the reason is; a change of place; I surrender to the decision of Jehovah, my way, He will bring about that which bears the greatest glory to Himself, and that which is of the greatest benefit to me;]

10. Saboath the L[or]d looks towards mee and upholds mee; buisinesses in hand are ready to hinder mee;
11. I goe to my Lady Veres; the L[or]d helpes mee in the ordinance and wee strike up the match
12. I goe from Hackney to Colne, M[r] Harlak:[enden] sad at my departure;

13. I goe to sudbury to that desolate creature Hanna; the Lord helps mee that I loose not all in journyes; and to Mr Harrison for my Lady[506]
14. I come to wethersf:[ield] to shew buisinesse to my father; he approves, I rejoice; a sad thing with Ez2k:[iel] the L[or]d layes yet sorrowes upon him; both knee and hip out of joint;[507]
15. I come home reveale to my Lady shee begins to stir, but I quiet her;
287. 16. I attend upon god, and the L[or]d gives mee favour in my Lady Dennys eyes, that I goe away suddenly shee pardons;
17. Saboth, many ocasions are ready to trouble mee but my thoughts are upon thee;
18. yet ocasions take up my thought; oh a mercy that I have but litle to doe in the world; at that time when I shall be past all;
19. I am still hurrying, but my heart is some measure kept up, and inlarged toward this pore unfruitfull familye; and I mourne to thinke the L[or]d removes mee in anger to them;
20.[508] Full of businesse in the day, posting away things; yet the L[or]d brings things to my mind, and guides mee to
288. the 20. Acts; 32.[509] the L[or]d opens my heart, and mouth to speak a word in season, and melts there hearts, L[or]d some true fruit pickes them; M1r: M45nt:[510] &c: mournes bitterly; remarke it; and pray
21. now I part with my Lady Denny the L[or]d hath guided mee with wisdom, in returne to prayer to part so lovinglye; shee gives mee 20l; and mrs Earle; 11;[511] I come to my Lady Veers; god is with mee; and I rejoice in it;

506 Richard Harlakenden is sad about not having Rogers in his mother-in-law's family and in as close proximity. Rogers then travels from Earls Colne, Essex, to Sudbury, Suffolk where Hanna, his sister, may be sorry to hear of his move. Rogers must also have given a message to Mr Harrison either from Lady Vere or Lady Denny. Given his location, rather than this being James Harrison, the minister of Hatfield Broad Oak, this could be the elderly John Harrison, the curate of St Peter's, Sudbury who had numerous difficulties with the episcopal authorities in the 1630s: Smith, *Ecclesiastical History*, p. 45; Shipps, 'Lay patronage', pp. 170ff.; BL Harl. MS 589 fos. 137–40; *Winthrop Papers*, III, 390.
507 Rogers receives a fatherly blessing for his move. He then makes comments about Ezekiel Rogers, his uncle, who had certainly suffered during the 1630s. From 1634 onwards he had numerous citations and articles to answer from the bishop's courts. He suffered inhibitions, suspensions and eventually excommunication. As he later stated, he did not have the liberty to preach as he wished. He had his ministry suspended in 1636 and lay under that condition until he emigrated to New England in 1638. Also, during his last months at Rowley, Yorks., he had a dispute with the son of his former patron, Sir Thomas Barrington, over whether Rogers would resign and the terms of such a resignation. Sir Thomas offered to pay money to Rogers for the rebuilding of the rectory house, but they disagreed on the man Barrington wanted as a successor. When Rogers did resign, Barrington's man received the place and Rogers wrote futile letters from New England about the agreed sum of money: Ronald Marchant, *The Puritans in the Church Courts in the Diocese of York, 1560–1642* (London, 1960), pp. 96ff., 274; BL Egerton MS 2646 fos. 104, 108, 109, 111, 163.
508 In margin: large '*'.
509 Acts 20:32 – 'And now, brethren, I commend you to God, and to the word of his grace, which is able to build you up, and to give you an inheritance among all them which are sanctified.'
510 Mary Mountfort.
511 Elizabeth Earle, the daughter of Lady Denny.

22. G.[od] caryes mee thorough the services of the family with new grace and supply; inlarges mee to speak clearlye; the L[or]d hath most sweetly smiled upon mee in secret witnessing peace; shewing mee his goodnes in this place;

289. 23. my rejoicing is in G.[od] my strength, who gives mee new supply, now hee hath called mee to new worke;

24. Saboath, the first at Hackney, the L[or]d draws neere to mee, is all sufficient, he gives mee great comfort in my Lady oh most difference between L. M.[argaret Denny] and her; oh my happy change;

25. miror certe dei summam erga me bonitatem: ille enim preces meas (quas extremus ego emisi) librè exaudiuit; Liberauit dominus nus seruum suum a miserâ seruitate spirituum carnalium; Deus certè irascitur illis; non enim auscultant vertitati in authoritate diuinâ; nota finem

[25. I surely wonder at the highest goodness of God towards me; for he has freely heard my prayers (which I, in my extreme state, have sent forth); the Lord has freed his servant from the wretched servitude of carnal spirits; God is surely angered against them; for they do not attend to the truth in the divine authority; take note of their end]

26. Exultat cor meum plurimum in deo turre mea; nec habeo ullum in cælis, aut on terris cui adhæreo præterquam tibi, domine

[26. My heart exults most greatly in God, my tower; nor do I have anything in the heavens, or on the earth, to which I adhere except you, O Lord]

290. 27. Eo Londinum ad audiendum D[r]: Staughton;[512] benedicat mens mea domine meo, qd dignum me put auit verbo suo in spiritus demonstratione; pugnam hac nocte habeo cum carne, corpore mortis; non appropinquat dominus, ut solet; atque doleo;

[27. I go to London to hear Dr Stoughton; may my mind praise my Lord, for he has thought me worthy of his word in the demonstration of the spirit; I have a battle this night with the flesh, the body of death; the Lord does not draw near, as he is accustomed; and I grieve;]

28. Onera externa leuiora sunt, quam solent esse; Laboram tamen sub onere interno; spiritus cum corpore mortis, atque hoc cum illo mutuò proæliantur; Dedit tamen Xtus meus hac nocte victoriam super superbum spiritum; atque humilior evado;

[512] This is Dr John Stoughton, the minister of St Mary Aldermanbury, London, one of the most popular godly preachers in England, a graduate of Emmanuel College.

[28. The external burdens are lighter than they are accustomed to be; nevertheless, I labour under an internal burden; the spirit with the body of death, and the latter with the former, mutually do battle; nevertheless, my Christ has given, this night, victory over the prideful spirit; and, more humble, I go forth;]

29. Deo meo non possum non inniti, etiam sub nebulis nigerrimis; atq Quia adhuc laborandum est cum meipso? ego a me consolatio nem cælestum aufero; ego me quaero et me perdo; fac Domine, ut ego omnia perficiam mea in Christi virtute, ut gloriam attribuam Christo mihique risus cælestes recuperem;

[29. I am not able to lean upon my God, even under the blackest clouds; Why thus far have I had to labour with my self? I carry off from myself celestial consolation; I seek my self, and I lose my self; cause, Lord, that I complete all my affairs in the virtue of Christ, that I might attribute the glory to Christ and recover to myself the celestial smiles;]

291. 30. plenitudo Lætitiæ meæ a christo meo est, Iustitiâ meâ; in cuius veste appareo (niger ego) pulcherrimus; Doleo certè sub angusto spiritu meo, et sub reatu quodam contracto mihi, qd non omnia facio ex christi sed meis, viribus; condona domine, et remove a me reatum hunc magnum, et libera me ad libertatem servorum tuorum;

[30. the plenitude of my joy is from my Christ, my justice; in whose clothing I appear (I am black) most beautiful; I surely grieve under my narrow spirit, and under the particular guilt [which is] contracted to me, because I do not do all out of the powers of Christ, but my own; pardon Lord, and remove from me this great guilt, and free me to the freedom of your servants;]

31. D.D. In quo passus sum fluxum et reflexum gaudij cælestis; appropinquat dominus Christus mihi oranti privatim, defunditque amorem suum per totum me, subtrahit se mihi publicè oranti in cubiculo Dominæ Veere, quia in meis viribus ago nimium; fac Domine, ut reatus totus condonetur; et omnia ab hinc in tuis agam viribus;

[31. The Lord's Day, on which I have suffered the flowing and ebbing of heavenly joy; the Lord Christ draws near to me praying privately, and He pours down His love through my whole being; He withdraws Himself from me publicly praying in the bedchamber of Lady Vere, because I act too much in my own powers; cause, Lord, that the whole guilt may be forgiven; and henceforth may I perform all in your powers;]

Finis Anni; 1637.

292. Jan: 1. Quia adhuc laborum est sub angustijs internis? quis me liberabit a corpore mortis; gratias ago tibi domine, qui me aliquo modo liberasti; perfectam concede libertatem;

[January 1. Why thus far have I had to labour under internal limitations? Who will deliver me from the body of death; I give thanks to you, Lord, who has in some measure liberated me; grant me perfect liberty;]

2. vita mea, est, per fidem in Christo Iesu meo, in promissionibus evangelij; sum in tenebris, at per fidem sum in luce, sum in cælis, per quam, (h. E. xires) victoriam aliquam super terram super peccatum atque omnia sum consequutus;

[2. My life is, through faith in Christ my Jesus, in the promises of the Gospel I am in shadows, but through faith I am in light, I am in the heavens, through which[513] some victory over the earth over sin and all I have obtained;]

3. verbum (hodie datum per fidelem dispensatorum D^{rm} Staughton)[514] vivificat me modo cælesti; In cælis sum nam sum in deo; radij solis non magis semen, quam radij solis iustitiæ me irradiant;

[3. The Word (given today by the faithful steward, Dr Stoughton) vivifies me in a heavenly manner; I am in the heavens for I am in God; the rays of the sun do not [shine on] a seed any more than the rays of the sun of justice shine on me;]

4. Dominus, deus, meus, non deerro animam meam, fruor deo hodiè orans, vivens; quid reddam Iehouæ, qui tantum sui mihi revelavit, qui botros dedit, cælestis Canaan Arrhabonem? ego me dabo, et iuvencos labiorum;

[4. The Lord, my God, will not stray from my soul, I enjoy God today praying, living; what shall I render to Jehovah, who has revealed so much of himself to me, who has given the grapes, of heavenly Canaan the pledge? I shall give myself, and the sacrifices of my lips;[515]]

---

[513] That is, faith.
[514] John Stoughton.
[515] Literally 'the young bullocks of the lips'.

293. 5. Audio hodiè magistrum Sedgewick[516] prædicantem, pium quidem ut spero sed non plenum dei; nimium se sapit; nec ipsam conscientiæ medullam attingit; Ego acquiesco per totum diem in deo, rupe meâ, in cuius ulnis securè dormiturus sum;

[5. I hear today Master Sedgwick preaching, pious, to be sure, as I hope, but not filled with God; he excessively savours himself; nor does he touch the very marrow of the conscience; I rest through the whole day in God, my rock, in whose arms I am going to sleep securely;]

6. if deus deserat me parum, nihil sum; preces meæ sunt preces mortuæ, etiam vita mea mors est; Condona domine peccata rerum sanctarum; lachrymas meas lava atque preces; ablue reatum, aliquem; oh da mihi, faciem ut videam tuam;

[6. If God disinherits me a little, I am nothing; my prayers are dead prayers, even my life is death; Forgive, Lord, the sins of holy things; wash my tears and prayers; wash away some guilt; oh grant to me, that I may see your face;]

7. D. D. negat equidem deus verbum externum, vividum; habemus Downing,[517] hominem dubium generalum sui sapidum; non negat tamen deus seipsum atque suam præsentiam, In veni (querens) dominum in via suâ hac nocte publice; Lauda dominum, Anima mea, qui te coronavit benignitate;

[7. Sunday. God indeed denies the external, vivid word; we have Downing, a doubtful man generally self-important; Nevertheless, God does not deny Himself and His presence, I (seeking) found the Lord in His way, this night, publicly; Praise the Lord, my soul, who has crowned you with blessing;]

294. 8. Eo visum M^{rm} Laurence,[518] qui penitus servat se a Leturgiâ; hominem non naturâ fortassis sed gratia ingenuum, cordi dunque

---

[516] This 'magistrum Sedgwick' is likely to be Obadiah Sedgwick, rather than William Sedgwick of Farnham. Obadiah was a graduate of Magdalen Hall, Oxford (BD 1630) and had served as a chaplain to Horatio, Baron Vere in the Netherlands. In 1630 he became the curate and lecturer of St Mildred's, Bread Street, London, close to George Hughes at All Hallows, Bread Street. He went on to be a prominent figure in the 1640s, not least in the Westminster Assembly. Another possibility is Richard Sedgwick, the pastor of Wapping Chapel in London from 1617 to 1643.

[517] Calibute Downing, the minister of St John's, Hackney, in Middlesex from 1637. He could be seen as something of a trimmer, with godly roots and ambitions for the episcopate, not necessarily conflicting interests earlier in the century but a more difficult line to follow in the 1630s.

[518] There is a chance that this may have been Henry Lawrence, later President of Cromwell's Council of State. Another possibility is that it was Simon Lawrence, a merchant on the committee of the East India Company and a radical from the St Stephen's, Coleman Street,

optimis; dat mihi dominus libertatem maximam hac nocte; appropinqua domine, atque adhuc magis; te da mihi sit anima mea templum
tuum;

[8. I go to see Master Lawrence, who utterly saves himself from
lethargy; a man not by nature, perhaps, by grace noble, and finally
pleasing the best men; the Lord gives me the greatest liberty on this
night; draw near, Lord, and even more, up to this point, give yourself
to me; may my soul be your temple;]

9. Possum omnia per Christi vires qui libertatem dat coram Comitissâ
Clarensi;[519] nihil est homo, si deus præsens sit; tuam concede
præsentiam, protege me hac, hac nocte; in ulnis tuis acquiesco, sub
onere corporis mortis ingeniscens;

[9. I can [do] all things through the powers of Christ who gives liberty
in the presence of the Countess of Clare; man is nothing, if God be
present; grant your presence, protect me, this night; in your arms I rest,
under the burden of the body of death sighing;]

10. Deus fortis mihi omni = suficiens est; corona gaudij mei in deo est,
in christo meo qui mihi vis est in imbecillitate, dat protectionem,
libertationem a malis diaboli; oh quando videam te in gloria tua?
anhelat anima;

[10. The mighty God is all sufficient to me; the crown of my joy is in
God, in my Christ who to me is strength in weakness, [who] gives
protection, liberty from the evils of the devil; oh when may I see you in
your glory? My soul pants;]

295. 11. Fixum adhuc est cor meum in deum, doleo qd gloriam nominus
illius affere non possum, oh quando? quamdiu tardas ad ventum tum
Iesu mi? ego lubens in ulnis tuis morer ut gloriam tuam videam, atque
ut gloriam reddam,

[11. Thus far my heart is fixed on God; I grieve because I cannot utter
the glory of his name; oh when? how long do you delay until your
coming, my Jesus? I willingly would die in your arms, that I might see
your glory, and that I might render glory,]

---

parish: David Kirby, 'The radicals of St Stephen's, Coleman Street, London, 1624–1642',
Guildhall Miscellany 3 (April 1970), *passim* and esp. p. 119. There is, however, too little here
to indicate in either direction and a third possibility, of course, that it was a completely
different Mr Lawrence.
519 The Countess of Clare was Lady Elizabeth married to John Holles, and the daughter of
Lady Vere.

12. Lætitia mea patitur reflexum In angustijs sum, quis me liberabit; D4m3na disserit mecum de puribus longis; pertvrbatur mens mea; a precibus sp:[es] quem vincere vix possum, sæpius vidi in me; infirmitas mea est non pudentia; non zelus purus; Domine Condona, sana;

[12. My gladness suffers an ebbing; I am in the straits, who will free me; Madam [Vere] discusses with me about the enduring bitterness; my mind is troubled; there is hope from prayer which I am scarcely able to conquer, more often I have seen [it] in me; my weakness is not a shameful matter; it is not pure zeal; Lord, forgive, heal;]

13. Cogitationes meæ sunt de te Domine; Lex tua metitatio mea est eritque die et nocte; doleo quod afectiones meæ ardentes non sunt, non sunt vivaces satis; vivifica cor meum [inked out] o deus; [inked out] quia tecum est fons vitae;[520]

[13. My thoughts are about you Lord; your law is, and will be, my my meditation, by day and by night; I grieve because my feelings are not burning, they are not vigorous enough; vivify my heart, o God; because with You is the fountain of life;]

296. 14. D. D. Deus satis est mihi qui se manifetat, video te domine, quasi per ænigma, oh quando videbo te in gloria, ubi omnis cessabit labor, dolor, præsertim peccatum, oh Dies Lætitiæ per petuæ

[14. The Lord's Day. God is enough to me who reveals himself; I see you, Lord, as through a mystery, oh when shall I see you in glory, when shall cease all labour, sorrow, especially sin; oh day of perpetual gladness]

15. Lætor multum in Christo, qui iugum obedientiæ reddit quotidie facile; mandata tua Domine non sunt gravia, dixti tu atque dixisti; (quod ego expertus sum, esse) verum; [esse] subijce tibi Domine in me omnes vanas imaginationes, quæ vijs tuis aliquo modo non auscvltant; ut adhuc liberior evadam;

[15. I rejoice greatly in Christ, who daily renders the yoke of obedience easy; Your mandates, Lord are not heavy, You said, and You spoke the truth (for I have experienced [it] to be [so]) subject to yourself, Lord, in me all vain imaginings, which in any manner do not attend to your ways; that even more free I might go forth;]

16. Laboro sub difficili, inconstanti, superbo, et exvînde, obscuro

---

[520] 'The fountain of life' is a fairly common image in Scripture. See, for instance, Psalm 36:9; Prov. 13:14, 14:27; Rev. 21:6.

spiritu; væ mihi misero sub hoc onere peccati, quia sol iustitiæ non mihi splendescit in gloriâ suâ; immitte Domine radios tuos in terram hanc, atque semina gratiarum irradia, ut crescant in messem magnam, ad nominis tui gloria, atque ad gloriam meam;

[16. I labour under a difficult, inconstant, proud, and consequently, darkened spirit; woe to me, wretched, under this burden of sin, because the sun of justice does not shine on me in its glory; send, Lord, your rays into this earth, and irradiate the seeds of grace, that they may grow into a great harvest, by the glory of your name, and to my glory;]

297. 17. Cum minimum habeam creaturæ, fruor Christo maximè; inconstans spiritus, et obscurus perturbat me; nec traho liber sub onere (corporis mortis,) superbiæ meæ, in pietatis operibus, ne derelinquas seruum tuum Domine; nihil sum; omnia possum assistente Christo;

[17. When I have a minimum of the creature, I enjoy Christ in the greatest degree; an inconstant and dark spirit troubles me; nor do I move freely under the burden (of the body of death) of my pride; in the works of piety; may you not abandon your servant, Lord; I am nothing; I can [do] all, Christ assisting;]

18. prædicat obscurus, voluminus M^r: Goodwin;[521] de fide; duos tantum errores exaudio; nec unquam post preces tales, exaudiverim tam confusum chaos; Deus mihi omni = suficiens est, ego miser in Christo Iustitiâ meâ tutus acquiesco;

[18. Master Goodwin, obscure, voluminous, preaches; about faith; I hear only two errors; nor even after such prayers, might I have heard such confused chaos; God is to me all-sufficient, I, wretch, in Christ, my justice, rest safe;]

19. Lætor multum in humili societate Dominæ veere; cuius molle cor ostendit se hac nocte per lachrymarum rivulos, in consideratione suiipsius; Euince domine per hoc exemplar, imaginationes meas superbas; nihil sum; sive in meis oculis verè nihil ut onere per christum evadam;

[19. I rejoice greatly in the humble society of Lady Vere; whose soft

---

[521] John Goodwin had been elected as minister to St Stephen's, Coleman Street, London as the successor to John Davenport in 1633. The parish was renowned as a centre for puritan radicalism. Theologically, Goodwin took the preparationist theology of Hooker and his East Anglian acolytes to an extreme degree, eventually stepping over the line that took him into that unusual breed, the puritan Arminians. At this stage he was not completely clear in his position but there were concerns among the godly and it was a difficult line to walk in the conditions of Laudianism; perhaps this accounts for Rogers' choice of the adjective, 'obscurus' and his noting of 'errores'.

heart displayed itself this night, through streams of tears, in
contemplation of herself; subdue, Lord, through this model, my proud
imaginings; I am nothing; or in my own eyes truly nothing that
through Christ I might go forth from [this] burden;]

298. 20. magnæ, densæ que nubes faciem solis iustitiæ obfuscarunt; onus
intolerabile est ira patris cælestis; ego interim indignationem domini
feram submisse, ego enim merui, qd magis est, quod æternum est;

[20. Great, and dense clouds block the face of the sun of justice; an
intolerable burden is the wrath of the Heavenly Father, I, meanwhile,
shall bear submissively the indignation of the Lord, for I have deserved
what is greater, what is eternal;]

21. D.D. Onus insupportabile super me est ira, et indignatio domini,
premit me multum hodiè; Laboro sub angesto spiritu; corde durissimo;
reiquit me deus, ut videam quod in me est; (ut Hezekiah)[522] oh nihil est
in me; omnia possum per Christuum; infirmitous, sum atque ipsa
imbecillities sine Christo; auscultabo tamen qd loquutus dominus, ille
enim creabit mihi pacem;

[21. Lord's day. An impossible load to carry is the anger, and indignation
of the Lord, it oppresses me greatly today; I toil under spiritual distress;
[under] a very heavy heart; rest me Lord, as to show what is in me; (as
Hezekiah) oh nothing is in me; I can do all through Christ; I am weakened
and just weakness without Christ; I shall, however, hearken to what the
Lord [has] spoken, for he will create peace for me;]

21.[523] Sol iam post noctem langam exoriturus est; ego aliquos radios e
longiquo vidi; ego et adhuc in deo credam, qui mihi vita est, se dedit,
dabitque gloriam;

[21. the sun new, after a long night, is going to rise; I have seen some rays
from a distance; even thus far may I believe in God, who is life to me, who
has given himself to me, and will give glory;]

299. 22. Dolor dentium perturbat me, interpellat me in divinis; oh miserum
me, quantillum gratiæ, patientiæ, fideique, habeo; vix enim submissè,
possum ferre, qd minimum est; Storfordiensem zelum non invenio, nec
Christuam tam aperte; sic sine onere vel interno, vel externo, non
vivam; nec grata sit patria; oh quamdiu; quamdiu?

---

[522] This may be a reference to the time when Hezekiah rested on his laurels and responded to
Isaiah's threats regarding the consequences for the next generations by saying, 'Is it not
good, if peace and truth be in my days?' (II Kings 20:19), thus showing that the good of his
reign was due to God rather than any good in himself.

[523] Successive entries are numbered 21.

[22. A toothache troubles me, it interrupts me in divinity; oh wretched me, how little grace, patience, and faith I have; for scarcely can I bear submissively what is most slight; I do not find the Stortford zeal, nor Christ so openly; thus I might not live without either, the external or internal burden; nor would the homeland be pleasing; oh how long; how long?]

23. Anhelat anima mea post te Domine, qui hodie pacem dedisti, consolatus es animum meum per evangelizationem Drs Staughton;[524] Ego vestigij tuis insequar in vijs sanctitatis; vt te tandem aliquando videam, non per aenigma, sed aperte;

[23. My soul pants after You, Lord, who today has given peace, consoled my soul through the evangelising of Dr Stoughton; may I follow in your footsteps in the ways of sanctity; that finally I may see you sometime, not through a mystery, but openly;]

24. Angit me plurimum vehemens dentium dolor; interrumpit me inter studendum; video tamen amorem dei patulum in acerbitate hac; exinde conticescam

[24. The vehement toothache hurts me more; it interrupts during my studies; I see, however, the love of God revealed in this bitterness; therefore I shall be silent]

300. 25. nubes obscuræ tegunt faciem patris mei; Ego nihil sum, superbiam meam domat et adhuc dentis vexatio; Ego ad te aspicio, qui mihi omni = sufficiens est;

[25. Dark clouds cover the face of my Father; I am nothing, even thus far the pain of the tooth subdues my pride; I look to you, who are all-sufficient to me;]

26. Doleo multum, qd frigent affectiones meæ; nec ridet (secundum solitum) dominus in me; Adhuc tamen cor meum fixum est in Jehovan, qui adhuc me tentat dolore meo in solito, atque magno; sed morbi aculeus non est in me, sed in Christo; ego ergo patiar qd prudentissimus deus mihi imponit;

[26. I grieve greatly, because my feelings are cold; nor does the Lord smile on me (according to his custom); nevertheless, thus far my heart is fixed on Jehovah, who thus far tests me with my unaccustomed and great pain; but the sting of disease is not in me, but in Christ; may I therefore suffer what the most prudent God imposes on me;]

524 John Stoughton.

27. D.D. calor adhuc in me est, cælestis certè; extra porum habeo omnia in christo;

[27. Lord's Day, the warmth is thus far in me, surely heavenly warmth; beyond I have all things in Christ;]

28. Qui nomen tuum sciunt, confident in te; turris enim est, et sanctuarium tuis, in qua tuti tui latitant, etiam in temporibus mali;

[28. [Those] who know your name trust in you; for it is a tower, and a sanctuary for those who are yours, in which yours are safely concealed, even in times of evil;]

301. 29. sub onere hodie ingranui, ad hac nocte, aperui ut cum Dominâ, veere, et multum consolata est me; (egoque vicem illam) lætor multum in Iehovah rud in me; in Iustitiâ meâ; Lætor multum in Dominâ meâ; indignus ego, ut sub tectum eius dormiam; Lauda dominum quodcumque in me est; qui se dedit mihi, atque gloriam dabit;

[29. under a pressing load I groaned today, from this night, I revealed myself with Lady Vere, even much consolation is to me; (I consoled her in turn) I rejoice greatly in Jehovah in me; in my justice; to rejoice much in my Lord; I, unworthy, that under His roof I might sleep; Praise the Lord, whatever is within me; who has given himself to me, and will give glory;]

30. Exultat anima mea in domine, qui appropinquat ad me hodie in ministerio verbi (Dr Staughton)[525] oh quam anhelat spiritus meus post deum * sanctitatis, post sanctum sanctorum in quo nihil pollutum habitat;

[30. My soul exalts in the Lord, who draws near to me today in the ministry of the word (Dr Stoughton) oh how my spirit pants after the God * of holiness, after the holy of holies, in which nothing polluted dwells;]

Feb: 1. In extremitate meâ levat me deus; apostemem, depositum; doloris dentium emulveret lauda dominum [anima?][526] mea; reus iam;

[February 1. In my extremity, God raises me; He appeases the abscess, the deposit of the toothache; praise the Lord, my soul; guilty now;]

[525] John Stoughton.
[526] This section is seriously smudged.

302. 2. Non invenio continuum istum fervorum in me; refluxum patior; nec possum me in pulverem conijcere post res sacros; oh duplicitatem spiritus mei atque superbiam; Ad mensam sacramentalem advenio domine, ut Christum inveniam omni = suficientum;

[2. I do not find this continuous ardour in me; I suffer the ebbing; nor can I hurl myself into dust after sacred things; oh the duplicity and pride of my spirit; I come to the sacramental table Lord, that I may find Christ all-sufficient;]

3. spes mea in deo est; desiderio desidero sacramentum, foederis sigillum;

[3. My hope is in God; by desire I desire the sacrament, the seal of the covenant;]

4. D.D. accedo iam ad mensam domini in congregatione Colmaneas[527] oh quam tripudiat mens mea in risu Christi; accedit ad me familiariter deus, atque exultat anima mea; præsentia tua domine vita mea est;

[4. Lord's Day, I approach now to the table of the Lord in the congregation of Coleman oh how my mind dances in the smile of Christ; God approaches me familiarly, and my soul rejoices; your presence, Lord, is my life;]

5. In negotijs meis (Instruo enim; D[om] Rogerum Townshed)[528] spiritus meus evanescit, vix vitam servare possim, adhuc tamen vivo, atque tuus totus sum ut disposæ sigillum in turrem sacram

[5. In my affairs (for I am preparing[529] Lord Roger Townshend) my spirit disappears, scarcely may I preserve life, yet thus far I live, and I am all yours, that places the seal into the holy tower]

303. 6. 7. spiritus meus in fervore suo fluit, refluitque; oh miserum me; adhuc motum meum cælum versus retardat corpus mortis; pulverizetiam hoc mortum corpus qd pessime olet in naribus novi hominis; tandem, domine;

[6. 7. My spirit ebbs and slows in its ardour; oh pity me; thus far, the body of death slows my movement towards heaven; may I pulverise this dead body which smells very badly in the nostrils of the new man; at last, Lord;]

---

[527] St Stephen's, Coleman Street, London.
[528] Roger Townshend was the son of Sir Roger Townshend of Rainham, Norfolk and young Mary Vere, the second daughter of Lady Mary Vere, Rogers' patron. Rogers presumably began the instruction of young Townshend when the boy was perhaps eight years old.
[529] That is, instructing.

8. Elevatur spiritus meus per humilem societatem D^{os} Staught[on][530] qui nobiscum hodiè edit: cogitatio mea in te fixa est domine, qui solamen neum es, rupis, in temporibus malis;

[8. my spirit is raised through the humble company of Dr Stoughton who dines with us today: my thought is fixed on you Lord, who are my solace, [my] rock, in evil times;]

9. 10. Deus mihi et adhuc omni = suficiens est, qui ridet in me; Doleo tamen sub corpore hoc mortuo; caro naxi me resistit spiritum; spiritus tamen carni opponit; ego in hac pugnâ stabo, usque dum completam mihi deus dabit victoriam;

[9. 10. Even thus far God is all-sufficient to me, who smiles on me; nevertheless I grieve under this dead body; the flesh within me resists the spirit; the spirit, however, opposes the flesh; I shall stay in this battle, until God will give complete victory to me;]

11. D.D. M^{ra} D45nin:[g][531] (ut patet) hodiè prædicat; tinea frigidæ certe, Ingemisco sub hoc; Deus tamen so consedit; atque Lætor multum; Ad huc tamen non invenio zelum stortfordien sum, oh domine;

[11. Sunday, Mr Downing (as it appears) preaches today; a cold bookworm, surely, I groan under this; God, however, grants himself; and I rejoice greatly Thus far, however, I do not find Stortford zeal, oh Lord;]

304. 12. Adest nobis Mr Sedgewicke,[532] aliquo modo levis, plausum querens; perdit quidem mecum aliquid; ingenuus quidem atque bonus socius; reatus etiam rerum sacrarum me premit, usquedum dominis levat; atque iam cælo sereno inspiciam atque videbo lucem vultus divini; usque ad satietatem;

[12. Mr Sedgwick is with us, frivolous in some manner, seeking applause; indeed he wastes some time with me; honourable, to be sure, and a good companion; guilt even of sacred things oppresses me, until the Lord relieves me; and now I shall look into the clear sky and I shall see the light of the divine countenance; up to the point of satiety;]

13. Eo Londinum ad meros emendas; et ecce terrenae affectiones meæ

---

530 John Stoughton.
531 Calibute Downing.
532 It is not clear which Sedgwick this is, but if it is one of the ministers identified above, then it is more likely to be Obadiah than William, as it would be surprising if William Sedgwick, not having been seen for so long and so highly valued, would have not been seen as more noteworthy and received such a bad review.

fixæ ament in creaturis; eleva domine spiritum meum; quia adhuc deus
spes mea est in quo acquiesco;

[13. I go to London for pure corrections and, behold, my earthly
feelings remain fixed in the creatures; raise, Lord, my spirit; because
thus far God is my hope, in whom I rest;]

14. Quotidiè doleo sub onere corporis mortis; oh quando liber evadam;
anhelat anima mea post te Domine; eleva cor meum ad te; atque non
admirabor visibilea;

[14. Daily I grieve under the burden of the body of death; oh when
shall I go forth free; my soul pants after you, Lord; raise my heart to
you; and I shall not admire visible things;]

15. Factum est cor meum pro te, et irrequietum est donec veniat
ad te; anhelo multum, oh quando viderim te in æterna luve;
perturbat me hac nocte melancholius humor, atque reddit me
incongruum, difficilem (non facile); libera me domine ab onere
meo;

[15. My heart is made for you, and it is restless until it may come
to you; I pant greatly, oh when shall I have seen you in eternal
light; a melancholy humour troubles me this night, and it renders
me disagreeable, morose (not easy); free me, Lord, from my
burden;]

305. 16. Laboro sub duritie mea; possidet me reatus levitatis meæ, atque
premor tristitiâ; Eo Londinum cum Dominâ veere, quæ me corroborat
atque consolatur; Revertere domine ut videam vultum tuum, cuius lux
totum me irradiabit, recreabit;

[16. I labour under my hardness; the guilt of my levity possesses me,
and I am oppressed with sadness; I go to London with Lady Vere, who
strengthens and consoles me; return, Lord, that I may see your
countenance, whose light will irradiate, recreate my entire being [lit:
revive me];]

17. Fluo, refluoque; sic deus vult, ut grata sit patria, in viâ tam difficili;
acquiesco tamen in te; oh spes mea;

[17. I flow and ebb; thus God wishes, that the homeland may be
pleasing, in such a difficult way; I rest, however, in you; oh my
hope;]

18. D.D. Ingemisco sub corpore mortis; Infidelitas me turbat
multum; atque superbia; Dominus adhuc me aspicit in Iehovâ,

Iustitiâ meâ; Mr Housman[533] ad est nobis; præsentia eius me exinanivit; ego parum habeo, ille multum;

[18. The Lord's day, I groan under the body of death; faithlessness disturbs me greatly; and pride; the Lord thus far considers me in Jehovah, my justice; Mr Housman is with us; his presence has emptied me; I have little; he much;]

19. Opprimor ferè hodie, vix preces effundere possim; ut columba [questionable bit] in montibus, sic ego gemebun dus doleo; dominus rugas ostendit mihi;

[19. I am nearly overwhelmed today, scarcely may I pour forth prayers; as the heights in the mountains, thus I to be lamented, grieve; the Lord shows his anger to me;]

Attamen iam

306. [534] ridit, atque ego glorior in facie eius, cuius facies recreat subsidentes spiritus; lauda dominum, cor meum; qui me coronavit misericordia; cui ego Beulah, atque Hephtzibah sum;[535]

[but yet now he smiles, and I glory in his face, whose face revives [my] sinking spirits; praise the Lord, my heart; who has crowned me with mercy; to whom I am Beulah and Hephtzibah;]

20, 21, 22, 23, 24, 25, 26, 27. 28. March 1. 2. 3. 4. 5. 6. 7. 8. 9. 10. 11. 12. 13. 14. 15. 16. 17. 18. 19. This day An Ague; Burning; tertian (Epidemicall a gentle warning) takes mee, the first lasting sicknesse, that ever I was acquainted with; and hath lasted mee a moneth; At the first I found my heart wonderfull unwilling to stoop to the dealing of G.[od] (no afflict:[ion] is joyous but greivous) I would faine have kept in my heart but I found it ready to murmure; but I blesse G.[od] the longer I remained under his hand, the more willing I found my self to stoop to him; Our family hath bine much afflicted with it also;

306a. [536] 20, 21, 22, 23, 24, 25. I blesse the L[or]d who hath spared mee, and recovers strength to mee; but especially in that a gracious maner he manifests hims:[elf] and sanctifies his chastening to me so as that I am made in some measure partaker of his Holinesse; and that it yields the peacable fruits of righteousnesse to mee, who in some weake measure

---

[533] Unidentified.
[534] In margin: two large '*'.
[535] Beulah and Hephtzibah were Old Testament figures who symbolically expressed the return of God's delight. Beulah was a land no longer deserted by God and Hephtzibah (Hebrew for 'my delight is in her') was the renaming of 'Forsaken': Isaiah 62 and, in particular v. 4.
[536] Following p. 306, also numbered 306.

have bine exerci[se]d therby; Heb: 12. 10. 11.[537] Now L[or]d grant that it may much more; and that now I may lay up much Grace, against greater tryalls that they may not take mee unarmed, as this did in a great maner; L[or]d grant that I having tasted of a gen:[eral] desease, which is as a punishm:[ent] to our land, may see more into nat:[ure] of the cause, myne owne and nationall sine;

307. I will now sever my covenant with thee; Oh L[or]d; I am thyne thyne; [sic] who hast shewne mee such mercy; who hast afflicted mee for my good; I will walke before thee in the land of darknesse in my Integritye; oh that I might cleave[538] closer to thee forever to thee, even in that distraction, or separation;

26. In this sicknesse of mine upon the 18 March: king [sic] the sab: at 12. at night L.[ady] Townsh:[end's][539] chimny was a fire, and the soot set wood a fire that went thorough the chimny, being unwisely put in; the Lord delivered us strangely; if it had burnt a litle longer wee might have bine burnt; espec:[ially] I that lay sole et, [on my own] as I could not have gone downe to escape it; Let us render the Calves of our life; give up ourselves, which is better than the offering of an oxe that hath hoofs;[540] my spirite is flat; I am yet in my chamber, and not come into publique service; which is a wonderful quickning;

308. 27. Last night, I was distempered and could not sleep, much troubled and by reason of myne intemperance, I moderate not my selfe in diet; and so have litle comfort, if distresse should returne; but the Lord I believe hath put away my sin: oh that I might sin no more ag:[ainst] him in this kind;

28. I goe downe a litle, and catch cold, and a new fit of an agie [sic] assaults mee I find my head yet stubburne and loath to stoop; L[or]d make mee willing;

29. Ready to be discontented and melancholye for feare of more fits; but comforted and raised by 12. Heb: fit to be read of all afflicted ones;[541] and unbeliefe somew[ha]t beat downe; and my soule tender, and desirous to stoop;

---

[537] Hebrews 12:10–11 – 'For they verily for a few days chastened us after their own pleasure; but he for our profit, that we might be partakers of his holiness. Now no chastening for the present seemeth to be joyous, but grievous: nevertheless afterward it yieldeth the peaceable fruit of righteousness unto them which are exercised thereby.'

[538] See Glossary.

[539] Lady Townshend was Mary Townshend, the second daughter of Lady Mary Vere, who had married Sir Roger Townshend on 17 May 1627: Calder (ed.), *Letters of John Davenport*, p. 30n.

[540] Psalm. 69:30–31 – 'I will praise the name of God with a song, and will magnify him with thanksgiving. This also shall please the Lord better than an ox or bullock that hath horns and hoofs.'

[541] Heb. 12 explains that suffering can be seen as a suitable chastisement sent to the chosen people by God and is something to be learned from rather than simply mourned. It is a good thing, as any father will deliver chastening to his children, whereas 'if ye be without chastisement, whereof all are partakers, then are ye bastards, and not sons'.

309. 30. The L[or]d exercises mee with a 2d; fit; somewhat sharp; but I find more of his grace, and presense; he hath granted in my intermission some affliction grace which now I will try; oh lord give now, before new trialls; strengthen thou the hands that hang downe; my greatest burden is; that I can doe no good in my place; but it is thy will; makes mee lay my hand upon my mouth; I with Aaron will hold my peace;[542]

31. Still shall my mind depend upon him in whom I have believed; and I rest satisfied in that promise; that blessed is the man, whom the Lord corrects; and therefore I will not despise the chastening of the Lord;

April. 1. Saboth; wherin the L[or]d makes a reall sermon to mee by a third fit; but he moderates his hand graciouslye and supports mee with grace, and new supply of strength to beare the crosse; oh the sting is gone it is in X; the waspe cannot hurt mee; but it shall doe mee good;

310. 2. I still am in dependence upon G.[od] I have no whether else to goe; in affliction wee dare not looke away from him who beates us;

3. The L[or]d yet exercises mee with a 4th fit; yet moderate; L[or]d the use; he thaws my heart, and I yield, yet I feele another law in my members;

4. I stand yet in awe of G.[od] and find comfort in him; I mourne after recovery; for this glory sake Lord; for the fruit and this pore familye;

5. the Lords hand is upon mee in a 5. fit; but gentle still; I find my heart ready to be weary, and cast downe, but I gather up my selfe in the Lord, and have new comfort, and strength in him;

311. 6. I lye downe rejoicing in god; whose mercye, and truth failes mee not; whose lovingekindnesse hath shined upon mee and I lye downe in thyne armes;

7. Now the L[or]d tryes mee with a 6. fit but still nowe moderate a greate deale; and makes up all in that sweet, and constant communion, that I have with himself; thus the L[or]d traines mee up to have a greater burdens then these; oh Lord suffering grace, affliction strength;

8. Saboth, a day of rest, and comfort to my soule in reg:[ard] of the most gladding presence of Christ to mee; I am yet shut up in my chamber and without imployment, but the L[or]d is very gracious, and meanes mee to beare greater crosses;

9. this day, in the time of my fit, I had only an anguishnes, no distinct fit; the L[or]d is good to mee, gives mee hope of a perfect recovery, and now reveales himself and most sweetly to mee;

312. 10. The Lord is graciously neare to mee; and my heart waites upon him in the way of his judgements;

---

[542] Leviticus 10:3 – 'The Moses said unto Aaron, This is it that the Lord spake, saying, I will be sanctified in them that come nigh me, and before all the people I will be glorified. And Aaron held his peace.' This is when Aaron's sons, Nadab and Abihu, had been killed because they offered sacrifices contrary to the commandment of the Lord, so Rogers is hoping for similar acceptance of suffering.

11. my Ague still hangs upon mee and I am troubled with faint spreading sweat, but oh pore wretch that I am; I find in mee, a rebellious sp:[irit] lo[a]th to stoop, and wait gods laisure; but I moane under it; L[or]d quell it; I am yet thine;

12. Another Ague comes upon mee, the L[or]d will have mee stoop;

13. And still another fit, my flesh is weak, and ready to resist; but the L[or]d brings downe my heart low by Job; la:[st] cap:[chapter] I abhor;[543] Xt after G.[od] had sp:[oken] out of the whirlewind;[544]

313. 14.[545] Another sad fit comes; but the grace of g.[od] is allsufficient, I find abundance of gods presence, and my head lye in the dust, I have bine in an agony but god sent an Angel Mr Dod[546] to comfort mee; he sayes drink the cup that g.[od] gives without any mixture of oil as X did; and bec:[ause] g.[od] never punishes his people but chastises; 4 diff:[erences] 1. chastisements from a fountaine of love; punishm:[ent] a contra 2. g.[od] chastises in measure, and for a good end; he punishes the wicked, as malfactors; 3. chastisem:[ents] are mingled with blessing (Blessed is the man;[547] &c.) the other with cursing; 4. chastisements newest: δοκίμιον τῆς πιστεω;[548] is more precious than gold; the very tryall itselfe is the chastisement; then he said cast all your care and burden upon G.[od]; nigh sone; [sic] and so blessed mee for my grandf:[ather] and father each; and the L[or]d much refreshed mee by him; 85 y:[ears] old next May;

313a. [549] 15. Saboth another fit; Dr Clarkes physicke;[550] powder; blest to my great ease; All my care is now at length upon god; and I am at ease; car[e] of body; car[e] of soule; goods, yea of familye; and account too, which I did take upon my self and could not beare; Now I am eased; G.[od] cares for all; and I will wait to see the salvat:[ion] of g.[od];

---

[543] As far as can be ascertained, Rogers is brought low by the inadequacy of his willingness to embrace suffering according to the model of Job. The last section refers to Job 42:6 – 'Wherefore I abhor myself, and repent in dust and ashes.'

[544] Here Rogers is trying to take on the lesson of Job 40:6–8 – 'Then answered the Lord unto Job out of the whirlwind, and said, Gird up thy loins now like a man: I will demand of thee, and declare thou unto me. Wilt thou also disannul my judgment? wilt thou condemn me, that thou mayest be righteous?'

[545] In margin: 'Dod *'.

[546] John Dod was one of the greatest of the godly ministers of the first part of the seventeenth century. He was best known as a preacher and devotional writer at Hanwell, Oxon., and then at Canons Ashby, Northants., but he worked as a spiritual and, on occasion, political counsellor to both lay and clerical puritans: Samuel Clarke, A Generall Martyrologie (1677), pp. 168–78; Webster, Godly Clergy, pp. 11, 25, 58, 277–8, 301–5.

[547] Probably a reference to Psalm 94:12 – 'Blessed is the man whom thou chasteneth, O Lord, and teachest him out of thy law; That thou mayest give him rest from the days of adversity, until the pit be digged for the wicked.'

[548] δοκίμιον τῆς πιστεω: a testing of faith.

[549] Also numbered 313 in text.

[550] A Dr Clarke appears in the Hackney parish register: GLRO P79/JN 1/22.

16. Another moderate fit; comfort sent bef:[ore] by Mr Sedgewicks[551] coming and by the gracious presence of god; who constantly reveales his lovingk:[indness] to mee; ther[e]f:[ore] I put my trust under the shadow of his wings;[552]

17. This day the L[or]d moderates his hand for fit; very litle; but my teeth ake violentlye; I will stoop; I mourne that my sp:[irit] is something flat, and faith not a foote

314. 18. Now I take a vomit; oxynel scyllit: from Dr Clarke; it workes not, but by violence, and I am much disquieted; and flesh and blood resists; oh how hard a th:[ing] it is in such a pinch, to lye low, and submit without fretting L[or]d pardon what in mee is flesh and give more grace;

19. I am weake in stomacke, and bodye, and a grudging of fit comes; and flesh out of frame; but my heart is fixed upon him, who is my all = sufficiency;

20. Now an imposture breaks in my mouth, and I eased thorough mercye, yet much troubled with teeth, and the unfitnes of body makes mee out of frame to pray; but still the L[or]d is gracious, and my bent, and confidence the same; this was my last Ague day; blessed be G.[od];

21. In the last night perplexed with teeth, and [inked out] aguishe sweating in the morning now refreshed with the kindnes of the Lord, and in him I will rejoice evermore, be carefull in nothing; but rather give thanks; and pray;

315. [553] 22. Saboath; in the morning in head an anguish sweat (a consequent upon an old ague) comes upon mee, no fit; and my heart loath to stoop to it, and g.[od] in it, but I stoop ag:[ain] and awcke,[554] and have found much of g.[od']s presence in the latter part of this day, cheared, and refreshed;

23. weakely, yet recovering strength, but illish, and mind something unwilling to stoop to god; yet sp:[irit] is willing;

24. I grow stronger still, I blessing this a chearfull day to mee; oh mercye, to injoy one day; blesse the L[or]d, oh my soule; L[or]d an heart to walke worthy of thy kindnesse;

25. this day the L[or]d sends my father by providence to mee; who quells my spirit; and the L[or]d now is pleased still to strengthen mee in

---

[551] Obadiah Sedgwick; see above p. 133n.

[552] The term 'shadow' is common in Scripture as a word for 'shelter'. The full phrase is probably taken from Psalm. 36:7, particularly as it is also the source of 'lovingkindness', another favourite of Rogers: 'How excellent is thy lovingkindness, O God! therefore the children of men put their trust under the shadow of thy wings'.

[553] Numbered 215 in text but changed here to 315. From here onwards Rogers sticks to this misnumbering by one hundred, and for the sake of clarity the numbering in the three hundreds will be adopted.

[554] See Glossary.

body, and to refresh my soule daily with his peace and lovingkindnesse; oh bless the L[or]d, oh my soule;

316. 26. Still the L[or]d refreshes mee with recovering strength, gives mee a day of libertye; and comfort 1. from hims:[elf] (oh that my soule may walke in awe, and feare of him recovering, and in health as well as in sicknesse) 2. from the joy of my fathers presence;

27. In the morning in my bed warmed and thawed, with my fathers prayer, in private; who prayed most effectually for mee; espec:[ially] that I may not loose that after recovery which I have got in sicknesse; and for present that I should wait with patience upon g.[od] in this time, when I can doe litle; oh: * I asked what I should doe ab:[out] 45r f1sh34ns[555] heere; he says; pray; never medle except very excessive in such th:[ing]s my father would never; content your selfe; and say nothing; and ag:[ainst] try a moderation; sad at departure, but rejoicing in g.[od] my father, who leaves mee not; Full of joy in prayer this night; oh blesse;[556]

317. 28. The L[or]d is very graciously neere to my soule this day; and comforts mee in bodye; oh I have chastisements, and hope of recovery from a promise;

29. Saboth, something ill in body, and flesh, and blood is ready to be full of feares; oh yet I gather up my selfe; and find abund:[ance] of sweetnesse in G.[od] and his promise; A comfortable saboth though in my chamber; G.[od] is All;

30. yet rejoicing in G.[od] being much cheered with strength, and revived in sp:[irit] yet some flaggings, but I gather up my selfe, and rejoice in the promise;

May; 1. This day, an ague of mind distempers mee something, but my peace is in G.[od], in whom is all my comfort; oh L[or]d I am lose; why shouldest thou regard a worme; oh an heart inlarged to praise thee;

318. 2. In the night perplexed with many thoughts, ready to be discontent, for want of rest, but I checke Flesh; In the day I take a purge; the L[or]d blesses it to mee; and cheers my sp:[irit] this evening, and in his armes I lye downe;

3. the coast yet cleare betweene the L[or]d, and mee, though yet weake in bodye; I wait for strength;

4. the L[or]d continues gracious, I get strength and my heart is inlarged, and I meet the L[or]d drawing near to mee in the day, and this evening, sweetlye;

5. the Lord causes mee yet to attend upon him, and he causes mee to be

---

[555] In inquiring about 'our fashions', Rogers was asking if he should correct what he saw as the inappropriate clothes of his employers, and his father, probably wisely, suggested that he should be cautious.
[556] In margin: '* nota'.

quiet, and thankfull; oh my soule mourns after exercise; L[or]d by thy loving chastisement fit mee for great service;

6. * Saboath; wherin the L[or]d is good to my soule in my privacye still; but oh he hath given mee leave to praise him in the familye; 1. Timo;[557]

319. he gives strength, and assistance to feeblenesse, L[or]d goe on to give strength, that I may give it to thee; I lye downe in thyne armes;

7. the L[or]d is yet my portion; I goe to publique supper with a great company, and vanities and my mind ready to goe after the creat:[ures] but they are too empty;

8. much refreshed by societye, at mr Davis[558] his house; the L[or]d hath yet granted libertye ag:[ain] to come publiquelye, and caryes me thorough the dutye with alacritye, and comfort;

9. yet god is good, and quickens, and joyes mee in the performance of my exercise; oh I yet joy in G.[od] and feare him, never let mee loose the fruit of thy chastisement oh Lord;

320. 10. I visit freinds, with godly cheere, Mr Crooke;[559] but needing to mope out of company; and be very thoughtfull; (oh my unbelieving care; L[or]d purge it) but yet in the multitude of my thoughts within mee thy comforts refresh my soule; and I joy in thee, lying downe;

11. the Lord yet affords strength; yet weaknesse in bodye; oh by this the L[or]d awes mee; and yet is gracious to mee;

12. my heart is not so close to g:[od] as faine I would have it; yet is it fixed; companyes, and ocasions are ready to flat the sp:[irit]lesse the Lord be wonderfull gracious; yea so he hath bine, and so he is;

13. Saboath, the 1. I goe abroad; blesse the L[or]d, oh my soule, who accord:[ing] to his promise hath dealt with thee delivered thee thus far; pore means without; but G.[od] All = sufficient is neere mee, and chears mee; and I roule my selfe upon him;

321. 14. the L[or]d is yet gracious, and my heart much refreshed in secret by the presence of god; wee part with m[r] Glover;[560] oh L[or]d pitty us wee are very weake; and goe with them; and shew us all thy way;

15. A litle distempered, and many unbeleiving thoughts come in upon mee doubtfulness, and anxietye, but I gather up my selfe, and rejoice in G.[od] and his promise; no evell shall come neer mee;

---

557 This may be a reference to the first epistle of Timothy.

558 Perhaps Mr Davis was William Davis, a resident of Clopton, Hackney: GLRO LB/P79/JN1/22.

559 Both a William and a George Crooke lived in Clopton, Hackney. William Crooke was a member of Lincoln's Inn and Sir George Crooke was a judge of the King's Bench: GLRO LB/P79/JN1/22. Of the two, the first is the more likely, given Rogers' usual devotion to giving his characters their proper titles.

560 Jose or Joseph Glover was the rector of Sutton, Surrey from 1628 to 1636. He resigned in 1636 and then preached in London, travelling and soliciting funds for the college that was to become Harvard. He was probably pursuing such work in the Vere household. In May 1638, as Rogers notes later, Glover and his family, Stephen Day, a printer, and three male servants boarded a ship bound for New England: Anna Glover, *Glover Memorials and Genealogies* (Boston, Mass., 1867), pp. 560–1.

16. the L[or]d yet upholds my spirit, and causes mee to rejoice in himselfe; and to be glad at this that he is a Blessed man, whom the Lord choses and * causes to approch to himselfe; (65. psal:[m] 4:)[561]

17. thou art yet neere to mee, deare G.[od] and I am under the shadow of thyne hand, and I shall be safe;

18. yet is my soule fixed upon my G.[od] and I walke with him with full hearte though weakely, but the savour of my chastisement is upon mee;

322. 19. Still I bend towards my center, and fly to my [inked out], I am weary with flut[te]ring over the waters; oh when shall I rest in thee and never fly out more;

20. Saboath, much revived, my soule joyes in G.[od] myne habitation, to whom I resort; (71. psal;[m] 3.)[562] I am much caryd in a way of praising god, and thankfulnes; I cannot love thee, oh my g.[od] I cannot praise thee, as I would; Did I ever injoy more of God constantly? I thinke no;

21. I walke yet with the sense of gods favour, though with much weaknes; the L[or]d pittyes and knows my mould;

22.[563] this day have I payd my vows, that I made to G.[od] in my sicknesse; that if he would restore mee, then would I give the calve of my life and I have found the presence of G.[od] graciouslye; I have bine espec:[ially] once in the suburbs of heaven; oh it is most excellent being in heaven, where I shall doe nothing else and that without flagging or wearing which I mourne under heer;

323. 23. I heare Dr Staughton;[564] no peace with the pap:[ists] and come home in coach late, and no family duty, and I untoward in private after supper ready to sinke, L[or]d be gracious, and recover life, and strength, I am thyne, and thy presence is sweet;

24. my confidence is not removed, but is daily in G.[od] my portion; I mourne that my heart is ready to be hurryed, and cannot so cleave[565] to the L[or]d without separat:[ion]

25. sadded, thorough the darke, dusty, dulsome cariage of these women L1d:[y] V[ere]; and Prisc: W1stn[566] L[or]d thou wouldest humble mee and doe mee good by all; oh thy selfe more, and let mee not flag;

26. though neither head in the stall; nor figtime blossome &c; yet in the L[or]d alone does my soule rejoice;

---

[561] Psalm 65:4 – 'Blessed is the man whom thou choosest, and causest to approach unto thee, that he may dwell in thy courts: we shall be satisfied with the goodness of thy house, even of thy holy temple.'

[562] Psalm 71:3 – 'Be thou my strong habitation, whereunto I may continually resort: thou hast given commandment to save me; for thou art my rock and my fortress.'

[563] In margin: '* A day of thanksgiving'.

[564] John Stoughton.

[565] See Glossary.

[566] Lady Vere and Priscilla Watson, the servant identified above, p. 123n.

27. Saboath, my sp:[irit] seems something flattish; and not that close acquaintance with G.[od] which I faine would have; but my heart is fixed;

324. 28. A litle sunke; I cannot apply my selfe constantlye to any thing; oh L[or]d pitty mee; my thoughts yet resort to thee as my habitation;

29. much adoe to keep above; oh that I could walke closer and more clearelye; yet this I have found in G.[od] that I would not part withall for a world;

30. I goe to London; heare Dr Gouge;[567] thy vowes oh Lord; &c: and Dr Staughton;[568] my heart is thawed and inlarged to praises, and thanks to the god of my chastisem:[ent] deliverance, and comfort; oh that I could walke before the Lord in the land of the living;

31. my soule glories in Christ not in selfe; I am nothing; vile; my services sinfull, I every way awcke[569] but my thoughts are upon god; my habitation; oh when shall I come; &c:

325. June: 1. refreshed by publique meanes, mr sedgewicke;[570] and my soule longs for a sacrament;

2. my heart is extraordin:[arily] inlarged in dutyes, and raised; L[or]d how sweet is it to converse with thee?

3. Saboth; sacram:[ent] at Coleman Street libertye; and the L[or]d refreshes mee more and stirs up faith to trust in him; and quickens my affections; and now L[or]d I am thyne for ever;

4. I injoy some sweet communion with god; and the L[or]d is still my portion; oh that I could walke before him in the land of the living;

5. my heart is somewhat downe the wind; oh I cannot cleave[571] so close; I mourne; yet my joy is in the L[or]d my Righteousn[ess] and my heart, and confidence fixed;

326. 6. Dr Staughtons[572] * Irenicum: for Lutherans; I something downe; and untoward L[or]d smile and comfort, in thee is my life, and peace;

7. somewhat downe, and untoward; but my thoughts, and eyes towards him now;

8. sunke; and the Lord seems in some maner to stand aloofe of[f]; and to shew mee what is in my selfe; oh L[or]d a lump of miserye; all my hope is in free mercye;

9. I injoy G.[od] in some measure though the coast be not so cleere; oh that it were; L[or]d I am thyne, give mee my sicknesse grace; that tedeous [sic] feare to offend thee, faith to trust thee;

---

[567] William Gouge was an important figure of moderate puritanism. He served as lecturer at St Anne's, Blackfriars from early in the century until his death in 1653. He had been one of the ministers involved in the Feoffees for Impropriations and went on to work for Presbyterianism in the Westminster Assembly.
[568] John Stoughton.
[569] See Glossary.
[570] Obadiah Sedgwick.
[571] See Glossary.
[572] John Stoughton.

10. Saboth, the L[or]d is gracious; though I conflict with an untoward heart yet it is overcome by lying downe; oh more of thy selfe, and subdue my selfe dailye;

327. 11. now comes the Earle of Westmorl:[and][573] ab:[out] the match; and I am full of distractions; and melancholye; oh sad; sad; the L[or]d pitty her, that shee may never loose any motions; but stir them up;

12. now comes the sad newes of my sister Marys mortall sicknesse;

13. 14. 15. And I ride home and find her somewhat cheered, yet scarse knowing mee, but roving and ering in g.[od] and goodnes; the promises that were her studdye, and joy in health now vent thems:[elves] As the name of the L[or]d; &c: G.[od] All suffic:[ient] et:

16. now she begins to change; and our hearts are filled with sorrow; and yet wee break our hearts in gods bosome, and are eased;

17.[574] Now is the saboath, and the L[or]d takes away our beloved Jonathon;[575] He gives her saboth, upon saboth; I am distressed for thee oh my sweetest sister;

328. very pleasant hast thou bin unto mee oh my darling thy Love to mee was wonderful passing the love of women (oh my deare) for thy love was divine, and from above; thou oh Lord hast taken away thyne owne; for parents are but nurses, and from nurses are the children taken at their fathers command;[576] wee will stoop bec:[ause] it is thy will; but wee will lye downe and mourne for her and humble our soules under thy hand;

This Saint departed; was by nature; something reserved, and not active; in her youth violently impatient, and by reason of it very litle regarded of us; but after the L[or]d had wrought his mighty worke of grace in her; these things vanished and the quite contrary appeared;

329. for she (by grace) was v[er]y active, and never well, but when shee was doing for god; either doing, or receiving good, or both together if possible; A most hungry soule after more, more; much acquainted with self denyall; and the life of faith in the *parish, which was her soules delight and savored promises, as much as ever any that I knew; shee was acquainted with the most close, and spiritual wayes of god; increasing daily in divine knowledge; surely by prayer and Obed:[ience]

---

573 The second Earl of Westmorland was Mildmay Fane, a graduate of Emmanuel College, Cambridge and an MP in the early 1620s. He married Lady Mary Townshend on 21 June 1638. Rogers is concerned that Mary Townshend will lose her religious zeal in such a marriage.

574 In margin: '*'.

575 Jonathan was David's close friend, seen to represent love, faithfulness, disinterestedness and self-sacrifice: I Sam. 18:1; 20; II Sam. 1:26.

576 A fairly common source of comfort among the godly: Houlbrooke, *Death, Religion and the Family in England, 1480–1750*, p. 241.

Jer. 33.3.[577] If you doe; A most publique sp:[irit] shee had for the church of G.[od] and tenderly affected with the evell of the times, from which now the L[or]d hath hidden her, with himselfe; (oh my sister of delights) I thinke long to be with thee out of a miserable world;

330. shee was a substantiall grounded Christian, of a solid temper (oh that wee may inherit her graces) eminently gifted, as in dayes of humiliat:[ion] with Mrs Clench[578] (who is to be sp:[irit] of her (as her freind most constant, and deare) with respect) appeared; the L[or]d hath inlarged her by the 3. or 4. houres together; shee was a most dutifull, and loving child, as I thinke lived upon the earth, for shee loved in the L[or]d; A most tender, and loving sister to her brothers, and sisters, ever studying, and praying for there good; An intire freind to the worship of Xt; and shee againe, was the daughter, and sister, and freind of Delights; where shee saw no savor of G.[od] shee could not love, though other things were ab:[ove] common; when shee spyed the image of G.[od] (as the L[or]d gave her a discerning sp:[irit] in an eminent way) shee clave to them, though never so neare; (Remdmb 44: Is: 3.4:5:)[579]

331. 18. upon the 18. wee buryed her by my grandfather; (oh that her graces may not be buryed from us) and the bitter mourners goe about the streets; wee returne home, and brake our hearts in the bosome of the L[or]d; and the L[or]d graciously inlarges mee to set it home in prayer in the familye; And the L[or]d in mercye of his abundante grace sanctifie this chastisement to all that survive;

19. Upon the 19. I am constrained to returne home to Hackneye by reason of my place; and the mother ading ocasions; oh woe is mee that I am come out of the house of mourning into an house of rejoicing;

20. now preparations for the great mariage of Lady townshend with E.[arl] of Westmorland, and my heart is sad, and above

332. these things that perish with the using;

21. And now the wedding is; and my heart; yet the L[or]d is with mee to carrye mee thorough the service of my place, with life and some sweetnes; undaunted before great ones;

---

[577] Jer. 33.3 – 'Call unto me, and I will answer thee, and shew thee great and mighty things, which thou knowest not.'

[578] Mrs Clench may be Jane Clench, who by the 1650s was of Halstead, Essex. She helped Mary Josselin, the wife of Ralph, in her final hours in 1650: Alan Macfarlane (ed.), *The Diary of Ralph Josselin 1616–1683*, Records of Social and Economic History n.s. III (London, 1976), pp. 203, 711.

[579] Isaiah 44:3–5 – 'For I will pour water upon him that is thirsty, and floods upon the dry ground: I will pour my spirit upon thy seed, and my blessing upon thine offspring: And they shall spring up as among the grass, as willows by the water courses. One shall say, I am the Lord's; and another shall call himself by the name of Jacob; and another shall subscribe with his hand unto the Lord, and surname himself by the name of Israel.'

22. I am nothing, all my joy is in thee; the lesse I have of the creature; oh L[or]d the more let mee find in thy selfe;

I am bereft of my sister, but I am not bereft of my g.[od] I now studdy the use of this affliction, it is to no purpose to pore upon the losse and goe no further; oh L[or]d bring my heart daily more and more into a profiting frame; I will reste upon thee now oh L[or]d a few dayes, and then also my desired charge ever the day of my redemption shall come;

333. 23. my sp:[irit] much sadded; yet I gather up my selfe in the Lord my portion; though freinds, and heart failes, yet G.[od] doth faile mee never; oh Lord, mee thinkes I want that stortford compassionate sp:[irit] and sp:[irit] of zeale; oh poure it downe deere G.[od] upon dry ground;

24. Saboath, drooping, and downe, but myne eyes are fixed, to attend what g.[od] the L[or]d will doe for my soule;

25. straitned, and untoward; by multitude of company, and some profane; (oh it vexes my soule) by the grim spirits ordinary; which I am to deale withall; L[or]d give a blessed use of there darknes; L[or]d be thou mine All = sufficiencye for thou hast removed my darling sister; and givest mee small hopes under the sun;

26. much discontent, and moping, being crost in myne expectation of L1d:[y] T4wnsh:[end's] g3ft: a pore

334. requitall for l1b:[our] p t4ng[ue] L[or]d raise up my thoughts to thee;[580]

27. Drooping, and sad still; the L[or]d seems to be far of[f]; and crosses, are upon mee; oh what shall I doe; I will looke up, and waite patiently for the G.[od] of my salvat[ion];

28. the L[or]d now somewhat eases mee, and cheers my sp:[irit] lets in some light; speakes though somewhat far of[f]; oh blessed mee, that the L[or]d should refresh mee;

29. I will lye downe in the arms of g[od] who hath spoken peace to mee, and hath supported mee by his grace to walke with him this day though weaklye; L[or]d forgive; L[or]d I believe;

30. All my joy is in the L[or]d my G.[od] I am nothing; L[or]d make mee to trample upon selfe more, and more; I am thyne, and I lye downe with my heart fixed upon thee;

335. July. 1.[581] Saboth; and sacrament at Coleman: broken to peices with joy; drunk with comfort; this is a day of rejoicing, and strength; for the joy of the L[or]d, hath bin my strength; A sweet communion of Saints, at mr Roules his house at dinner;[582] a sweet refreshing at mr

---

[580] The expression 'p tong' may be an abbreviation for 'practising tongue'. Rogers expected rather more for his services. He seems to have given some instruction to young Townshend and may have played some part in the marriage service.

[581] In margin: '*'.

[582] After the service at St Stephen's, Coleman Street, Rogers stayed on for dinner. 'Mr Roules' may have been Owen Rowe who had moved into the parish sometime in 1632. His family had been prominent in the government of London for several generations and he was related by marriage to the godly Earl of Warwick. He went on to be famous as one of those

Simonds;[583] one of a most sweet, godly spirit; and now I lye downe with praises;

2. Somewhat down ag:[ain] oh L[or]d thou liftest mee up, and casteth mee downe; yet will I look towards thee; and in thyne armes will I lye downe;

3. This day I view the towre of the great sights there; and I see that the time is coming that one stone shall not be left upon another; L[or]d thou art my towre, enduring in whom I will dwell safely, and lye downe in peace;

4. I sinke, and find this dead body annoying mee; L[or]d subdue it then shall I praise thee freely;

336. 5. Tyred by going to London, and unfit for any th:[ing] sp:[iritual] bec:[ause] of untowardnesse in body; Lord smile; I am thyne; I visit Dr Laiton[584] in the fleet; a scotch sp:[irit] right; but sure upright, and one that hath tasted of the sweetnes of X, even in this affliction;

6. untoward by a cold; and awcke[585] to good; but my heart brake somewhat; the remembrance of my sister is mournefull; yet I can joy in G.[od] here, and my salvation;

7. my soule exalts it selfe in the L[or]d; who hath graciously satisfied mee with his lovingkindnesse oh that I could walke worthy of it;

8. Saboath, wherin the L[or]d hath given some support, and strength to attend upon him; a great fit of wind, and loosenes, and it makes mee stoop more to god;

337. 9. somewhat eloofe of; somewhat more common, in company, and giving my selfe scope in mirth; and I am downe; but my heart is fixed;

10. I joy in the L[or]d, who is my strength, and though I am very weake in dutyes, and pore in my obedience, yet will I rejoice in the L[or]d my portion, who forgives those, and accepts freelye;

11. 12. supported thorough daily grace given, to attend upon the L[or]d with full bent, and purpose; and some sweet refreshings I find by Xs smiles;

13. still I depend upon him, who is my strength, and hold, even in the time of trouble;

14. There is a comfortable serenitie upon my soule; and my heart is

---

who signed the death warrant of Charles I in 1649. Valerie Pearl, *London and the Outbreak of the Puritan Revolution* (Oxford, 1961), p. 324; Kirby, 'The radicals of St Stephen's', pp. 104, 110, 112–13.

583 Joseph Simonds, the rector of St Martin's, Ironmonger Lane, London. After his education at Emmanuel College, he went on to study under Thomas Gataker at Rotherhithe. Shortly after this entry, he emigrated to the Netherlands: Shipps, 'Lay patronage,' pp. 353–6; Seaver, *Puritan Lectureships,* pp. 195, 259–60.

584 Alexander Leighton, the radical puritan and polemicist, who was imprisoned in the Fleet prison, fined and branded for his scurrilous and controversial writings against bishops and members of the royal court: see Foster, *Notes from the Caroline Underground,* pp. 14–39.

585 See Glossary.

soft, and awefull of god; I thinke of my sister, and I looke up, and lye downe pore, nothing;

338. 15. saboth, when I am much downe, in reg:[ard] of means dead and dry; but my heart is yet hankering after G.[od]; and unquiet without him;

16. Now wee see the Queene, at Mr Basses;[586] oh how happy am I, that know the court tumult so litle, as I doe; oh blessed be thy name oh L[or]d, who hast denyed mee much in the creature but hast supplyed all in thy selfe;

17. my soule is somewhat of[f], and downe; but yet melting after my beloved; and in him alone yet doe I comfort my selfe;

18. my heart is yet fixed in god and comforted in him in regard of my selfe, and my deare sister departed;

19. I find it hard to keep close to the Lord; I mourne under a flagging spirit; L[or]d raise mee up and hold mee;

339. 20. my heart still goes on, and something rejoices in god my portion; though something damped by the darke solemnes of our people;

21. the Lord is my Rocke, into whom in these sorrowfull times I will run, and lye safe; oh that I could serve him, and Love him more;

22. Saboth, wherin the L[or]d is to mee above meanes dry doings with pore D4wn3ng;[587] but supported inwardlye; oh I will waite till my charge shall come, and then I shall need no more meanes;

23. Mourning under an untoward auck spirit, a body of death, that makes mee sullen, and untoward, Lord ease mee, and comfort mee;

24. yet does the L[or]d support mee in a dependance upon himselfe; though I am weake, yet does he pardon, and accept me in X; but I see him not so clearlye;

340. 25. A litle downe, but hanging upon him who is my all-sufficiencye; and in his armes I sleepe;

26. The name of the Lord is my tower, and in the saddest times I will run therinto, and be safe;

27. I find not that heate of spirit;

28. and neernes to god, yet my soule stay it selfe upon him, and is safe;

29. Sab:[bath] the coast not so cleare but my heart is fixed, and the Lord gives mee a desire earnest for the good of this pore familye; but mee thinkes I want the bleeding affections, that I found at stortford;

30. pore in services, if the Lord withdraw, I draw on heartilye; oh Lord I am nothing; thou art all;

31. my soule stayes it selfe upon god my All-sufficiencye, and I am established with perfect peace, in his armes I rest;

[586] Mr Bass was a resident of Hackney: GLRO P79/JN 1/22. The queen, to state the obvious, was Henrietta Maria.
[587] Calibute Downing.

341. August: 1.[588] my heart is not so full of joy in god, as I would faine have; I find a lazy, luskish,[589] dead, base heart, warping[590] from god; oh Lord drawe mee neere, and hold mee close to thee; I am comforted with a letter from M W1k2r:[591] wherin is signified that I have bin as one of 1000. to her;

2. I have got somewhat neere to G.[od] and rejoice in him; and am comforted in the hope of sacrament coming; oh Lord, as thou hast bin to mee, so be;

3. Refreshed with John wright, an old zelot; the L[or]d grant more life, and sweetnes to mee, for I am under a cloud; yet mee thinks the sun glimpses thorough it;

4.[592] this day fasting and prayer private for preparat:[ion] to sacram:[ent] I find the L[or]d very gracious; he makes my heart bleed for the times and inlarged mee yet to mourne, and wrestle; and hath given some hints; and a sweet comfortable confidence in him that I am his, and shall be refreshed at his Feast;

342. 5. Sab:[bath] this day sacrament, at Coleman, and Spurstow afternoone;[593] I am refreshed with the fat things of the house of my God, this day; Blesse the lord oh my soule, and all that is within mee pay tribute to him; * this is a day of gladnes and joy;

6. my heart is ready to flag, I mourne that so quickly after a sacrament; my heart should grow dull, and untoward; but Lord I trust in thee;

7. my heart, downe, and the L[or]d seems to leave mee; but it is to shew mee my nothingnesse, and that I must live by a moment[ar]y dependance upon him;

8.[594] This day I was at mr Crooks; and confer[e]d with mrs Keeling his daughter;[595] one in the saddest condition, that ever I knew any; one that breaks much, but shee cryes out, all is but passion; and shee can have no rest, for shee is not sanctified; shee hath kept from ch:[urch]

---

588 In margin against the section about the letter: '*'.

589 See Glossary.

590 See Glossary.

591 'M Waker' is Lady Anne Wake, the daughter of Edmund Bray of Barrington, Glos. and Berks., the step-daughter of Sir Edward Conway and the widow of Sir Isaac Wake. Conway was the brother-in-law of Lady Vere: Calder (ed.), *Letters of John Davenport*, p. 77; Kirby, 'The radicals of St Stephen's', p. 100n; see below, pp. 160, 162.

592 In margin: '*'.

593 'Spurstow' was probably William Spurstow, one of the wealthiest parishioners of Coleman Street. He was a mercer and merchant and went on to be MP for Salisbury in the Long Parliament: Kirby, 'The radicals of St Stephen's', p. 119.

594 In margin: '*'.

595 See p. 149 above. This Mr Crooks was William Crooke of Chilton, Bucks. He was a member of Lincoln's Inn and a resident of Clopton, Hackney. Mrs Keeling was his daughter and married to John Keeling, a barrister of the Inner Temple: J. J. Howard (ed.), *The Visitations of London* (1883), II, 25, 204. Either Crooke or a relation of his may have partaken in the negotiations with the Feoffees for Impropriations about All Saints, Hertford, where John Archer was chosen as lecturer: I. M. Calder, *Activities of the Puritan Faction of the Church of England* (London, 1957), pp. 55, 80, 89–90, 103. See above, p. 30.

unfit for calling; overwhelmed with temptat:[ion] condemning herselfe for the comforts shee hath had

343. and says, they were but meere contemplations; and they are not the th:[ing]s to comfort her, but she must find those graces in her selfe, before she can find comfort; I prayed, and the L[or]d directed mee strangely; L[or]d pitty this pore Heman;[596] my heart, and bowells earne[597] towards her;

9. I cannot walke with G.[od] so closely as faine I would; the L[or]d seems to stand afarr of[f], but my heart is fixed;

10. somewhat darke, and much adoe to keep up a flagging unbelieving heart, and I am ready to goe out in mine owne strength to dutyes, and I loose of my comfort, L[or]d heale all Breaches, and yet will I lye downe in thee;

11. the Lord shimmeres through the clouds, and I am glad; oh it is uncomfortable to live a day without a sun;

12. Saboth, inlarged much in publique, yet straightnd at home, L[or]d loose this bound up sp:[irit] and remove all guilt;

344. 13. I am in a cloud and much straitned; the L[or]d pitty mee, unloose mee, and inlarge mee; and I will run;

14. 15. Troubled ab:[out] sick folk, at my Ladys going to Northamptonsh:[ire][598] and my thoughts disordered; oh how unfit am I for tumultuous ocasions; oh a mercye that I may live quietlye, and injoy peace from thee;

16. An awck[599] heart to that which is good, and very eloofe, by reason of ocasions; oh L[or]d persuade mee neere to thee I see that tumultuous thoughts awaite mee and I find it difficult to walke with god in the midst of them

17. I ride to mrs Baringtons, and so to wethersfeild, and see my father yet mourning for that precious pledge, Mary, and I mourne with him;

18. preparation for preaching: I find a good deale of straitnes;

345. 19. Saboth, I preach at wethersfeild twice, upon 53. Is:[aiah] 5. chastisement;[600] &c. I find sweet assistance, but I have found more inlargement at home a great deale;

20. seing freinds; and at cousen Suttons[601] inlarged in dutye, and something revived;

596 See above, p. 5n.
597 See Glossary.
598 Lady Vere must have gone to visit her daughter Anne and son-in-law, Sir Thomas Fairfax. The two were at Knaresborough, Northants.
599 See Glossary.
600 Isaiah's 'suffering servant' figure suffered for the sins of the people but the sufferings were, in the long term, profitable. The application to the present state of the Church of England and the persecution of the godly are, from Rogers' point of view, fairly plain.
601 One of the offspring of Daniel Rogers' sister Mary married a Daniel Sutton: Waters, *Genealogical Gleanings*, I, 210. Sutton was probably the same man who was the curate of Wethersfield in 1637. He later became rector of Cavendish, Suffolk in 1645: Matthews, *Calamy Revised*, p. 470. See above, p. 11.

21. I goe to my Lady Dennys with my father, and am refreshed to see my startford freinds, yet once againe, I revive them, and am revived;

22. I returne home by Epping sermon, and find my selfe much straitned, L[or]d inlarge mee;

23. dumpish, and dull, and the coast is not cleare, the L[or]d beats mee to shew mee what is in my heart;

24. I sup with mr sedgewicke,[602] and I see I have lost of my stortford zeale; but yet I hanker after thee, oh L[or]d, and am not well but in thee;

346. 25. Lady comes home, and the Lord inlarges mee in duty, and somewhat refreshes my soule;

26. Saboth, and we stay at home, and I speake, and the Lord is with mee to preach X; oh I rejoice in X, my peace, and righteousnesse;

27. I am ready to flag, and grow dead, and dull; I mourne after the Lord, but mee thinkes he is afar of[f]; Lord draw neere, Lord come neere; thy presence shall abase mee, and I shall be nothing;

28. sweetly thawed this day, and drawing toward heaven; the Lord clears the coast, and I behold him with comfort;

29. the Lord upholds mee graciouslye; but I find not that Savor after ordinances, which faine I would; Oh I goe out in mine owne strength, and also am ready to rest in the duty done;

347. 30. Something sinking; oh mee thinkes I see not so much of G.[od] in an ordinance as I was wont to doe, L[or]d thy countenance, or grant more of thy selfe though I am less of the creature;

31. I heare Dr Staughton;[603] of whom I thinke as my father said, there is yet aliquid amplius[604] to be desired, but learned, witty, and godly; my heart is naught, naught, I know not what to doe;

September 1. I have bin downe this day much, and heartlesse, and dull of hearing and speaking; but the L[or]d hath in some measure drawne neere, and given mee hope of much in his word, and Seale to morrow;

2. Saboath; sacrament, at Coleman refreshed, and quickened and joyed Oh that it might hold, and that I might walk worthy accord:[ing] to my covenant sealed;

348. 3. oh how soone does my hearte sinke, and grow dead, and dull againe; oh Lord, I have need of thy daily support, and grace;

4. I cannot live above, nor joy in the clearenes of G.[od] as I was wont to doe; yet Jehovah is my Hope; mr sedgewicke, and I went to Mrs Keeling;[605] and shee holds still her owne; ever this for one; that all that

---

602 William Sedgwick of Farnham.
603 John Stoughton.
604 Something more.
605 Obadiah Sedgwick, lecturer of St Mildred's, Bread Street, London assists Rogers with Mrs Keeling, on whom see above, p. 157.

are elect have some seeds of grace from the childhood; and shee had none; &c, L[or]d pitty;

5. Oh how dead; oh how Dull am I I mourne under a cursed proud dedolant[606] spirit; and am no way so heavenly as I was after my sicknesse; L[or]d recover mee; and restore light to mee;

6. I mourne under the sense of myne owne vilenesse; but yet I rejoice in gods free grace; and admire at the transcendant Love of my Lord Jesus;

349. 7.[607] this day G.[od] hath looked upon mrs St Johns,[608] and delivered her; L1d:[y] tells mee I was t4 l4ng at pr1y[er] and my heart boiles ag:[ainst] her; most bitterly; A sad w4m1n, that will have her w3l, and will not give in an 4nch;[609] the Lord give mee a meeke, and a wise sp:[irit] to doe service in my place;

8. the Lord yet seems to stand afar of[f] from mee, and I long after him; I will yet looke towards him though he kill mee;

9. Saboth, the L[or]d causes mee to adventure all upon him; yea in thee will I trust, though I dye; I was with Lady wake sicke, and prayed with her, and dealt impartially with her, and I have comfort in it;

10. Oh I find sin very strong and my heart awck;[610] but yet looking upon him, whom my soule loves;

11. supported in seeking god, yet I find much straitned, and dulnes Lord help my weaknesse;

350. 12. I injoy not so cleare a communion with god, as I was wont to doe; oh pressed, and awcke,[611] L[or]d w[ha]t looke I for, surely my trust is in thee, yea though in darkenes, yet in thy name; &c

13. Now the Lord hath sweetly thawed my soule, and let in some beams of hims:[elf] and cheared mee, so that I lye downe with Light, and Joy; oh that it might hold; oh that I might walk worthy of it;

14. my soule still stayes upon god; the creature is a pore reedy staffe and cannot sustaine the soule but I trust in the L[or]d Jehovah and he is, and will be Everlast:[ing] strength;

---

[606] 'Dedolant' means feeling no compunction, insensible or callous (*OED*). As a matter of little more than simple interest, it might be noted that one of the contemporary examples in the *OED* is taken from Daniel Rogers, *A Treatise on the Two Sacraments* (1635), second pagination, p. 23, where he castigates those who come to the sacraments 'with an insensible, dedolant, heart, with a dead, benumbed spirit'.

[607] In margin: '*'.

[608] Mrs St Johns was Catherine, married to Oliver St John, son of John St John of Lydiard Tregoz, Wilts. She married St John on 30 January 1634; after his death, she married John, Lord Paulet: Calder (ed.), *Letters of John Davenport*, p. 77. This Oliver St John is not to be confused with his more famous namesake of Long Parliament fame.

[609] It seems Lady Vere complained that Rogers was too long at prayer during the family exercise. He claims that she is a sad woman who will have her will and will not give in an inch.

[610] See Glossary.

[611] See Glossary.

15. I am something eloofe of againe, but thinking on G.[od] depending on god, adventuring upon his promise running into his name;

16. Saboth; something downe, yet my soule is fixed and comforted in faith; Mr Sedge:[wick] Bredstreet[612] preaches, strangely ut solet[613] But I trust in God;

351. 17. This day the Lord makes a breach upon us; Mrs Makepeace dyes of the pox,[614] one that wished, oh that I might heare let mr Rogers voice ag:[ain] though at the dore, oh how would I prize, yet the Lord tryes her not; Lord teach mee to live for the lost; yea give mee some token from thee that may be sweeter than life, and stronger than death;

18. now my brother comes,[615] and I am refreshed; but much adoe to keep up a flagging spirit;

19. 20. Brother continues with us, and on 21. I goe to wether:[sfield] to

22. visit my father sicke of a sad quartane ague;[616] A man of himselfe unfit to beare sicknesse, and unwilling, but the Lord brings him downe by grace;

23. Saboth, brother and I preach at wethersf:[ield] and much inlarged, and wee refresh the saints there my aunt Hosther,[617] and others are comforted;

352. 24. now wee visit freinds, and

25. recreate our selves at C.[ousin] Suttons;[618] &c:

26. but I find it hard to walke

27. closely with G.[od] in such ocasions; wee see desolate sister Hanna and comfort her, and cheare her weary spirit;

28. wee goe to colne, and the L[or]d was with mee in the ordinance there and wee rejoice much in each others companyes;

29. I returne home, and the L[or]d is good to mee, I find it hard to keep up my sp:[irit] in riding; and am saluted with the sad newes of pox in familye, but thou oh Lord art my hiding place in life, and death;

30. Sab:[bath] mr Spurstow, refreshes us he savors X much: thus the Lord provides, but I mourne under a cursed streight spirit; though I have great inlargemente in publique, yet streightned in soule; L[or]d pitty mee;

353. Octob: 1. This day is something cloudy, and I droop, for I see not with clearenes, the presence of God, yet my heart hangs upon the promise;

2. I am much straitned, and dumpish, yet faith is comfort, and I will trust in the Lord, though he kill mee;

---

612 Obadiah Sedgwick of Bread Street.
613 As usual.
614 Frances Makepeace or Makepeall, buried at St John's, a parish in Hackney: GLRO P79 JN 1/22.
615 Presumably his brother Daniel.
616 By 'quartane ague', Rogers means a fever or 'ague' where the increase of the acuteness comes on every fourth day.
617 Aunt Hosther is most likely to be the daughter of Richard Rogers named in his will as Hasselder: Waters, *Genealogical Gleanings*, I, p. 210.
618 Daniel Sutton.

3. I have bine much kept downe in spirit this day, even in hearing Dr Stoughton;[619] but this evening I have bin something refreshed, Oh w[ha]t an hell is the absence of Jesus Christ, and his presence heere, the suburbs of heaven;

4. very dulsome, and sad againe, oh the Lord seems to be absent, I find not that sweetnes in ordinances nor life in a Xian[620] course, as I once found at startford in the midst of opposition;

5. Oh how heavily doe I draw on in dutyes, my heart is strait, and the Lord seemes to be afar of[f], oh w[ha]t is the presence of g.[od] worth;

354. 6. wee hurry to Lady wakes for feare of small pox; and I am cast downe in my thoughts, and very low, but my confidence is in G.[od];

7.[621] Saboth, ravished with exceeding joy in meditation in the morning; upon that promise; I will be a dew, and he shall grow as the lillye;[622] Lord thou hast bin a dew upon my fleece this day, when others have bin dry; Ravished by Mr Goodwins prayer (but odde preacher[)][623] and at sacrament; and much thawed by mr John Sedgwick,[624] and inlarged at home; oh how shall I blesse the Lord, who hath done thus much for mee, oh to let mee dwell in the suburbs of heaven this day;

8. still remaines some sweetnes, and comfort in god, and his promise stays, and cheeres my soule; and I rejoice in the Lord Jesus, yea, and in him I will rejoice;

355. 9. I doe yet attend upon thee, and I doe still rejoice in Jesus Christ, my sorrow is; oh Lord I cannot serve thee, as I would; oh when shall I come unto thee; How long? how long?

10. somewhat downe; oh Lord inlarge mee; I rest upon him in whom I have beleived he hath caryed mee on, and he will doe; I find an unbeleiving heart distrusting god for the future; but my heart is fixed;

11. this day, I goe to westminster; to the Hall; to the minster, see the monuments; I was refused of the popish Clarke to go to the sword; &c: bec:[ause] I would not put of[f] my hat before the Altar; from here to a place called Hell, and thence to Lambeth to Caiphas Hall (out of the frying pan into the fire) where sat those 2. cursed traitors to X; W.[illiam of] C.[anterbury] and M.[atthew] wren with there hangbyes; I look above them, and have joy in G.[od] and I shall dye better then

---

[619] John Stoughton.

[620] Christian.

[621] In margin: '*'.

[622] Hosea 14:5. To make his meaning plain, the previous verse needs to be included: 'I will heal their backsliding, I will love them freely: for mine anger is turned away from him. I will be as the dew unto Israel: he shall grow as the lily, and cast forth his roots as Lebanon.'

[623] John Goodwin, see p. 136 above.

[624] John Sedgwick, the younger brother of Obadiah, BD from Magdalen Hall, Oxford. He was, at this time, lecturer at St Giles, Cripplegate, London: Seaver, *Puritan Lectureships*, pp. 131, 344.

they; I come home; and my mind hurrys over these th[ing]s: strangelye;[625]

356. 12. the Lord is yet good unto mee, and I rejoice in his promise, and in Jesus X, my portion, and joy;

13. this day, the Lord is pleased to be with mee, to keep up my spirit in some measure; but yet I want what I have injoyed, I cannot find, what I would doe;

14. Saboath, I am sadded under a dead lumpish spirit; and litle healed by mr St Hills sermon,[626] though sweete; P. W1ts4n, comes to mee before repetition and tells mee; L. M1r5: would not have mee 1d: any th:[ing] to s2rm:[on] and I was much v2x2: but cr4s:[627] in actions, the best way to deale with such sp[irit]s:

15. I am very dull and dumpish, and cannot be cheerful in god; I labour under a weight; oh when will I be rid of it, oh when shall I appeare in thy sight;

16. some thoughts for good, but oh I cannot doe what I would, oh wretched man that I am; L[or]d help mee, and ease mee of this loade; and this body of death;

357. 17. my heart is fixed; and I would faine wind up my affections to god, but they are ready to flag againe; oh Lord I thinke long to come to injoy thee in perfection without sin;

18. the Lord does uphold mee in depending upon him; and though I find not that Joy, which sometimes I have; yet I find joy in nothing else; I make hast after no other gods, for so, I know my sorrows are multiplyed;

19. I am much sunke, and pressed in spirit, and mourne under a dead, unbeleiving, disturbed heart, oh Lord, heale mee; oh when shall I come unto thee to be perfectly cured, and dwell with thee in Light;

20. I am something straitned, but my confidence is in God, who supports mee in all estates when I am in the deeps, as well as when I am out; oh one day, one day I shall be past all; then shall I triumph gloriouslye;

[625] Rogers visits Westminster Hall where he is told off for failing to remove his hat at the altar, thus judging the minister to be 'popish'. He then crosses the Thames to Lambeth Palace, where he sees William Laud and Matthew Wren, newly translated to the diocese of Ely. His condemnation has to be made plain. He refers to Lambeth Palace as 'Caiphas Hall', thus comparing Laud and his acolytes to Caiaphas, the high priest who 'gave counsel to the Jews, that it was expedient that one man should die for the people' (John 18:14). Hence Laud and Wren are 'cursed traitors to [Christ]'.

[626] Peter Sainthill was the son of Peter Sainthill of Southwark, Surrey. Lady Vere had presented him to the rectory of Ovington, Essex in 1635: Venn; BL Add MS 4276 fo. 112; GL 9539 A/ 1 fo. 63.

[627] Priscilla Watson, the servant in the Vere household, told Rogers that Lady Mary (possibly Lady Mary Westmorland) did not feel that he needed to add anything to the sermon, that is, any commentary. Rogers was vexed by this order which he felt rather crossed him.

358. 21. Saboath, very much downe, and straite, and mourning under a sad ministrye; of pore D4wn:[ing]⁶²⁸ the Civilian; caryd on in dutye (here at Lady wakes⁶²⁹ still) and discourse with those 2. Ladyes; being much of a temper, and way in Religion; sincere, I hope, and for god, but want that simplicitie, and fervencye, that is in pore ones; this is the Resolution of great ones, that Religion must complye with there state and some of there bredths yet I say not all of them bredths are sinfull; Oh L.[ady] V.[ere] s1d m1tches for h2r ch3ld:⁶³⁰

22. I have my thoughts upon the Lord, and mourne that I should any way warpe⁶³¹ from him, in whom is all my peace, and comfort;

23. I find not so much of the comforting presence of god in my life, nor ordinances, as I was wont to doe; I mourne, yet looke toward sion, for my help comes from on high; I am greived much at the sad l2tt2r and these 2. husw3f2s L. W1k:[e] and V2r:[e]⁶³²

359. 24. 25. I have bin sunke in spirit much both these dayes, and have had a feverishnes in the night, lost my sleepe, and my base heart is unwilling to stoop unto gods dealing;

26. I have a very giddy, inconstant sp:[irit] and cannot fixe upon God by faith, as faine I would; I am inlarged in performance of dutyes, but straitned within; having not that savor, and sweetnes in god as I have found, L[or]d draw neere, for myne expectation is from thee;

27. The Lord seems to stand afar of[f] from mee; oh justly; for oh what a lazy heart have I in dutyes, oh how doe I slubber⁶³³ with the Lord, oh I find not so much of god in secret, as I was wont to doe;

28. Saboath, wry untoward under sad helps, Light Downing;⁶³⁴ oh Lord help, for thou art my portion and my god, with means, without; and ab:⁶³⁵ them;

29. much hurryed at London, L[a]d[y] M. show; I see a good deale of the bubbles of the world, and hate it and rejoice in someth:[ing] better;

360. 30. Troubled ab:[out] mr Saint Johns small pox;⁶³⁶ the Lord follows us with sad afflictions, though wee fly from them; oh that I had more to

---

⁶²⁸ Calibute Downing.

⁶²⁹ For Lady Wake, see above, p. 157.

⁶³⁰ In his conversation about religion with Lady Vere and Lady Wake, Rogers finds them somewhat lacking, according to his taste. They seem to be engaged in negotiations regarding a marital union, for he ends with fears about Lady Vere making 'sad matches' for 'her children'.

⁶³¹ See Glossary.

⁶³² It is not clear what the 'sad letter' was that grieves Rogers, but for him to refer to Lady Vere and Lady Wake as 'huswives' is a serious social insult.

⁶³³ When Rogers castigates himself in the observation 'oh how doe I slubber with the Lord', he seems to be accusing himself of 'darkening' or 'obscuring' the Lord, of imposing distance between the Lord and himself. See Glossary.

⁶³⁴ Calibute Downing.

⁶³⁵ This may be 'about'.

⁶³⁶ Oliver St John was the husband of Catherine, the third daughter of Lady Vere. He died on 3 November 1637. See above, p. 160 and Introduction.

dye withall; L[or]d herein will I rejoice, ever in thy selfe;

31. I find corruption much stirring, and can scarse master it, unlesse the Lord should be gracious to mee, what should a pore worme doe with such an unbeleiving barren, earthly, giddy heart, oh when Lord, oh when shall I be rid of these, and injoy thee in perfect Holinesse;

November 1. Drooping under the burden of a body of death, but fighting against it, mourning under it, and rejoicing in hope of that day of Refreshing, and perfect Redemption;

2. Some thawing, and breaking in gods bosome oh who am I, that should injoy but any bunches of grapes in earnest to the whole of vintage;[637] Oh Lord more, Lord more; I looke up to thee, thou art my God, in life, and death;

361. 3. this day the Lord takes away Mr St. Johns, ab:[out] 2. in the morning; A sad thing, that the Lord should come and take three in lesse than 7. weekes; from us; oh that wee could live for our lost; in this will I rejoice, that the Lord is my portion and life, and Death shall be Advantage to mee;

4. Saboath, and sacrament at Coleman: and the L[or]d is most sweet ever in the ordinance; and as my sister Mary said to my father, that shee seldome received, but shee found much in that Ordinance; so I blesse God, I have received very often, and the L[or]d hath bin abundantly gracious to mee; I visit mrs St. Johns, and exercise with her, and pray, and the L[or]d is with us, and the truths have taken hold of them;

5. This is the day of rejoicing in that great deliverance of P.[owder] Treason, never to be forgot; oh I cannot be thankfull enough; this day I richt[638] my leg sadly and I am kept from service;

362. 6. I mourne that I cannot hold that sacramentall joy and strength; oh that I were with X which is best of all (if the Lord may have most glory that way) then should I have holinesse without addition of sin, and joy without mixture of sorrow;

7. I mourne with the mourners this day, pray with them Mrs St. Johns; &c: the Lord graciouslye drawes neere to mee, and causes mee to rejoice in himselfe; oh blessed be his name;

8. Tossed in London ab:[out] many ocasions, and I am ready to be lost; oh blessed mee god, who hath not laid many things upon one so unfit; now Lord, what waite I for, surely my confidence, and Joy is only in thee;

9.[639] My soule still leanes on God, and in some weake measure I rejoice

---

[637] This may be taken from Micah 7:1 – 'Woe is me! for I am as when they have gathered the summer fruits, as the grapegleanings of the vintage: there is no cluster to eat: my soul desired the first ripe fruit.'

[638] Rogers has 'richt' his leg, that is, he has sprained it. The term is close to 'wrenched' (*OED*).

[639] In margin, in later hand: 'the Scots'.

in g[od] and this day my heart hath bine inlarged to peice in with the Sc4ts who begin their Synod with F. this weeke and nexte;[640] L[or]d hasten them, Lord some ease, and good ever so oh Lord; to thy church;

362a. [641]10. my heart is downe; and I mourne I drive on but heavily in dutyes for the Lord stands far of[f], yet my confidence is in him; and I will waite till my charge shall come; L[or]d bring good to thy church out of this Scotch buisinesse;

11. Saboath; wherin the Lord is graciously with mee in a private exercise with the desolate widow Mrs St. Johns; (out of the Depths &c:) but my heart is strait, and I mourne under a dedalent[642] spirit; and the distance of god;

12. A litle in the suburbs of heaven in the house of mourning with Mrs St. Johns; but quickly downe againe; oh that it might continue of when shall I appeare in thy presence never to be separated;

13. the Lord drawes neere in some measure to mee, and supports my spirit in a fixed way of dependance upon him; oh I reioice above all the B[isho]ps in England, for I have the Lord to joy in, and the feast of a pure conscience;

363. 14. the Lord in mercye lets mee out a litle; though I have cause to mourne, for myne owne saplesse, unbeleiving giddy heart, oh Lord, once, once, ease mee of these, yet oh Lord thou upholdest mee in my integritie;

15. I yet hold on my course, and am upheld through mercye in this wofull world from perishing in the sins of the world; yet the Lord hath kept mee from the evell, and at last I shall have perfect redemption;

16. Dull of spirit, dead to dutye, the Lord is pleased to absent himself to shew mee myne owne emptinesse well, I will then be vile, and the Lord is holy; I am weake the L[or]d strength I nothing but the Lord is Allsufficiencye;

17. I mourne still under a strait, dead, hard heart, but my confidence is in the lord my salvation in whose armes I lye downe;

364. 18. Saboath, pore day, dull doings with pore C1l3but:[643] the L[or]d help us, and grant to mee a constant powerfull ministry; oh how happy were it; but I can rejoice still in the L[or]d, who is my g.[od] though he seems to stand something afar of[f], yea and ab:[ove] means;

19. I am much straitned, and the Lord seems to be absent; but I will goe no whether else; my confidence is only in him;

20. this day a litle cheered, and refreshed, and I can rejoice in the L[or]d my portion; oh I will never depart from the Lord, for he never failes the soule, that waites upon him;

[640] The General Assembly had been called after the National Covenant.
[641] Numbered 262 again.
[642] See above, p. 160n.
[643] Calibute Downing.

21. Sometimes ebbing, and againe flowing sometimes; oh that the comforts I find in the Lord might but endure; L[or]d pardon my sin, whereby I cause thee to depart from mee; and * Abide with mee;

22. I yet depend upon god, my Rocke and rejoice, that I have an hiding place, in these stormy sad dayes;

365. 23. I am something downe in affections, and feeling; but though heart failes, yet God failes mee never; he is my portion, and my covert [sic] from raining, and storme;

24. This day L. M1r3. and S1: have a c4nt3ntl4n s1d enough behind great p1rl4r d4re; ab:[out] generalls in pr15: oh a s1d m2l1nch: t1mer5s, sp:[irit] I g3e n4t: in and 45erc4m; I rejoice in the l[or]d, and delight myself in him;[644]

25. Saboth, sad without, and much deaded by reason of, our sad pastor; a right Ἀμφίβιον; an ambidexter;[645] oh L[or]d how sad a deep is this world unto thy servants; wee cry unto thee, L[or]d for food; oh it is for bread wee are pincht, oh help us;

26. Somewhat cheered, and well apaid in god, and his favour; I am much inlarged to thankfulnesse; oh one day, one day, I shall praise my god my gracious, and tender god;

366. 27. I goe to mr Suetosse honest, and plaine; and m^rs Marsh, teachable; and sober;[646] I am dead, and dull, Lord help mee; I find a cursed spirit in mee to looke at some str1ng2r: that heare pr15:^ts and aime at th4, rather than g4d;[647] I goe out in myne owne strength, and am in bitternes; [in margin:] tut soleo; oh mirum![648]

28. I am nothing I am much straitned, but my confidence is in thee oh my strength; the Lord upholds mee (and will uphold mee) to pray; to Believe, and to walke uprightly;

29. A strait heart, but my confidence is still on high in his name, who is my portion, and my reward;

30.[649] vidi iam annos viginti quinque; perdidi certè multos horum; ignosce mihi domine; atque posthac fac, ut redimam tempus, præsertim quia

dies mali sunt;

---

644 Rogers seems to have overheard a 'contention sad' behind the 'parlor door' between 'Lady Mari' and 'Sa[rah]', presumably a household servant over something to do with 'prao', possibly 'prayer', which he ascribes to a 'sad melancholy timorous spirit'. He is resolute and manages to 'give not in' and to 'overcome'.

645 Rogers calls Calibute Downing 'a right amphibian, an ambidexter', which is as much as to say he cut his cloth according to his company, in effect that he was a trimmer.

646 Mr Suetosse and Mrs Marsh seem to have been local residents. Marsh, at least, was a common name in the area.

647 This coded section is difficult to interpret. He complains that he finds it hard to see some stranger that here prays without focusing on those, that is, such like strangers, rather than God.

648 Always watch; oh strange!

649 In margin: '*'.

hodiè Laboro sub gravi onere; Corpus mortuum me premit multum non upprimit tamen; nomen enim domini Iehovæ turris est robusta mihi;

[30. I have now seen twenty five years; I have surely wasted many of these;
forgive me, Lord; and hereafter cause that I may redeem the time, especially since the days are bad;
today I labour under a heavy burden, the body of death oppresses me greatly it does not overwhelm me, however, for the name of Jehovah is a strong tower to me;[650]]

367. Decemb: 1. Cor saxeum hoc, prorsus ineptum est sabbatho, verbo atque sigillis fœderis; conteras domine cor meum [inked out] verbo tuo; fac ut appropinquam tibi; appropinqua mihi, domini ut ex sacramento atque verbo, tanquam ex ubere lac consolationis atque nutritionis, exugam;[651]

[December 1. This stony heart is especially unsuitable for the Sabbath, the Word, and the seals of the covenant; may you wear away my heart, Lord, by your Word; cause that I draw near to you; draw near to me, Lord, that from the Sacrament and the Word, just as from a breast, I may suck the milk of consolation and of nourishment;]

2. Dies dominicus; in quo Christo fruor in verbo suo, atque sacramentis; quis ego sum (miser) domine, ut mei memoresses; benedictum sit nomen tuum quia præsentiam tuam hodie, publicè, privatimque mihi gratis concesseres; ego tuus sum in æternum;

[2. Lord's Day, on which I enjoy Christ in his Word and in the sacraments; who am I, wretched, Lord, that you are mindful of me; blessed be your name because you have freely granted to me your presence, today, publicly and privately; I am yours, throughout eternity;]

3. Ego imbecillis sum, robur meum est Christus meus; qui mihi adhuc suppetias dat; adeo ut portae viferorum nihil possunt; nec mordi turres peccati; ego tutus hac nocte acquiescam in brachijs Christi providentiæ;

[3. I am weak, my strength is my Christ; who thus far gives help to me; so much that the gates of flesh can do nothing; nor the towers of sin; I shall this night rest safe in the arms of the providence of Christ;]

---

650 Psalm. 61:3; see above, p. 122n.
651 Isaiah 60:16 – 'Thou shalt also suck the milk of the Gentiles, and shalt suck the breast of kings: and thou shalt know that I the Lord am thy Saviour and thy Redeemer, the mighty one of Jacob.'

4. Ingemiscit domine anima humilli servi tui, sub corpore mortuo, vivo spiritui coniuncto; perturbat me, male olet in naribus spiritus putridum hoc corpus; oh quam anhelo post te, oh quando apparebo in conspectu tuo;?

[4. The soul of your now most humble servant groans, under a dead body, which is joined to a living spirit; this putrid body troubles me, it smells badly in the nostrils of the spirit; oh how I pant after you, oh when shall I appear in your sight?]

368. 5. O quam sitio post aquas vitæ, atque rivos pacis; gustavi parum, admiror su avitatem aquæ istius cælestis; non admiror furtivas aquas, non suaves sunt rivi voluptatum carnalium; nec habeo hos rivos, neque eo nec cvro;

[5. O how I thirst after the waters of life, and the streams of peace; I have tasted too little, I admire the sweetness of that heavenly water; I do not admire the furtive waters, the streams of carnal pleasures are not sweet; nor do I have those streams, nor do I care for them;]

6. minima ocasio me impedit in rebus divinis; beatus sum ut qual^e humili statu sim;

[6. the slightest occasion impedes me in divine matters; I am blest that I might be in such a humble position;]

7. miserum est deo servire animo distorto, beatum est, servire placido et libero animo,

[7. it is wretched to serve God with a perverse soul, it is blessed to serve with a quiet and free soul;]

8. O quam densæ sunt nubes hae, inter solem, et opacam terram hanc, h: est inter Christum, et animam meam, vix possunt radij aliqui nubes dividere vel pertransire; Ego tamen intentus ora teneo cælum versus vel opacum, vel serenum; tandem expectans videbo cælestes radios;

[8. O how dense are these clouds, between the sun and this dark earth, that is between Christ and my soul, scarcely are any rays able to divide or to go through the clouds; I nevertheless intently hold my face towards heaven whether it be dark or clear, finally, hoping I shall see the heavenly rays;]

9. D.D. quem dulcem fecit verbum sane prædicatum per D.^{ro} Stauton; nomen domini mihi est turris roboris; ego sane hodie lætor multum, in hac turre; cor meum molle fit lætumque in Iehovah Deo meo;

[9. Lord's Day, which the Word makes sweet, reasonably preached by Dr Stoughton; the name of the Lord to me is a tower of strength;[652] I indeed rejoice greatly today, in this tower, my heart becomes softened and glad in Jehovah, my God;]

369. 10. Remanet certè aliquid hesterni caloris; præsentiam tuam domine inveni hodiè in publico; privatimque; Lauda deum anima mea; et quiquid intus est magnifica nomen turris meæ, in qua tutus hodie dormitabo;

[10. There surely remains something of yesterday's ardour; your presence, Lord, today in public and privately; praise God, my soul; and whatever is within me, magnify the name of my tower, in which today I shall sleep safe;]

11. vidi hodie Invisibilem deum; atque gavisus sum; super omnia visibilia iam sum; non admirantur certe candelæ lucem qui solis splendorem intuiti sunt;

[11. I saw today the invisible God, and I am gladdened; now I am above all visible things; they certainly do not admire the light of a candle, who have gazed at the splendour of the sun;]

12.[653] Hodie Ieiunantes nos, preue effendimus non ieiunas; in domu nostrâ; liqua facit dominus corda nostra in pectore suo; ille gratium habet abunde satis; liquantem gratiam; candescentem sanctificantamque; ex abundanti spiri tuc suum effedit super me; Ynvenio certe confidentiam magnam in Iehovah nomine; fastam solitum suppressit gratissime; atq[ue] consolationem in gratiosâ affectiae eius in rebus de ne, de familiâ; de Dominâ Veere, De Ecclesiâ nostra, atque scoticanâ; ego tutus fidusque in Iesu ulnis Latiao etiam in temporibus pessimis; R[egis?]: es nostris;

[12. Today, we, fasting, pour forth prayers which are not scanty, in our house; the Lord melts our hearts in his breast; he had grace abundantly enough, melting grace; shining and sanctifying; out of the abounding spirit he has poured forth his spirit upon me; surely great confidence in the name of Jehovah; he has suppressed the accustomed fast most willingly; and the consolation in matters concerning me, the family; concerning Lady Vere; of our church, and the Scottish [church]; I, safe and faithful, lie hidden in the arms of Jesus, even in the worst times; You are [king?] to us;]

---

652 Psalm. 61:3; see above, p. 122n.
653 In margin: '*'.

370. 13. Adhuc etiam manet consolatio, atque deus mihi turris est; Adverarius ille me tentat; sed ego confido in illo; tristia nos hodie salutat nova: m^r Glover mortuus est; super mare, itinerus novem Angliam versus; sic iusti eripiuntur (manu se: amoris) a malis imminentibus; quin adque domine, aliquid pro Anglia nostrâ; sit paxa æterna, ut sancta; sion, olim delicijs tuis; purga ecclesiam, atq rempublicam; funda super unctum tuum, atq nos spiritum Lætus manum, supplicationum; atq adhuc Domine nobiscam habita;

[13. Even thus far there remains consolation, and God is a tower to me;[654] the adversary tempts me with those things; but I trust in him; new sorrowes greet us today; Mr Glover is dead;[655] on the sea, travelling to New England; thus the just are snatched away (by the hand of love) from imminent evils; why not even now, Lord, something for our England, may there be peace, eternal and holy; Sion, once your delight; purify the church, and the state, found them upon your anointing, and your welcome blessed hand we beg; thus far Lord dwell with us;]

14.[656] Affligimus nos Ecclesiâ ciborum percibisq hodie, in domu (o bed Edom)[657] Mr Staughton; vix unquam plus spiritus supplicationum; tamen, iam recubiturus, spiritum superbientem invenio; Deus tamen possit, et vult subijcere impium spiritum perié [?inked out], et preces;

[14. The relief of our church is damaged today, at home (o [---?---] Edom) Mr Stoughton, hardly ever prayed; now, however, going to bed, I find a proud spirit; God, however, may and desires to cast down the impious spirit through [?] and prayers;]

15. Interpellat solationes meas, reatus elati animi hesterni; non est hic dies hemene dies? ut priore due; ego ploro sordidum meum spiritum; Quin adhuc confido in nomini Xi;

[15. the shame of yesterday's elated soul disturbes my consolations; this day is not as before; I deplore my sordid spirit, because thus far I trust in the name of Christ;]

371. 16. D. Dominicus * moralis; in quo ingemisco sub onere ministerij tristissimi, Calebut: miserere mei Domine, cor durum fuit hodie, mollius est mihi recubanti; lugeo sub reatu hesterno

[16. The Lord's Day, * dead; on which I groan under the burden of the

---

654 Psalm. 61:3; see above, p. 122n.
655 See above, p. 149 and n.; Glover, *Glover Memorials*, pp. 560–1.
656 In margin: '*'.
657 Edom is the alternative name for Esau, although the nature of the analogy is not clear.

saddest ministry, Calibute [Downing;] have mercy on me Lord, the
heart has been hard today, it is softer as I lie down; I mourn under [Lit:
'to me lying down'] yesterday's shame]

17. Bonum est deum quærere, etiam et expectare; non deest dominus,
animæ quærenti, et expectanti eum; ego hodiè viam; perspicuum
magis est est [sic] cælum, et intueor solem, et tutus sub umbra eius
delitescam;

[17. It is good to seek God, and even to hope for Him; seeking and
hoping for him; I today [the right way?]; the sky is more bright, and
safe under his shadow I shall take refuge;]

18. Ergo certè (servorum Isaaci instar in 26. Gen: 20 ff) in hac valle
Gera, in hac tristi terrâ puteos fodio, Esek, et Sitnah, * Contentionis, et
Ofij Satanae,[658] et peccati, et * Odij, mundi se: periculosissimi; solatio
est deus mihi fodit puteum Rehoboth (Dilatationum, ubi ampla sunt
loca) Fœderis se: et gratæ promissionis; cuius aquæ, amaras
contentionis, ut odij aquas reddunt, dulces, mellitasque;

[18. I surely (the likeness of the servant of Isaac in Gen. 26:20 ff), in this
valley of Gera, in this sad land I dig wells, Esek and Sitnah, of striving,
and obstructions of Satan, and of sin, and * of hatred of the world
most dangerous; God is a consolation to me he digs the well Rehoboth
(of extensions, where the places are ample) the well of covenant and of
pleasing promise; whose waters render the bitter waters of strife and
hatred sweet and honeyed;]

19. Insultant super me aliquidando melancholicæ apprehensiones et
conceptus; phantasiam putiunt; et reddunt me ineptum ad agendum;
tristis, et umbratilis * Incolarum nostrum mos me perturbat valde; sic
non est hoc in mundo quiescendi locus; at ego confido in te;

[19. there leap upon me sometimes melancholic apprehensions and
conceptions; they worry[?]; and they render me unfit for business; the
gloomy and retired custom of our natives troubles me greatly; thus
there is not in this world a place of resting; but I trust in you;]

372. 20.[659] Lugeo et adhuc sub mole corporis mortui; o quando liber
evadam; an helat anima mea post te Domine, in hoc infrugifero et sicco
desero; o quando apparebo in conspectu tuo; perturber sanè sub cum

658 Rogers is drawing on Gen. 26:16–22. Once Isaac had been sent into the valley of Gerar by
Abimelech, his servants dug wells to provide water. The first two attempts were named Esek
and Sitnah because the local herdsmen laid claim to them. The third well was called
Rehoboth because it was not fought over and reflected God's approval.
659 In margin: '*'.

difficili hoc Spiritu D4m: m2d: [Dom: med:]⁶⁶⁰ neque certe vivere possim sine onere; Des mihi Domine sapientiam supernam, consistentiam, patientiam fidem; et aliquid fructus in hoc loco vocationis meæ; Doleo certè in spiritu imo meo, videns sterilitatem magnam; Consumpsi iam annum, et quid egi; (quis credidit fearæ nostrae; nihil tum habes quam quod prophetæ doluere) merces mea tecum est domine; Condona domine quod in meo est, ne faciat peccatum meum ordinationes tuas inanes alijs;

[20. I mourn even thus far under the difficulty of the dead body; oh when shall I go forth free; my soul pants after you, Lord, in this barren and dry desert; oh when shall I appear in your sight; I am indeed troubled with this obstinate spirit Lord [?] nor surely might I be able to live without the burden; may you give to me, Lord celestial wisdom, constancy, patience, faith; and some measure of profit in this place of my vocation; I surely grieve in my deepest spirit, seeing the great sterility; I have now spent a year, and what have I done; (who believed our [—?—]; you then have nothing but what the prophets mourned) my reward is with you, Lord; forgive, Lord, what is in me, lest my sin make your ordinances empty to others;]

21. Innititur Iehovae anima mea; et verbo eius et nomini eius; non est spes mea (frustra certe) in brachio carnali, in creaturis manibus; in te acquiesco domine, etiam in hisce temporibus; prævideo certe malum venturum, et abscondam me in te, et tutus ego evadem aut in vitâ, aut per mortem;

[21. my soul leans on Jehovah and on his Word, and on his name; my hope is not (surely in vain) in the fleshly arm, in created hands; in you I rest, Lord, even in these times; I surely foresee the evil that is going to come, and I shall conceal myself in you, and I shall go forth safe, either in life, or through death;]

373. 22. Disservi hac nocte de beatâ unione cum christo; et exultat cor meum in Christo, capite, meo, vite, coniuge, fundemento, magistro, Rege meo; non habeo id quo gloriatur mundus, sed habeo Christum, maritum meum, in cuius ulnis hac nocte totus Latebo;

[22. I have discussed, this night, of the blessed union with Christ; and my heart rejoices in Christ, my head, vine, spouse, foundation, teacher, my king; I do not have that in which the world glories, but I have Christ, my husband, in whose arms this night I shall safely be sheltered;]

⁶⁶⁰ The abbreviation may be for something along the lines of 'medeor', to heal, or 'medicor', to cure.

23. D.D. Onustus redeo a cæta nostro, a Xristi Generali (1λ3β5);⁶⁶¹ premor multum diu in domestico exercitio, miseretur mei tandem dominus, molle reddit cor durum; pacificat me; Lætor multum in meditatione, et apertos cælos video; deumque invisibilem;

[23. Lord's day: burdened, I come back from our meeting, ah Christ is everything; I am oppressed greatly, for a long time in domestic exercise, the Lord finally has mercy on me, he renders soft the hard heart; pacifies me; I rejoice greatly in meditation, and I see the heavens opened, and the invisible God;]

24. Certè deus spei, meæ, satisfecit mihi pace sua per fidem; adhuc mihi turris est, et nihil indigebo;

[24. Surely God has satisfied my hope for me by his peace through faith; He is a tower to me,⁶⁶² and I shall lack nothing;]

25. Premor aliquo modo; societas multa me disturbat; atque effusus animus quietem non auget, sed diminuit; oculi tamen sunt in Deum, tanquam solem nubilatum;

[25. I am oppressed in some fashion; much company disturbs me; and my soul, when poured out, does not increase quiet, but diminishes it; my eyes, however, are towards God, just as towards the clouded sun;]

26. Obtundit animum meum, sermo obloqu[or?] caro infirma est, spiritus quidem facilis est; acquiesco in domu mʳⁱ Haught:⁶⁶³ societas est suavis fidelium; extollit se animus aliquo modo etiam in exercitijs, supprime domine, condona domine;

[26. It dulls my souls, the discourse abuses me the flesh is weak, the spirit indeed is willing;⁶⁶⁴ I rest at the house of Mr Haughton, it is a

---

661 This term is particularly difficult, being in Greek and in code and, perhaps, an abbreviation. If the second letter is indeed λ, there are two possible solutions: it could be 'αλιεύς', which means 'fisher', as in 'fishers of men', plainly appropriate for Christ. An alternative, basing the Greek letters on phonetic resemblance rather than visual similarity, would be 'αληθως', which means 'truly'. This is to understand the '3' as 'η' (which has the same sound as an 'i' in Greek), and the '5' would be representing 'ω' (which has the sound of an 'o'). The last option means that '5' represents an 'o' sound rather than its usual 'u' sound. The overall difficulty is the opening of 'αλ', in that there are not many words that begin in this way.
662 Possibly Psalm. 61:3; see above, p. 122n.
663 Mr Haughton could be William Houghton who was admitted as curate at St Mary, Colechurch, London in 1633: GL 9539 A/1 fo. 26v. It may be that it was the home of John Holles, the husband of Elizabeth Vere, as he had been Lord Houghton, but by this point he was the second earl of Clare and Rogers is usually sensitive to social titles: Calder (ed.), *Letters of John Davenport*, p. 29n.
664 Matthew 26:41 – 'Watch and pray, that ye enter not into temptation: the spirit indeed is willing, but the flesh is weak.'

sweet society of the faithful, the soul raises itself in some manner even in exercises, restrain Lord, forgive, Lord;]

374. 27. Durum certe est cor meum, et ad exercitia divina, ineptum prorsus; nebulæ sunt, o densæ, densæ! et ego confido in nomine tuo;

[27. my heart is surely hard, and for the divine exercises, utterly unsuitable; the clouds are, o dense, dense! but I trust in your name;]

28. non habeo tandem semper libertatem cum Christo; iam sum super astra, iam subter agros, etiam in aquis imis; at ego adhuc caput extollo, et extollam cælum versus, et inspiciam spem meam;

[28. I finally do not always have freedom with Christ; now I am above the stars, now beneath the fields, even in the deepest waters; but I thus far raise the head, and I shall raise it towards heaven, and I shall look upon my hope;]

29. Immittit Sol iustitiæ radios suos, sed per nebulas, non video vt vidi olim, sed adhuc anhelat anima mea; oh quando apparebo in conspectu tuo; ut videam in perfectione Lucis, et Gloriæ;

[29. The sun of justice sends in its rays, but through clouds, I do not see them as I saw them once, but thus far my soul pants; oh when shall I appear in your sight; that I might see you in the perfection of light, and of glory;]

30. D. D. Ingemisco multum sub gravidine peccati, habitantis in me (nolente tamen) o quis liberavit me;? Ille certè, qui Redemit me a potestate tenebrarum, et transtulit in Regnum filij sui;

[30. Lord's Day: I groan greatly under the weight of sin, which is dwelling in me (despite my unwillingness) o who shall free me? He, surely, who had redeemed me from the power of the shadows, and has conveyed me into the kingdom of his son;]

31. Magna est intemperies spiritus mei, non habeo illos risos condonanti dei; attanem video solem per nebulas et certe dissapabit sol tandem nebulas hasce; lætor tamen dum meditor de æternâ Christi fruitione, in cuius ulnis in æternum Delitescam;

[31. Great is the intemperance of my spirit, I do not have those smiles of the forgiving God; but yet I see the sun through the clouds, and surely the sun will at last disperse these clouds I rejoice, however, while I meditate about the eternal enjoying of Christ, in whose arms I shall take refuge throughout eternity;]

Finis Anni 1638.

Index

INDEX   181

Church of England Record Society

COUNCIL AND OFFICERS FOR THE YEAR 2002–2003

'The object of the Society shall be to advance knowledge of the history of the Church in England, and in particular of the Church of England, from the sixteenth century onwards, by the publication of editions or calendars of primary sources of information.'

Membership of the Church of England Record Society is open to all who are interested in the history of the Church of England. Enquiries should be addressed to the Executive Secretary, Miss Melanie Barber, at the above address.

PUBLICATIONS

1. VISITATION ARTICLES AND INJUNCTIONS OF THE EARLY STUART CHURCH. VOLUME I. Ed. Kenneth Fincham (1994)
2. THE SPECULUM OF ARCHBISHOP THOMAS SECKER: THE DIOCESE OF CANTERBURY 1758–1768. Ed. Jeremy Gregory (1995)
3. THE EARLY LETTERS OF BISHOP RICHARD HURD 1739–1762. Ed. Sarah Brewer (1995)
4. BRETHREN IN ADVERSITY: BISHOP GEORGE BELL, THE CHURCH OF ENGLAND AND THE CRISIS OF GERMAN PROTESTANTISM 1933–1939. Ed. Andrew Chandler (1997)
5. VISITATION ARTICLES AND INJUNCTIONS OF THE EARLY STUART CHURCH. VOLUME II. Ed. Kenneth Fincham (1998)
6. THE ANGLICAN CANONS 1529–1947. Ed. Gerald Bray (1998)
7. FROM CRANMER TO DAVIDSON. A CHURCH OF ENGLAND MISCELLANY. Ed. Stephen Taylor (1999)
8. TUDOR CHURCH REFORM. THE HENRICIAN CANONS OF 1534 AND THE REFORMATIO LEGUM ECCLESIASTICARUM. Ed. Gerald Bray (2000)
9. ALL SAINTS SISTERS OF THE POOR. AN ANGLICAN SISTERHOOD IN THE NINETEENTH CENTURY. Ed. Susan Mumm (2001)
10. CONFERENCES AND COMBINATION LECTURES IN THE ELIZABETHAN CHURCH: DEDHAM AND BURY ST EDMUNDS, 1582–1590. Ed. Patrick Collinson, John Craig and Brett Usher (2003)
11. THE DIARY OF SAMUEL ROGERS, 1634–1638. Ed. Tom Webster and Kenneth Shipps (2004)

Forthcoming Publications

LETTERS OF THE MARIAN MARTYRS. Ed. Tom Freeman

THE PARKER CERTIFICATES. Ed. Ralph Houlbrooke and Helen Parish

THE BRITISH DELEGATION AND THE SYNOD OF DORT. Ed. Anthony Milton

THE UNPUBLISHED CORRESPONDENCE OF ARCHBISHOP LAUD. Ed. Kenneth Fincham

THE DIARY OF JOHN BARGRAVE, 1644–1645. Ed. Michael Brennan, Jas' Elsner and Judith Maltby

THE 1669 RETURN OF NONCONFORMIST CONVENTICLES. Ed. David Wykes

THE CORRESPONDENCE OF THEOPHILUS LINDSEY. Ed. G.M. Ditchfield

AN EVANGELICAL MISCELLANY. Ed. Mark Smith and Stephen Taylor

THE PAPERS OF THE ELLAND SOCIETY. Ed. John Walsh and Stephen Taylor

THE DIARY OF AN OXFORD PARSON: THE REVEREND JOHN HILL, VICE-PRINCIPAL OF ST EDMUND HALL, OXFORD, 1805–1808, 1820–1855.

Ed. Grayson Carter

ANGLO-CATHOLIC COMMUNICANTS' GUILDS AND SOCIETIES IN THE LATE NINETEENTH CENTURY. Ed. Jeremy Morris

Suggestions for publications should be addressed to Dr Stephen Taylor, General Editor, Church of England Record Society, School of History, University of Reading, Whiteknights, Reading RG6 6AA.